YORK NOTES COMPANIONS

Renaissance Poetry and Prose

June Waudby

Longman is an imprint of

Harlow, England • Lon
Sydney • Tokyo • Sing
Cape Town • Madrid •

York Press

YORK PRESS
322 Old Brompton Road, London SW5 9JH
PEARSON EDUCATION LIMITED
Edinburgh Gate, Harlow CM20 2JE. United Kingdom
Tel: +44 (0)1279 623623 Fax: +44 (0)1279 431059
Website: www.pearsoned.co.uk

First edition published in Great Britain in 2010

ISBN 978–1–4082–0478–8

British Library Cataloguing in Publication Data
A CIP catalogue record for this book can be obtained from the British Library
Library of Congress Cataloging in Publication Data
Waudby, June.
Renaissance poetry and prose / June Waudby.
p. cm. -- (York notes companions)
Includes bibliographical references and index.
ISBN 978-1-4082-0478-8 (pbk. : alk. paper)
1. English literature--Early modern, 1500-1700--History and criticism--Handbooks, manuals, etc. 2. English poetry--Early modern, 1500-1700--History and criticism--Handbooks, manuals, etc. 3. Literature and society--England--History--16th century. 4. Literature and society--England--History--17th century. 5. Renaissance--England. I. Title.
PR411.W38 2010
820.9'003--dc22
2010008776

10 9 8 7 6 5 4 3 2 1

14 13 12 11 10

Phototypeset by Carnegie Book Production, Lancaster
Printed in Malaysia, CTP-KHL

Contents

Part One
Introduction

The volume is intended as a guide for students of Renaissance poetry and prose, providing sections of close analysis and contextualisation of notable works. The intention is to introduce students to the specialised terminology appropriate to discussion of the literature of the era and which they are expected to develop during the course of their studies. In particular, rhetorical terms are used where appropriate, but always glossed in the footnotes, to familiarise both the vocabulary and usage. Part Three's 'Epyllia' section pays particular attention to this aspect of Renaissance literary expression.

The underpinning framework of the volume is drawn from practical teaching experience and represents many of the established canonical authors of the period encountered on English Literature study programmes. These range in time from the early part of the reign of Henry VIII (1509–47) through the reigns of the Tudor and Stuart monarchs and the period of the Civil War to the Protectorate (1642–60).

One of the primary intentions of this Companion is to demonstrate the widening parameters of the canon by including work that is sometimes not considered 'high' literature, such as the seventeenth-century marriage guides discussed in the 'Life Guides, Mother's Advice and Conduct Books' chapter of Part Three and the controversial 'Woman Debate' pamphlets of Part Four. By definition, Renaissance literary studies are fragmentary, consisting of typical, atypical or innovative examples of a genre and so can seem disconnected and impenetrable to the newcomer. Populist texts, such as the marriage guides, Mother's Advice manuals and explorers' records of voyages of discovery, can often provide a grounding insight into the era, 'patching' the gaps, and helping to contextualise the more literary works. In selecting material, a further consideration was that of including female authors wherever possible, to be read alongside their male counterparts. Greater numbers of early modern female authors appear in the scholarly anthologies with each new edition; irrevocable evidence that the parameters of the canon are widening. Aemilia Lanyer is now firmly entrenched and is discussed in the 'Woman Debate' chapter of Part Four, but Anne Locke,[*] Anne Bradstreet,[†] Dorothy Leigh, Elizabeth Joscelin[‡] and Rachel Speght,[§] all less familiar authors, are also introduced in this volume. It is hoped that a more balanced impression of the individuals who were involved in literary activities and their motives can be achieved by this approach.

Part Two [illegible] ovides a backdrop to the literary texts discu[illegible] ng sections. The central place of the classics i[illegible] which can be a challenge to the student reader, is identified here as being linked to humanist educational strategies. Sir Thomas More's influential fictional work, *Utopia* (1516), is then discussed in Part Three within this context. The gender-specific education of children discussed in the Overview reveals patriarchal attitudes, which are interrogated in Aemila Lanyer's *Salve Deus* (1611) in Part Three and Rachel Speght's refutation in the 'Woman Debate' chapter of Part Four. The theme of travel and international relations, also introduced in the Overview, are further developed in Part Four's 'New Worlds'. Part Two also outlines the religious strife which characterises the period, to be further illustrated in the 'Religious Works

* Locke's Psalm paraphrase is discussed in the 'Religious Verse' chapter of Part Three.

† Bradstreet's poetry is discussed in the 'New Worlds' chapter of Part Four.

‡ Leigh and Joscelin's 'Mother's Advice Books' are discussed in the 'Life Guides, Mother's Advice and Conduct Books' chapter of Part Three.

§ Speght's articulate response is discussed in Part Four's 'Woman Debate' chapter.

and Controversy' chapter of Part Four and in the examples of religious poetry discussed in Part Three.

Detailed discussion of works of poetry and prose under six genres is found in Part Three: 'Texts, Writers and Contexts'. The first chapter provides an outline of amatory verse conventions from the era and Sir Thomas Wyatt's importation of the Italian sonnet form to England during the reign of Henry VIII. The fourteenth-century sonnets of Francesco Petrarch which Wyatt introduced to the court had a wide-reaching influence on European Renaissance love poetry generally. The chapter moves on to illustrate the trajectory of imitation, adaptation and innovation in the sonnets of Wyatt, Sir Philip Sidney and, finally, Shakespeare. Despite their originality – and concerted efforts to seem so – the poems of the later sonneteers nonetheless demonstrate their debt to the inherited Petrarchan conventions, whether this is acknowledged or parodied.

Three Elizabethan epyllia are discussed in the following chapter. The form has a close relationship with the sonnet, often parodying the, by this time, tired Italian conventions. The epyllion is sometimes termed 'minor epic' or 'erotic verse narrative' and was often used by aspiring young poets to demonstrate their classical knowledge and literary skills. The wit, humour and risqué content, with occasional homo-erotic allusion, were particularly appealing to urbane university-educated men, who are generally considered its target audience. If the sonnet owes a debt to Petrarch, the epyllion's main benefactor was the Roman poet, Ovid (43B.C.–17A.D.). His *Metamorphoses* provided over two hundred classical myths, all of which described transformations arising from the complications of love. The work offered Renaissance authors a rich source of inspiration, but his *Amores* (Loves or Passions) provided stimulation of a more erotic nature, evident in most Elizabethan epyllia. Thomas Lodge's *Scylla's Metamorphosis* (1589) is based on the myth of Scylla from the *Metamorphoses*, revealing her punishment by the gods for refusing the love of Glaucus. Shakespeare's *Venus and Adonis* (1593) offers the most humour of the three epyllia discussed, in its raucous depictions of Venus, the goddess of love, and her determination to seduce the innocent and uninterested youth Adonis. Marlowe's *Hero and Leander* (published

1598) takes as its source a tragic Greek myth of lovers parted by a dangerous stretch of water. Marlowe's narratorial presence creates much of the humour through asides and comments on the protagonists' naivety. An uncomprehending Leander, for example, is pursued by the god Neptune in a sensuous homo-erotic encounter and, although determined to 'bed' Hero, he is not sure what is to be done once they arrive there.

The following chapter, 'Pastoral to Epic', introduces the classical theories of literary hierarchy which were adopted in the era. This so-called 'Virgilian path' traces a poet's development from the humble pastoral to the elevated form of the epic. Spenser's *Shepheard's Calendar* (1579) combines both classical Arcadian epic features, such as the praise of rustic activities, with the Mantuan moral influence of the fifteenth centu [illegible] entury, Marvell's 'Garden' poems were ofte [illegible] s in praise of rustic retreat, but reveal simila [illegible] Spenser's impressive epic poem *The Faerie Queene* (1590–6), despite its misleading title, is a consciously patriotic endeavour, which deals with serious political and religious issues allegorically. It is modelled on the Arthurian chivalrous romance and is an interesting read on this level. Its elaborate and intertwined plots introduce a range of colourful characters and gripping adventures. The extensive *dramatis personae* include battling knights in dastardly plots, an evil enchanter, an evaporating giant, a monster which is half serpent and half woman and a powerful dragon. The final text discussed in this chapter is Milton's powerful and more sombre *Paradise Lost* (1667, 1674).* His patriotic intention was to create a great work of literature for the glorification of the nation, with the pious aim of 'justify[ing] the ways of God to man'. The work takes as its theme the biblical account of the creation of mankind and its fall from Eden. Despite this religious endeavour, however, the impressive revolt of Lucifer and, in particular, the engaging character of Satan, led William Blake to declare that Milton was unwittingly of the Devil's camp.

Religious works, whether translations or paraphrases, were often the vehicles which enabled Renaissance women to enter into print.

* *Paradise Lost* originally appeared in 1667 as ten books. Milton introduced new material and reorganised these to create a twelve-book epic in the classical format in 1674.

Although both female writers discussed in the chapter on 'Religious Verse' published Psalm paraphrases, their motivation and circumstances were markedly different. Anne Locke was from an affluent merchant background and wrote her *Meditation* on Psalm 51 during her time spent as a religious exile during the reign of the Catholic Mary I (1553–8). A penitential sequence marked by its extreme Calvinism, it was published within a volume of sermon translations. By contrast, the Countess of Pembroke's metrical Psalms, written during Elizabeth I's reign and established state Protestantism, are overtly elaborate and literary. While Locke intended to provide a pious framework for an austere programme of self-reckoning, Mary Sidney Herbert's Psalms were admired by esteemed contemporary poets for their extraordinary control and dexterity. George Herbert's religious poetry demonstrates a similar interest in elaborate form and experimentation, while John Donne's devotional sonnets unite many aspects of the work of the writers discussed earlier in this chapter. His abstract concepts and metaphysical conceits reveal an acute intellect interest in poetic expression, particularly the impossibility of capturing thought and e[illegible] intense personal struggle of the individual v[illegible]rtainty echoes the frantic despair of the s[illegible]*editation.*

The following chapter is concerned with humanist prose and rhetoric. Humanism was the catalyst which enabled the great literary works now considered representative of the era.* Humanist scholars rediscovered and re-translated lost classical works, encouraging their intensive study in extensive educational programmes. The modes of linguistic study and habits of thought it engendered moulded the minds of generations, creating a shared repository of classical knowledge. Sir Thomas More was the most prominent of the early English humanists, and his fictional commonwealth, *Utopia*, is in the classical tradition in its reflection on ideal systems of government. The intense humanist interest in expression and the power of language is exemplified in the various published 'Defences' of poetry, grammars and dictionaries, and especially the self-

* The term humanism was originally associated with the formal university study of the humanities. See Part Two: 'A Cultural Overview' for further discussion.

help manuals of writing skills and oration. Sidney's *Defence of Poesy* e role of the poet and poetry in society, basing and classical examples. Thomas Wilson's *Arte of* George Puttenham's *The Arte of English Poesie* (1589) serve an egalitarian aim as handbooks of practical assistance, but are also nationalistic works which aim to promote the creation of high literature in the vernacular tongue.

The final chapter of Part Three is concerned with the genre known generally as 'Conduct Books'. These were handbooks to guide the reader through most aspects of life; spiritual, moral, medical, social and commercial. Their popularity can be attributed to a number of converging factors, including a rapidly changing society, lack of traditional support through familial fragmentation due to migration to the cities, a more literate populace and the wider availability of cheap printed books. Sir Thomas Hoby's *The Book of the Courtier* (1561) was a translation of an earlier Italian work considered to be the definitive guide to the profession. William Whately's *A Bride-Bush* (1617) and William Gouge's *Of Domesticall Duties* (1622) are both concerned with household governance, but are effectively marriage guides written from an extremely patriarchal perspective, while Mother's Advice Books were intended to provide maternal guidance in the event of the mother's death. Dorothy Leigh's *Mother's Blessing* (1616), for example, was written for her two young sons, although it was published to popular acclaim. Elizabeth Joscelin's *A Mother's Legacy to her unborne childe* (1624) has a more poignant provenance in that it was written secretly by a young woman convinced that she would die in childbirth. It was discovered by her husband upon her death, occurring nine days after the birth of her first child.

The four areas considered in Part Four: 'Critical Theories and Debates' are central to an understanding of the Renaissance world view and inform the close analysis of the texts which appear in the previous section. The first chapter discusses perceptions of and the tensions between the city, court and country. Although city life, especially life at court, was uniformly considered to be hazardous to moral, physical and spiritual health, to those who aspired to self-advancement it was a magnet representing ease, wealth and recognition. By contrast, in literary works and the popular imagination the country was often idealised; associated with the simple life, honest work and absence of corruption. This ideological dichotomy was foregrounded as divisions appeared between supporters of the king and parliament in the seventeenth century, antipathies and divergent loyalties eventually escalating into wholescale conflict with the onset of the Civil War.

'The Woman Debate' chapter discusses cultural representation of women's perceived inferiority from their classical and biblical origins to the implications for women's everyday lives. Defences of women and the infamous *querelle des femmes** pamphlets are discussed, including Aemilia Lanyer's proto-feminist *Salve Deus* (1611), Joseph Swetnam's uncompromising *Arraignment*† *of Lewde, idle, forward, and unconstant women* (1615) and Rachel Speght's polemical response, *A Mouzell for Melastomus* of 1617. Despite their articulate arguments and proto-feminist intentions, however, the female-authored responses are perhaps unsurprisingly predicated on the same values as those of their male contemporaries, demonstrating the power of the prevailing ideology.

The third chapter in this section considers some of the implications of Renaissance exploration and expansionist policies, whether on the literary imagination or in terms of colonisation and trade in newly discovered assets. The accounts of 'discoveries' recorded in navigators' journals included sensational lands and inhabitants, such as the Blemmyae, supposed inhabitants of Guyana, who managed without heads and wore their features on their torsos. Behind the hazardous voyages, into literally uncharted oceans, was the intention to claim land for monarch and nation, the hope of saving 'heathen' souls for a Christian God, and dreams of unimaginable wealth.

The final chapter of Part Four traces some of the most significant reforms and religious controversies of the era. Martin Luther's call for an end to corruptive practices within the Catholic Church is identified as the catalyst from which the Protestant Church eventually developed. Calls for reform percolated throughout Europe, including England,

* French: literally 'Quarrel about Women' but more appropriately, 'Woman Debate'.

† Arraignment: Trial.

generating heated and complex theological debate. This chapter traces the course of English state religion from Henry VIII's establishment of the Church of England, through the various permutations of Protestantism and the brief re-establishment of Catholicism during the reign of Mary I (1553–8).

Part Five introduces a chronology of important literary and cultural events, ranging from Columbus's 1492 voyage to the 'New World' through to the death of Andrew Marvell in 1678. Including all of the texts discussed in the volume, it is intended to illustrate their historical and cultural contexts, providing useful cross-references. The Further Reading section revisits some texts referenced in the various chapters and introduces further works, providing helpful annotations. There are also some URLs of reputable electronic resources, such as the Spenser Home Page, which is based at the University of Cambridge, and hosts the Spenser Journal and the Spenser Society. Throughout the volume there are also references to Early English Books Online. This valuable resource is an electronic database to which organisations such as universities and colleges subscribe on behalf of their students. It enables users to search for and read original publications from the era, including any illustrations, preliminary letters, introductions or disclaimers, and is an important resource for students of this fascinatingly rich era of English literature.

June Waudby

Part Two
A Cultural Overview

Although the period of European history usually referred to as 'the Renaissance' dates from the fourteenth century in Italy, the English Renaissance is generally considered to have begun at the beginning of the reign of Henry VIII (1509–47).

Italian influences gradually percolated through Europe over the next two centuries, informing and transforming native culture. The description 'Renaissance' is often considered unwieldy and imprecise, however, as it implies a unified and universal movement. It refers rather to intellectual ideas and vision, and the works arising from these, rather than any precise temporal parameters. The discoveries, rediscoveries and opportunities which may have changed lives among the rising bourgeoisie are also difficult to quantify lower down the social order. In 1977 Joan Kelly-Gadol most famously asked if women had a Renaissance at all and in what terms this might be measured.[1] It may be more helpful, therefore, to think of the Renaissance in terms of a variety of new advances in diverse fields which affected lives in a multiplicity of ways, although sharing some important features.

The Rediscovery of the Classics

One of the defining characteristics of the era is an intense interest in the retrieval of ancient classical culture. This interest was considered to have been lost in the so-called medieval 'Dark Ages',[*] hence, the name Renaissance, or 're-birth' of learning. Although monasteries and other religious houses contributed to the preservation of classical works during the medieval centuries, the range of texts studied was limited and tended towards conservatism; the primary interest of the twelfth and thirteenth century scholars was to align classical Aristotelian philosophy with Christian tenets. Greek works, moreover, were most usually studied in Latin translation and, from concern to adhere closely to the sense of the original works, were translated as literally as possible. By contrast, the Renaissance scholars brought to these texts advanced linguistic knowledge and a deep-seated interest in eloquent style and expression. Most importantly, there was a passionate interest in rediscovering lost examples of ancient literature. Classical literature studied in the Renaissance universities included works of philosophical, ethical and political theory by Plato, Aristotle and Cicero, medical treatises by Galen and Hippocrates, poetry and drama by Homer, Virgil, Plautus and Seneca, satires by Aristophanes, Juvenal and Horace, works of literary theory by Aristotle and Horace and the histories of Livy and Tacitus.

A fundamental difference between the scholarship of the medieval and Renaissance eras was in the perceived purpose of learning. Whereas previously those engaged in studies had often been destined for a life in the Christian ministry, from the sixteenth century onwards scholars often came from secular walks of life and had aspirations towards professional lives in law and diplomacy. Enabled by a humanist educational programme which saw a rise in grammar school provision, the sons of the bourgeoisie and gentry became involved in the administrative machinery of government. Their knowledge was therefore to be put to active use, to inform decisions in the material world, rather than the spiritual.

* Modern medieval scholars often object to this term which is, more usually, used to refer to the period between the sixth and tenth centuries.

The Training of the (Male) Mind

There were similarities between the education of young men during the medieval and Renaissance periods, in that both followed classical precedents. The two courses of university study were known as the *trivium*, or three subjects, and the *quadrivium*, four subjects. During the later period the focus moved to bring different emphasis on the components of the *trivium*. In medieval times the latter consisted of grammar, logic and dialectic, or disputation, whereas Renaissance humanist study emphasised the stylistic and oratorical aspects of persuasive argument within poetry, history and moral philosophy.* The subjects studied in the *quadrivium* were arithmetic, geometry, astronomy and music. The combined courses were known as the humanities or the 'liberal arts', indicating the course's encouragement of a certain freedom of intellect. As Elizabethan playgoers knew, there could also be an implication of too liberal knowledge, which trespassed into the realms of the occult, as in the cases of Marlowe's Faustus and Shakespeare's Prospero.†

Whether the classical works were histories, dramas, epic poetry, works of moral philosophy, theology or politics, their form as much as their content was studied minutely as part of the students' training in grammar and rhetoric.[2] Besides the concentrated analysis of the grammatical structure of works, to help students to acquire eloquence they were required to keep commonplace books into which fine examples of speeches, phrases or rhetorical figures were to be transcribed. Even in the mid-seventeenth century Charles Hoole would stress the importance of this and other forms of imitation of classical works, as a way of acquiring fluency and eloquent style:

* The term 'humanist' was not in use at this time, but derived from the name of the liberal arts' study, the humanities. Classical authors Cicero, Scipio and Gellius, however, all refer to courses of study which are termed *studia humanitatis* and relate to the subjects of the liberal arts programmes. See Joanna Martindale (ed.), *English Humanism: Wyatt to Cowley* (London and Sidney: Croom Helm, 1985), p. 18.

† See Christopher Marlowe's *The Tragical History of Doctor Faustus*, scene 1, *passim*; Shakespeare's *The Tempest*, I.ii.73.

> Let them pick out the phrases and more elegant words as they go along and write them in a paper book, and transcribe what sentences they meet withal into their commonplace book.[3]

The practice of imitation is a constant in Renaissance literature which is difficult to access for modern readers. *Imitatio* (Latin for imitation) was a crucial and central part of training in rhetoric and oration, defining the mindset of scholars who had passed through a grammar school or university education. Likewise, the gathering and appropriation of noteworthy sections of the work of admired writers was endorsed and encouraged. What to a modern reader may seem reprehensible borrowing in an Elizabethan poem or play therefore was not exceptional to a contemporary audience and indicated the writer's wide literary knowledge.

The Instruction of a Christian Woman

The education of girls was quite different to that of young men.* Girls were generally educated within the home, perhaps later being put into service in a household of similar or higher status, to learn etiquette and gain access to social advancement.† Within a familial context the wife of the household was responsible for teaching her young children, servants and retainers to read, often using the Bible as a primer. In some cases young people in service could gain from more extensive training or educational opportunities than were available at home. The poets Aemilia Lanyer and Isabella Whitney are both considered to have benefited from an advanced education most probably gained in this manner. Just as a family of humble background might seek to place a daughter with a family who would teach her to read and further her

* See Part Four: 'The Woman Debate' for detailed discussion of Jean Luis Vives's *Instruction of a Christen Woman* (1523).

† Boys and young men often followed similar periods of training. See, for example, Sir Thomas More's allusion to his own service with Cardinal Morton in *Utopia*.

religious knowledge, Lady Lisle* was similarly eager to place her two daughters in the royal household, in this case not only for the polishing of manners, but also for the promise of favour, impressive social connections and marriage prospects.[4]

The subjects which girls and young women might study were, of course, mainly dictated by their social status. In all cases, however, the primary concerns were their training in religion, morality, obedience and modesty. As Juan Luis Vives emphasised, in his *Instruction of a Christen Woman* (1523), 'As for a woman she hath no charge to se to but her honestie and chastyte'.[5] The book is sometimes referred to as a conduct book, in that, rather than merely attending to a girl's education, it is a direction towards a modest and godly life, from weaning to widowhood, as is partially indicated in the extended English title: *Whiche boke who so redeth diligently shall haue knowlege [sic] of many thynges ... and specially women shal take great co[m]modyte and frute towarde the[n]crease of vertue & good maners.*[6]

Reading and writing were taught as separate skills at this time, and therefore an ability to read did not necessarily indicate that an individual could also write.† Except where necessary in their work, the lower classes were unlikely to be able to write at all. As the sixteenth century progressed, in the rising merchant class boys most usually attended grammar school or were tutored at home, before being apprenticed within a trade. Young women of gentry and middling class may have been fortunate enough to be permitted to study at home with either a female or male tutor, focusing mainly on religious works, but also tutored in Latin, a modern foreign language and classical works of literature, although always avoiding the risqué.‡ Training in rhetoric and oratory were to be avoided as wholly unsuited to a woman's private role

* For more on Lady Lisle, see Part Three: 'Life Guides, Mother's Advice and Conduct Books'.

† Literacy figures are difficult to estimate accurately and are often based on signatures on legal documents. This system is very unreliable, however, as the ability to provide a signature does not indicate any greater writing ability.

‡ Girls' schools did exist in the early seventeenth century but were greatly outnumbered by boys' grammar schools, many of which were established by the fervour of humanist activity in the sixteenth century.

within the household, as was any text which might encourage thoughts of love or romance, especially Ovid's works. Vives reserves particular venom for Ovid whom he terms 'a schole maister of baudry, a common corrupter of vertue'.[7]

Whilst men were associated with the rationality and intellectual abilities necessary for public life, authority and study, widespread belief still held that the majority of women were incapable of benefiting from a formal education. As they were primarily associated with the home, their basic areas of instruction were concerned with practical household management, bearing and raising children, extensive needlework and the preparation of simple medicines. In the wealthier classes 'household management' was complex, however, and could amount to the organisation of near self-sufficient communities: raising ducks and chickens for eggs and meat, brewing ale, growing and preserving fruit, making butter and cheese, processing wool from sheep by spinning, weaving and the making of garments, 'stillroom'* tasks of gathering, drying and processing herbs for culinary and medicinal use, besides supervising the necessities of the household, including the daily provision of bread.[8]

Women and Public Life

During the early Renaissance the medieval trade guilds continued to exert a powerful influence on commercial structures, safeguarding areas of production and trading privileges, effectively creating self-contained monopolies which both policed their own members and protected their livelihoods from external influences. Joan Kelly-Gadol's criteria for assessing the historical experience of Renaissance women included examination of their economic roles and their access to 'education or training necessary for work'.[9] Selective modern day discussion of the lives of literary Renaissance women may imply acquiescence to the silent, private, chaste and obedient preferred model of femininity, but

* 'Stillroom' comes from 'distil', which is a room where preserves and medicines were made.

women of the labouring classes often lived very public lives in trade and manufacturing. Women's status as putative 'dependents' could effectively bar them from participation in male-dominated areas of commerce, although throughout the country guild regulations were surprisingly diverse as to whether women could serve apprenticeships, whether they could participate fully in guild activities and what their trade rights were as *feme sole*[*] or as dependents of male members of the guild. A girl might be trained in a family trade to assist a prospective husband, and many urban women, especially, did engage in business on these terms. There was some controversy, however, regarding the possible neglect of her primary duties as wife and mother if a woman were to engage in public life:

> Daughter, for those that has been brought up to a trade,
> When they are marry'd what use can be made
> Of this imploy, when they have a Family,
> To guide and govern as it ought to be.[10]

Evidence of women's participation in trades shows that they were active in most, not only those considered as traditionally female work, but also plumbing, plastering, gardening, the upkeep of firearms and machinery, printing and painting.[11]

Within the prevailing patriarchal ideology it was always preferable for women to be under the authority of the male members of her family, however, whether her father, brothers or husband. Feminist scholars have suggested that the emerging Renaissance concept of personal identity largely excluded women, and most cannot be said to have participated in the determining factor of the era: the rebirth of classical culture and learning. In the sixteenth and seventeenth centuries women were defined by their relationship to authoritative males as daughters, wives or widows and in legal terms they were considered to be the property or 'chattels' of their male relatives. The definitive example of this concept is found in judicial proceedings

* This Norman French expression means an independent single woman under common law (as opposed to civil law).

arising as the result of rape. Incredible as it may seem to modern day sensibilities, compensation could be paid to the male relative, rather than the female victim, arising from the loss in the woman's value as 'spoiled goods'. Women could not plead cases in law courts and in legal situations were viewed as equivalent to children and mentally-deficient males. T. E.'s *The Lawes Resolutions of Women's Rights* (1632) supports this dependence unequivocally, stating 'All are understood either married or to be married',[12] verifying an ideology which promoted a model of female activity which was secondary, supportive and maternal, and confined to the domestic unit.

Masculine Roles and Education

It is difficult for us to ascertain precisely what 'masculinity' meant during this era, but some idea can be pieced together from historical documents and cultural artefacts. An active public life was considered essential to young men to avoid the feminising effect of remaining within the household. In Shakespeare's *Two Gentlemen of Verona*, for example, Proteus is chided for wishing to remain at home, rather than going out into the world to gain knowledge and experience and to advance his fortunes. Andrew Marvell's 'Horatian Ode' similarly calls upon the 'forward youth' to engage in active life:

> 'Tis time to leave the books in dust.
> And oil the unused armour's rust.
> Removing from the wall
> The corslet of the hall. (ll. 5–8)

A regime of kindness in austerity was encouraged towards children generally, but especially boys. This is encapsulated in Christine de Pisan's *Here begynneth the booke whiche is called the body of polycye* (1523). She looks back to the ancients for models of governance, including the raising of boys as good subjects of the sovereign, discussing 'theyr introduccyon in vertue and good maners specyally in ye feate of knyghthode whiche is taken & deputed for the saufegarde of the comon welthe'.[13] The system that she recommends leaves little room for sentiment, prescribing the Roman method of removing children from their mothers as early as possible to present them with 'payne and travayle accordyng to their strengthe'. From their earliest days their lives were to be strictly governed and austere, lacking all delicacy, whether in diet or dress. They were denied all but 'gross meats' and their clothes, though of the cut appropriate to their status, lacked furring or embroidery. Put to task, to bear arms and labour 'after their strength', they should be 'acustomed .... to lye harde & to goo late to bedde & aryse erely. And ... suffre al maner of other possible paynes that belonged to the feate of armes.'[14] In short, the boy was in training for an honourable life of combat dedicated to his nation. Sir Thomas Elyot's translation of Plutarch similarly endorses classical precedent for the training of boys, stating that it is 'most expedient to exercise children in feats of arms, such as riding and chasing, casting of javelins and darts, shooting in the long bow and such other martial acts'.[15] The value of victory was quickly learned as the victor was to be awarded the personal effects of the vanquished, even at an early age. The active nature of a boy's training did not overlook the moral or spiritual, so heavily endorsed in the training of young women, but emphasised his preparation for a physical and public role in society.

Renaissance culture tended to espouse classical theories corroborating patriarchal authority. Under these terms a binary model of male authority and superiority, both physical and intellectual, was endorsed alongside concepts of corresponding female weakness and dependence. The Platonic theory of creation expounded in *Timeus*, for example, holds that the original being was male and those individuals who did not conform to classical models of masculinity were transformed into women: 'those who were cowards or led unrighteous lives may with reason be supposed to have changed into the nature of women in the second generation'.[16]

Medicine and the Four Humours

In the early Renaissance, before the dissemination of scientific discoveries enabled by the pioneering work in human dissection, medical knowledge was dependent upon classical medical texts.[17] Galenic* medical theory, upon which early Renaissance medicine depended, also endorsed patriarchal doctrine in that it claimed that a diminutive but perfect male child seed was implanted in the female body at conception. Man, in the image of God, was therefore the creator. A successful pregnancy was founded upon appropriate incubation, in which case a male child was produced. The child was literally the imprint of his father and replaced him in the world, continuing his father's role. It is to this concept that Shakespeare alludes in the early sonnets of his sequence:

> … your sweet semblance to some other give;
> So should that beauty which you hold in lease
> Find no determination; then you were
> Yourself again after yourself's decease. (Sonnet 13: 4–7)

In adverse circumstances, however, a girl, an imperfect male child, resulted from the defective performance of the maternal role. This gives some insight into Henry VIII's frustration with his wives who could not give him a living male heir, but only 'misbegotten males': in other words, daughters.

It was believed that the body was composed of four elements or humours: black bile, yellow bile, phlegm and blood. The humours were understood to contribute to an individual's disposition and an imbalance to cause ill-health. Within these theories men were considered to be predominantly 'hot' and 'dry', whereas it was held that women were subject to cold and wet humours, which led to them being changeable and deceptive. The preoccupation with women's biological functions

* Claudius Galenus was a first-century Roman physician (originally from Greece) on whose medical theories European medical practice was founded.

also generated the theory that they were dominated by their wombs, which might migrate around their bodies, impairing rational processes:

> … when remaining unfruitful long beyond its proper time, [the womb] gets discontented and angry, and wandering in every direction through the body, closes up the passages of the breath, and, by obstructing respiration, drives them to extremity, causing all varieties of disease …[18]

These issues are central to the prevailing notions of 'natural' order, which were largely predicated upon medical knowledge and contemporary biblical interpretation. These in turn helped to shape the construct of 'woman', and define the nature of the relationship between the sexes.

Religious Strife

The Renaissance era saw cataclysmic religious upheavals which profoundly changed concepts of man's relationship with God and with his fellow man. It also affected human relations and had a lasting effect on western Christianity. Although Martin Luther's questioning of ecclesiastical authority, which ultimately led to the Reformation and the creation of the Protestant Church, is often traced to his reaction to the sale of Papal indulgences in 1517, there were more complex forces at work.* Endemic corruption of the Church was a grave concern shared by many within the ministry, but the fundamental problem that Luther identified pertained to man's relationship with God and with his fellow man. The medieval Church emphasised the Mosaic Law† and the impossibility of mankind's ever sufficiently satisfying God's demands for retribution. No matter how pious, or how steadfastly an exemplary a life of good works was led, mankind was always divorced from God through its transgressions.

* See Part Four: 'Religious Works and Controversy'.

† Mosaic Law refers to the ancient Hebrew law, given to Moses on Mount Sinai, according to the first five books of the Bible (the Pentateuch).

Luther's breakthrough enabled him to perceive the centre of the Gospel's message to be love and forgiveness, rather than anger. The righteousness of God was interpreted not in the satisfaction of the Law, but in His freely-given forgiving grace. This radical concept fundamentally undermined Catholic Church doctrine in the sacrament of penance. The doctrine behind concepts of 'imputed grace' and 'imputed righteousness' teaches that, in His mercy, God accepts mankind as if it were not sinful, despite its faults, there could be no need for the ritualised performance of penitence, no necessity to obtain papal indulgences, or even sponsor masses for the dead, as purgatory* itself could not exist. The controversial religious debates sparked by Luther's demands eventually generated the European Reformation of the Church. Its radical impact seeped into England during Henry VIII's reign and found state-endorsement during the reign of Edward VI.

The central importance of religion during the era, whether Catholic or Protestant, cannot be overemphasised. It formed an influential undercurrent to all Renaissance life and was linked to theories of 'natural' order and authority. Under Protestantism an extensive knowledge of the Bible was usual rather than exceptional and quotations found their way into texts of every genre as example and endorsement. A Renaissance concept that is largely lost to modern readers is that the Bible was also read for historical exempla. In His providential care of mankind, God had caused the Bible to be written to form a template by which to live one's life, whether in the form of caution, prophecy, practical advice, encouragement in adversity, or promises of the hereafter.

The Bible also provided a primary example of social hierarchy in the relationship between Adam and Eve. Before their disobedience and exile from Eden, Eve was understood to be in willing subservience, but upon being cast forth into the world she would henceforth be subjugated to Adam's authority. Milton's Book IX of *Paradise Lost* explores these concepts as part of his endeavour to 'justify the ways of God to men'.†

* Under Catholic doctrine purgatory was the place of suffering and purification where one made retribution for sins not fully compensated for by penitence whilst alive, before gaining admission to heaven.

† See Part Three: 'Pastoral to Epic'.

According to contemporary interpretation of the Genesis account of creation, Eve was responsible for mankind's Fall from perfection. Due to her disobedience, foolishness and guile, humanity was driven out of Paradise to a life of suffering and death. Her punishment was threefold; to share Adam's penalty of earning food by the sweat of the brow, to have pain in childbirth and to be subjected to the rule of Adam, her husband. By divine will she and her female descendents were to devote themselves to redemption through childbearing and consider themselves to be in subjection to their husbands. In his *Basilikon Doron*, for example, James I advised his son in precisely these terms:

> ... command [your Queen] as her Lord: cherish her as your helper: rule her as your pupil ... ye are the head, shee is your body: it is your office to command, and hers to obey.[19]

Postlapsarian* mankind was considered to be totally corrupted, apparent not only in the estrangement from God, but also in a tendency towards evil. Women particularly were considered to have inherited Eve's negative attributes and this, amplified by the current medical theories of gender, advocated a need for women's close governance, to remedy their perceived threat to good order.

Although Protestant doctrine theoretically advocated 'companionate' marriage, the husband had absolute power over his wife and household in a microcosmic echo of the monarch's divinely-ordained power over his subjects. This is the world-view presented in the austere domestic guidance literature generated in the seventeenth century, such as William Whateley's *A Bride-Bush* (1617) and William Gouge's *Of Domesticall Duties* (1622).† The patriarchal dogma represented in prescriptive texts of the era presented considerable challenges to women's agency and expression, although it is not possible to know how far they represented the actual life experience of women of different status and circumstance. As the experiences and expectations of women of the nobility and the

* Postlapsarian means 'After the Fall from Eden'.

† As discussed in the marriage guides featured in Part Three: 'Life Guides, Mother's Advice and Conduct Books'.

poorest sectors of society differed greatly, it is unfeasible to try to create a composite and unified picture.[20] The domestic advice literature mentioned above was didactic, rather than reflective, for example, and was aimed at a literate rising middle class readership. The relative obscurity in which the majority of underprivileged people lived, by comparison, left little trace on history, as Amanda Shepherd states quite rightly, 'it is impossible to know how the illiterate majority responded to official expectations of behaviour, except where their response landed them in the court'.[21]

Theories of Order

Particularly under Protestantism, the family was understood both as a microcosmic echo of the hierarchy of state governance and of God's majesty in heaven. Just as God ruled over the assembled angelic orders, it was held that the King should rule over his subjects and the father rule over his household. Thus, God, the monarch and the father were tied together in an echo of the Holy Trinity that enmeshed divine and civil authority. Wider concepts of this theory of order, referred to as the Great Chain of Being, placed all parts of creation in harmonious relation to all other, in a hierarchical arrangement stretching from the pebbles on the ground through all mineral, plant, animal and human life. The concept of a harmonious tension between each element of the social fabric held that each served a purpose within God's great plan, and loss of order in any part threatened the whole of society with collapse. The concept was diligently enforced, even to the extent of policing sartorial appearance, in the form of sumptuary codes, laws which delineated precisely what fabrics, styles of clothes and value of accessories could be worn by individuals of different levels of social status. This discourse of 'natural', or divine, order was promoted by Church and state and preached from the pulpit on a weekly basis in sermons, or 'homilies'.* If all had subscribed willingly to the theory, however, such themes as

* The Elizabethan homilies (sermons) were added to the earlier collection written in Henry VIII's reign, but not preached until the reign of his son, Edward VI. Their intention was to promote social control as much as conformity of religion.

castigation for 'disobedience and wilful rebellion', 'idleness', 'strife and contention' would not have appeared alongside more conventionally religious exhortations in these didactic sermons. The high profile of such strategies of enforcement bears witness to political anxieties regarding civil disorder, social mobility and loss of cultural coherence.

Duty to God and Monarch: *The Obedience of a Christian Man*

Issues of secular authority were debated fiercely throughout the period, from the reign of Henry VIII, who erased the spiritual authority of the Pope in England when he assumed the title Head of the Church of England, through to the Civil War period, culminating with the execution of Charles I in 1649. Religious works of the early Reformation frequently discussed the seeming dislocation between loyalty owed to the monarch and the duty due to God and his representatives on earth, in particular the Pope. With consistency, the reformers endorsed the divinely decreed authority of the sovereign and his magistrates, with the proviso that in a religious context it may be possible to disobey and follow the conscience. William Tyndale's *The Obedience of a Christian Man* (1528) provides an illuminating insight into contemporary attitudes to both divinely-ordained power and a stalwart belief in the beneficial working of God's Providential design for mankind's ultimate benefit. Following biblical precedents, he charges the populace to recognise the authority of the higher powers and submit even to the will of a tyrannical ruler, for example, as part of God's unfathomable scheme. William Baldwin's *Mirror for Magistrates* (1559) similarly delineates the concept of a divinely-ordained terrestrial hierarchy of power:

> For as justice is the chief vertue, so is the ministracion therof, the chiefest office: & therfore hath God established it with the chiefest name, honoring & calling Kinges, & all officers under them by his owne name, Gods. Ye be all Gods, as many as have in your charge any ministracion of justice.[22]

The premise of the *Mirror* was to caution those in authority by means of verse 'histories' of rulers who met inglorious ends through mismanagement or abuse of power. It is a site of tension, however, in its stated adherence to the status quo of God-given power, as reiterated in the opening epistle, and its didactic mission to exhort and compel those who occupied positions of authority. These conflicting and dangerous objectives, which drew attention to errors of governance and focused attention on the personal failures of monarchs, were responsible for its suppression under Mary I. Problems of legitimate rule, political stability and divine right are rehearsed within the verses, sometimes with surprising boldness. The fifth cautionary 'history' is of 'Howe Kyng Richard the seconde who for his evyll governaunce was deposed from his seat and miserably murdred in prison'.[23] The account emphasises the dichotomy between the sovereign role, ordained by God, and the physical body of the man, driving a wedge between the two, forming the prelude to Henry Bolingbroke's usurpation and the eventual regicide. The relation of such contentious material is further complicated for Baldwin in that the lineage of Bolingbroke, later Henry IV, is the ancestry of his own queen, Elizabeth I. Shakespeare's own interest in these issues is apparent in his *Richard II,* the second play of his second tetralogy of history plays. John of Gaunt simultaneously endorses Tudor orthodoxy while declining to avenge the deposed Richard, his nephew:

> God's is the quarrel; for God's substitute,
> His deputy anointed in His sight,
> Hath caused his death; the which if wrongfully
> Let heaven revenge, for I may never lift
> An angry arm against His minister. (I.ii.37–41)

In effect, Shakespeare balances the outrage by paraphrasing Romans 12:18: 'Vengeance is mine: I will repay, saieth the Lord'.

Such issues of divine will versus a government based on social contract between the governors and the people would assume crucial importance during the reign of Charles I, and would later be developed by Thomas Hobbes and John Locke.[24] In 1642 Charles I declared war on Parliament and the country was plunged into the Civil War, which culminated in the execution of the king and the establishment of Oliver Cromwell's Protectorate. Andrew Marvell's 'Horatian Ode', whilst ostensibly lauding Cromwell's recent victory in Ireland, looks back to Charles's death, demonstrating ambivalence and possible unease with the outcome, in his ambiguous approach to both the victor and the deposed.

Towards a Modern Society: Status Quo versus Social Mobility

Set against the discourse of order endorsed by Tudor and Stuart polity, however, was a state of social upheaval, as society gradually moved towards a more recognisably modern form, based on capitalism rather than feudal rule by the nobility.

Webs of patronage and service still held Tudor society in a fragile balance within which literary works were often commodities or units of exchange. Within these networks of interrelated dependence and reciprocity the court was both a powerful epicentre of cultural life and of national patronage and favour. Petitioners for royal preference, monopolies, rights and licences, rubbed shoulders with the nobility, holders of lucrative commissions, civic dignitaries and powerful members of the court household. The court and its ordinances represented the epitome of order and the enforcement of obedience in a rigidly hierarchical society while, paradoxically, becoming for many a means of attaining an entirely altered life to that decreed by accident of birth and social degree.

Although the fortunate achieved self-advancement, social tensions were created as sectors of society with a vested interest in maintaining the status quo attempted to re-assert hierarchical tradition. The increase in large-scale organised production in many areas, but particularly in fine woollen fabric, created greater European trade and speculation opportunities, and massive wealth for some merchants, brokers and bankers. A pool of talented and educated young men who had experienced a humanist education had been created through improved educational opportunities, and they were eager to obtain patronage, coveted diplomatic and magisterial posts, or positions at court. The nobility retained respect and status, but as they were required to maintain the façade of luxurious living and conspicuous consumption, in reality they were often indebted to the *nouveau riche* grand merchants to support their lifestyles. The founder of the German Fugger company, for example, was a weaver who was also involved in trading endeavours. By 1525, a century later, his descendent Jakob Fugger had become the wealthiest merchant banker in Europe, managing Papal funds and frequently involved in raising massive loans for European monarchs.[25]

Relations with Europe

Much of the new wealth which flooded the country from the sixteenth century was generated within lucrative trade consortia, whether through investments in the voyages to the New World or in trade with nearer neighbours in Europe. Reflecting the changing attitude to the production of wealth, sixteenth-century merchants developed a new economic ethic which lauded trade as honest toil and read divine approbation in their profit. The London Company of Mercers was at the centre of this mercantile Christian tradition, investing in the voyages to Virginia, founding St Paul's and the Mercers' schools, operating loan systems to enable young people to set up in trade and creating several charitable trusts which supported needy individuals, including poor widows and the children of clergymen.

Many of these merchants were obliged to spend most of their lives in the great trading centres of western Europe, such as Frankfurt and Antwerp, and at the beginning of the English Reformation were very much implicated in the import of outlawed religious texts from the Continent. As Henry VIII's Lord Chancellor, Sir Thomas More was acutely aware of the reformist support networks which spread throughout Europe and penetrated not only into London but to the very centre of the royal court. His painstaking pursuit of those he suspected is documented in the State Papers of the reign of the king.

The Mercers[*] employed by the royal household supplied Anne Boleyn with not only fine cloth of silver and gold, but also books deemed heretical by More and the king, her husband.[†]

Despite the knowledge of Latin, shared by educated (male) Europeans, merchants needed skills in foreign languages to pursue their work efficiently. Some of the earliest books to be printed by Caxton's press were French Dictionaries, one appearing in 1480 and a second in 1497.[‡] The latter of these was an anonymous rhymed phrase book, aiming specifically to address the needs of merchants, which appeared under the title *Here is a good boke to lerne to speke French*.[26] In 1516 a particularly innovative phrase book was published by Roger William, entitled *A key into the language of America, or, An help to the language of the natives in that part of America called New-England*. Intended not only to enable trade negotiations but also to convert the 'heathen', it quickly progresses from salutations and practical matters to issues of whose God made the moon and stars.[27] As the sixteenth century progressed dictionaries of other European languages became available, facilitating ease of travel and conversation within the broader parameters of what would become known as the Grand Tour.

Travel was an important part of the education of a young man of means, as alluded to in Shakespeare's *Two Gentlemen of Verona*, mentioned at the beginning of this chapter. It was considered broadening to the mind, albeit with attendant moral and spiritual dangers. Typically a young man, overseen by a sober attendant, would travel through Europe to visit centres of culture, especially the Italian cities of Pisa, Florence, Padua, Venice and Rome. An uneasy tension existed under Protestantism, however, between the era's fascination with Latin culture and the perceived danger of seduction to a dissolute life and the Catholic faith. Roger Ascham's *The Scholemaster* (1570) illustrates these contemporary fears in its endorsement of the

* Members of the prestigious Mercers Guild which dealt in fabric, especially luxury fabrics used by the nobility.

† See the circumstances of Anne Locke's family in Part Three: 'Religious Verse'.

‡ William Caxton was a successful merchant and the first native English printer, establishing his press in London in 1476.

discriminating use of Latin texts in boys' education but also gives grave warnings against the corrupting influence of travel, and overmuch liberty, to an untrained mind. Referring to Italy as an enchantress's court, he expostulates against the 'Englishman Italianated', condemning 'the religion, the learning, the policy, the experience, the manners' as 'enchantments of Circe brought out of Italy to mar men's manners in England'.[28] On some level, at least, a similar outlook is at play in the notorious Jacobean revenge tragedies, where all manner of depravity is depicted as being perpetrated in the courts of Spain and Italy. No doubt appealing to the xenophobic attitudes of their audiences, which ensured commercial success, these works also commented on affairs closer to home, beneath their sensational wraps.

Without doubt, themes of foreign cultures and travel engaged the popular imagination in this era, whether in the guise of an account of shipwreck and hardship off the coast of Bermuda, such as Strachey's *True Reporatory* (1610) or a travelogue of a gentleman's journey through Europe, such as Coryat's *Crudities* (1611). The pleasure of acquiring knowledge of far-flung places for most was spiced by the exoticising tendencies of authorial strategies and habits of categorisation. 'Otherisation' of alien races, focusing on perceived differences, served to define concepts of national identity by comparison. Thus Francis Osborne's advice to his son warns against the 'levity of France, pride of Spain and treachery of Italy', by definition affording the English nation a monopoly in soberness, humility and honesty.[27] Paradoxically, Elizabethan and Jacobean ethnocentricity whilst delighting in tales of the exotic, and aspiring to the pre-Christian classical ideals of Ancient Greece and Rome, simultaneously read non-Protestant cultures as inferior and hazardous.

Notes

1 Joan Kelly-Gadol (1977), 'Did Women Have a Renaissance?' in *Women, History and Theory: The Essays of Joan Kelly* (London: University of Chicago Press, 1984), pp. 19–50.

2 For examples of elaborate rhetorical devices commonly used in Elizabethan literature, see Part Three: 'Renaissance Epyllion'.

3 Charles Hoole, *A new discovery of the old art of teaching school* (1660), 'The programme for the fifth form', excerpt in Martindale (ed.), pp. 85–97, p. 89.

4 See *The Lisle Letters, An Abridgement*, Muriel St Clare (ed.), selected and arranged by Bridget Boland (London: Secker and Warburg, 1983), vol. 3. The Lisles are also mentioned in 'Religious Works and Controversy', in Part Four.

5 Richard Hyrde's translation of Juan Luis Vives's *Institione Foeminae Christianae* as *The Instruction of a Christen Woman* (c. 1529), cited in Valerie Wayne, 'Some Sad Sentence: Vives' *Instruction of a Christen Woman*' in Margaret Hannay (ed.), *Silent But For The Word, Tudor Women as Patrons, Translators, and Writers of Religious Works* (Ohio: Kent State University Press, 1985), pp. 15–29, p. 15. Also available via Early English Books Online, http://eebo.chadwyck.com/home, STC 24856.5. Early English Books Online is hereafter referred to as EEBO.

6 See Valerie Wayne's discussion in, 'Advice from mothers and patriarchs' in Helen Wilcox (ed.), *Women and Literature in Britain 1500–1700* (New York and Cambridge: Cambridge University Press, 1996), title as given by EEBO, STC 24856.5.

7 Vives in Hyrde's translation, STC 24856.5, p. Bii *verso*.

8 See Sara Mendelson and Patricia Crawford's excellent *Women in Early Modern England 1550–1720* (Oxford: Clarendon Press, 1998), pp. 305–7.

9 See Joan Kelly-Gadol's seminal essay, 'Did Women Have a Renaissance?' available in various publications, including Renate Bridenthal and Claudia Koonz (eds), *Becoming Visible: Women in European History* (Boston: Houghton Mifflin Company, 1977), pp. 148–52, 154–61 and reprinted in The Norton Critical Edition of Baldessare Castiglione's *The Book of the Courtier*, ed. by Daniel Javitch (New York and London: W. W. Norton and Company, 2002), pp. 340–51.

10 An extract from *The Good Wife's Fore-cast* in *Roxburghe Ballads*, W. Chappell and J. Ebsworth (eds), 9 vols (London and Hertford, 1866–99), vol. 8, vi, pp. 349–50 in Mendelson and Crawford, *Women in Early Modern England 1550–1720* (Oxford: Clarendon Press, 1998).

11 Mendelson and Crawford, pp. 330–1.

12 See Catherine Belsey, *The Subject of Tragedy: Identity and Difference in Renaissance Drama* (London: Methuen, 1985) p. 153.

13 Christine de Pisan, *Here begynneth the booke whiche is called the body of polycye* (1523) Book II, 'Howe the noble auncyentes enduced theyr chyldren', p. 53, available via EEBO, STC 7270.

14 Pisan, p.53, available via EEBO, STC 7270.

15 Sir Thomas Elyot, *The education or bringinge up of children, translated oute of Plutarche* (1532), chapter 8, 'Of the commoditie of virtuous exercise', spelling modernised in quotation, available via EEBO, STC 20057.
16 Plato, *Timaeus,* 'Creation of the Animals', 90e–92c.
17 See Valerie Traub, 'Gendering Mortality in Early Modern Anatomies' in *Feminist Readings of Early Modern Culture,* Valerie Traub, M. Lindsey Kaplan and Dympna Callaghan (eds), (Cambridge: Cambridge University Press, 1996), pp. 44–92.
18 Extract from Plato's *Timaeus*, 'Creation of other animals', 90e–92c, as above. The 'Mother', or hysteria, was recognised as a medical complaint which involved the rising of the womb, which caused a sensation of suffocation. See Shakespeare's *King Lear* Act II.iv.54–5.
19 James VI, King of Scotland (and later James I of England), *Basilikon Doron Devided into three bookes* (Edinburgh: 1599), available through EEBO, STC 14348, Book Three, pp. 97, 99.
20 See Hilary Hinds, *God's Englishwomen, Seventeenth-Century Radical Sectarian Writing by Women* (Manchester: Manchester University Press, 1996), pp. 18–50.
21 Amanda Shepherd, *Gender and Authority in Sixteenth-Century England* (Keele: Keele University Press, 1994), p. 8.
22 William Baldwin, the opening epistle, *Myrroure [Mirror] for Magistrates* (1559), available via EEBO, STC 195.16. The work is a continuation of John Lydgate's *The fall of princes* (1431–9) which itself is a translation of Boccaccio's *De casibus illustrium virorum* (*The fate of illustrious men*) (1335–74). Note, Baldwin was the editor and compiled the volume but there were a number of contributors.
23 Baldwin, Folio xvi *recto*, available via EEBO, STC 1247.
24 See Thomas Hobbes's *Leviathan* (1651) and John Locke's *Second Treatise of Government* (1689).
25 See Eugene F. Rice, *The Foundations of Early Modern Europe, 1460–1559* (London: Weidenfield and Nicholson, 1970, reprinted 1978), pp. 44–6.
26 Anon, originally published in 1497, 1500 edition available via EEBO, STC 24867.
27 Roger William, *A key into the language of America, or, An help to the language of the natives in that part of America called New-England*, available via EEBO, Wing (not STC) 2766.
28 Roger Ascham, *The Scholemaster*, excerpt in *The Norton Anthology of English Literature*, vol. 6 (New York and London: W. W. Norton, 1993), pp. 994–5.
29 Francis Osborne, *Advice to a Son* (1656) in Louis B. Wright (ed.), *Advice to a Son, Precepts of Lord Burghley, Sir Walter Raleigh and Francis Osborne* (New York: Cornell University Press, 1962), p. 73.

Part Three
Texts, Writers and Contexts

The Sonnet and Amatory Verse: Wyatt, Philip Sidney and Shakespeare

There is a tendency to read love poetry as the sincere outpouring of the soul, but all is often not as it seems, especially with amatory verse of the Renaissance. Along with other types of literary expression, it was also often a vehicle of self-aggrandisement in career terms. Gary Waller suggests that patterns of patronage and poetry radiated out from the court, from the central 'courtier poets', such as Sir Thomas Wyatt, through lawyers or gentlemen like John Donne, who hoped to share in the court's munificence, to those of lower social rank, like William Shakespeare, whose livelihood was directly influenced by the patronage of the nobility.[1]

The ability to express oneself in eloquent prose and verse were social graces expected of educated individuals, and advancement often depended upon self-display. Exceptional literary prowess in these circumstances could make the difference between a successful suit for patronage and graceless anonymity. Close reading of love poetry often reveals subtle political tensions, religious or social comment and anxieties, within conventional structures or through subtle manipulation of predictable tropes.

Sir Thomas Wyatt and the Forerunners to the English Sonnet

Sir Thomas Wyatt (1503–42) was a young courtier at the court of Henry VIII in 1527 when, uninvited, he joined a diplomatic mission to Rome and Venice. This characteristically impulsive act was to have a profound influence on the subsequent development of English poetry. The verse of the English court at the beginning of Henry's reign fell into two broad types; the eloquent courtly style, dealing with the arts, courtesy or virtuous love, and the popular, often raucous, ballads of sexual adventure, hunting and other 'country' pursuits. Aspects of the more sophisticated Italian verse forms such as the *frottoli* of Serafino,* however, were being enthusiastically assimilated into the native lyric by the mid 1520s.

Whether during the diplomatic visit to France of 1526 or to northern Italy the following year, Wyatt's poetry was influenced by the *strombotto*, a type of verse form that was often accompanied by lute music and the defining aspect of which is its alternating *ab ab ab* rhyme scheme culminating in the couplet *cc*. Wyatt's best-known example is 'She sat and sowed', which appears in the Devonshire Manuscript, a court compilation of popular verse.[2] The light-hearted rhythm and witty handling belies its sardonic and ultimately vengeful content:

> She sat and sowde that hath done me the wrong
> Whereof I plain and have done many a daye,
> And whilst she herd my plaint in piteous song
> Wisshed my hert the samplar as it lay.
> The blynd maister whom I have served so long,
> Grudging to here that he did here her saye,

* Serafino de'Ciminelli (1446–1500) also known as Serafino dell'Aquila. The term *frottola* is generic and used for a variety of types of songs which mixed courtly and folk traditions; they may include snatches of 'folk wisdom' in proverbs, shreds of contemporary songs of the day, improvisation and more formal types of song or verse. They were witty and urbane and often performed to the lute. Although they had no fixed stanzaic format, they often had an amusing refrain. The *strombotto* comes under this general heading. See Elizabeth Heale, *Wyatt, Surrey and Early Tudor Poetry* (London: Longman, 1998), pp. 78–86.

Made her own wepon do her fynger blede,
To fele if pricking were so good in deed.[3]

It is tempting to read the poem within the context of the hothouse atmosphere of a court life of display, flirtation and frustration and, no doubt, this allusion would be recognised by its first readers. The culture of service and imposed idleness was often considered effeminising and the male voice of the poem could be seen as powerless in his suffering. The initial couplets of the complaint introduce a conventional courtly theme of unrequited love, but the 'turn' of the third line instigates a more sinister and cruel shift. Focalised through the rejected lover's eyes, the woman's diffident stitching at her embroidery frame becomes a violent attack on his heart. With great economy of expression the direction of the poem veers from bitter vulnerability to forceful revenge as the speaker attempts to seize control, albeit through the intervention of his 'blynd master', Love. In a neat epigrammatic flourish, the final couplet turns the woman's needle upon herself, 'To fele if pricking were so good in deed' (l. 8). To achieve any coherence this has to be read as sexual innuendo, suggesting that the withheld 'love' that the speaker so desires is of a carnal nature and that it has been freely given elsewhere. In the manuscript version the last two syllables are transcribed as separate words ('in deed'), with forceful emphasis on the last and the betrayal of the 'deed' done. The revelation of the final line disrupts the primary understanding of the relationship between the two characters, necessitating re-evaluation and a new reading. The lover's brooding re-enactment of the assumed act of infidelity is replicated in the reader's return to the beginning of the poem. The worldly astringent humour of the poem is typical of the *strombotto*, but also draws upon existing ideas about women's supposed libidinousness, unfaithfulness and manipulative tendencies, often found in contemporary ballads, rhymes and jokes.

The Italian Sonnet and Petrarchan Influences

Whilst in Italy Sir Thomas Wyatt encountered the impressive sonnet sequence of Francisco Petrarch (1304–74). The courtly love conventions of the French Troubadour and German Minnesang[*] poets which Petrarch inherited were characterised by profound, wounding and quite ecstatic desires for the idealised Lady. Her presence is often endowed with a religious profundity which guides the Lover towards a spiritual understanding of love, crystallised in the moment of the poem.[4] His own influential sonnet sequence was addressed to 'Laura' but she may have been unaware of Petrarch's enduring devotion, which prompted him to write the cycle of three hundred and sixty six sonnets, continuing even after her death.[†] The sequence, which was widely imitated throughout Europe, is composed of sonnets and other poetic forms, including *canzoni* (songs), ballads, sestina[‡] and madrigals,[§] creating a garland of praise and reflection.

Typical features of the Petrarchan sonnet which would be emulated by later European poets include stylised images of physical beauty and allusions to spirituality and moral growth inspired by the *donna angelicata*.[¶] Nonetheless, the focus is firmly on the male experience of love. Tensions generated between physical desires and the aspirational moral aesthetic find expression in characteristic use of oxymora and antitheses.

Typical tropes such as the rhetorical figure of partheniade became commonplace and were eventually parodied in the work of later English sonneteers such as Shakespeare.[**] This literary device is also known as

* The German Minnesang poets were performers of original music and lyric, flourishing between the twelfth and fourteenth centuries. The Troubadours were the northern Italian and southern French equivalent.

† Petrarch's sequence is known as *Canzoniere* or *Rime Sparse* ('Scattered Rhymes'), it is comprised of 317 sonnets, 29 *canzoni*, or songs, and 4 madrigals. The term *canzoni* is used to describe a range of medieval poetic forms and has links with the Troubadour poets of Provence. See Michael Spiller, *The Development of the Sonnet: An Introduction* (London: Routledge, 1992). Laura is believed to have been the young wife of Hugh de Sade, born in Avignon, whom Petrarch met when she was seventeen.

‡ A sestina is a tight arrangement which revolves around the figure 6: it has six verses which each have six lines; within the poem there are six key words, two of which appear in each verse; the poem ends with a triplet which must contain all six of the key words.

§ A madrigal is an unaccompanied song sung in several harmonising or counterpoint parts. The term is also used for poems which could be sung in this way.

¶ This means 'angelic woman' in Italian.

** See his Sonnet 130 discussed later in this chapter.

the blazon* and metaphorically associates the beloved's attributes to precious commodities. Attention is directed to the alluring, but ultimately fragmented, charms of the beloved, such as forehead and breasts of alabaster or ivory, eyebrows of ebony, hair of golden wire, lips of coral or rubies, and teeth as small pearls. Importantly, her eyes are considered to be the windows of the soul and are Neo-platonically† associated with light and spirituality. Consequently, her gaze may bathe the onlooker in light, literally shining like cosmic bodies such as the sun or stars. The themes, imagery, structure and literary techniques of these poems became codified into a system of amorous lyricism termed 'Petrarchism' which was introduced to the English court by Wyatt, but also had a profound effect upon love poetry throughout Europe.

The 'Englishing' of Petrarch‡

When Wyatt returned to England and began 'translating' Petrarch's sonnets he maintained the octave's structure but, perhaps influenced by the possibilities of the neat *strombotto* ending, introduced a final couplet.§ Wyatt's modified structure anticipated the creation of the English sonnet, with a rhyme scheme of *abbaabba cddc ee*. Wyatt's reworking of Petrarch's sonnets should not be considered merely translations, however, as the sentiment moves subtly from the aesthetic Neo-platonic concerns of the originals to encompass a more worldly and grounded perspective. Wyatt's slight reconceptions often transpose the idealised

* A list of physical attributes, sometimes glossed as a 'top to toe' description.

† The Renaissance saw a renewed interest in the classics which included Plato's theories of love, discussed in his *Symposium*. See Hoby's translation of Castiglione's *Book of the Courtier* in Part Three: 'Life Guides, Mother's Advice and Conduct Books'.

‡ This is a contemporary term used in the sixteenth and seventeenth centuries to mean translation, but in fact the term was loose enough to encompass paraphrase and more creative interpretation.

§ The normative structure of the Italian sonnets was an octave rhyming *abbaabba* with a sestet rhyming either *cdecde, cdcdcd* or *cdedce*. Henry Howard, Earl of Surrey, Wyatt's friend and admirer, was responsible for dividing the octave of the inherited Petrarchan sonnet into two more manageable quatrains, rhyming *abab cdcd*. He then changed the pattern of the sestet to follow suit, thereby developing the form now recognised as the English or Shakespearean sonnet: *abab cdcd efef gg*.

vision of timeless devotion to a compromised social situation which is redolent of English court intrigue.*

Wyatt's version of Petrarch's *Rime* 19, '*Son animali al mondo*',† as with many of his works, is often interpreted as referring obliquely to his ill-fated association with Henry VIII's second wife Anne Boleyn. Petrarch's octave presents a typically Neo-platonic motif; the extended metaphor of animals who, in varying degrees, can withstand the brilliance of the 'sun' which, in the second line of the sestet, is revealed to be the glance of his Lady. Aligning himself with those who misjudge its danger, the speaker admits that, although he knows that he will be burned, with weeping eyes he must still follow (her). The passive resignation of Petrarch's Lover is subtly manipulated, affording the voice of Wyatt's poem a more assertive persona as he embraces his doom in the burning embers. The suffering victim of Petrarch's lament is shaped by Wyatt into a more heroic and active Lover who is nonetheless similarly infatuated. Read in autobiographical terms, at Henry's court to pursue the prohibited – whether Anne Boleyn's charms or a more prosaic desire – could be dangerously self-destructive.‡

Wyatt's 'Whoso list to hounte' [hunt] similarly reworks the Petrarchan '*Una candida cerva*' (A white hind), *Rime* 190.[5] In Petrarch's sonnet the pure white hind with golden horns evokes the unicorn, associated with virginity in contemporary myth. It wears a golden collar, embellished with diamonds and topazes, which clearly states that 'Caesar' declares it to be free. The text on its collar also has biblical associations, linking it with Christ in the Garden of Gethsemane.[6] The overall impression is of spiritual ethereality, whereas Wyatt employs the virile semantic field of the hunt, one of the most popular pastimes at Henry's court. Wyatt's 'Dier' [dear] by contrast, is not the distant and saintly Lady of the Italianate sonnet tradition; she is wild, untameable, and her pursuers are figured as the hunt in full cry. Contrary to Petrarchan sonnet

* See discussion of the precarious nature of the courtier's life in the 'City, Court and Country' chapter in Part Four of this volume.

† The first line of Wyatt's version is '*Som fowles there be*'.

‡ See discussion of Wyatt's '*V. Innocentia Veritas Viat Fides*' in Part Four: 'City, Court and Country'.

expectations the speaker does not declare abiding love and willing service; from the opening lines he declares his exhaustion, 'the vayne travail hath wearied me so sore' (l. 3). Despite trailing behind the pack, in itself an unchivalrous aspersion on the Lady's honour, he is still compelled to follow. The octave's end recognises his certain failure with the despairing 'in a nett I seke to hold the wynd' (l. 8). To this point the sonnet seems to imply merely a wayward liberty in the hind, however the precise reason why she is so unattainable is written in the diamonds of her necklet which transcribe a stark warning: '*Noli mi tangere* for Caesar's I ame' (l. 14).* It is usual to read this as referring to Henry VIII's 'ownership' of Anne Boleyn and a warning to prospective lovers, Wyatt included. We should be wary, however, of allowing biographical reflection to undermine its literary value. Given the fact that she wears the ruler's mark, and yet still seems willing to participate in the chase, the implication of inconsistency at least, if not outright infidelity, seems all too clear.

Faithless Friends

In 'They flee from me', one of Wyatt's most popular poems, he continues the unfaithful lover theme, albeit draped in some ambiguity. As indicated in the opening to this chapter, love poetry, like any other, carries the imprint of its time and may carry complex references to external factors. The first stanza of the poem is often read as a critique of the shifting factions of alliance and intrigue at court. The three movements of the poem represent, firstly, a reflection on the fickleness of unnamed individuals who shun the speaker; a fond dream-like remembrance of a specific sexual liaison with an attractive and accommodating woman; and her rejection of him, followed by his rejection by her, ending in a direct address to the reader which elicits judgement upon her behaviour.

An atmosphere of indistinct danger is suggested in that the unnamed 'They' of the first stanza is said to have put his/herself at risk through

* 'Don't touch me for Caesar's I am.' This sonnet is the seventh in the Egerton Manuscript.

their associations with the speaker in former times. In a troubling mixed metaphor these visitors are represented as tame deer, willing to 'take bread at [his] hand' (l. 6) and simultaneously hunting beasts 'stalking in [his] chamber' (l. 2). By the stanza's final line, however, the animal imagery is abandoned to the pressing issue of human inconstancy in seeking fresh adventure. The two remaining stanzas describe one such specific circumstance, initially lingering voyeuristically on the charms of a past lover, alighting on her 'armes long and small' (l. 12), as she permits her loose gown to fall from her shoulders, and asks softly 'dere hart, how like you this?' (l. 4). The woman is indisputably in control of the situation, however, there is no ambiguity regarding her sexual availability. Moreover, having enjoyed the liaison, she dismisses the speaker, in his terms, following what he terms a new promiscuous fashion at court. This may be an oblique reference to the sexual dalliances of Wyatt's contemporaries, or even criticism of the king, but the uncertainty defies explanation. Wyatt pays no lip-service to the courtly love conventions of chastity or suffering in celibacy. Predatory and fully aware of her power, his woman overthrows contemporary gender conditioning, becoming the lover, rather than the passive beloved. Unlike in the Petrarchan traditions, however, her victim does not suffer in silence, but bitterly demands of the reader, 'I would fain knowe what she hathe deserved' (l. 21).

The acidic tone continues in 'She sat and sowed', where the woman is imagined enclosing her admirer's heart in her embroidery frame, the better to stab it with her needle. By contrast, this poem foregrounds the woman in an intimate moment of sexual fulfilment, framing her within the two more abstract verses. The gaze of the reader is invited to view the woman's vulnerable unclothed body, whilst the rejected partner solicits compliance to his call for revenge. In an ironic contradiction between sentiment and expression, the semantic field of this last stanza emphasises the gracious courtly speech of service and submission.

Although it is not possible to date most of the poems accurately, Wyatt's 'They flee from me' appears in his own Egerton Manuscript which was begun early in 1535. If the wild and provocative woman portrayed is Anne Boleyn, as is often suggested, she did call down judgement on herself in May of the same year. Accused of adultery with several courtiers, including her brother, she was beheaded. Wyatt was imprisoned in the Tower of London and fully expected to follow his fellow courtiers to the block, as his letters to his father reveal.*[7] After a period of rustication at his father's estate in Kent, however, most probably due to the intervention of patrons at court, he was readmitted into the king's service. Shortly before his death, he was restored to favour, receiving a royal pardon, and returned to diplomatic duties in 1542. The contradictory juxtaposition discussed above in 'They flee from me' evokes just this type of political instability, arbitrary danger and the duplicity of court life. The intimate microcosmic exemplar of powerlessness and rejection in the poem can be read against the shifting political alliances and self-seeking power-games of Henry VIII's court.

Sidney's *Astrophil and Stella*: 'Strife Growne Between *Vertue and Love*'

Sir Philip Sidney's Petrarchan-inspired sonnet sequence *Astrophil and Stella* was written after a lull of around a quarter of a century, and inspired a new Elizabethan interest in sonneteering. The work circulated in manuscript form until his sister Mary, Countess of Pembroke, published his collected works posthumously in 1598. *Astrophil and Stella* is the first English sonnet sequence to adopt Petrarch's model of true sonnets linked by other types of lyric verse forms, although Sidney uses the connecting poems to different effect. The sequence of a hundred and eight sonnets and eleven songs traces Astrophil's infatuation with Stella, his attempts to engage her attentions, the ethical struggle between desire, duty and virtue, his attempts to seduce her and his ultimate failure. The sequence does not impose an obvious moralising closure, through acceptance of the error of his judgement or elevation to a Christian or Neo-platonic level, for

* Wyatt is thought to have written '*Circa Regna tonat*' whilst in the Tower, witnessing the executions from his window: 'These blood days have broken my heart … The bell tower showed me such a sight / That in my head stick day and night', ll. 11, 16 and 17. See Muir, *Life and Letters*, and Part Four: 'City, Court and Country'.

example. The eleven 'songs' allow extended development of themes, difficult in the compact form of the sonnet, such as Song 10's teasing and decidedly erotic fantasy of love's consummation.

The sequence represents a complicated relationship between the conventions of courtly verse and biographical details of Sidney's life in the early 1580s, often being read as a *roman-à-clef*,* detailing his supposed rebuffed advances to Penelope Devereux. In part this rests upon her father's wish that they might marry, expressed shortly before his death. In fact, there seems to have been no contact between them in the ensuing five years until January 1581 when Penelope arrived at court, aged eighteen, as the ward of Sidney's aunt, Lady Huntingdon. By November of the same year she was betrothed and married to Robert, Lord Rich. Michael Spiller reads the sequence as autobiographical but points out that neither Sidney's wife, Frances Walsingham, Sidney's family, nor Penelope Rich herself seem to have objected to her being identified as Stella, or to the information being broadcast by publication, despite some *risqué* implications.[8] Gary Waller, however, points out that the two sonnets most transparent in their identification of Penelope Rich (24 and 37) did not appear in the first volume. For untraceable reasons Sidney seems to have enjoyed fuelling his readers' speculations by inserting clearly identifiable allusions to Penelope's new name 'Rich' into Sonnets 24, 35 and, most uncompromisingly, Sonnet 37:

> My mouth doth water, and my breast doth swell,
> My tongue doth itch, my thoughts in labour be:
> Listen then Lordlings with good eare to me,
> For of my life I must a riddle tell.
> Towards Aurora's Court a Nymph doth dwell,
> Rich in all beauties which man's eye can see:
> Beauties so farre from reach of worlds, that we
> Abase her praise, saying she doth excell:
> Rich in the treasure of deserv'd renowne,

* French: *Roman-à-clef* means 'novel with a key', indicating that there are embedded clues which allow the reader to identify real historical personages within it.

Rich in the riches of a royall hart,
Rich in those gifts which give th'eternall crowne;
Who though most rich in these and everie part,
Which make the patents of true worldly blisse,
Hath no misfortune, but that Rich she is.

The sequence does present itself as an account of lived personal passion, with direct allusion to Sidney's own name in 'Astrophil' and Sonnet 83's references to 'Good brother Philip' and 'sir Phip' (ll. 1, 14). Although ostensibly directed at Stella's pet sparrow, to an informed reader the humorous warning that it takes liberties with Astrophil's patience is read as witty self-reflexive censure:

Cannot such grace your silly selfe content,
But you must needs with those lips billing be?
And through those lips drink Nectar from that toong;
Leave that, sir Phip, lest off your necke be wrong. (ll. 11–14)

On many levels a sense of court life, with its social, amatory and political rivalries, which Sidney knew and participated in, is captured in the poems. A biographical reading is encouraged in the vivid glimpses of a courtier's life which provide vehicles for introspection on the effect of Astrophil's passion. These include amorous dalliances and rivalry (Sonnet 54), feats of horsemanship (Sonnet 49), popular interest in astrology (Sonnet 26); the 'discourse of courtly tides' (Sonnet 51); the gossip of 'courtly nymphs' (Sonnet 6); discussion of topical events in Europe (Sonnet 30); and staged trials of combat (Sonnets 41 and 53):

Having this day my horse, my hand, my launce
Guided so well, that I obtained the prize,
Both by the judgement of the English eyes,
And of some sent from that sweet enemie Fraunce ... (Sonnet 41)

Two such tournaments in which Sidney participated, and which French diplomats attended, were staged at court in 1581, before Penelope

Devereux was betrothed to Lord Rich.[9] If the context of the sonnet evokes contemporary activities at Elizabeth's court, the couplet identifies the infatuation as *amour courtois* (courtly love). The concluding lines reveal that the reason for Astrophil's good fortune is not, as the gathered audience variously state, his horsemanship, his strength, nor parrying skills or luck, but Stella's illuminating and inspiring presence: 'her heav'nly face / Sent forth beames, which made so faire my race' (ll. 13–14). This is clearly alluding to the Neo-platonic sonnet conventions of the 'Angelic Lady'.

The sequence's opening sonnet encapsulates the tensions between the inherited schema of Petrarchism and Astrophil's (and perhaps Sidney's) personal drive towards originality. It announces the paradoxical situation of one who loves sincerely but is entrapped within an amatory convention which undermines its expression. In order to gain the attention of his beloved, and convince her of his spontaneous love, he must 'paint the blackest face of woe' (l. 5), but in order to find the inspiration he needs to do so, ironically, he needs to search the works of other poets. The reader is struck by the embellishment required, not only in the expression of Astrophil's pain, but in the necessary rhetorical display indicated in the 'inventions fine' (l. 6) that he studies. Moreover, the entire focus is on the difficulties of expression – on the writing of the sonnet, in fact – rather than the beloved or the love. Drawing attention to itself in Alexandrines* rather than the pentameters of the other sonnets, this poem 'sets out the stall' for the entire sequence. The embedded incongruity is that, despite the first line's declaration of heartfelt sincerity and the last line's seeming resolution to ignore the stilted conventions of contemporary love poetry, the sonnet is loaded with predictable allusions and copious rhetorical devices such as might be found in the Petrarchan imitators. The first part of the octave provides an abstract of the whole sequence, delineated in the steps of the rhetorical figure of anadiplosis,† which leads to the goal of gaining Stella's 'grace' (l. 4). Sidney frustrates his creation's indicated plan, however, subjecting him to lack of inspiration and paucity of

* In English poetry the Alexandrine uses six iambs per line.

† Anadiplosis: chaining effect, achieved by the repetition of the word at the end of one phrase to begin the next.

eloquence. In the over-theatrical stilted conceit used by Astrophil to describe his state Sidney lampoons the far-fetched devices of past and contemporary poets, gained from 'turning others' leaves' (l. 7):

> But words came halting forth, wanting Invention's stay,
> Invention, Nature's child, fled step-dame Studie's blowes,
> And others' feete still seem'd but strangers in my way. (ll. 9–11)

Despite this sonnet's bid for sincerity and seeming rejection of the circus of Petrarchism, in fact, Petrarch's own Sonnet 20, originally intended as the first in his sequence, traversed similar ground:

> Many times I have begun to write verses:
> but the pen, the hand and the intellect
> fell back defeated at their first attempt. (ll. 12–14)[10]

Astrophil's literary anxiety regarding the articulation of his passion is a dominant theme throughout and a significant component of his obsession with the enactment of love. A brief examination discloses this enduring trope: Sonnet 6 reviews the content of other lovers' poems, noting their genre and style; Sonnet 58 reflects upon the orator's powers, as he attempts to write the 'anatomy' of his 'woes' in 'piercing phrases' (ll. 10, 9); the rules of grammar which decree that two negatives (Stella's repeated refusal) generate a positive are wittily described in Sonnet 63; while Sonnet 70 finds Astrophil considering the sonnet form itself, maintaining that it is not bound 'in sad rhymes to creep' (l. 2). Despite his admission in several sonnets that he 'engarlands' his own speech with the 'choicest flowers' of others' words (Sonnet 55, l. 2), Astrophil is at pains to claim that he is 'no pick-purse of another's wit' (Sonnet 74, l. 8), which is clearly untrue. The dichotomy between Astrophil's speech and action, his self-deluding claims and lack of self-awareness, is often a source of humour and serves to highlight the distance between Sidney and Astrophil. The untrustworthiness of appearance is a familiar preoccupation in Renaissance drama but the self-conscious parody within the sequence draws attention to the constructed nature of the text – or art as technique, in Victor Shklovsky's terms.[11] The artifice constructs the 'reality' presented, hence the reader becomes aware of the poesis rather than mimesis of life, neatly underlined in Sonnet 45's paradoxical 'I am not I, pity the tale of me' (l. 14).

More typically adhering to the sonnet traditions, in Sonnet 9 Stella's beauty is praised in an elaborate blazon:

> Queene Vertue's Court, which some call Stella's face,
> Prepar'd by Nature's choisest furniture,
> Hath his front built of Alabaster pure;
> Gold is the covering of that stately place.
> The doore by which sometimes comes forth her Grace,
> Red Porphir is, which locke of pearle makes sure:
> Whose porches rich (which name of cheekes endure)
> Marble mixt red and white do interlace. (ll. 1–8)

To its first readers the opening epithet no doubt evoked the court of Queen Elizabeth and her assiduously-maintained persona as the Virgin Queen, which in itself is most probably a wry reference to Stella's perceived over-zealous protection of her honour. Elizabeth had not only read Petrarch in the Italian but also wrote poems within the tradition herself, readily discernible in the couplet 'On Monsieur's Departure': 'I am and not; I freeze and yet am burn'd; / Since from myself, my other self I turn'd' (ll. 5, 6). She encouraged her male courtiers to participate in courtly love dissemblance, expecting and manipulating their devotion to political ends.

The effect of Sidney's blazon is slightly grotesque to the modern reader, however, and such elaborate blazons were already being parodied in verse and image, as is evident from Thomas Lodge's *Scillaes Metamorphosis* (*sic*) (written c.1584–8).* The semantic field used in the octave of the blazon is of architecture, appropriate to the embellishment of a palace, delineating the exquisite beauty of the façade, roof, porches,

* See the discussion of Lodge's Scylla in Part Three: 'Renaissance Epyllion' and Shakespeare's parodies in his sonnets, discussed in the same chapter.

portal and door furniture. At this point the reader may begin to suspect an element of gentle burlesque humour: would Stella be flattered to hear that her mouth was like a door which her teeth kept firmly locked? Moreover, the suggestion which is developed in the sestet is that Stella dwells within this artificially-erected and guarded structure. This semblance of propriety and Vertue is 'built' (l. 3), moreover, it is cold – calling into play the dichotomy between cool virtue and hot desire which pervades the sequence. The sestet interacts with the Petrarchan conceit of the *donna angelicata*, naming Stella 'this heav'nly guest' (l. 9) and developing the familiar conceit of the illuminating and transporting gaze, associated with the spirit. Nonetheless, as she surveys the surrounding countryside there is a sense that Stella is trapped within the edifice. Employing the rhetorical figure of polyptoton* in keeping with the sophisticated but artificial celebration of Stella's beauty, the convoluted word play insistently dwells on the idea of sensory gratification: 'Of touch they are that without touch doth touch' (l. 12), ostensibly referring to Astrophil's emotional response to her glance. The concluding line, however, demolishes his painstakingly-created monument to virtue, revisiting the theme of suppressed desire. Astrophil's control of the situation is lost as the final 'touch' [of Stella's eyes] is revealed to be the tinder which reignites his passion: 'Of touch they are, and poor I am their straw' (l. 14), which incidentally evokes Petrarch's Sonnet 90.

Sidney's application of what Leonard Forster has termed the 'arsenal' of conceits, gathered from Petrarch and other Italian sonneteers, was complex.[12] Whilst employing the conventions he simultaneously undermines, parodies or even refutes them. Sonnet 15 addresses other poets engaged upon writing love poems in a series of apostrophes,† deriding their methods.‡ He upbraids them for forcing the conventions artificially into their verse, searching for the 'purling spring', driving in

* Polyptoton: repetition of a word in different forms in a sentence.

† Apostrophe: an exclamation turning away from the subject in hand to address a person or entity (such as the gods or Nature).

‡ It is not clear to whom Sidney alludes here, it could be Chapman, Marlowe or Jonson, but it is more likely to be a composite or even merely a literary device. There does not need to be a 'real' poet any more than one Dark Lady or a Beautiful Boy in Shakespeare's Sonnets.

wild flowers 'not sweet perhaps', scouring the dictionary for alliterative adornment, and particularly for recycling 'poore Petrarch's long deceased woes' (ll. 1, 3, 5, 6 and 7). Unusually, in this sonnet the rhyming couplet appears after the octave, in the French style, rather than at the end of the poem. As Sidney knew and admired the French poets of the French *Pléiade* group, this may have been a gesture towards Joachim du Bellay's anti-Petrarchan poem 'Against Petrarchists', which culminates:

> And in short, to listen to their songs
> one would think that their love was nothing but flames and icicles,
> arrows, chains and a thousand other
> such pretentious nonsense.[13]

Sidney's well-known *The Defence of Poesy* similarly castigates contemporary poets for using clichéd and artificial conceits which do not convey true sentiment or passion. Shakespeare's sonnets also reveal the artificiality of the conventions in witty parody.

Astrophil and Stella prompts lively critical debate including whether it should be read sequentially, if it has an overall binding narrative structure, or if it represents 'snap shots' representing a fusion between Petrarchan and contemporary love conventions. Lacking neat closure, the sequence requires the reader to supply a resolution. It can be read, for instance, as reiterating a Petrarchan perspective of the enduring and incapacitating effect of love, or even as an illustrated negative exemplar of stages towards the despair which arises from the corrupting effects of carnal desire, hence accommodating a moralistic or Christian reading.

William Shakespeare's 'Sugr'd Sonnets'

William Shakespeare's collection of sonnets generates ambiguities to an even greater extent than Sir Philip Sidney's. Without doubt they interact with the Petrarchan conventions, but often indirectly through the works of earlier poets. Modern scholarship especially draws attention to the model of Samuel Daniel's *Delia* and *The Complaint of Rosamund*, published together in one volume in 1592, as were *Shakespeares Sonnettes* and *A Lover's Complaint*, which were finally published under the one title in 1609. By this time William Jaggard had already printed four of the sonnets, without authorisation, in editions of *The Passionate Pilgrim By W. Shakespeare* of 1599, implying that the entire contents of the volume were by the same author.[14] Although these dates are verifiable due to external references, the dates of the sonnets' composition have been widely debated. One of the main reasons for this is the longstanding tendency to read the sequence as autobiographical; if dates can be established for particular poems, they may be related to the known facts of Shakespeare's life. In this way Shakespeare scholars have attempted to discover the recipient of the dedication affixed by the printer, to 'Mr. W. H.', and the addressees of the poems.

The first section of the sequence as we now have it, from Sonnet 1 to 126, is addressed to a beautiful young man and this has particularly occupied such investigations, as an autobiographic reading may suggest that Shakespeare was bisexual or homosexual. These poems are regarded as a sub-collection and are assumed to be in the order which Shakespeare intended. Colin Burrow points out that they can be quite confidently dated as being composed between 1595 and 1596, but may have been revised up to the point of publication.[15] Critics often speculate that they may have been written for Henry Wriothesley, the young Earl of Southampton, to whom Shakespeare's *Venus and Adonis* (1593) was dedicated.

According to evidence revealed through lexical analysis, it is very probable that one of the earliest groups written contained the so-called 'Dark Lady' Sonnets, from 127 to 154, beginning as early as 1591, and that there was an overlap between these and some of those to the young man, 61 to 103, written from the end of 1594 to 1595. The sonnets which now appear first, 1 to 60, are believed to have been written the following year. After a gap of around three years the final section, from 104 to 126, was written, from 1598 to 1604.[16] Although this information may seem a little dry, it does provide a useful insight into Shakespeare's interests and the development of his themes. A composition guideline also demonstrates the futility of trying to calculate the addressees of the sequence as it now stands by aligning it with Shakespeare's sparse biographical information. He did not produce the sequence in a linear fashion, beginning at our Sonnet 1 and ending at Sonnet 154.

The first section of sonnets is unusual in being addressed to a young man, but is not unique within the sonnet tradition. In 1595 Richard Barnfield had included some quite explicit love poems to 'Ganymede', a lovely young man, in his *Affectionate Shepherd*. Michelangelo, the great Italian artist, also wrote a series of three hundred love sonnets to the young Tommasio de'Cavalieri, using Petrarchan conventions. The first seventeen of Shakespeare's sequence initially adopt a fraternal or even paternal tone, urging the young man to marry in order to reproduce his own beauty in his children. Henceforward the relationship between the speaker and the addressee becomes more ambiguous; in some poems the word play is light-heartedly erotic, in others the fear of loss lurks beneath the praise. As with many of Sidney's sonnets, there is also self-reflexive comment on the act of writing and, particularly in these early sonnets, the trope of cheating time through fixing the young man's image eternally in verse, as discussed below.

'Wasteful time debateth with decay'

The quotation is from Sonnet 15 and summarises one of the central themes of the entire early section of the sequence. Sonnet 12 is also typical of the earlier group, maintaining that all things on earth have their moment of perfection, beyond which they must ripen and decay:

> When I do count the clock that tells the time,
> And see the brave day sunk in hideous night;
> When I behold the violet past its prime,
> And sable curls all silvered o'er with white;
> When lofty trees I see barren of leaves,
> Which erst[while] from heat did canopy the herd,
> And summer's green all girded up in sheaves,
> Bourne on a bier with white and bristly beard … (ll. 1–8)

In both sonnets the argument is presented in the familiar three-stage syllogism,* coinciding with the beginnings of the three quatrains. The theme of mutability pervades the entire Sonnet 15 until the final line, beginning in a general consideration of the life cycle of all natural things in the first two lines. The second half of this quatrain introduces a theatrical metaphor deprecating the 'shows' of the man-made world, observed by higher powers. By the second quatrain Shakespeare has begun to texture the imagery by conflating the two themes already introduced, the lives of men are become indistinguishable from plants', in that they, too, have 'sap' in their veins and 'increase' under the same sky. Conversely, the lexical choices suggest that the plants are cheered or jeered by the same theatrical audience, like swaggering actors who brag and display themselves in early life at the height of their careers but then, quite poignantly, given Shakespeare's profession and maturity, in decline are left only with ephemeral memories:

> When I consider everything that grows
> Holds in perfection but a little moment;
> That this huge stage presenteth naught but shows
> Whereon the stars in secret influence comment;
> When I perceive that men as plants increase,
> Cheered and checked by the self-same sky,
> Vaunt in their their youthful sap, at height decrease,
> And wear their brave state out of memory. (ll. 1–8)

With great economy Shakespeare has succeeded in presenting two intertwined discourses of vegetation and theatrical performance in only eight lines, the weight of which is brought to bear on the young man in the next quatrain. Punning on the 'conceit' of his imagery, the speaker pointedly addresses the young man, declaring that these natural rhythms, the decay of beauty, the swagger of youth, and the decline of worldly reputation, all bring him to mind. At once he is revealed as vain, conceited, showy and shallow, trapped by nature's course but

* Syllogism: three-stage deductive reasoning, usually from a general concept to the more specific. Sometimes used to demonstrate seemingly rational but spurious reasoning.

unnatural for not participating in its renewal. Moreover, in a morality play fragment, Time and Decay already lurk at his shoulder ready to claim him, very much as the skeleton images of Holbein's series of woodcuts of the *Dance of Death* haunt the daily lives of the unsuspecting. The melancholy tone is only relieved by the deliverance of the last line, where the Lover claims that, like a Good Angel – albeit a horticulturally-inclined one – he can intercede on the young man's behalf: 'And, all in war with Time for love of you, / As he takes from you, I engraft you new' (ll. 13–14). This image of rebirth or regeneration, however, is not from seed – which the young man has avoided setting – but by grafting, perhaps a pun on the colloquial term for hard work.

This method of propagation takes a desirable but often weak scion from one plant and binds it to the stronger and older root stock of another, to create a hybrid plant with the best qualities of both. The transitive verb 'engraft' is unusual for the time, its first appearance recorded in the late sixteenth century, but the art of grafting was a valuable skill in the great gardens of the nobility. In 1568 Leonard Mascall translated *The Arte and Manner Howe to Plant and Graffe all Sorts of Trees*, in which he describes a method of prolonging the 'fruiting' of cherry trees in precisely the approach that Shakespeare advocates: 'graffe them upon a frank mulberry tree … and they shall endure unto Allhallowstide'.[17] The analogy is that the older poet will be the 'frank mulberry tree' to the decorative youth and the fruit of their union will be his beautiful image, recreated in verse.

The entangled natural and human imagery of the first quatrain is fulfilled in the bond of the graft, which entwines lover and beloved but also, on a metaphysical level, in the triumph of man's ingenuity in manipulating nature and time. The structure and the usual *abab cdcd efef gg* rhyme scheme of the sonnet are by this time unexceptional, but the ingenuity and economy of the tightly-packed conceits are admirable. Apart from the possible pun already noted and a second on 'you, most rich in youth' (l. 10), which may refer to the wealth and lineage of the young man as much as to his abundance of youthful beauty, there is less ambiguous word play and innuendo than characterises many sonnets in the sequence.

The deliciously playful and provocative Sonnet 20, by comparison, tests the skills of the reader on every line. Opening with a compliment that may seem to be directed at the Lover's mistress, 'A woman's face with nature's own hand painted', the poem introduces ambiguities before reaching even the end of the first phrase. The face is said to be beautiful and 'painted' by Nature, but the verb actually destabilises the phrase, implying negative connotations with the cosmetic enhancement that unnamed 'others' may use. The smooth movement of the enjambment of the first line ends on the address to the beloved, creating a perplexing paradox: 'A woman's face with Nature's own hand painted / Hast thou, the master mistress of my passion' (ll. 1–2).

The epithet is confusing and offers a number of possible readings: it may refer to the relative dependence of the speaker and his socially-elevated addressee or perhaps it alludes to a courtly-love convention in which the poet demonstrates his devotion to his mistress in verse. There may be homo-erotic implications or perhaps the person has characteristics of both genders. Clearly the phrase needs interrogation and may prompt a re-reading of the first line. The gender of the addressee is in flux throughout the first two quatrains and the entire sonnet is replete with such knots of interpretation which may be termed 'impeded form'. Russian Formalism draws attention to such literary strategies which prevent the 'automisation of perception', curbing unreflective assimilation, and so compelling the reader to participate actively in unravelling meaning.* The rhyme scheme also draws attention to the gender confusion in that this poem alone in the sequence uses only 'female' rhymes.†

The sonnet reworks many Petrarchan conventions using paradox, antithesis, the blazon and Neo-platonic allusion in the heavenly light which emanates from the beloved, 'Gilding the object whereupon it

* The technique of *ostranenie* (making strange) slows reader perception, defamiliarising and forcing closer engagement with the text *as a created artefact*, rather than the language being invisible and simply carrying a message, as in usual conversation. See Victor Shklovsky's 'Art as technique' (1917), excerpt reprinted in David Lodge (ed.), *Modern Criticism and Theory: A Reader* (London: Longman, 1988), pp. 15–30.

† The 'female' rhyme falls on the penultimate syllable, rather than the last: for example, *paint*ed / *aquaint*ed; *pass*ion / *fash*ion; and *pleas*ure / *treas*ure.

gazeth' (l. 6), for example. However, the ambience of the sonnet is far removed from the Italian conventions, eventually constructing a series of strongly misogynistic binaries between the beloved young man and 'false' women, whilst presenting a plethora of sexual innuendo. The concealed puns in 'not aquainted / with shifting change' (ll. 3–4), for example, contain bawdy references to female genitalia and undergarments in 'aquainted' (a-*quaint*-ed) and 'shift'. In the last quatrain the gender of the beloved is revealed to be male, however the ambiguities and lightly-concealed erotic innuendo continue. The elaborate conceit has the goddess Nature form a being of such beauty that she is compelled to add 'one thing' to change the gender of, and – ironically – prevent her same-sex love for, her creation. In case the hint has been overlooked, the nature of the addition is underlined less subtly in the couplet: 'But since she pricked thee out for women's pleasure, / Mine be thy love, and thy love's use their treasure' (ll. 13–14).

The final line is read differently according to different critical perspectives. For those who wish to avoid the possibility of a homo-erotic reading the couplet is interpreted to mean that, due to this addition, the young man does not excite any sexual interest in the speaker. Given the linguistic acrobatics and the same-sex eroticism of the rest of the sonnet, however, this argument seems not particularly persuasive. As Colin Burrow points out, in the 1609 Quarto edition there are no apostrophes, indicating that the 'pleasure' may mean that of other women, or 'the type of pleasure enjoyed by women', suggesting a homo-erotic theme.[18] Similar themes are revisited in Sonnets 42, 133, 134 and 144; these refer to a *ménage à trois* between the speaker of the poem, the desirable young man and an unfaithful mistress.

'Dark Lady' Sonnets

Perceptions of beauty, natural, literary and counterfeited, resurface in the so-called 'Dark Lady' sonnets, beginning with Sonnet 127 and most famously in Sonnet 130. It should be noted that the appellation 'Lady' is hardly appropriate for these poems since, as we shall see, the woman addressed in this section is clearly not of noble birth or disposition. In

Sonnet 127 the speaker specifically interrogates the blazonic descriptions of synthetic and idealised beauty esteemed in the amatory verse traditions. Like Sidney's Stella, the female addressee has dark eyes, 'not counted fair' (l. 1) by Petrarchan standards. Throughout the poem the word 'fair' carries the double signification of 'blond' and 'beautiful'. The woman's darker complexion is celebrated by the lover, however, as being a more modern and natural beauty. Linking with Sonnet 20's reference to 'painted' beauty, the second quatrain reveals that public opinion coerces women to apply cosmetics, in order to be considered beautiful, 'Fairing the foul with art's borrowed face' (l. 6). For this reason the eyes of the beloved assume mourning black, all the same inspiring comment on their beauty. The sonnet relies on the paradoxical concept that 'fair' ('beautiful') is foul and that considered foul is actually fair – prefiguring the weird sisters' assertion in *Macbeth* – and may allude to the disordered mind of the Lover, whose perceptions of reality may be compromised by his condition. Feminist critics may also note that the sonnet draws attention to the constructed nature of models of female desirability, which are then playfully hijacked by the speaker.

Beginning 'My mistress' eyes are nothing like the sun', Sonnet 130 develops these themes to an extreme extent, in effect creating an anti-blazon. Evoking the sonnet conventions on every line, the voice of the Lover undermines each of the now commonplace metaphors. The fragmented attributes of the mistress – eyes, lips, breasts, hair, complexion, breath, voice and gait – are all revealed to be either unremarkable or actually unattractive. A number of contested readings offer themselves in this and similar sonnets. One response, for example, may be to conclude that the lover eschews fashionable ideas of beauty, and appreciates his mistress as being as attractive as any woman either falsely enhanced (by use of cosmetics) or over-praised in conventional verse. The tone, however, can be interpreted as either sincere or jocund.

Underlying these matters, however, is a wider debate on the unreliability of language, facilitating the familiar Renaissance theme of the variance between surface and actual content: duplicitous façade and inner truth. Duplicitous linguistic expression may also be an indication of tensions arising from inequalities of power in relationships of dependency, whether of patronage or romantic/sexual liaison. Sonnet 129, in very negative terms, debates the force of lust which 'Is perjured, murd'rous, bloody, full of blame, / Savage, extreme, rude, cruel, not to trust' (ll. 3–4). Interestingly, Sonnet 93 addresses the young man in similar terms; suspicious lest the face of virtue hides deceit.

Reversing the Ancient Greek theory of inner purity shining through to create physical beauty, the misogynistic maxim of the untrustworthiness of women's appearance often arises in literary works of the era. This finds expression in the dichotomy of attractive and virtuous appearance which hides 'all hell below', eventually at its most extreme being condensed synecdochically* in the vagina equating hell, as rehearsed in the final line of Sonnet 129; 'To shun the heaven that leads men to this hell' (l. 14). King Lear, for example, condemns 'simp'ring dames' who 'mince virtue' proclaiming, 'But to the girdle do the Gods inherit, / Beneath is all the fiends': there's hell' (*King Lear*, IV.vi.117, 119, 125, 126). Although Sonnet 130 interrogates these anxieties and cuts a swathe through the binary definitions which either idealise or vilify women as angels or whores, it is still unsettling in its extreme imagery. The message of the sonnet may simply be that the wooing of women through romantic verse and even an abundance of beauty is superfluous to the object, as Katherine Duncan-Jones suggests, 'all that is necessary is that the object of desire is female and available'.[19]

'False Bonds of Love'

Shakespeare's sequence is most unusual in that not only does it address beloved 'friends', of different genders, but there are also sonnets which speak of a rival poet (Sonnets 77 to 87), others which reveal the woman's repeated unfaithfulness, and even sonnets which speak of her infidelity with a young man who is also beloved of the speaker: these last are often termed the 'triangle' sonnets and include Sonnets 42, 133, 134 and 144.

* Synecdoche: a condensed metaphor which uses a part to represent the entire. The symbolism can be quite extended, as in a handkerchief representing its owner, for example.

Sonnet 142, for example, opens quite conventionally and is quite Sidneian.* The first quatrain is laden with paradox and antithesis and the rhetorical device of polyptoton in repetition of 'sinne' and 'sinful' (ll. 1, 2). The ending of the final quatrain is also very reminiscent of the first sonnet of *Astrophil and Stella* in the chaining effect of the rhetoric: 'Roote pitty in thy heart that when it grows, / Thy pitty may deserve to pittied be' (ll. 11–12).

Between the two, however, the second quatrain unexpectedly demolishes the expectation set up at the beginning of the sonnet. The woman is no cool and distant paragon; rather she is addressed as a liar, a frequent maker of false promises and an adulteress. Sonnet 142 is probably the best known of this group:

> ... those lips of thine,
> That have profan'd their scarlet ornaments,
> And sealed false bonds of love as oft as mine,
> Rob'd others' beds' revenues of their rents. (ll. 5–8)

The last line quoted suggests that women were seen as commodities within Renaissance society. Viewed as the chattel of her husband this woman is not free to dispose her favours. The implication is that she is robbing her husband by sleeping with another man: her favour is not hers to give. The female addressee of the 'triangle' series is even further removed from the idealised and distant beloved of the sonnet conventions:

> Two loves I have, of comfort and despair,
> Which, like two spirits, do suggest me still:
> The better angel is a man right fair,
> The worser spirit a woman coloured ill. (ll. 1–4)

* Adjective used by literary scholars to describe the literary style or accomplishments of Sir Philip Sidney and /or his sister, Mary Sidney Herbert.

The imagery again evokes the medieval Morality Play in its battle between good and evil to win man's soul. The imagery of this psychomachia* may have been prompted by Christopher Marlowe's *Doctor Faustus* (performed 1592) as this sonnet is considered to have been written between 1591 and 1595.† In the first quatrain the lovers take the roles of good angel and evil spirit, tempting in opposite directions, however the situation is radically altered in the central quatrain which posits the speaker literally between the two 'friends'. Amid a plethora of references to salvation and damnation, it is divulged that the 'female evil' (l. 5) has enticed the beloved young man away from the speaker, 'wooing his purity with her foul pride' (l. 8). The final movement of the sonnet discloses that, despite the vindictive tone and considerable anxiety compacted into the four previous lines, the accusations are based on conjecture. The heightened sense of psychological torment is not dissipated, however, as the speaker goes on to imagine the pair engaged in the sexual act in his absence, 'But being both from me both to each other friend, / I guess one angel in another's hell' (ll. 11–12). The final couplet offers no respite: 'Yet this shall I ne'er know, but live in doubt, / Till my bad angel fire my good one out' (ll.13–14). Ironically, despite what may seem a complete dissimilarity in sentiment from the Italian conventions, the couplet reveals the lover to be in the same vulnerable and impotent state of stasis as the Petrarchan lover. Shakespeare could therefore be said to rework the conventions of a more innocent past to accommodate the familiar brutal realities of his experiences in contemporary London.‡

* Psychomachia is a battle for the soul between good and evil, from a fourth century poem by Prudentius.

† The play traces Dr Faustus's journey towards destruction after he sells his soul to the Devil. It has strong links with the medieval Morality Plays' theme of the battle for man's soul and interacts with contemporary anxieties about religious reform and changing state religion, including both Catholic and Protestant referents.

‡ See the introduction to London of the late sixteenth century in Part Four: 'City, Court and Country'.

Extended Commentary: Sidney, *Astrophil and Stella* (1598)

The various simple ballad-type structures of the songs which link the sonnets in Sidney's sequence invite engagement on a more familiar level than the compact but formal form of the sonnet. Read alone they provide a useful counterpoint to the more prescribed conventions of the sonnets and encourage a linear reading of the lack of development of the love affair. This is not to say that they resist the familiar Petrarchan tropes such as Cupid's feats of archery, the beloved's illuminating eyes, the classical references or the flourish of the blazon and rhetorical embellishment. They do deal much more directly with Astrophil's unruly passion, however, including his partially successful attempts to seduce Stella and a vitriolic condemnation of her when he loses patience. The brief indication given in the songs below should indicate not only Astrophil's psychological disturbance and insecurity, but also the carnal rather than aesthetic focus of his desire.

The second song represents Astrophil's inner dialogue as he debates with himself to what extent he should take advantage of Stella's vulnerable sleeping form.* The opening stanza clearly indicates retaliatory intention for denying his advances. As the focus glides over her sleeping eyes, her tongue and her hand, which he notes he may now fondle freely, he eventually aspires to 'invade the fort' (l. 15). Chastened by the thought of Stella's anger, however, he steals only a kiss, which wakes her. The final line rejects the opportunity for moralising remorse as he makes his retreat regretting 'Foole, more foole, for no more taking' (l. 28).

* The first song appears between Sonnets 63 and 64, beginning, 'Doubt you to whom my Muse these notes intendeth'. It addresses Stella obliquely without revealing her name, hyperbolically praising her to near-divinity. It is well-crafted, using a variety of rhetorical figures and, unusually, employs female rhymes throughout, rather than the more usual male rhyme. The closing line refers to his song beginning and ending in her; it literally represents her, which is neatly embodied in the feminine rhyme scheme. It does not provide insight into the psychological conflict afforded by the other songs discussed, however.

The fourth to ninth songs represent a cluster of frustrated desire, beginning with an evening encounter which promises 'large offer of [their] blisse' (l. 32) in a moonlit garden ornamented with flowers. Despite the perfect opportunity, however, Stella's insistent refrain in all nine stanzas is 'No, no, no, no, my Deare, let it be'. Loss of hope and favour prompts Astrophil's next song, which warns that henceforth his pen will no longer praise her 'glory' (l. 3), but will record her faults. The fifteen stanzas release a tirade of acrimonious invective, naming Stella a 'theefe', 'murdrer', 'Tyran[t]', 'Rebel', 'Vagrant', 'witch' and 'Divill', which is however undercut by a final besotted '(alas) you still of me beloved' (l. 87). The disparity between Astrophil's perverse taunts and his usual high-flown rhetorical eloquence are a source of humour to the reader, but one also senses Sidney's own amusement in their melodrama. Some stability has been restored by the eighth song when Stella's voice is again heard, most unusually, admitting that she loves Astrophil, but still resisting his flattering speech and physical advances. In the ninth he is found rejected and somewhat forlornly addressing sheep, pondering 'Why alas doth she then sweare, / That she loveth me so dearely' (ll. 31–2). The overtly sexual fantasy of Song 10 imagines the consummation of desire in a crescendo of impressions which are sent to Stella in his absence:

> Thinke of my most Princely power,
> When I blessed shall devower,
> With my greedy licorous sences,
> Beauty, musicke, sweetnesse, love
> While she doth against me prove
> Her strong darts, but weake defences. (ll. 31–6)

The transparently orgasmic transport of the following verse leaves Astrophil admitting 'Thy delights my woes increase, / My life melts with too much thinking' (ll. 44–5), as he paradoxically instructs 'Thought' to think no more. The final song sees decorum restored, creating a Romeo and Juliet-type balcony scene featuring a colloquy between Astrophil and Stella. Her voice reasonably directs Astrophil to other love objects, demanding, 'Be not yet those fancies changed?'

(l. 9), but is resisted by his claim, which he also expresses in Sonnet 91, that all others are mere counterfeits of her greater perfection. The final stanzas intimate that their clandestine relationship may be suspected by others. Fearing that his continued attentions might endanger her, he is therefore persuaded by Stella's 'Well be gone, be gone, I say, / Lest that Argus* eyes perceive you' (ll. 41–2). This final rejection leads directly to the last despairing sonnets of the sequence in which Astrophil laments Stella's absence, whilst somewhat forlornly still taking pleasure in memories of her.

The sequence is characterised by contradictions, which are frequently attributed to Sidney's consummate handling of the motifs of the Petrarchan tradition. He delineates the emotional turmoil of all-consuming passion from which he, nevertheless, maintains an ironic distance. This often arch and witty undermining of Astrophil's condition has enduring appeal and is similar to Marlowe's handling of Leander's amorous ineptitude in *Hero and Leander* (c.1593). Astrophil's contradictory sentiments and irresolute moral stance mimic his vacillating and disordered emotions. He debates his situation with unnamed others, including the reader and, in Sonnet 14, a well-intentioned but infuriating 'friend':

> Alas have I not pain enough my friend,
> Upon whose breast a fiercer Gripe doth tire
> Then did on him who first stale down the fire,
> While Love on me doth all his quiver spend,
> But with your rhubarb words yow must contend
> To grieve me worse, in saying that Desire
> Doth plunge my wel-form'd soule even in the mire
> Of sinfull thoughts, which do in ruin end? (ll. 1–8)

The entire octave of this sonnet forms in effect one sense paragraph as Astrophil reacts hotly to the unsolicited and unwelcome comment on

* Jupiter's amorous passion for Ios prompted his wife, Juno, to set Argus, a hundred-eyed monster, to guard her. When he died his eyes were placed in the tail of the peacock to commemorate his service.

his enamoured state. The call is for Astrophil to renounce his 'sinfull' course which threatens irretrievably to damage his 'wel-formed soule' (l. 7). Reading 'soule' as 'person', the warning may be understood as a sharp and apposite reminder of the precariousness of his position at court. Sidney's own potential was never fully realised, for despite his manifold abilities his career never flourished and he was considered to be undervalued in the English court by his Continental acquaintances.

Alternatively, the friend's exhortation is entirely in keeping with Calvinist directives to 'admonish, accuse and correct the bad' in a general sense, but especially in subduing the flesh 'that it may not be wanton'.[20] The devout Protestantism of Sidney's family was unassailable and aspects of these religious undercurrents also appear in Sonnet 5, albeit accompanied by Neo-platonic references.* The discord between repressed desire and imposed celibacy erupts most famously in Sonnet 71's final line, '"But ah", Desire still cries, "give me some food"', which underlines the difficulties of aligning spiritual idealism with the passion of lived experience. This can be read as personal conflict between physical passion and the moral prompting of conscience and that this is the impression that Sidney wishes to create. It can also be seen as a sophisticated literary strategy, however, and a demonstration of the persuasive power of rhetorical device.

Although the opening apostrophe of the sonnet is in a colloquial register and the verse's iambic pentameters mimic an enjambed indignation which replicates speech, nonetheless the lines are 'coloured' with hyperbolical classical allusion. Astrophil pathetically claims that his suffering is greater than that of Prometheus, whose liver was torn out daily by an eagle (miraculously restoring itself at night), as punishment for stealing fire from the gods. Copiously exaggerating his case, he adds that Cupid did not loose the customary single dart to his heart, as with most lovers, but the entire contents of his quiver. In an abrupt descent to more sordid matters, he proceeds to accuse his friend of wishing to

* Sidney's maternal Dudley uncles and grandfather were deeply embroiled in the plot to crown the Protestant Lady Jane Grey as Queen, after the death of Edward VI, in 1533, in order to prevent the accession of Mary I who considered it her sacred duty to return the country to Catholicism.

torment him further with a medicinal purge of rhubarb, used to sluice out troublesome intestinal problems. This bathetic slippage exemplifies the descent from the sublime to the lowest registers and in Elizabethan terms represents an offence against decorum.* The engaged reader is invited to participate imaginatively in Astrophil's exasperation, but simultaneously to admire Sidney's humorous sleight of pen in Astrophil's dramatic outburst. Throughout the sequence there are similar episodes where the reader is placed in a situation of complicity between Sidney and his creation and is aware of two very different perspectives. Although not fully realised within the action as an assumed persona, the author guides the reader in a similar way to the framing characters used in Renaissance drama, employed to distance and comment upon the action.†

The sonnet has a clearly identifiable *volta* or change of direction in the sestet as Astrophil demonstrates that his love is not sinful. Using the rhetorical device of anaphora,‡ repeating 'If that be' at the beginning of lines 9 and 12, leading to the conclusion of line 14, he then creates a syllogism, articulately arguing his case in three points (emphasis added):

> *If* that be sinne which doth the maners frame,
> Well staid with truth in word and faith in deed,
> Readie of wit and fearing naught but shame,
> *If* that be sinne which in fixed hearts doth breed
> A loathing of loose unchastitie,
> *Then* love is sinne, and let me sinful be. (ll. 9–14)

* A concept derived from classical theories of literature concerning the concordance of appropriate style, tone, form, vocabulary and subject matter within a work of literature.

† Most famously, Thomas Kyd's *The Spanish Tragedie* (*c*.1582–92), uses two characters from the main action on stage, Revenge personified and a ghost, Don Andreas, as a framing device for the play. Such characters can distance and comment upon the action and may take the form of individuals – human or otherwise – or a Chorus (adopted from Ancient Greek drama). They can be used to outline the pre-history of the play, condensing the action, or to guide the audience in 'correct' interpretation. The 'position' of these characters is interesting in that they are neither fully inside nor outside the play. Some more sophisticated dramas do have characters which blur these boundaries by leaving the middle ground and either entering into the action of the play, or – more rarely – coming from within the audience.

‡ Repetition of the same word at the beginning of successive lines, phrases or clauses.

The paradoxical conclusion may be representative of Astrophil's delusion or Sidney's own frustrated comment on a courtly society that judges others by its own tarnished integrity. The elaborate rhetorical embellishment of heated individual opinion in idiomatic speech sets up a tension between public performance and personal integrity. In fact, as noted previously, preoccupations between outer semblance and inner truth arise persistently in the literature of the period. Generally, the inner aspect is exposed as immoral and corrupt, whilst the outer presents the contrary. In John Webster's *White Devil* (1612), for example, the central female character is denounced as 'the devil in crystal' (IV.ii.86), referring to her external beauty which is considered to hide an evil and dishonest heart. Astrophil's argument insists on the contrary, however: outer appearances are tainted by the perceptions of the beholder, whilst his true inner sentiments are honourable.

Notes

1 Gary Waller, *English Poetry of the Sixteenth Century* (Harlow: Addison Wesley Longman Ltd, 1986), 2nd edn, 1993, pp. 103, 104.

2 The manuscript sources for Wyatt's poems are the Egerton (*c.*1537), the Blage and the Devonshire Manuscripts. Tottel's *Songes and Sonettes* (June, 1557), otherwise known as *Tottel's Miscellany* was published almost 25 years after Wyatt's death and contained 90 of Wyatt's poems and is the main printed source of his poetry.

3 Devonshire Manuscript LIV, K. Muir and P. Thompson (eds), *Collected Works of Sir Thomas Wyatt*, (Liverpool: Liverpool University Press, 1949 rev. 1969), p. 40. The original spelling has been retained in all quotations excepting the correction of 'u' for 'v'.

4 See Petrarch's Sonnet 90, for example, which contains many aspects which later resurface in the English sonnets. 'Petrarch, *Canzoniere* Sonnet 90', in Stephen Minta, *Petrarch and Petrarchism: The English and French Traditions* (Manchester: Manchester University Press, 1980), pp. 47, 48.

5 See Rachel Falconer's reading of this poem in *A Companion to English Renaissance Literature and Culture* (Oxford: Blackwell, 2000, reprinted 2003), pp. 176–86.

6 See Elizabeth Heale, *Wyatt, Surrey and Early Tudor Poetry* (London: Longman, 1998), pp. 57, 58.

7 See Kenneth Muir, *Life and Letters of Sir Thomas Wyatt* (Liverpool: University of Liverpool Press, 1963).

8 See Michael Spiller, *The Development of the Sonnet* (London: Routledge, 1992), Chapter 7 *'I am not I': The Sonnets of Sidney*, p. 107.

9 See William A. Ringler (ed.), *The Poems of Sir Philip Sidney* (Oxford: Oxford University Press, 1962), pp. 473, 474.

10 Frederic J. Jones, *The Structure of Petrarch's Canzoniere* (Woodbridge, Suffolk: Boydell and Brewer, 1995), p. 214.

11 See Victor Shklovsky, 'Art as technique' in David Lodge (ed.), *Modern Criticism and Theory: A Reader* (Harlow: Addison Wesley Longman, 1988), pp. 15–30.

12 Leonard Forster, *Icy Fire. Five Studies in European Petrarchism* (London and New York: Cambridge University Press, 1969), p. 73

13 Joachim du Bellay, *'Contre les pétrarquistes'*, quoted in Forster, p. 39.

14 See Colin Burrow (ed.), *William Shakespeare: The Complete Sonnets and Poems* (Oxford: Oxford University Press, 2002), p. 111; Katherine Duncan-Jones (ed.), *Shakespeare's Sonnets*, The Arden Shakespeare edition (London: A. & C. Black, 1997), p. 44.

15 All dating references stem from this source and Burrow's discussion of recent stylometric testing, Burrow, p. 107.

16 Note Sonnet 104 which may refer to a gap of three years in composition: 'Three April perfumes in three hot Junes burned, / Since first I saw you fresh, which yet are green.' (ll. 7, 8), cited in Burrow, p. 109.

17 The first recorded usage was in the late sixteenth century: Leonard Mascall, Clerk to the Kitchens of the Archbishop of Canterbury, *The Arte and Manner Howe to Plant and Graffe all Sorts of Trees* (1586) translated from a French text by David Brossard, cited by Mavis Batey, 'Basing House Tudor Garden', *Garden History*, 15:2 (1987), pp. 94–108, p. 101.

18 Burrow, p. 130. Burrow goes on to discuss Stephen Orgel's interpretation which elaborates on this reading.

19 Duncan-Jones, p. 374.

20 John Calvin, *Institutes of the Christian Religion*, vol. III, Bk IV, Chapter XII: 11, 15.

The Renaissance Epyllion: Lodge, Shakespeare and Marlowe

In Ancient Greece and Rome the epyllion was a recognised genre with its own conventions, only some of which the Elizabethans adopted, and for this reason the label is sometimes contested.[1] The classical epyllion, or 'minor epic', was typically only around five hundred lines in length and took its subject matter from mythology, often including forbidden amorous passions. It employed a wide range of different poetic styles and literary techniques, and used the epic form of dactylic hexameters.* The Elizabethan poets rejected this form, usually opting instead for the more accessible iambic pentameter and heroic couplets (Marlowe) or six line stanza, something like a reduced *strombotto*, rhyming *ab ab cc* (Lodge and Shakespeare). Their works are generally much longer than their Greek and Roman models, ranging from Lodge's *Scylla's Metamorphosis* at a relatively short 786 lines to Shakespeare's extended *Venus and Adonis*, weighing in at 1,194 lines. Apart from these differences the term is quite apt and it is useful to bear in mind the classical models when reading the Renaissance works. Specific traits of the form which can seem over-long or irrelevant, such as characters' lengthy monologues and digressions from the main storyline, for example, are in fact, rhetorical devices intrinsic to the genre. Young male writers of the late

* A dactyl is a metrical foot which has three syllables, one stressed syllable followed by two unstressed short syllables and there are six feet in a hexametrical line.

Elizabethan period consciously chose this new genre to showcase their talents, although the classical term of epyllion was not in contemporary use.

Thomas Lodge's *Scylla's Metamorphosis*

Thomas Lodge's verse narrative, written *c*.1584–8, is considered to be the first of the popular poetic form now referred to as epyllia, but it is untypical in some respects. *Scylla's Metamorphosis: interlaced with the unfortunate love of Glaucus* (published in 1589) rehearses many of the familiar sonnet conventions and embellishments:

> Ay me, my moanings are like water drops
> That need an age to pierce her marble heart;
> I sow'd true zeal, yet fruitless were my crops:
> I plighted troth, yet falsehood wrought my smart:
> I prais'd her looks, her looks despised Glaucus;
> Was ever amorous sea-god scorned thus? (ll. 355–60)

Glaucus's lamentations are stereotypical of a Petrarchan lover, as he wanders among 'hapless men', warbling 'songs of remorse' (ll. 409, 411). The heartless object of his love, Scylla, is portrayed as the familiar proud ice maiden whom the reader glimpses in the *Cazoniere*: 'Here I saw her all humble and there haughty, / Now harsh, now gentle' (Petrarch, Sonnet 112, ll. 5–6). Lodge's beloved, however, does not merit the positive values of these antitheses. Despite Glaucus's praise in speech and verse, her 'marble heart' remains untouched, as he regrets above.

In the extract above Lodge manages to compact conventional themes, conventions and familiar rhetorical embellishment of the amatory verse tradition.* Apart from the antitheses noticed, for example, there is the association of the lover with nature, and therefore the suggestion that the beloved is unnatural in her rejection of him; the

* See Part Three: 'The Sonnet and Amatory Verse'.

revelation of his enduring true love and praise of her beauty; her unfaithfulness and scorn; and the rhetorical devices of chiasmus,* in the mirrored 'her looks', and the culminating apostrophe,† addressed to the narrator.[2] Lodge's entire poem can be read as a literary exercise, laden as it is with embellishment and literary exemplar. Critical opinion diverges, but some scholars read the poem as satirical, due to its copious exaggeration and tenacity of metaphor, which is sometimes pursued to ridiculous lengths. This reading is plausible since Sidney's *Astrophil and Stella*, broadly contemporaneous with Lodge's epyllion, also mocked aspects of the Petrarchan conventions.

Literary Platform and Intended Audience

As Lodge performs his literary portfolio there is a sense of audition. It is particularly appropriate, therefore, that the tale of the eponymous couple is displayed within the framing device, not only for the audience to enjoy the exploits therein, but also to admire the techniques of execution. His flourishes include the set speech and mythical allusion; numerous rhetorical figures; incorporation of the conventions of other popular poetry, including the pastoral, the love complaint, and the sonnet; descriptive tableaux; and poetical artistry in metre and rhyme, all identified as components of classical epyllia.

Lodge is sometimes termed a 'university wit' and his epyllion was written in his youth at Lincoln's Inn, as is apparent from its dedication to his fellow students, Ralph Crane and the 'Gentlemen of the Innes of Court and Chancerie'.[3] This is the type of audience for whom the genre was primarily intended: well-educated, witty and lively-minded young men who could appreciate the classical allusions, poetic aspirations and sometimes raunchy and subversive implications within the texts. Lodge's work may have originally been intended for private manuscript circulation among his friends, rather than for general publication.

* Chiasmus: two sets of corresponding terms 'back-to-back' in inverted order *(ab-ba)*.

† Apostrophe: speech turning away from the main issue to address an outside entity, as in a sudden address to the gods or Nature.

Lodge's opening finds the narrator in an English pastoral setting, with shepherds and flocks, 'walking', 'weeping', 'wailing' and 'wringing' his arms with insistent alliteration. The generic symptoms are so familiar to his intended readership that his lovesick state requires no glossing. It is so obvious to Glaucus, upon his appearance in the second stanza, that he and the narrator bond in their misery, pausing in a sorrowful intimacy:

> And as I sat under a willow tree …
> Repose'd his head upon my faintful knee:
> And when my tears had ceas'd their stormy shower
> He dried my cheeks (ll. 13–17)

Henceforth, there is a sense that the narrator's own tale is absorbed into the greater afflictions of Glaucus, just as the Ovidian tales – and their protagonists – mutate and transform.

Ovidian Influences

Along with most of the later epyllia writers, Lodge found his plot in Ovid's *Metamorphoses*, all fifteen books of which were translated into English by Arthur Golding in 1567. Both the subject matter and the complex structure of this work, which is presented in fragmented and interwoven form, provided inspiration for the young Elizabethan poets. Ovid's version of the Scylla and Glaucus story appears in Books 13 and 14 of *Metamorphoses*. In this work the nymph Scylla is admired by many suitors but rejects them all, gossiping about them with the Nereïds.* Glaucus was originally human but elected to 'belong to the sea' (13: 945), becoming transformed into a merman sea god, as he relates to Scylla upon their first encounter:

> … my body was totally different
> from what it had been before; and I wasn't the same in my
> mind. It was then that I first set eyes on this beard encrusted

* Nereïds are ocean-nymphs.

> with green, on the hair which sweeps in my wake as I swim far over the sea, my colossal shoulders, my blue-coloured arms and my curving legs which vanish away to a fish with fins. (*Metamorphoses*, 13: 957–62)[4]

Unsurprisingly, perhaps, Scylla rejects the aqueous and amorous sea-god, which prompts him to seek magical assistance from Circe. Incensed by Glaucus's vow of enduring passion for Scylla, compounded by his rejection of her own advances, the enchantress wreaks revenge on her rival, turning her lower body into 'a cluster of gaping hell-hounds' (14: 64). Although Ovid does not describe her final transformation explicitly, he mentions in passing that she eventually becomes fused into the rocky crag which overlooks the Straits of Messina, between Sicily and mainland Italy.* Lodge, by contrast, passes over the first transformation, focusing on Scylla's apt metamorphosis into the stony [hearted] cliff:

> … her locks
> Are chang'd with wonder into hideous sands,
> And hard as flint become her snow-white hands. (ll. 736–7)

Lodge's poem is Ovidian in its subject matter, in its source and theme of protean† change, indicated above, but it is not overtly erotic, which is one of the defining terms of the Renaissance epyllia. It deals with love, but not the Ovidian 'wanton love-tricks' of the worldly *Ars Amatoria* and *Amores*, nor the explicitly sexual. The textured narrative is tendered as a central classical myth within a pastoral frame. As Paul Miller points out, in classical epyllia the 'digression' may be as important as the main storyline, often elaborating or paralleling it.[5] This is the model of Lodge's poem, as the 'digression' is in fact the main focus and the narrator's tale of thwarted love acts as a slim framing device to the story

* Different versions of the myth exist; in Homer's story Circe performs both transformations, whereas in others Scylla's metamorphosis into the treacherous rock which guards the seaway is the work of a rival Nereïd.

† Adjective derived from the name of the Greek sea-god, Proteus, meaning changeable or able to take on various shapes.

of Scylla and Glaucus. The narrator and Glaucus are presented in the manner of the heterosexual Petrarchan lover, largely without the 'Ovidian' lust and carnal desire found in later examples of the genre.

The narrator's opening speech beginning 'Within a thicket near to Isis' flood' (l. 2), which also introduces his own love-sick state, goes on to announce his position as an Oxford scholar. This was no doubt intended to be read as humorous *poesis-à-clef.** As William Keach points out, although there was an Italian pastoral tradition of creating a 'myth of locality' the reference was, no doubt, 'intended for the enjoyment of the ex-University men in Lodge's Inns of Court audience'.[6] Significantly, in the familiar 'reason versus emotion' dichotomy, despite the knowledge and skills gained from his studies, the narrator has not learned a fundamental truth of nature: 'times change by course of fate' (l. 41). He is encouraged, therefore, to learn from Glaucus's paradigm of mutability, which demonstrates the gods' somewhat heartless championing of the lover's cause to the grievous destruction of the haughty female in question.

Literary Contexts

The blazon of Scylla seems to parody the sonnet traditions, in its hyperbole and the absurdity generated by over-laborious conceits. Predictably, her hair is 'soften'd golden wires', 'scatter'd on her brow', through which Glaucus peers to discover her 'ivory-shadow'd front' (ll. 284, 282, 291). A conventionally complimentary description of her complexion is halted briefly by the rather awkward – or humorous – observation that her nose divides her cheeks (l. 295). The parodic tenor is affirmed in the metaphors by which Glaucus describes Scylla's mouth: rather than the more conventional precious jewel imagery of coral or ruby, he uses the metaphor of a purple violet. Somewhat bafflingly, it is also referred to as 'the ocean's pride' (l. 300), which may obliquely evoke the clichéd allusion to her teeth as small seed pearls, but the

* French: *Roman-à-clef* means 'novel with a key', indicating that there are embedded clues which allow the reader to identify real historical personages within it. *Poesis-à-clef* is a coinage meaning 'poetry with a key' sharing the same characteristic.

metaphor of 'ivory' prompts an unwelcome vision of elephantine tusks, while the ocean connotations suggest foam. Stanza 52 continues the satiric experimentation, as the beloved's long and delicate arms, reminding the reader of Daphne's metamorphosis, spread 'like two rare branchy saples in the spring' (l. 308).* The conceit becomes strained as it figures the branching fingers as twigs topped with rosebuds; the mixed metaphor pointing up the parodic intent: 'Which featly sprout in length like spring-born friends, / Whose pretty tops with five sweet roses ends' (ll. 311–12). A further witty self-referential allusion is embedded in this image. By Apollo's decree the leaves of the Laurel, into which Daphne was transformed, were used to crown poets of the highest calibre.

Despite an otherwise conservative approach, at the point where Cupid punishes Scylla by causing her to desire Glaucus, the gender coding is reversed. Although offering comic potential, this aspect also held erotic appeal, possibly due to its fantasy-fulfilment potential in a largely male readership, but also through its inversion of conventional cultural codes. The female pursuit of an uncooperative male love object also appears in Shakespeare's *Venus and Adonis* (1593) and Francis Beaumont's *Salmacis and Hermaphroditus* (1602), which both take their themes from Ovid's *Metamorphoses*. Moralists condemned exactly this type of inversion as salacious and corrupting, nonetheless, poets consciously manipulated the subversive erotic potential, as is evident in Beaumont's opening address to the reader: 'I hope my poem is so lively writ, / That thou wilt turn half-maid [mad] with reading it.'

Scylla's charmed pursuit of Glaucus is channelled through the narrator's perspective, his voice often discernible in the interjections and the refrain of the verses. Scylla's ineffective quest in many ways prefigures Venus's lost cause in Shakespeare's *Venus and Adonis*:

* See for example, Bernini's sculpture of Daphne's metamorphosis as she is pursued by Apollo (1622–4), which is in the Galleria Borghese in Rome. This image is used on the cover of the Penguin Classics edition of *Metamorphoses* (2004).

But fruitless hopes and fatal haps deceive her.
Lord, how her lips do dwell upon his cheeks;
And how she looks for babies in his eyes:
And how she sighs, and swears she loves and leeks,
And how she vows, and he her vows envies:
Trust me, the envious nymphs, in looking on,
Were forc'd with tears to assist her moan.
How oft with blushes would she plead for grace,
How oft with whisperings would she tempt his ears;
How oft she wip'd them with her amber hairs:
So oft, methought, I oft in heart desir'd
To see the end whereto Distain aspir'd.
(*Scylla's Metamorphosis*, ll. 618–30)

Shakespeare handles similar material with more humour and economy, but close analysis reveals obvious parallels of imagery between sections of the two works, suggesting that he was influenced by Lodge's epyllia, rather than there simply being generic similarities:

Now doth she stroke his cheek, now doth he frown,
And 'gins to chide, but soon she stops his lips,
And kissing speaks, with lustful language broken:
'If thou wilt chide, thy lips will never open.'

He burns with bashful shame, she with her tears
Doth quench the maiden burning of his cheeks;
Then with her windy sighs, and golden hairs,
To fan, and blow them dry again she seeks.
(*Venus and Adonis*, ll. 45–52)

There are many such echoes between the two works, although Lodge's poem does not generate the same sense of urgency or passion. As is frequently noted, the poem is more concerned with its literary performance than in extensive exploration of the characters' emotions.

Scylla's eventual despair is played out in a poignant duologue with Echo, prefacing the appearance of the Morality Tale figures Fury, Rage, Wanhope, Despair and Woe, who appear from hell to bind her to the rocks into which she will be received (ll. 715–32). M. C. Bradbrook has pointed out that the medieval 'persuasion to love' tradition is alluded to in the figures of Wanhope and Distain.[7] * This intention is affirmed in the Envoy's cautionary message, conveyed from Glaucus, to 'Ladies' who may be condemned to live with 'Scylla in the rocks', should they mistreat admirers (ll. 781–5). The pseudo-moralising conclusion does not make literal sense, however, as it condemns ladies who 'backslide', presumably from promises given, although Scylla gave none. Nonetheless, it does formally complete the claim of the extended title, which identifies the poem as being instructional and 'very fit for young courtiers and coy Dames to remember'.

William Shakespeare's *Venus and Adonis*

Venus and Adonis was the first of Shakespeare's poems to be published, under his own name, in 1593, and as such represented a claim for poetic reputation. The epigraph in the dedication to Henry Wriothesley, Earl of Southampton, quotes Ovid, unequivocally highlighting both his aspiration and his debt: 'Let the common herd be amazed by worthiless things; but for me let golden Apollo provide cups full of the water of the Muses' springs'.[8]

The poem is commonly considered to have been written during the closure of the theatres due to a protracted outbreak of plague, which raged through London with only brief periods of respite, from September 1592 until the summer of 1594.[9] It is likely that the first of Shakespeare's sonnets were also being composed around this time, as it is assumed that those at the beginning of the sequence were written from around 1595.[10] This provides a useful insight. Firstly, it suggests

* The tradition of the 'persuasion to love' includes the concept that it is natural and desirable to love and procreate, which is sometimes manipulated to endorse the *carpe diem* (sieze the day) attitudes of later love poetry.

that Shakespeare consciously strove to gain recognition as a serious poet, when already a successful dramatist. Secondly, there is a time overlap with the earliest of his sonnets which are in the 'persuasion to love' tradition, urging a beautiful young man to procreate. Colin Burrow convincingly argues that *Venus and Adonis* may also be read as belonging to this tradition as there are topical references within the poem to the refusal of Shakespeare's youthful dedicatee to marry Lady Elizabeth de Vere. Rather than this being the simple *raison d'être* of the work, however, he suggests that it was written in the spirit of literary rivalry in response to a less skilled poem on this theme.[11]

Literary Contexts

To a large extent enjoyment of the epyllion depends upon an appreciation of the mythological references and implication within the poem. From their schooldays Elizabethan boys studied the classical authors intensively and were thoroughly versed – literally – in Ancient Greek and Roman myths. A. B. Taylor points out that Shakespeare, like his contemporaries, studied Ovid's *Metamorphoses* from the age of eleven or twelve, rigorously examining passages for their rhetorical features, metrical patterning, mythological content and moral implications, before copying out impressive sections and committing both the poetry and explication to memory, for testing the following day.[12] Consequently, a generation of young men from relatively bourgeois backgrounds shared not only knowledge of classical authors and their works, but also a web of associations and patterns of thought about them. This had implications for representations of classical figures in subsequent works of literature, as each brought their own matrix of associated connotations. Hence, to a readership of shared familiarity, a figure can be evoked by the associated and expected symbols or attributes, in a type of metafictional code. Sidney's 'Love born in Greece' would be readily recognised as Cupid, Shakespeare's 'the war-like god' as Mars and Marlowe's 'sapphire-visag'd god' as Neptune.[13] Shakespeare relied on this shared language of symbol and allusion for much of the humour in *Venus and Adonis*.

Ovid's version of the story appears in Book 10 of *Metamorphoses*, narrated by Orpheus, whose own tale of tragic love may have inspired Shakespeare's reinterpretation. The Ovidian version states that Orpheus, after losing his wife to the underworld, renounced love of women and instigated a practice of 'turning for love to immature males and of plucking the flower of a boy's brief spring before he has come to manhood' (ll. 84–5). Upon his death Adonis's transformation was into an anemone and Venus does, in fact, pluck him – quite literally – at the end of *Venus and Adonis.* Although Shakespeare plunges into his story of ill-fated love, *in media res*,* the pre-history to Venus's infatuation with Adonis is given in Ovid: whilst Cupid was kissing his mother (Venus), he accidentally grazed her breast with one of his arrows. The Ovidian Venus consequently neglects her former haunts to accompany Adonis, 'roaming the mountain ridges and forests' (l. 535), and expresses fear for his safety which she enhances with a story of wild beasts who will not be charmed by his beauty. Importantly, Venus does not lose her dignity, except in wandering in the bright sunshine with her dress tucked up around her knees. Her sole amorous advance is to nestle against Adonis, resting her 'burning cheek' on his 'naked breast', while 'interspersing her words with kisses' (ll. 558–9). By comparison, Shakespeare's Venus, although ostensibly the exquisitely beautiful ethereal goddess of love, whose chariot is drawn by swans, is depicted by an amorous harlot.

Lack of '*Decorum* and good proportion in every respect'

After the description of a purple sunrise, the compound adjectives quickly identify Venus as 'sick-thoughted'† and liken her to a 'bold-faced suitor' (ll. 5, 6), in contrast to the fresh-faced youth, Adonis, who scorns love and desires only to go hunting with the boys. The colours of the dawn introduce an extended theme of blushing, which is used to express both embarrassed modesty and, conversely, the heat of erotic

* Latin: 'in the middle of events'. This is traditionally the opening strategy adopted by writers of epic.

† '[S]ick-thoughted' refers to Venus's love-sickness.

passion, throughout the work.* White and red, acting as conventional descriptions of a beautiful complexion, occur frequently. Skin is described as 'More white and red than doves or roses are' (l. 10), conflicting emotions are painted 'white and red' (l. 346), 'pale' cheeks are slapped red (ll. 271, 472), and the pressure of forceful kissing alternated with teasing dalliance causes lips to 'red and pale, with fresh variety' (l. 21). The conceit tragically comes full circle in Adonis's death and Venus's lasting tribute to her love. The mouth of the boar which gores Adonis to death is 'frothy ... bepainted all with red, / Like milk and blood being mingled both' (ll. 901–2), Adonis's 'lily white flank' weeps 'purple tears' (ll. 1053, 1054) and he is finally transformed into an anemone:

> A purple flower ... chequered with white,
> Resembling his pale cheeks, and the blood
> Which in round drops upon their whiteness stood. (ll. 1168–70)

The incongruence of Venus's opening speech, which immediately tumbles into insistent and elaborate erotic persuasion, no doubt thrilled and amused its first readership on at least two planes. The less obvious to a modern reader concerns the Renaissance concept of literary decorum,† which was based on classical prescription and demanded concord in appropriate subject-matter, form and register. The *Arte of English Poesie* (1589) devotes an entire section to the subject 'to the intent the stiles may be fashioned to the matters, and keepe their *decorum* and good proportion in every respect'.[14] As Pauline Kiernan points out, Ovid himself self-consciously paraded his own poetical impropriety in his *Amores* and Shakespeare's own distortion of literary boundaries and expectation can be read as a continuation of this practice.[15]

* In itself the blush is an acknowledgement of a classical conceit and is used in Ovid's *Amores* (II.V, 33*42) and Virgil's *Aeneid* (xxii, 64–9).

† Decorum: a classical literary term which decrees that within a hierarchical model, with tragedy and epic as the highest forms, the style, vocabulary, characters, action, and all other aspects of a work are appropriate to all the other elements.

Venus, the 'Bold-faced suitor'

Venus is overstated in every way; she has a physically impressive presence, forcefully entrapping, stroking and planting unwanted kisses on her victim. Her monstrous desire lends Amazonian strength, as she lunges forward, unseating 'the tender boy' from his horse, and stowing him under her arm (l. 32). That she has the presence of mind to tie up his horse before turning her attentions to the captive adds to the humour. All demand and activity, her passions cause her to sweat, faint melodramatically and, alarmingly, take on the characteristics of a bird of prey as she feeds upon Adonis's lips:

> Even like an empty eagle, sharp by fast,
> Tires with her beak on feathers, flesh, and bone,
> Shaking her wings, devouring all in haste,
> Till either gorge be stuffed or prey be gone –
> Even so she kissed his brow, his cheek, his chin,
> And where she ends she doth anew begin. (ll. 55–60)

Similar imagery accompanies the second ravishment, as Adonis wearily endures her attack in order that he might leave:

> … glutton-like she feeds, yet never filleth.
> Her lips are conquerors; his lips obey,
> Paying what ransom the insulter willeth:
> Whose vulture thought doth pitch the price so high
> That she will draw his lips' rich treasure dry. (ll. 548–52)

The volatility of her behaviour, which fluctuates between eloquent good-natured persuasion and threatening obsessive dominance, is theatrical and compelling. Whilst plainly rapaciously out of control in some stanzas, 'Her face doth reek and smoke, her blood doth boil' (l. 555), at other times she frames her desire to conform to Petrarchan manners: tender, petitioning and entreating. Critics point to the difficulty of interpreting the poem, not least because of the brutal aspects of Venus's predatory lusts and the inequality of her apparent experience and Adonis's innocence. The reader is invited to enjoy the comic spectacle of an older female's lecherous appetites for an adolescent boy, which the power dynamics render quite grotesque and exploitative. Combined with the maternal reference to Venus as a 'milch doe' (l.875), very much uncharacteristic of her earlier seductress persona, this can evoke the theme of incest, resurrecting Adonis's own inheritance.[*16] As Jonathan Bate notes, the transgression of Adonis's mother, Myrrha, creates 'contextual pressure' on the narrative and is referred to by Venus (ll. 203, 204), albeit in ambiguous terms. Bate draws attention to Ovid's perspective of poetic retribution in Venus's unreciprocated love for Adonis; the goddess of love herself was responsible for the devastating passion experienced by Adonis's mother which precipitated her downfall.[17] Readers versed in Ovid's *Metamorphoses* would be sensitive to these implications, which underwrite the epyllia, providing a nuance of tragedy beneath the witty and amusing superficial aspects, most apparent in the closing section of the poem. Venus is further discussed in the Extended Commentary at the end of this chapter.

Adonis, 'The field's chief flower'

For all of her prolixity, Venus's rhetorical acrobatics are scathingly discounted by Adonis as an 'idle over-handled theme' (l. 770), underlining their formulaic nature. He remains disdainful of the goddess's erotic motivation throughout the poem, ironically in the manner of a virtuous sonnet maiden. His character is framed by his delicate feminine beauty and helplessness, which only later in the poem is developed to incorporate a moral stance. Adonis represents the type of youthful androgynous beauty admired in Ancient Greece and Renaissance Europe, neither woman nor yet man. His complexion is 'rose-cheeked' (l. 3) and fresh, his face is dimpled (l. 242) and 'hairless' (l. 487), and he indulges in teenage 'sullen' 'lours' (l. 75). Repeatedly

* Myrrha committed incest with her father, Cinyras, and Adonis was the offspring: 'born of his sister and sired by his grandfather', Ovid, *Metamorphoses*, 10: 521.

citing his youth and lack of experience in matters of love, he uses a series of metaphors to describe his immature state, such as a bud unopened, fruit yet sour, an unfinished garment and 'ungrown fry' (ll. 413–20, 527, 523–8).

Critical opinion often focuses on Adonis's determination to preserve his own sense of identity and avoid change, in itself unnatural according to the concept of mutability which underwrites Shakespeare's sources, and contemporary theories of natural regeneration. Adonis's delight is to hunt with male friends in a homo-social group, bonded by active masculine and character-forming pursuits, rather than submit to the passive recreation of amatory dalliance, identified with femininity in the era. Coppélia Kahn draws attention to these two different ways of delineating the self which 'define the male passage into maturity that are aligned with gender-specific pursuits. For Venus it is carnal knowledge that ought to initiate Adonis into manhood; for Adonis it is the hunt'.[17]

That initiation is Venus's aim is confirmed in her acknowledgement of his pubescent status in her addresses as 'sweet boy' (l. 583), her remark upon his downy skin and persistent dwelling upon her anticipated sexual enjoyment, which here links lip, food and oral pleasure: 'That tender spring upon thy tempting lip / Shows the unripe; yet mayst thou well be tasted' (ll. 127–8). Despite the blandishments, boasts of past conquests, and honeyed invitations to 'Feed where thou wilt' (l. 232) or 'stray lower, where the pleasant fountains lie' (l. 234), Adonis remains unmoved. In the two tableaux of consummation contrived by Venus her own sexual fervour is simply intensified without any reciprocal passion. Early in the poem she 'plucks' Adonis from his horse and pushes him roughly backwards on to a grassy bank, 'as she would be thrust' (ll. 30–41), only to discover that she cannot compel his active participation. Adonis's revelation that he intends to hunt boar the following day prompts a desperate struggle to detain him, which culminates in his falling on top of her, humorously reported by the narrator in the discourse of chivalric combat:

> Now she is in the very lists of love,
> Her champion mounted for the hot encounter.

All is imaginary she doth prove;
He will not manage her, although he mount her,
That worse than Tantalus is her annoy,
To clip Elysium, and to lack her joy. (ll. 595–600)

Keach notes a sense of physical struggle in the rhythmic assonance of 'push'd', 'thrust' and 'lust', all of which are held in an antithetical figure of passion and indifference.[18] To the first readers the absurdity of the Goddess of Love flat on her back, lusting after a recalcitrant youth, no doubt gave a great degree of salacious pleasure, as the narrator's polyptoton* underlines, 'She's love, she loves, and yet she is not loved' (l. 610). The imagery also analeptically† links back to the early digression of the sexual encounter between Adonis's horse and the jennet, which Venus endorsed as being healthy and natural (ll. 259–324). The horse himself acquires a fulsome blazon from the narrator, which underlines his magnificence and virility, pointing to the main difference between horse and rider. This lack is also lamented in Venus's later, 'Would thou wert as I am, and I a man' (l. 369) and an exasperated accusation that in resisting her he proved his inhumanity, the subtext being that a mere mortal could never resist her if even gods were overcome by her charms: 'Fie! lifeless picture, cold, and senseless stone, / Well-painted idol, image dull, and dead' (ll. 211–12).

The pale 'image dull, and dead' prefigures Adonis's death at the end of the poem in yet another prolepsis. Kiernan notes the tendency to halt living processes and fix them into figures of speech which refuse 'to accommodate organic processes, mutability and time', suggesting that Venus's own rhetoric creates the frozen image of Adonis.[19] By denying his corporeal, rosy presence and encasing him in the fantasy of her own poetic diction, Venus condemns Adonis to the same fate as the objectified lover of contemporary sonnets.

* Polyptoton: a repetition of words deriving from the same root but ending differently.

† Analepsisis: echoes, links back to earlier part of the work (Ant. Prolepsis: prefigures, looks forward).

Lust versus Love

Despite having claimed not to know what love was, Adonis launches a principled speech, claiming: 'I hate not love, but your device in love' (l. 789). The lexical choice of 'device' highlights the artificiality of Venus's invitations. Adonis's speech on the nature of true love can be termed gnomic* and facilitates a moral reading of the poem, albeit at severe odds with the more bawdy aspects, which then must be read as negative exempla:

> Love comforteth like sunshine after rain,
> But lust's effect is tempest after sun;
> Love's gentle spring doth always fresh remain,
> Lust's winter comes ere summer half be done;
> Love surfeits not, lust like a glutton dies;
> Love is all truth; lust full of forgèd lies. (ll. 799–804)

Like a seasoned orator, the idealistic youth creates a moving rhetorical display to rival the best of Venus's. Laden with antithesis, the entire speech can be considered a distinctio,† which takes a broadly similar theme, stage by stage, and undermines it: love does this, while lust does that; love is this, but lust is that.[20] It may also be interpreted as Shakespeare's judgement on the situation, in a formal prosopopoeia;‡ given the debauched tone of much of the epyllion, however, one would have to assume this to be satirical.

Adonis's claim not to know love, which he qualifies quite curiously as 'Unless it is a boar' (ll. 409–10) foreshadows the circumstance of his death, which Venus rationalises as the kiss of the boar, alarmingly aligning herself with the beast:

* Gnomic: an aphorism, something with a didactic purpose, intending to teach.

† Distinctio: highlighting of precise meanings between similar words to distinguish between them.

‡ Prosopopoeia: a rhetorical figure in which the speaker or writer assumes a persona in order to speak to the reader.

… by a kiss [he] thought to persuade him there,
And, nuzzling in his flank, the loving swine
Sheathed unaware the tusk in his soft groin.

'Had I been toothed like him I must confess
With kissing him I should have killed him first …' (ll. 1114–18)

Critics struggle to interpret the implications of Venus's reflection, although it is difficult not to find a cruel humour in it. Keach draws attention to the 'ironic significance … of the grotesque parallel to all the previous occasions when Venus's embraces were described as the attack of a wild beast'.[21] Kahn, however, proposes a psychoanalytical reading in which Adonis tries to kill that which he most fears: 'he projects his anxiety about being devoured by Venus on to the boar, and attempts to destroy the boar so that Venus will not destroy him.'[22] The final section of the poem focuses on Venus's grief and subsequent lengthy etiological[*] prophecy that love will henceforth cause humankind to suffer, presented in a series of antitheses which are introduced by the excessive alliteration of paroemion:[†]

'It shall be fickle, false and full of fraud,
Bud and be blasted in a breathing-while;
The bottom poison, and the top o'erstrawed
With sweets, that shall the truest sight beguile.
The strongest body shall it make most weak,
Strike the wise dumb, and teach the fool to speak.
(ll. 1147–52)

* Etiology: dealing with the origins or causes of things.
† Paroemion: excessive alliteration, sometimes to the point of relentlessness.

Christopher Marlowe's *Hero and Leander*

Scholars have deliberated throughout the decades the extent to which Shakespeare and Marlowe were influenced by each other's epyllion. Although *Hero and Leander* (*c*.1593, pub. 1598) was not published in Marlowe's lifetime, it appeared in the Stationers' Register in the autumn of 1593, following his death at the end of May. *Venus and Adonis* appeared in the same register the month before Marlowe's death and the quarto edition was being sold by June of the same year. As Robert Logan points out, opinion has come full circle, as modern interpretations tacitly re-affirm the claims of the 1960s scholars, that Marlowe's poem was at least a model for Shakespeare's. He also notes, however, that as the precise dates of the two authors' writing and reading of the poems is not verifiable, the debate must be speculative.[23] As all of the epyllia of the late sixteenth-century interacted with each other and their classical conventions, it is difficult to identify unequivocally specific parallels. *Hero and Leander*, like other examples of the genre, is a set piece which is intended to demonstrate the literary and rhetorical skills of the author and as such it is often considered to be the prime exemplar, outstripping even Shakespeare's epyllion.

Literary Contexts

Marlowe may have been influenced by Ovid's *Heroides*, which is a series of epistles purportedly written between mythical lovers. As Keach points out, however, the letters between Hero and Leander, 18 and 19, would logically belong to the period after their sexual union and Leander's leave-taking,[24] and so poignantly foreshadow Leander's death. Although critics note close resemblances between sections of the poem and both Ovid's *Ars Amatoria* and his *Amores*, the main source for the subject matter of the epyllion was not Ovid's *Metamorphoses*, but Musaeus's* version of the popular Greek myth. This fifth-century epyllion had been

* Little is known about the fifth century A.D. Greek poet Musaeus but he is usually credited with having written the version of *Hero and Leander* which inspired Marlowe.

available in translation in Latin and various European languages from the early sixteenth century. Hero is the beautiful and celibate votaress of Venus's temple in Sestos, where each year the men of the town hold a festival in honour of Adonis, whom Venus loved. Hero and Leander meet when she officiates at the rites and, upon the exchange of glances, they fall instantly in love.

Marlowe's version does not reach the tragic end of the Greek myth but it is not apparent if this was deliberate avoidance or if it was left unfinished at his murder. The epyllion ends at the dawn after the young couple finally consummate their love, causing some scholars to read it as celebratory, rather than tragic, despite Marlowe's dramatic opening 'On Hellespont guilty of true love's blood' (l. 1). The classical dénouement has Leander drowning swimming across the Hellespont to Hero, which prompts her subsequent suicide. George Chapman undertook to complete the poem. His section is characterised by a very different tone, however, with discernible movement towards the philosophical and moralistic. In the 1598 second edition Chapman also divided the poem into the stanzas which are termed 'sestiads' after the town, Sestos, the final four of which he wrote himself.

Hero, 'Venus' nun'

Hero is presented as beautiful, desired by gods and somewhat puzzlingly, 'Venus' nun' (l. 45), but to the Renaissance imagination Venus could represent pure chastity or conversely overt sexuality and eroticism.[25] A contemporary readership would also no doubt find sly humour in the 'nun', which was a vernacular term for woman of slack morals, if not actually a prostitute. The ambiguity sets in play a teasing anticipation which Marlowe exploits to the full, especially in his delay tactics, which include digressions, visual tableaux and extensive dilations.

The first of the tableaux is the portrait of Hero, which is intricately detailed and initially seems to present a vision of exquisite beauty, describing the textiles, colours and workmanship of each of the articles with which she is adorned. She wears fine lawn lined with purple silk which is covered in gilt stars; her blue tunic has wide green sleeves, heavily embroidered with classical scenes; from a crown of myrtle leaves her trailing veil is embroidered with life-like flowers and leaves; and her necklace, although made of pebbles, shines like diamonds, reflecting the luminosity of her skin. It is only as the reader's attention is directed to her buskins* that the parody is revealed: they are made of 'silvered' sea shells and coral, within which sparrows perch. If the playful travesty has not been recognised, the final touch makes it transparent: cups of gold and pearl are provided for the chirruping birds, which a handmaid fills with water each day (ll. 9–36).

The description is blazonic in that it describes Hero's appearance from 'top to toe', but this type of vivid verbal picture is also termed 'ekphrases', a poetic fanfare which demonstrates consummate poetic dexterity. Its fascination has the effect of slowing time and is used by Marlowe as a detour, something like the formal digression, along the route which the reader knows will eventually lead to the voyeuristic pleasure of watching the consummation of the young couple's love. As is frequently noted by commentators, it is also concerned with superficial somatic† detail, rather than the more expected description of Hero's attributes.

Leander, 'All that men desire'

The sensual and appealing portrayal of Leander emphasises his desirability to 'venturous' youths, gods, goddesses, peasants and even rough-hewn Thracian soldiers. The weighting is on homo-erotic allure, which Marlowe flaunts in the voice of the narrator, humorously undercutting the descriptions with asides which designate his poetic muse as 'slack' and his pen as 'rude' (ll. 55–73). The line caresses Leander's image, compiling an erotic blazon from the long 'dangling tresses', which have never been cut, down his straight body, over the delicious 'meat' of his shoulder, suggesting oral gratification, to his 'smooth breast' and white belly. The meandering line then guides the

* Buskin: a type of boot which has cloth or leather sides over-laced to the knee, traditionally worn by classical tragedian actors.

† Somatic: referring to the outer, physical bodily make up as opposed to the mind.

gaze of the reader, tracing the indentation of his spine, 'That heavenly path, with many a curious dint, / That runs along his back' (ll. 68–9), in a patently subversive gesture which encourages desire towards sexual gratification. The teasing narrator offers and yet withholds information, drawing attention to his strategies whilst denying access to further indulgence with an abrupt change of direction:

> ... but my rude pen
> Can hardly blazon forth the loves of men,
> Much less powerful gods; let it suffice
> That my slack muse sings of Leander's eyes,
> Those Orient cheeks and lips ... (ll. 69–73)

This overtly homo-erotic section at the threshold of the epyllion introduces a theme which is glancingly acknowledged in a description of Jove 'dally[ing] with Idalian Ganymede' (l. 148), again in the wood god Sylvanus's 'weeping for the lovely boy', Cyparissus (ll. 154–5), to be further developed in the digression, or parecnasis, of the second sestiad. All of these allusions introduce a more extended treatment of the theme in Neptune's seduction attempt as Leander swims across the Hellespont. Despite the underlying threat, the episode is humorous; it also is very evocative of fishlike movement as Neptune, 'the lusty god' (l. 67), steals kisses, thrusting between Leander's strokes and darting to and fro around his swimming form. The sense of movement is created partly through the rhythm of the couplet format, but is also aided by the rhetorical devices of sinathrismus,* which loads the sentences with information, and the breathless repetition of the polysyndetic† 'And':

> He watch'd his arms, and as they opened wide,
> At every stroke betwixt them he would slide,
> And steal a kiss, and then run out and dance,
> And as he turn'd, cast many a lustful glance ...
> ... And dive into the water, and there pry

* Sinathrismus: the gathering or heaping of words.

† Polysyndeton: multiplication of conjunctions, in this case, 'and'.

Upon his breast, his thighs, and every limb,
And up again, and close behind him swim ... (ll. 183–90)

The foil for Neptune's brazen and lecherous aims is Leander's innocence, which does not permit him to believe that the god sexually desires a youth, prompting his cry 'You are deceiv'd, I am no woman, I' (l. 192). The reader is complicit with the narrator and enjoys the situation's dramatic irony, knowing that Neptune's proclivity is aroused precisely because Leander is not female. Marlowe's subversive digression can be read as an interrogation of heterosexual romantic conventions. Georgia Brown remarks upon his self-conscious modernity in the poem, suggesting that it deals in 'wantonness, ornament and excess', with specific intention to 'undermine social and political authority'.[26]

Invitations to Love

Much of the humour of the epyllion is predicated on a worldly readership's enjoyment of Hero and Leander's relative inexperience, sometimes amounting to ineptitude, in sexual matters. Although Leander understands well enough the conventions of love poetry and formal courtship, he is not so sure what should follow. His *carpe diem* encouragement to abandon chastity and taste the pleasures of married love is delivered 'like a bold sharp sophister' (l. 197), underlining its literary origin. A sophister is a teacher of rhetoric and, as such, associated with university scholarship, rather than sincere passion, as Hero impatiently points out in her, 'Who taught thee rhetoric to deceive a maid?' (l. 338). Nonetheless, when her reluctance is overcome, and she throws herself upon him, Leander is unsure how to proceed:

And as a brother with his sister toy'd,
Supposing nothing else was to be done,
Now he had her favour and good will had won. (ll. 52–4)

The charm of the narrative lies in the couple's naïve awakening to desire, particularly in the depiction of Hero's complex psychological response to first sexual attraction. Elizabethan cultural expectation would demand that she remained aloof to Leander's obvious adoration and amorous persuasion, but she is unable to prevent her blush of acknowledgement and is given to soft encouraging asides, which the narrator implies are designed to be just audible. Although later in the poem Hero may be manipulative, her bashful attraction seems genuine early in the encounter. Keach highlights Marlowe's indebtedness to Musaeus for this 'simultaneous fear and desire, uncertainty and curiosity', but also includes 'naiveté and *sophistication*' (emphasis added), suggesting that Hero eventually recognises and exploits her power over Leander.[27]

Tragic Undertones

The puella* mentality, however, is strangely at odds with the undertones of menace and tragedy suggested by aspects of Hero's attire, past and the temple with which she is associated. On her feet are not decorative sandals, to compliment her sumptuous and feminine robes as might be expected, but the buskins worn by male actors in classical tragedies. They do, of course, add to the incongruity of Hero's presentation, but they also allude to a more disturbing aspect of her makeup as a tragic character. As the reader – and Leander – first discover her she is sacrificing turtle doves (ll. 157–8), but the gory bloodstains on her tunic are not the result of this occupational hazard; amid her captivating blazon it is revealed that they are in fact 'made with the blood of wretched lovers slain' (l. 16). No explanation is given as the description of her luxurious robes sweeps on in tautological† excess. Whether these lovers are, in fact, Hero's lovers or lovers in the general sense, who have sought her assistance in her professional capacity, or perhaps have been sacrificed themselves, is not clarified, nor is any explanation given regarding the manner or circumstances of their deaths.‡ All the same, she is tainted by association at the least, at worst she may be considered a murderess.§

* Puella: young sweetheart or new wife.

† Tautology: repetition of an idea in different words, perhaps to the point of redundancy.

‡ Note also lines 117–130, which detail the dreadful results of those enamoured of her.

§ Juliet finds herself in a similar predicament in the balcony scene in *Romeo and Juliet* (II.ii).

The exceptionally vivid imagery of sexual violence and exploitation which embellishes Venus's temple is in itself alarming and does not bode well for Hero and Leander's relationship. Presented in a further *pictura poesis** the building's materials, colours, carvings and statues are described in close detail, but in such a manner that the unruly and lascivious performance of the gods depicted seems to escape the semantic boundaries of descriptor and verse. It becomes unclear if the disorderly behaviour is represented in carving, paint or reality.

From the exotic natural beauty of coloured 'jasper stone', 'green sea-agate' and 'crystal', the narrator guides the reader along a twisting carved vine to find the tipsy god of wine, Bacchus. Mythologically-literate readers would recognise that the god, also known as Dionysius, is associated with sexual licence, excess, ecstasy and fertility. He proves to be an appropriate doorman, as the narrator passes on to introduce a fantastical scenario: beneath the crystal pavement all manner of 'heady riots, incest, rapes' (l. 144) are being committed by the gods, overseen by a statue of Dánaë, who was herself raped by Jupiter. The licentious acts outlined are from the well-known stories of Ovid's *Metamorphoses* but the presentation is calculated to defamilarise them as threatening and sinister.

In a similarly unsettling episode, the tragic end of the young couple's love is alluded to in the digression introduced by Cupid's errand to the Destinies, seeking their favour for Hero and Leander. As their own love was rejected by Mercury, the petulant Fates deny their assistance. In a prolonged deferment of reader gratification, the narrator playfully leads the reader further from the central love affair, in order to explain not only the reason for the Fates' obstruction to love but also, preposterously, the reason why all scholars are poor (ll. 369–83).

The imagery of the eventual sexual encounter is contradictory. Hero is presented as both desiring and yet wishing to appear reluctant, which is misogynistically commented on by the narrator as true to form, while Leander's passion draws forth the observation that 'Love is not full of pity … / But deaf and cruel' (ll. 287–8). The couple eventually mutually enjoy the consummation of desire, which is couched in terms of a pagan

* *Pictura poesis*: a vivid picture created through poetry.

paradise and the seizing of forbidden fruit, although Hero's joy is marred by the approaching dawn for two reasons. She regrets the end of their night of love-making but it is also implied that she is ashamed, as she slips from the bed 'mermaid-like' (l. 315), to be revealed naked and blushing. Her glow creates a false dawn which illuminates the chamber, calling forth the true dawn, not of a bitter-sweet lover's alba,* but a more ambiguous and ominous scenario. The pathetic fallacy paints the spectacle of the night's shame and guilt across the sky:

> [Hesperus] ran before, as harbinger of light,
> And with his flaring beams mocked ugly Night,
> Till she, o'ercome with anguish, shame, and rage,
> Dang'd down to hell her loathsome carriage. (ll. 331–4)

Extended Commentary: Shakespeare, *Venus and Adonis* (1593)

Although Venus's character is in constant flux, perhaps intending to denote the destabilising nature of love, one facet of her nature that Shakespeare maintains throughout is her rhetorical skill. Kiernan convincingly argues for the entire poem as an exploration of the possibilities of rhetorical display, in a popular field that borrowed themes and loosely-defined literary strategies from Ovid, but paid less attention to his 'consummate practition [...] of rhetorical poetics'.[28]

Venus's speeches, which form the greater part of the narrative, are elaborate persuasions to love, exemplified in the forms of *carpe diem*, Petrarchan and Ovidian discourse, and lover's complaint. In order to give full rein in this persuasive oratory, Adonis needed to be recalcitrant, hence Shakespeare's manipulation of his source material. Although Adonis is not presented as enthusiastic in *Metamorphoses*, neither is he vehemently adverse to Venus's love-making as in the Shakespearean version. Book 4 of *Metamorphoses* did however present a besotted

* Alba: a love song at the parting of lovers at dawn, especially in Provençal poetry.

nymph, Salmacis, who pursued the fifteen-year old Hermaphroditus who 'didn't know what love was' (l. 330) in a similar fashion to Shakespeare's persistent goddess.*

The rhetorical overload of the epyllia generally has prompted the comment that it is 'rigid with rhetorical constructions and studded with compound and decorative epithets'.[29] This section will identify some for illustrative purposes; a brief survey of Venus's opening speech will demonstrate the case. She can be read as a parody or caricature of the Petrarchan lover, employing the same highly ornate rhetorical figures and persuasive devices, ultimately to the same aim. The incongruity of her situation is emphasised not only by her own lumbering physicality, but also Adonis's deflating rejection of her artificial entreaties in bathetically practical terms: 'you hurt my hand with wringing. Let us part' (l. 421), 'you crush me. Let me go' (l. 611) and, insultingly, in his petulant cry that all he is interested in is trying to recapture his horse:

> 'For shame,' he cries, 'Let me go, and let me go.
> My day's delight is past; my horse is gone,
> And 'tis your fault I am bereft him so.
> I pray you hence, and leave me here alone,
> For all my mind, my thought, my busy care,
> Is how to get my palfrey from that mare.' (ll. 379–84)

As Lucy Gent has painstakingly catalogued,[30] Venus employs a surfeit of rhetorical devices in this first address, which in itself demonstrates copia,† and the excess of compliments addressed to Adonis is hyperbolic in entirety. Her address to Adonis as 'The field's chief flower, sweet above compare, / Stain to all nymphs, more lovely than a man' (ll. 8–9) is pleonastic,‡ in Puttenham's terms, the 'fault of [too] full speech' to the point of redundancy; it may also be termed tautological, in that it

* Shakespeare's model for his insistent love-struck goddess could have also been Lodge's Scylla, of *Scylla's Metamorphosis*, discussed in this chapter.

† Copia: expansiveness, richness through words.

‡ Pleonastic: piling up of words to the point of redundancy.

repeats the same idea in a different form.[31] The pre-figuring of Adonis as a flower, which points to his ultimate fate, is an example of prolepsis,* while the many comparisons (*comparatio*) load the verses to the extent that the subject of the speech – Adonis – becomes lost amid the plethora of generated images.

Out-Petrarching Petrarch

Venus's ironic position, as an aggressive female lover who desires to be wooed by a passive and basically uninterested boy, prompts her to enumerate her own charms, as she would wish a more experienced lover to manage for himself. She introduces her theme with what at first seems to be an anti-blazon, similar to Sonnet 130's, exhaustively enumerating no less than sixteen negative attributes which might prevent a suitor's love. The catalogue persuades by negation, however, in the figure of litotes,† as the argument triumphantly turns on the final line of the sextain,‡ 'But having no defects, why dost abhor me?' (138). The pleonastic display includes hard[harsh]-favoured, foul, wrinkled, old, ill-nurtured, crooked, churlish, thick-sighted and 'lacking juice' (ll. 133–8), and would be recognised as sinathrismus§ by its rhetorically-tuned readers. As George Puttenham wryly points out, the author goes about his business 'by heapes as if [he] would winne the game by multitudes of wordes'.[32] The effect of the heaping creates a breathless speed, as Venus hurries on, augmenting her argument with further exposition of her imagined flawlessness in the following stanza, which takes the form of a more conventional – if egotistical – blazon. Delineating her charms through unwrinkled brow, bright grey eyes to her skin in conventional sonnet-manner, her control begins to slip into a more lascivious tone, however, as her own sexual desires intrude into the self-display. The anaphoric¶

* Prolepsis: prefigures or looks forward (Ant. Analepsis: echoes or looks backward).
† Litotes: affirms something by denying its contrary.
‡ Sextain, also sixtain, sestina: a verse of six lines.
§ Sinathrismus: the heaping of speeches or words with similar meaning.
¶ Anaphora: the repetition of a word at the beginning of a line, phrase or clause.

repetition of 'my' dominates the stanza, insistently drawing attention not to the fragmented single features of the face, but rather to the uncontainable and more sensuous, 'beauty', 'flesh' and 'marrow', connoting sexual desire. This is not the *donna angelicata*[*] of the cool alabaster complexion and jewel-like features, but a glowing soft, plump and moist desiring female. Neither is she too coy to admit that her 'marrow burns' (l. 142) nor to fantasise about the melting pleasure of holding hands (l. 44). Apart from the indecorous eroticism and the seeming self-arousal, the goddess is also associated with natural processes. Kiernan points out that her own descriptions emphasise 'fluidity and change, organic process, physical growth and renewal'.[33] All of these aspects align with the traditional 'encouragement to love' debate, found, for example, in Shakespeare's early sonnets, but are complicated by being presented by the female who is encouraging the use of her own body.

Framing a more appealing vision, Venus casts herself as a fairy, and a nymph 'with long dishevelled hair' who dances along the sands, and is so insubstantial that she leaves no footprint (ll. 146–8). She goes on to develop the theme of lightness, entranced by her own inventiveness, suggesting that the delicate flowers upon which she reclines remain unbent by her negligible weight and that she is no burden to the weak doves which draw her chariot through the sky. The couplet of the stanza turns wittily upon the paronomasia,[†] generated on 'light' and 'heavy' imagery, demanding the reason why Adonis resists her. The effect of these puns is to compress several different meanings into two short lines; this in itself mimics the capacity of the classical epyllia. Self-engrossed oratory display propels Venus into more erotima,[‡] before embarking upon further ratiocination[§] in the conventional argument to procreate, as noted in Shakespeare's sonnets:

* This means 'angelic woman' in Italian.

† Paronomasia: word play, punning.

‡ Erotima: a rhetorical question.

§ Ratiocination: methodical and rational reasoning, sometimes parodied in love poetry to comic effect.

Upon the earth's increase why shouldst thou feed,
Unless the earth with thy increase be fed?
By law of nature thou art bound to breed,
That thine might live, when thou thyself art dead:
And so in spite of death thou dost survive,
In that thy likeness still is left alive. (ll. 169–74)

As Burrow points out, Shakespeare was no doubt familiar with Erasmus's 'Epistle to persuade a young man to marry' which rehearses the same metaphors of cultivation and the natural cycle of life in which, by analogy, the young man is urged to participate.[34] There are striking parallels between his Sonnets 1, 3 and 13 and this section of the poem, but all of the early sub-group, up to Sonnet 17, is informed by similar concerns. Nonetheless, Venus's solicitude seems hollow, given the extensive treatment of her overwhelming desire, and we are bound to read this as yet another manipulative rhetorical device.

Notes

1 Paul W. Miller discussed the controversy as long ago as the 1950s, comparing the classical model with Renaissance examples, in 'The Elizabethan Minor Epic', *Studies in Philology* 55:1 (1958), pp. 31–8, pp. 32, 33.

2 A useful and reliable glossary of rhetorical terms is available at this American university website: http://rhetoric.byu.edu/.

3 The work is available on the electronic database Early English Books Online (hereafter EEBO), Short Title Catalogue number 1820.09, complete with dedication. The main text can be found in *Amorous Rites: Elizabethan Erotic Verse*, ed. by Sandra Clark (London: Everyman, 1994), pp. 3–30. All quotations of the work are from this text.

4 Ovid, *Metamorphoses: A New Verse Translation*, translated by David Raeburn, Penguin Classics (London: Penguin Books, 2004), p. 544. All references to the work are from this source.

5 Miller, pp. 36, 37.

6 William Keach, *Elizabethan Erotic Narratives* (New Jersey: Rutgers Press, 1977), p. 40.

7 M. C. Bradbrook, *Shakespeare and Ovidian Poetry* (London: Chatto and Windus, 1951), p. 56.

8 '*Vilia miretur vulgus: mihi flavus Apollo / Pocula Castalia plena minister aqua,*' Latin epigram from Ovid's *Amores*, 1:15, 35–6, as translated in Colin Burrow (ed.), *The Oxford Shakespeare, Complete Sonnets and Poems* (Oxford: Oxford University Press, 2002, repr. 2008), p. 173.

9 Burrow, p. 41.

10 Burrow, p. 107; Bradbrook, p. 61.

11 John Clapham's poem, *Narcissus*, written in Latin, was also dedicated to the young Henry Wriothesley, Earl of Southampton. Burrow suggests that there are close resemblances in some areas of *Venus and Adonis* where Shakespeare seems to be 'consciously attempting to outdo Clapham's monochrome classicism in technicolour English', Burrow, pp. 10–12, p. 12.

12 A. B. Taylor (ed.), *Shakespeare's Ovid: The Metamorphoses in the Plays and Poems* (Cambridge: Cambridge University Press, 2000), p. 1.

13 Sidney, *Astrophil and Stella,* Sonnet 8, line 1; Shakespeare, *The Passionate Pilgrim,* Sonnet 11, line 1; Marlowe's *Hero and Leander*, line 155.

14 George Puttenham, *The Arte of English Poesie*, Book III, v, p. 150.

15 Pauline Kiernan, '*Venus and Adonis* and Ovidian indecorus wit', in *Shakespeare's Ovid: The Metamorphoses in the Plays and Poems*, pp. 81–95, pp. 85, 86.

16 See *Metamorphoses*, Book 10: ll. 604–5; Jonathan Bate, *Shakespeare and Ovid* (Oxford: Clarendon Press, 1993), pp. 54–5.

17 Coppélia Kahn, 'Venus and Adonis', *The Cambridge Companion to Shakespeare's Poetry*, Patrick Cheyney (ed.) (Cambridge: Cambridge University Press, 2007), pp. 72–89.

18 Keach, pp. 72–3.

19 Pauline Kiernan, 'Death by Rhetorical Trope: Poetry Metamorphosed in *Venus and Adonis* and the Sonnets', *The Review of English Studies*, New Series, Vol. 46, No. 184 (Nov., 1995), pp. 475–50, p. 481.

20 See Burrow's notes for further explanation and reference, n.ll. 799–804, p. 217.

21 Keach, p. 80. He points out that a poem attributed to Theocritus (*Id,* XXX, 26–31) used the conceit of the boar's kiss and several translations were in circulation during the sixteenth century.

22 Kahn, 'Self and Eros in *Venus and Adonis*', in Philip C. Kolin (ed.), *Venus and Adonis, Critical Essays* (New York and London: Garland Publishing, 1997), pp. 181–222, p. 197. Elsewhere she points out that the creature, considered to be overtly masculine and libidinous in this era, in fact, penetrates Adonis, in an encounter that can only be considered homo-erotic and as conforming to contemporary definitions of bestiality, both of which

represent 'an affront to political and moral order': Khan, 'Venus and Adonis' in *The Cambridge Companion to Shakespeare's Poetry*, p. 72.

23 See Burrow, pp. 6, 7, 17; Robert Logan, *Shakespeare's Marlowe: The Influence of Christopher Marlowe on Shakespeare's Artistry* (Hampshire: Ashgate, 2007), p. 57.

24 Keach, p. 87.

25 Keach, pp. 89, 90.

26 Georgia E. Brown, 'Marlowe's Poems and Classicism', in P. Cheyney (ed.), *The Cambridge Companion to Christopher Marlowe* (Cambridge: Cambridge University Press, 2004), pp. 106–26, p. 116, 108.

27 Keach, p. 98, citing Musaeus, lines 103–07.

28 Kiernan, pp. 475–501, p. 478. For some definitions of rhetorical devices see the University of Kentucky website.

29 F. E. Halliday, *The Poetry of Shakespeare's Plays* (London: 1954; repr. 1964), p. 62, cited in Kiernan, p. 476.

30 Lucy Gent, '*Venus and Adonis*: the Triumph of Rhetoric', *The Modern Language Review*, 69:4 (1974), pp. 721–9, p. 723.

31 Puttenham, Bk. III, xxi, p. 254.

32 Puttenham, Bk. III, xix, p. 236.

33 Kiernan, p. 481.

34 Burrow, p. 382.

Pastoral to Epic: Spenser, Marvell and Milton

Elizabethan poets who aspired to greatness attempted to follow Virgil's* path, beginning with the pastoral mode and progressing through the various genres to the epic, at the pinnacle of their careers. Within the classical pastorals there are constant references to the lowliness and simplicity of the form, compared with the poets' ambitions to write of more lofty themes in less 'rude' forms, indicating planned progression in the hierarchical scheme.

The Arcadian† pastoral of the classics celebrated an idealised country life of leisure (or *otium*), amid herders of goats. Characters' dialogues may be intellectual, however, including social or political debate, or poetry and singing contests. Given its 'low' designation, pastoral adopts simple rhyme schemes and language, sometimes even ventriloquising its simple characters in rustic idiom and dialect.‡ Despite the subject matter, its authors were highly educated and from the earliest examples the genre commented on political matters.[1] Virgil's inspiration was the Greek *Idylls*

* 'Virgil' is the anglicised name of the Roman poet Publius Vergilius Maro (90–70 B.C.). His most famous works are the *Eclogues*, the *Georgics* and the impressive epic poem, *The Aeneid*.

† 'Arcadian' means ideally rural or rustic.

‡ See Part Three: 'Humanist Prose and Rhetoric' for more detail on Renaissance theories of literary decorum.

of Theocritus,* but his Latinisation of the form emphasised the civic link, raising interesting tensions between city and rural matters.

The eclogues† of Mantuan made a significant contribution to the genre in mid-fifteenth-century Italy.‡ His eclogues, which he entitled *Adolescentia,* popularised a critical and morally-austere perspective. The pre-existing Arcadian critique of city life became foregrounded as a severe microcosmic representation of worldly corruption in general. In Mantuan's verse the love games of shepherds are not celebrated, in typical Arcadian pastoral mode, but seen as culpable, as a distraction from duty and responsibility. In his words, 'A hateful thing is Love' (II: 167), as sensual and emotional indulgence leads to loss of man's God-given reasoning capacity. This in turn instigates an abandonment of principles, morality and responsibility. The morally-uplifting content of Mantuan's eclogues made them popular as study texts in schools, and consequently they were well known among educated young men throughout the subsequent Tudor reigns.

Spenser's 'May' Eclogue: 'Shepheards and Wolves'

Edmund Spenser's eclogue 'May' in his *Shepheard's Calender* (1579) is a good example of combined Arcadian and Mantuan influences. Initially 'May' seems to present merely opposing views on the seasonal pastimes of the countryside, but a more didactic tone soon emerges. The contrasting dialogue is between Piers and Palinode, the perspective of the latter being that good things are God's gifts to us to be enjoyed. He enthusiastically describes the 'Maying' activities of the village:

* Theocritus was Greek but born in Sicily in 300 B.C. Little is known about him but his short pastoral poems influenced Virgil's eclogues.

† An eclogue is a short pastoral poem; Virgil's *Bucolics* is a good example. Note the term was written both 'eclogue' and 'eglogue' in the Renaissance. Debates about the etymology of the word recognise its root either in conversations between individuals or a link to goat-herding. Virgil's fourth and sixth eclogues deal with this theme and Spencer interacts with the concept in the 'June' section of *The Shepheard's Calender*.

‡ Mantuan's full name was Battista Mantuanus Spagnuoli (1447–1516). A member of the reformed Carmelites, he became their Vicar General for reform. In the mid 1480s he also preached before Popes Sixtus IV and Innocent VIII against papal corruption.

> Youghthes folk now flocken in every where,
> To gather may buskets and smelling brere;
> And home they hastes and posts to dight,
> And all the Kirk pillours eare day light,
> With hawthorne buds, and sweet Eglantine,
> And girlonds of roses and Sops in wine. (ll. 9–14)*

Piers attacks the celebrations, however, at first as young people's 'foolish' amusements, but as the poem progresses, the denunciation of the entertainments intensifies, and they become 'wanton' and eventually evil. Reading the eclogue in isolation, the slippage from irritation with rustic diversions to overt religious polemic can be puzzling, but Spenser's own introductory 'Argument' underlines the Mantuan thrust:

> In this fifte Æglogue, under the persons of two shepheards Piers and Palinode is represented two formes of pastours and Ministers, or the protestant and the Catholique: whose chiefe talk standeth in reasoning whether the life of one must be like the other …

The criticism of Catholic prelates' corruption aligns with Mantuan's own condemnation of the Church of fifteenth-century Italy. Spenser's diatribe against 'shepherds', whose fraudulent practices demonstrate their true wolfish nature, escalates in force as Piers accuses them of often 'devour[ing] their own sheepe' (l. 128). A modern-day reader may find this incomprehensible, but a contemporary readership was accustomed to reading allegorically. The biblical analogy of the Christian minister as the good shepherd – or not in this case – therefore, would be transparent. The anomaly of absent and non-preaching priests, who gained benefices

* The first of May marked the end of winter and the beginning of summer's fertility. Traditionally young people went out into the countryside very early on May morning to gather blossoming branches of hawthorn, known as 'May Blossom' as this is when it flowers. They returned home, singing seasonal songs, with flowers and greenery to decorate the home and church. Elizabethan May Day celebrations included Maypole and Morris Dancing, plays and mumming, and were associated with courting, drinking and youthful high spirits.

and lucrative offices but neglected their congregations, provoked fierce criticism. In the 1530s, for example, Hugh Latimer persistently chastised these 'lording loiterers and idle [Catholic] ministers … who seek only their own pleasure'.[2] Although at the time of Spenser's writing the state religion had been Protestant since 1558, an ardent Protestantism still felt the need to define its parameters and distance itself from Catholic practice.

Piers subtly undermines the Catholic Church by aligning its feasts and saints' celebrations with the pagan seasonal festivities, stating that he pities the foolishness of the clerics (ll. 37–40). Although the Argument denotes Piers and Palinode as rival ministers of religion, which clarifies some of the pressures in the debate, in fact, rather than a staunch theological opponent, Palinode seems relatively naïve and in need of guidance, as is confirmed in the closing section.

'The credulous kidde'

Presented as a parable, this final section introduces a Fox pedlar who persuades a kid (goat) to invite him into his home. Fox demonstrates his gaudy wares and cunningly leaves one item at the bottom of his basket for the kid to retrieve himself. As he leans into the hamper Kidde is trapped:

> … All save a bell, which he left behind
> In the basket for the Kidde to fynd.
> Which when the Kidde stooped downe to catch,
> He popt him in, and his basket did latch,
> Ne stayed he once, the dore to make fast,
> But ranne awaye with him all in hast[e]. (ll. 288–93)

Spenser's gloss identifies the pedlar's showy toys as being of the 'popish superstition', meaning reliquaries, rosaries and other accessories of ritual, which reformists condemned as worthless vanities (l. 240). Given Spenser's religious affiliations, the inclusion of the parable is ironic. The practice of including entertaining fabliaux* and fables in Catholic sermons, to make didactic content more palatable, was much criticised by religious reformers.

Although country life is championed over that of the spiritually-threatening court, Mantuanesque pastoral is hardly celebratory of its joys. It equates rustic existence with struggle against the elements – lack of warmth and threadbare clothes, inadequate nourishment and the danger of attack from wild beasts – more than simple rustic pleasures or the beauty of nature. Spenser's pastoral vision is more subtle than earlier examples, such as Mantuan's or Alexander Barclay's but, as Cullen identifies, the antithetical tension still remains, arising basically from an opposition between the pagan Arcadian outlook and the Christian, as he states: 'The best to be hoped for is a precarious balance of these polarities'.[3]

Marvell's 'Skilful Gardener'

Andrew Marvell's 'The Garden' is pastoral in subject matter. It still retains the critique of man's relationship with his kind and interacts with Renaissance concepts of Nature, but his perspective is conciliatory. Rather than emphasising the rifts between the Arcadian and Mantuan visions, Marvell writes of Christian resolution in images of Eden and return to God. At this time contemplation of nature and one's own place within it was thought to generate an appreciation of God and his divine scheme. The trope of the garden both illustrates and complicates this vision, as an earthly garden is created through artifice and imitation, rather than existing as pure and uncomplicated nature.†

The initial Arcadian impulse, to celebrate retired life in an idealised countryside, can clearly be identified in 'The Garden', as the ambitious activities of the city are denigrated:

* A usually satirical short story in verse form, originally from twelfth-century France, popular in the Middle Ages.

† A subtle consideration to bear in mind in Marvell's pastorals is the idea that mankind had already failed as a gardener once, in the shape of Adam and Eve, who were expelled from the Garden of Eden.

> How vainly men themselves amaze
> To win the palm, the oak or bays,
> And their incessant labours see … (ll. 1–3)

Renouncing this misdirected life the voice of the poem praises the quietness and innocence of retirement and solitude, announcing, 'Society is all but rude' (l. 15). This amusing reversal of the familiar claim of the pastoral to be a rude (lowly) poetic form, suggests that sophisticated city-dwellers are too insensitive to enjoy the subtle pleasures of the country. Stanza five's apostrophe* to the reader is the climacteric of Arcadian vision, as the fruits of the trees press themselves into the speaker's hands and mouth, in sensual abundance:

> What wondr'ous Life in this I lead!
> Ripe apples drop about my head;
> The Luscious Clusters of the Vine
> Upon my mouth do crush their Wine;
> The Nectaren, and curious Peach,
> Into my hands themselves do reach. (ll. 33–8)

This cornucopia of delight has obvious resonance with the concept of the classical 'Golden Age',† but can also be read as a vision of perfection as in the Garden of Eden: fertility and plenty with mankind at its privileged centre. In Neo-platonic escalation, the following stanzas move from the senses to the mind and then the soul.‡ Through contemplation of nature's beauty and bounty, the soul is able to 'Cast […] the body's vest aside' and soar heavenward like a bird: 'My soul

* A 'turning away' from the subject in hand to address someone or thing not present, as in an ejaculation to Nature or the gods.

† A time of perfection in all respects, nostalgically evoked in comparison to a less propitious era.

‡ Renaissance readings of Plato's theory of love maintained that love should move from the love of one individual, through to love in a more general sense, eventually progressing to love of the Creator. It should also develop from the carnal and mutable to unchanging spiritual perfection. See Plato's *Symposium* and Hoby's translation of Castiglione's *Book of the Courtier* in Part Three: 'Life Guides, Mother's Advice and Conduct Books'.

into the boughs doth glide. / There like a bird it sits, and sings' (ll. 52–3).

Cullen reads the poem as a statement of Christian faith, identifying the tree in which the bird-soul sits as Christ's cross and the flight as being 'to become one with the spiritual source of greenness, God'.[4] Other critics associate the repetition of the colour green with new growth, naïveté, and the symbolic hope of a new Eden.[5] Repeated praise of solitude, introduced in the second stanza, leads somewhat unexpectedly to Adam's pleasure whilst he dwelt in Eden alone, before he was joined by Eve. This is a male paradise, precisely because it lacks women: 'Such was that happy garden-state, / While man there walked without a mate' (ll. 57–8).

Perhaps wry humour is intended but, as Marvell's poetry was not primarily written for external circulation, it cannot be said to pander to the often misogynistic humour of a male readership. The poem denigrates women, firstly as unworthy of compare to the beauty of 'fair trees' (ll. 17–24) and later, obliquely, as the fortuitous absence. The overall stance seems be that women and paradise are incompatible and that amorous love is a distraction from a worthy life. Despite the sensuous imagery suggesting the classical bucolic pastoral, ambiguous Mantuan undercurrents can be discovered just beneath its surface.

Spenser's *Faerie Queene*: 'Clowdilly enwrapped in Allegorical devises'

In his opening to *The Faerie Queene* (1590–6) whilst humbly maintaining his novice status, Spenser draws attention to his high aspiration in abandoning pastoral for the epic:

> Lo I the man, whose Muse whilhome did maske,
> … in lowly Shepheards weeds,
> Am now enforst a far unfitter taske,

For trumpets sterne to change mine Oaten reeds,
And sing of Knights and Ladies gentle deeds. (Book I: 1–4)*

Continuity within Spenser's oeuvre can be identified in the themes of moral vision and sexuality, particularly in the focus on the conflict between desire and responsibility as highlighted in *The Shepheard's Calender*. Colin Clout of Spenser's earlier *Colin Clout Comes Home Again* (1595) also makes a guest appearance in Book VI, which is concerned with the virtue of Courtesy and has a pastoral theme. As is appropriate in this highest of literary genres, however, both the themes and the narrative mode are far more complex than in the pastorals. As Gary Waller comments: 'Of all the age's poetry, *The Faerie Queene* is at once the most grandiose in its claims for wholeness of vision and the most dislocated and disrupted.'[6]

Attacks on Catholicism continue in Spenser's allegory of Duessa, the 'Whore of Babylon'† in Book I, for example, but his attitude to the state religion and Elizabeth herself are still ambiguous. As John Watkins suggests, Spenser's approach, rather than the clear vision of dominant Calvinist thought that might be expected at this stage of Elizabeth's reign, often seems to have more in common with the medieval plays and tales of Jesus and the Apostles as miracle-workers.[7] Although a simplistic reading may suggest an obsequious eulogy to the queen, her lineage and her reign, there are also embedded implied criticisms of her politics, lack of religious fervour and her decision not to marry.

'A Letter of the Authors' and Self-fashioning

The prefatory letter to Sir Walter Ralegh, affixed to the first edition of *The Faerie Queene*, claims that inspiration for the work came from classical epic, such as Virgil's *Aeneid*, but also popular Continental

* *The Shepheard's Calender* was published anonymously, hence the reference to masked identity. The shepherds of pastoral poetry frequently played upon home-made pipes fashioned from the stems of plants, in this case oat straws.

† 'The Whore of Babylon' was a common Protestant term of abuse for the Catholic faith in sixteenth- and seventeenth-century England.

contemporary works. Spenser specifically names Lodovico Ariosto's *Orlando Furioso* (1532) and Torquato Tasso's *Gerusalemme Liberata* (1581), saying that he takes example from these 'excellente Poets'. The work operates on many levels: as a conscious attempt to create a patriotic epic celebrating the achievements of sovereign and nation; as a heavily textured work of high literature demonstrating his consummate literary skills; as a chivalric romance; and also as a 'Courtesy Book'.* In Spenser's words, 'the generall end therefore of all the booke is to fashion a gentleman or noble person in virtuous and gentle discipline'. Scholars draw attention to the possible ambiguities of this declaration of intent. As the work claims to portray examples of civil behaviour, it can be read as a social and spiritual guide for would-be courtiers, gentlefolk and the nobility. The work also addresses the queen, suggesting she views herself in several of the virtuous female characters; however, this prompts the question whether she is the named 'noble person'. If Elizabeth is indeed the intended recipient of Spenser's advice, clearly she is not in need of training in 'Temperaunce', 'Chastity' or the other virtues to which the books are devoted. Spenser's political counsel is more subtly delivered beneath the layers of allegory, as he himself suggests, in a 'darke conceit'. Although the 'Letter' is a useful outline, Spenser's plan was never fully realised.[8] He states that the epic will take the Virgilian form of twelve books, dividing each into twelve cantos, each to celebrate a noble attribute, represented by one knight. He clarifies that his work is not a chronological history, but begins *in media res*†. If he had adopted a linear perspective, he explains, the last section, the Faerie Queene's annual twelve-day feast, would have been the opening. In Arthurian fashion, each day a knight would undertake an 'adventure' or quest, as described in the twelve books, along with 'many other adventures … intermedled'. He evidently intends the work to be read in the spirit of heroic romance, although it also contains weighty moral and spiritual implications.

* See Part Three: 'Life Guides, Mother's Advice and Conduct Books', which is devoted to this type of literature.

† Latin, meaning 'in the middle of events'. This is traditionally the opening strategy adopted by writers of epic.

The 'Wandring wood and Errours den'

Book I concerns the 'Knight of the Red Crosse, or Holinesse', whose quest is to assist Una, a beautiful young woman of royal lineage, who arrived at the Faerie Queene's feast and requested aid to rid her country of a fierce dragon which had held her parents hostage for many years. The vivid and enigmatic episodes are entertaining even on a superficial level, involving a serpent which spews forth its offspring from its mouth, a baby (Redcrosse himself) stolen by the Faeries, a powerful enchanter, a colourful seductress, a giant who evaporates on death, a parade of the Seven Deadly Sins and a fearsome dragon which endures a three day onslaught before succumbing to a grisly death.

The book is also profoundly informed by reformed Protestant doctrine, however, and – in the manner of Bunyan's later *Pilgrim's Progress* (1678)– allegorically depicts progress through temptations and adversity towards salvation. Important aspects of the quest derive from St John's Revelations, the final book of the Bible, believed to predict the end of time and Christ's second coming. When Redcrosse and Una become lost in the forest, he discovers a monster named Erroure, 'Halfe like a serpent horribly displaide, / But th'other halfe did woman's shape retaine' (Book I: 124–5), for example. Apart from evoking parallels with Ovid's metamorphosed females,* the description suggests a fusion of erroneous Eve and the serpent of Eden, but also, to pious readers of the time, the serpent of Revelation 12. Spenser's allegory draws strongly on such iconic images, making use of his readership's *a priori* understanding of the apocalyptic symbolism. Redcrosse's death blow prompts the serpent to vomit 'A floud of poison horrible and blacke' (Book I: 172–3) which emits such a stench that he is almost overcome. The 'filthy parbreake' (vomit) contains not only blind frogs and toads, often associated with black magic and sorcery, but also strangely, 'bookes and papers'. This reference to Catholic theological texts is further reinforced, to the astute reader, by

* See the section on Thomas Lodge's epyllion *Scylla's Metamorphosis*, in Part Three: 'Renaissance Epyllion'.

the intertextual association with the 'false prophets' in the biblical source, Revelations.*

Numerous links and echoes such as this help to enhance the characters, themes and confrontations. The work resists clear cut definitions, however, working on the metonymic plane of allusion and montage, rather than direct equivalences. The 'woman clothed with the sun' of Revelations is beset not only by the serpent, but also 'The woman clothed in purple and scarlet' (the Whore of Babylon) and her steed, 'a scarlet-coloured beast ... having seven heads and ten horns'. Spenser's Una ('One') represents the One True Church (aligned with the women clothed with the sun) and Redcrosse's character is an amalgam of St George, the patron saint of England, and an exemplar of the ardent Protestant actively pursuing salvation.† Much like the medieval Everyman of the Morality Plays, he interacts with allegorical characters that he must recognise and overcome on his journey; these include the knight Sans Foy ('Without Faith'), the seductress Duessa ('False Religion' or the Whore of Babylon), the Archmagus ('Hypocrisy'), Orgoglio the giant (the papacy) and a monstrous red dragon (Satan).[9]

'Mighty charmes, to trouble sleepy minds'

Spenser's narrative strategies ensure that the reader participates in Redcrosse's confusion and tardy realisations, as the significance of events or characters is often only gradually revealed in retrospect. Thus, the pious hermit who invites Una and Redcrosse to rest in his dwelling and converses of saints and popes, strewing his speech with 'an *Ave-Mary* after and before', it is revealed, is an Archmagus (Book I: 313, 315). When his guests are sleeping, like Marlowe's Dr Faustus, he retires to his study to use 'Magick bookes and artes of sundry kindes' to summon

* The biblical inspiration speaks of unclean spirits like frogs which emit from 'the mouth of the beast, and out of the mouth of the false prophet', Revelation 16:13.

† Redcrosse does not hear of his real identity until, after his defeat of Orgoglio and his recuperation in the House of Holiness, he is shown a vision of New Jerusalem and his history and destiny are revealed to him: 'For thou amongst those Saints ... / Shalt be a Saint, and thine owne nations frend /And Patrone: thou Saint George shalt callèd be' (Book X: 455–7).

spirits to facilitate his plans (l. 323). One flies 'making speedy way through sperséd ayre',[*] through the 'world of waters' and into the bowels of the earth, to procure an erotic dream from the god Morpheus (ll. 333–96).[†] Meanwhile, the Archmagus's second spirit helper is transformed into a beguiling female clad in Una's white robes and black stole. Redcrosse's subsequent dream graphically 'bathes' him in 'wanton blis and wicked joy' (l. 420), further exacerbated by spirit-Una's urges to share love pleasures with her. Although he overcomes his own desire, his confidence in Una (the True Faith) is shaken, prompting the Magus to plan a second attack using his compliant evil spirits. The first is transformed into a young Squire whom the Magus arranges Redcrosse to see with the spirit-Una in bed, 'In wanton lust and lewd embracement' (Book II: 42). Anguished by the revelation, Redcrosse secretly abandons Una and becomes susceptible to the influence of Duessa. The deceptions of the Archmagus point to contemporary propaganda against the 'True Church' (according to the Protestant outlook of the era), and prefigures Redcrosse's fascination with and subjection to Duessa 'that fowle Lady faire', representing Catholicism (l. 328).

Redcrosse's susceptibility to *hubris*[‡] is indicated in his visit to the House of Pride, guided by Duessa. The episode parallels Book III's Castle Joyeous section and is described in similar heightened detail, or ekphrases, tableaux-style. The ruler is a beautiful, vain and haughty queen named Lucifera and her court parallels the iniquitous places of resort depicted in the Mantuan pastoral tradition:

> Her Lordes and Ladies all this while devise
> Themselves to setten forth to straungers sight:
> Some frounce their curled hair in courtly guise,
> Some prancke their ruffes, and others do trimly dight
> Their gay attire: each others pride does spight. (Book IV: 122–6)

* In modern orthography 'dispersed air'.

† Spenser's very detailed account might be considered a minor digression, as found in the epyllia of the period.

‡ Pride.

Lucifera's coach is drawn by 'six unequall beasts', each mounted by one of her aged counsellors, who are in fact the remaining six Deadly Sins, as she herself represents Pride, the greatest sin of all. In the Castle of Busyrane, of Book III, there is a similar vivid pageant, although in this first example, the rearguard is brought up by Satan himself, lashing his minions forward 'with smarting whip in hand' (Book IV: 317).

Importantly, Redcrosse's main encounter with 'the old dragon', Satan, does not occur until he has visited the House of Holiness with Una, where he is instructed in spirituality by personified virtues, Humility, Zeal, Reverence, Fidelia (Faith) and Charity. His true lineage and destiny is also revealed to him in this episode, when he views New Jerusalem from the hill and descends a new man. The battle itself employs imagery from Revelation, also interweaving aspects of St Paul's letters and Calvinist doctrine; this said, it is also a masterpiece of heroic romance. After three days, during which Redcrosse and his horse face great danger, including being 'Snacht up' and borne into the 'yielding aire' (Book I: 157, 162) and near-death experiences, the knight prevails and the dragon is overcome. His victory is only possible, however, through the restorative qualities of the ancient Well of Life, 'wherin he drenched lay' (Book I: 299) and the life-giving balm from the Tree of Life. Critics debate the significance of both, detecting references to Christian baptism and in the Calvinist doctrine of Predestination.* Although the dragon is vanquished, the emissary of Satan, Archimago, escapes to cause further strife later in the work, indicating the ongoing battle of the Christian against evil.

* According to Calvinist doctrine the individual was utterly corrupt and could not influence his destiny by good works or any other act, as all mankind was tainted by original sin. Only by God's free gift of Grace, which enabled complete faith in Christ's atonement for this sin, might he/she be saved; hence, the doctrine of *sola fides* (only faith). Despair, such as Redcrosse experienced, was a sin signifying lack of belief. God gave Grace to the Elect, who were chosen for Heaven, but the Reprobate were destined for Hell.

Milton's *Paradise Lost*: 'Of man's first disobedience ...'

In his *Areopagitica* (1644), Milton looks back at Spenser's epic poem from a distance of almost half a century and very much altered political circumstances. He calls Spenser 'our sage and serious poet', claiming that *The Faerie Queene* teaches the path of a true Christian better than works of theologians. Specifically citing Sir Guyon's quest, Temperance, he draws attention to the need to know the extent of vice in order to abstain, sentiments which Eve will voice in Book IX of *Paradise Lost*.[10] Michael O'Connell suggests that Milton's *Paradise Lost* further develops Spenser's 'pastoral inwardness' of Book VI to centre on 'the quiet assertion of 'a paradise within'.[11]

Milton's youthful poetry included the companion poems *L'Allegro* and *Il Penseroso* (*c*.1631) and the elegy *Lycidas* (1637), all of which contain elements of the pastoral.[12] When he published his great epic poem, in 1667, however, the restoration of the monarchy had ended his successful political career, he had become blind and had suffered imprisonment. His grandiose scheme, defined in Book I, was to write of 'man's first disobedience' as defined in the Bible and to 'justify the ways of God to man' (Book I: 1–26). Although he praises Spenser's epic, he specifically rejects the theme of 'fabled knights / In battles feigned' (Book III: 30).[13] Milton dilates the relatively short biblical episode of 'man's first disobedience' (which occurs in Book IX), to show its development in retrospect and project also forward to include its ramifications. In this way *Paradise Lost* seems to include all time, giving it epic proportions. Milton's aim was patriotic and devoutly Christian; he intended creating a national epic in the vernacular tongue to rival the pagan epics of the ancient world:

> That what the greatest wits of Athens, Rome or modern Italy, and those Hebrews of old did for their country, I, in my proportion … being a Christian, might do for mine … content with these British islands as my world …[14]

'Of satanic pride, humiliation and hierarchies'

The grand design begins amidst the rebellion of Lucifer and his followers, but told in retrospect. At this point, the reason for the challenge to God's authority for which they were 'Hurled headlong flaming from the ethereal sky … to bottomless perdition' (Book I: 45, 47) is not clear. As is often pointed out, a challenge to God's authority seems to be the ultimate folly on Lucifer's part, although we are to understand that his 'obdurate pride' has blinded him (Book I: 56). He is piqued, it is later revealed, that Christ was chosen as Head of the Angels and he feels a self-righteous indignation by which his revolt against God's authority is justified. Profoundly aware of hierarchical systems of authority and dignity, in Book IX he again criticises God's perverse attitude to Adam and Eve. He pitches himself as liberator, claiming that half of the Angels joined his rebellion, and he 'freed [them] / From servitude' in one night (Book IX: 140–1). God's intention, much to Satan's dismay, is to exalt mankind to the rank of the Angels, 'to repair his numbers' (Book IX: 144), if they prove obedient. Moreover, during their time on earth, Adam and Eve are watched over by the Angels, a task which Satan feels to be humiliating:

> … to spite us more –
> Determined to advance into our room
> A creature formed of earth, and his endow,
> Exalted from so base an original …
> … O indignity!
> Subjected to his service Angel-wings
> And flaming ministers, to watch and tend
> Their earthly charge. (Book IX: 147–57)

In the earlier books Adam had already been alerted by the angel Raphael that an enemy plotted his and Eve's downfall; he had also been reminded of the obedience that God requires and of their reward in Books IV and V:

Your bodies may at last turn all to spirit,
Improved by tract of time, and winged ascend
Ethereal, as we, or may at choice
Here or in heavenly paradises dwell,
If ye be found obedient, and retain
Unalterably firm his love entire
Whose progeny you are. (Book V: 493–503)

The theme of proper attitude to authority and status, also found in Mantuan pastoral, surfaces persistently, as in Book V, where Raphael emphasises the movement from 'various forms, various degrees / Of substance' (Book V: 473–4) which grow more spiritual the nearer to God they are in the hierarchy. He stresses the correlation between the Soul and Reason; only mankind received these gifts and both are presented as defining features. The relationship between power and reason arises again in Book VIII, when Adam tells Raphael of his response to Eve when she was first created:

… transported I beheld,
Transported touch; here passion I first felt,
Commotion strange, in all enjoyments else
Superior and unmoved, here only weak
Against the charm of beauty's powerful glance.
(Book VIII: 529–33)

Raphael's consternation is apparent from his 'contracted brow' (Book VIII: 560) and he issues a stern warning against loss of judgement, warning Adam that Eve must be managed properly in order to acknowledge Adam's authority and yield to 'reality'. In order to exert his divinely-ordained power it is vital that Adam is not overcome by passion. Raphael's lesson on appropriate love alludes to Neo-platonic theories, as a vehicle 'By which to heavenly love [one] may'st ascend' (Book VIII: 592), and also solidly prescribes the era's contemporary vision of the companionate marriage, as a microcosmic echo of the divine hierarchy.

The constant reminders for Adam to use his God-given power of reason highlights the issue of Free Will, central to the entire work and foregrounded in Book IX. Ironically, it is Adam himself who lectures Eve regarding the possibility of reason being deceived. In a charmingly domesticated vision, Eve suggests that the pair work alone in different parts of the garden, because whatever gains they make are quickly lost, due to its abundant fertility:

> ... til more hands
> Aid us, the work under our labour grows
> Luxurious by restraint: what we by day
> Lop overgrown, or prune, or prop, or bind,
> One night or two with wanton growth derides,
> Tending to wild. (Book IX: 207–12)

Adhering to a typically Protestant work ethic, she claims that their 'casual discourse', looks and smiles slow down the work until 'the hour of supper comes unearned' (Book IX: 225). This, of course, is entirely reasonable, as her thought processes generally are. The frequent allusions to the theme, highlighted by Adam's caution, are designed to elicit an appropriate reader-response through reflection: Eve uses the gift of reason but it is flawed:

> God left free the Will; for what obeys
> Reason is free, and Reason he made right,
> But bid her well beware, and still erect,
> Lest, by some fair appearing good surprised,
> She dictate false, and misinform the Will
> To do what God expressly hath forbid. (Book IX: 351–6)

Despite numerous warnings, the couple separate for a morning's gardening, intending to meet for lunch. Pointing out her poignant innocence, the omniscient narrator dramatically interjects, addressing her as 'much deceived, much failing, hapless, Eve': she will never return because the flourishing vegetation conceals the 'hellish rancour' of Satan's ambush (Book IX: 404–9). Eve's indignation at Adam's perceived faithlessness in her integrity was the catalyst which prompted capitulation to her request to work apart. This rested on the point that 'faith, love and virtue' untried cannot reasonably earn their names and that God would not have left them so imperfect as to be unable to withstand attack (Book IX: 335–8). Although the arguments are plausible, the implication is that Adam was overcome by Eve's charms, rather than her logic.

Eve: the 'fairest unsupported flower'

Satan's initial strategy to gain Eve's attention fails, as he coils and recoils his 'rising folds', splendid in 'a surging maze' of pleasing form, coloured 'verdant gold' with luminous fiery-red eyes (Book IX: 497–504). Commendably, Eve does not notice as she is too absorbed in her work, which is described as propping up the luxurious and beautiful flowers. Eve's vulnerability and the appropriate relationship between man and wife is alluded to as the narratorial voice points out that she herself is the 'fairest unsupported flower, / From her best prop so far, and storm so nigh' (Book IX: 432–3). In her first introduction, her hair was likened to the tendrils of a vine, as 'dishevelled' and in 'wanton* ringlets' (Book IV: 306–7), implying that it is also in need of control. Moreover, the couple are explicitly introduced as not being equal:

> For contemplation he and valour formed,
> For softness she and sweet attractive grace;
> He for God only, she for God in him. (Book IV: 296–9)

The proper governance of Eve as his inferior is Adam's duty, as he has been reminded. Eve's reliance upon her own independent moral and intellectual resilience will become her downfall, as will Adam's overwhelmed attraction to her become his:

> Her loveliness, so absolute she seems
> And in herself complete, so well to know

* 'Wanton' can be read as 'unrestrained' but also carries undertones of libidinousness.

> Her own, that what she wills to do or say,
> Seems wisest, virtuest, discreetest, best:
> All higher knowledge in her presence falls
> Degraded … (Book VIII: 547–52)

Satan's guile targets Eve's vanity, a characteristic already implied by her narcissistic attraction to her reflection in a pool shortly after being created (Book IV: 460–70). Addressing her as 'sovran mistress', he admires her 'celestial beauty', suggesting that she should be seen 'As Goddess among Gods, adored and served / By Angels numberless' (Book IX: 532–48). Although the narrator informs us that the words entered Eve's heart, her immediate response is to his use of speech, which she had considered to be God's gift to humankind alone. Satan flatters not only Eve's physical attributes, but also appeals to her faculty of reason. He presents an ostensibly plausible theory of his elevation through the natural order to a superior status, as a result of eating the fruit of the Tree of Knowledge. Created a brute beast, the fruit has ennobled him to the extent that he has gained speech and reason; he is now capable of abstract thought and 'speculations high or deep' (Book IX: 599–602). Milton points to Eve's defective reason and manifest disobedience in planning to overturn divinely-ordained natural order by aspiring to achieve godly status, as prompted by Satan:

> … your eyes, that seem so clear
> Yet are but dim, shall perfectly be then
> Opened and cleared, and ye shall be as Gods,
> Knowing both good and evil, as they know.
> That ye should be as Gods, since I as Man,
> Internal Man, is but proportion meet;
> I, of brute, human; ye, of human Gods. (Book IX: 706–12)

Compounding her digressions, Eve consents to Satan's denigration of God's motives in denying mankind knowledge and accepts that God would be unjust to destroy mankind for disobedience. As she reaches for the fruit, Milton explicitly indicates that she anticipates transcending her present status of body and mind. Conversely, the fruit intoxicates her and, governed by appetite, she moves nearer to bestiality in the Renaissance concept of natural order. The perfection in which she was created is lost from this moment, as is Paradise for her.

The evidence of Eve's descent is apparent in her reprehensible impulses, firstly to worship the Tree of Knowledge, committing the sin of idolatry, secondly in her attitude to God, whom she now terms 'Our great Forbidder, safe with all his spies' (Book IX: 815) and thirdly in consideration of her status within her relationship with Adam. Eve debates whether to share the fruit and knowledge with him or maintain her advantage, 'to keep the odds of knowledge in [her] power'. Pondering that she can supplement female inadequacy 'the more to draw his love, / And render [her] more equal', she even contemplates having the ascendancy, 'for inferior – who is free?' (Book IX: 820–5). Although to a modern readership this may seem reasonable, this was not Milton's intention, as it would have been anathema to his seventeenth-century readers. Aware of her transgression, Eve considers God's punishment and the possibility that Adam may 'be wedded to another Eve' (Book IX: 828). Upon this unworthy sentiment she decides that he must share her fate and resolves to give him the forbidden fruit.* Adam was not deceived, as Eve was but, fully aware of his wilful disobedience, Adam accepts his fate for the love he bears her, 'fondly overcome with female charm' (Book XI: 999). As anthropomorphised Nature groans and weeps at their offence, they are overcome by carnal desires, indulging in amorous games driven by lust, rather than the earlier 'Rights mysterious of connubial Love' (Book IV: 743). Book IX closes amid discord between Adam and Eve, as he misogynistically predicts the continuing tensions between the sexes in an etiological† summary:

* Note, by contrast, Aemila Lanyer's positive reinterpretation of Eve's motive in her *Salve Deus Rex Judaeorum* (1611).

† A rhetorical figure, 'etiology' is the study of causes. Therefore in this case Milton offers an explanation of the reason for women's wayward nature, according to ideas of the time, based on contemporary readings of Genesis. See Part Four: 'The Woman Debate'.

> ... Thus it shall befall
> Him who, to worth of women overtrusting,
> Lets her will rule: restraint she will not brook,
> And, left to herself, if evil thence ensue,
> She first his weak indulgence will accuse. (Book IX: 1182–6)

Milton's version of God's anger focuses on the dereliction of reason, which leads to misguided action and disobedience. Germaine to this debate is the acceptance of theories of 'natural' order and hierarchy, to which women pose a threat:

> Was she thy God, that her thou didst obey
> Before his voice? or was she made thy guide,
> Superior, or but equal, that to her
> Thou didst resign thy manhood ... (Book X: 145–8)

Whether Milton's epic vindicated God's actions to men – as was his stated intention – or not still provides grist for critical debate. What can be recognised by a modern reader is an embedded misogyny, which reveals a society which accepted Eve's biblical transgression as a wholly legitimate reason to subject women to patriarchal control.[*] In terms of the genre, as C. S. Lewis pointed out, Milton very deliberately evoked the grandiose and solemn style of the secondary epic.[15] Above all, *Paradise Lost* is a long continuous narrative, which needs to be read as such in order to comprehend its grand design and intricate plot. Its extraordinary complexity and erudition identifies it as the acme of poetical achievement, according to the Virgillian model identified at the beginning of this chapter, and is all the more impressive given Milton's blindness when the work was composed.[†]

* Although Milton goes to some lengths to provide Eve with plausible reasons for her actions, ultimately the message is that women's reason is flawed due to their impaired intellectual capacities and susceptibility to negative emotions, such as vanity, ambition and pride.

† Milton created the epic wholly in the mind and dictated to an amanuensis, an assistant.

Extended Commentary: Spenser, *The Faerie Queene* (1590–6), Book III

'The Legend of Britomartis, or, Of Chastitie'

Book III of *The Faerie Queene* is complex and can be more difficult to follow than Books I and II. Rather than authorial loss of control, this can be attributed to a different *modus operandi*.* The first books trace the quests of only one knight who possesses a single virtue, whereas the third book is a series of entangled adventures. There is no single clearly-defined quest and, although Britomart, the female knight, represents chastity, as indicated in the title, there are also several other examples of the virtue, both positive and negative.

Spenser's position was delicate; by this stage of Elizabeth's reign her astutely-maintained persona of the chaste Virgin Queen was somewhat hollow. Spenser was aware of the potential political ramifications of her unmarried and childless state. By 1590 she was almost sixty and her counsellors were acutely aware of the inheritance crisis which would arise at her death. Moreover, the Protestant ideal status was companionate marriage for all; the family represented God's hierarchy of heaven in microcosm.† Contemporary ideas of womanhood also defined women mainly through their reproductive function and according to these theories the ideal woman was a wife and mother.

The opening lines of Book III invite the queen to see herself as – the absent – Gloriana or Belphoebe, one representing her rule and the other her chastity. Chastity in these terms does not necessarily equate complete perpetual abstinence; it may denote chaste married love or the temporary containment of betrothed love. Several types of female

* Latin, meaning 'method of working'.

† This classical concept is called 'The Great Chain of Being' and defines all of creation as occupying its place in creation according to God's plan, each differing slightly from the next but interdependent, in hierarchical arrangement. The hierarchy of heaven, with God at the apex, was mirrored by the earthly rulers' chain of command, from the king to his lowest subjects, and this was echoed in the unit of the family, with the father at the head.

chastity are also found in Britomart, Florimell and Amoret, with negative examples in Malecasta ('Badly Chaste') and Hellenore.

'Faire Britomart' of constant mind

The book opens with Britomart's martial encounter with Sir Guyon, the knight from the preceding book who is dedicated to 'Temperaunce'* and Britomart proves victorious. Her invincibility is due to the armour from the Saxon warrior, Angela, which she wears and the 'enchaunted spear' (Book III:1, 81)† which she carries. This latter is symbolic of chastity, which cannot be beaten by mortal strength. The link with ancient Saxon sovereignty is important to Spenser's project, as Britomart's quest is to find Artegall, with whom she will found the lineage which will eventually lead to the House of Tudor and Queen Elizabeth herself. Artegall's image was revealed to Britomart as she peered into the 'glassie globe that Merlin made' (Book III: 2, 181), which she found in her father's room. Despite her warrior-like appearance during the quest, at this point, chronologically before the opening of the first canto, she is revealed to be innocent and immature. Falling sick from love and anxiety, in case the unfamiliar emotion is unchaste, she seeks assurance from Merlin, who reveals her destiny. Hence, her 'chastity' is directed towards love, marriage and procreation, to which she has unswerving devotion. The extravagant compliment to Queen Elizabeth contains its own dilemma, however, in that focus on lineage should also look forward to descendents, which it obviously could not do.‡

Britomart's first major test, which forms the first of the set-pieces, is at Castle Joyeous where she discovers the knight Redcrosse, under attack from six knights loyal to Lady Malecasta. Her knights demand

* Moderation or restraint.

† Note the reference 'Book III:1, 81' denotes Book III, canto 1, line 81.

‡ Spenser freely adapted material from Ariosto's *Orlando Furioso*, into *The Faerie Queen*. This romance celebrated the dynasty of the ruling family of Ferrara (in what is now Italy). Just as Spenser's mythical marriage between Artegall and Britomart establishes the Tudor dynasty, Ariosto's marriage of Ruggiero and the Lady Bradamante establishes the ruling house of d'Este.

that any knight who passes must forsake his own lady in favour of Malecasta. If he refuses he must enter into combat with her followers. As Redcrosse is outnumbered, Britomart takes up his cause and, winning the skirmish, enters the castle. As she fought so valiantly, is wearing armour and carrying weaponry, she is not recognisably female. The comedic possibilities are exploited in a bedchamber scene where Malecasta unwittingly attempts to seduce Britomart, thinking that she is a virile young male knight. Malecasta's six knights represent the stages of love-play, from Gardante, meaning 'looking' or 'gazing', to Noctante, representing the sexual pleasures of the night.* In the fight which erupts at the bedside, Britomart is grazed by Gardante's arrow, suggesting that, despite her chastity, she is guilty of this one transgression against virtue: amorous gazing. This is because she fell in love with Artegall at first sight in Merlin's glass.

Amoret and 'goodly womanhed'

The myth of Venus and Adonis appears in the luxurious tapestries which decorate the Castle Joyeous, and prefigures both the Garden of Adonis episode (canto 6), and the disturbing depictions of love in the House of the Magician Busyrane (canto 11). Amoret, the twin of Belphoebe, features in both of these latter episodes, representing fertile and faithful love, 'th' ensample of true love alone, / And Lodestarre† of all chaste affection, / To all faire Ladies …' (Book III: 6, 463–5). The twins were conceived when sunbeams impregnated their mother, Chrysogonee, as she slept beside a forest pool. While Belphoebe was raised by Diana, the huntress, Amoret was taken by Venus to the Garden of Adonis, to be 'trained up in true feminitee' (Book III: 6, 455). Critics interpret the Garden variously as the ambiguous metaphor draws upon different myths of regeneration. It is a place of change and renewal, linked to the cyclical nature of man's life and the seasons. It also represents on some levels, Eden, Platonic theories of form and matter and Christian ideas

* The knights are Gardante ('looking'), Parlant ('speaking'), Jocante ('playing'), Basciante ('kissing'), Bacchante ('drinking') and Noctante ('Night').

† Guiding star.

of heaven.[16] The atmosphere of the garden is idyllic; couples wander together in delightful surroundings, freely making love (Book III: 6, 365–7). The central part of the garden is a secret flowery grove, where Venus enjoys Adonis 'and of his sweetness takes her fill' (Book III: 6, 414). Quite plainly, Spenser's vision of love does not exclude the sexual.

The closing adventure of Book III is Britomart's rescue of Amoret from the House of Busyrane. Her capture during her own wedding celebrations is described analeptically,* in the first canto of Book IV:

> For that same vile Enchauntour *Busyran*,
> The very selfe same day that she was wedded,
> Amidst the bridale feast, whilest euery man
> Surcharg'd with wine, were heedlesse and ill hedded.
> All bent to mirth before the bride was bedded
>
> (Book IV:1, 19–22)

Scudamour, Amoret's husband, laments before Busyrane's house, unable to aid her as he cannot pass through the wall of 'flaming fire' and 'stinking Sulphur' (Book III: 11, 186–7) which blocks his path. Again, Britomart is preserved by her virtue and is able to penetrate through barriers to inner rooms which are decorated with numerous images depicting negative representations of lust and violent love.† Evocative of the masque of the deadly sins in Book I, the Masque of Love parades numerous personified psychological responses to love.‡ The bewitched Amoret is marched between Despight and Cruelty, with her breast exposed, her snowy flesh rent by an open wound, through which her 'trembling' heart has been drawn into a silver basin and pierced with a 'deadly dart' (Book III: 3, 181–3). Although Amoret is finally rescued

* Looking backward.

† The tapestries which bedeck the walls depict woven images of the sexual rampages of the gods reminiscent of similar scenes embroidered on Hero's garments in Marlowe's *Hero and Leander.*

‡ These are initially: Fancy, Desyre, Doubt, Daunger (Distain), Feare, Hope, Dissemblance (Pretence), Suspect (Suspician), Griefe, Fury, Displeasure and Pleasance. After the spectacle of Amoret and her torture, there follows a disorderly crowd of further personages.

by Britomart, her trials continue as Scudamour has vanished when they escape.* Spenser's intentions in the Busyrane episode are ambiguous. Thomas P. Roche suggests that within the name are connotations of abuse and love as war, and therefore Busyrane may represent distortion of the idea of love, or perhaps abuse of marriage.[17] Elizabeth Heale's understanding is that the masquers represent 'women's fears and regrets [on entering marriage] ... as well as the male experience of unrestrained desire and its consequences'.[18]

Belphoebe: 'perfect Maydenhed'

By contrast, Belphoebe, Amoret's twin, avoids the sexual victimisation suffered by Florimell and Amoret. Her virginal state is seen as a vocation, exceptional, and part of her heroic character. Wounded in his fight to protect Florimell against the foresters, Timias falls in love with Belphoebe as she tends his wounds; she, by contrast, is impervious. In a five-stanza encomium† to Queen Elizabeth, thinly disguised as extolling Belphoebe's virtues, she is praised as a heavenly flower of 'chastity and virtue virginall' (Book III: 5, 467) with whom none can compare. Spenser's imagery of 'That dainty rose' (Book III: 5, 444) works on several levels: as a symbol of English beauty, as the emblem of the House of Tudor, but also as the virginal knot unbroken.

This is not to say that Belphoebe's portrait is entirely positive. In Book IV, Timias and Belphoebe both assist Amoret against her captor, Lust. Engrossed in the pursuit, Belphoebe leaves Timias comforting Amoret and on her return suspects that they are lovers. Her 'deep distdaine, and great indignity' causes Timias extreme suffering. He incarcerates himself in a woodland cave, forgoing all human company, unshaven, dressed in

* When the first three books of *The Faerie Queene* were published in 1590, Amoret returned to the waiting Scudamour at the end of Book III. Spenser extended their trials into the longer version by having her captured again, this time by Lust, and having to be rescued by the combined efforts of Britomart and Timias. Critics assume that their difficulties would have been resolved in one of the incomplete books, perhaps as an example of 'Constancie' in what is known as the 'Mutabilitie Cantos', but may have been intended as Book VII.

† Formal high praise.

tatters, 'Wretchedly wearing out his youthly yeares / Through wilful penury' (IV: 7, 35–41). It is generally accepted that Timias represents Spenser's friend and neighbour, Sir Walter Ralegh, one time favourite of the queen who earned her displeasure by secretly marrying.* It is not difficult to discover Spenser's censure of the queen's actions in this section. Elsewhere he also suggests that virginity is not laudable for its own sake, as such restraint is in fact against nature and God's will, as the theme of Marinell's celibacy demonstrates.† The ostensible focus of the book is chastity, although its true core, as many critics have pointed out, is love in its many forms: positive, affirming, fertile and corrosive.

Notes

1 Bart van Es, 'Spenseran Pastoral' in Patrick Cheyney, Andrew Hadfield and Garrett A. Sullivan Jr (eds), *Early Modern English Poetry* (Oxford: Oxford University Press, 2007), pp. 79–89, 79, 80. In his *Arte of English Poesie* (1589), George Puttenham clearly recognises this covert aspect of Virgil's *Eclogues*, explaining that the superficial 'rustical loves' contain a serious message: 'under the vaile of homely persons, and in rude speeches to insinuate and glaunce at greater matters, and such as perchance had not bene safe to have beene disclosed in any other sort … in which are treated by figure matters of greater importance…', George Puttenham, *The Arte of English Poesie* (Cambridge: Cambridge University Press, 1936, repr. 1970), p. 38.

2 'Sermon of the Plough' preached in London, 1543, *Sermons and remains of Hugh Latimer, sometime Bishop of Worcester, Martyr, 1555*, G. E. Corrie (ed.), Parker Society (Cambridge: Cambridge University Press, 1845), p. 65.

3 Patrick Cullen, *Spenser, Marvell, and Renaissance Pastoral* (Cambridge, Mass.: Harvard University Press, 1970), p. 151.

* Ralegh's unsanctioned marriage to one of the queen's maids, Elizabeth Throgmorten, occasioned a period of disfavour which spanned five years. In 1597 he was finally permitted to return to court. For more detailed discussion, see Michael O'Connell, pp. 114–22. Note also the mention of tobacco as a medicinal plant (Book III: 5, 277) which alludes to Ralegh, as he is credited as bringing the commodity back from America.

† It was prophesied to Marinell's mother that he would be badly hurt or die through the actions of a woman and so warned him against love. The Protestant faith taught that the celibacy of religious orders under Catholicism was unnatural and did not regard such self-denial as laudable or desirable.

4 Cullen, p. 160.

5 Terence Dawson and Robert Scott Dupree (eds), *Seventeenth-Century English Poetry* (New York and London: Harvester Wheatsheaf, 1994), n48, p. 504.

6 Gary Waller, *English Poetry of the Sixteenth Century* (London: Longman, 1986, repr. 1993), p. 171.

7 John Watkins, 'Spenser's Poetry and the Apocalypse', in *Early Modern English Poetry*, pp. 90–101, p. 94.

8 The first three books were published in 1590 and Spenser was awarded an annual pension of £50 by Elizabeth in December 1591. Following an adjustment in the ending of the third book, all six books were published in 1596. The final section, the *Mutabilitie Cantos*, may have been intended as a seventh book or, as James Nohrnberg suggests, 'an epilogue to the poem, a final comment on all that has gone before', Elizabeth Heale citing Nohrnberg, *The Faerie Queene: A Reader's Guide* (Cambridge: Cambridge University Press, 1987), p. 171.

9 John Ruskin's excellent exposition, originally Appendix 3 in his *Stones of Venice*, Vol. III, is reproduced in Graham Hough's *A Preface to The Faerie Queene* (London: Duckworth, 1962), pp. 145–8. Elizabeth Heale considers Orgoglio to represent 'the flesh, the earthly part of ourselves' indicated by Redcrosse's carnal ensnarement by Duessa: Heale, p. 39.

10 Book II of *The Faerie Queene* deals with this virtue. See excerpt from *Aeropagitica* in M. H. Abrams (ed.), *Norton Anthology of Literature,* Vol. I, 7th edn (New York: W. W. Norton and Company, 2000), pp. 1802–11.

11 Michael O'Connell, *Mirror and Veil: The Historical Dimension of Spenser's Faerie Queene* (Chapel Hill: University of North Carolina Press, 1977), pp. 188, 189.

12 John G. Demaray, *Milton's Theatrical Epic: the Invention and Design of Paradise Lost* (Cambridge, Mass.: Harvard University Press, 1980), pp. 77–9. Demaray points out the parallels between Milton's masque, *Comus*, his *Song on a May Morning*, the pastoral elements of *L'Allegro* and the first theatrical appearance of Adam and Eve (Book IV: 288–319).

13 As C. S. Lewis points out, Milton's Preface to *Reason of Church Government*, Book II, also debates the choice of genre and subject matter, in some detail. See *Preface to Paradise Lost*, pp. 3–8.

14 John Milton, *Reason of Church Government* in *Milton's Prose Works* (Bohn), Vol. II, p. 118, cited Professor Basil Willey, *The Seventeenth-Century Background* (Harmondsworth: Penguin, 1962), p. 200. See also excerpt of *The Reason of Church Government* in *Norton Anthology*, pp. 1796–1801.

15 See the first seven chapters of C. S. Lewis's *A Preface to Paradise Lost* for a discussion of primary and secondary epic and Milton's task (London:

Oxford University Press, 1942, repr. 1967), pp.1–40.

16 See Plato's *Republic*, Book X, lines 614–21, for the Fable of Er, a meadow where souls are given bodies; and Virgil's *Aeneid,* Book VI: 329, 748, regarding wandering souls which will eventually be reborn.

17 Thomas P. Roche, Jr, *The Kindly Flame: a Study of the Third and Fourth Books of Spenser's Faerie Queene* (Princeton: Princeton University Press, 1964), pp. 82, 83.

18 Heale, p. 95.

Religious Verse: Locke, Mary Sidney and Donne

During the Renaissance religion was an inescapable part of most people's lives, and understandably within this culture, sacred poetry became an important genre. Extended biblical expositions, sermons and the scriptural works themselves provided inspiration for both male and female writers of the era. Especially after the printing of the Geneva Bible, a common parlance arose through allusion to a familiar mesh of interacting religious texts, enabling almost endless extension through a labyrinth of annotated linked biblical chapter and verse.* Levels of abstraction not apparent to most present-day readers extend the compacted forms of pious poetry infinitely and an attempt to articulate the unsayable often finds expression in mystical and partially-hidden devices.

Anne Locke: 'Woefull sighs and bitter penitence'

Anne Locke's mid-sixteenth-century emergence as the first English female poet to publish original devotional poetry can be attributed more to her unusual circumstances, than to driving literary ambition. She was born into a merchant family which lived and traded in Cheapside, close

* The Geneva Bible was translated, written and printed by English religious exiles in Calvin's Geneva during the reign of Mary I.

to St Paul's in London.* Along with her brother and sister Locke seems to have studied French and Latin, and perhaps even some Greek, from the family tutor, Mr Cobbe.[1] During the reign of the young Edward VI (1547–53), the country had fully embraced Protestantism and prominent European religious reformers were invited to help establish the new state religion. Trade generated strong links with the Continent and mercantile families had long been implicated in the importation of reformist ideas and texts, even in the reign of Henry VIII. Both Anne's family and that into which she married were staunch reformists and she was raised as a Protestant. When Mary I acceded to the throne on her brother Edward's death, however, she felt that it was her divine purpose to restore the Catholic faith and allegiance to the Pope. The religious strife which ensued had a direct influence on Anne Locke's life and literary output. As the situation deteriorated, Protestants faced capital punishment by burning for adhering to their faith. The diary of a London undertaker, Henry Machyn, records at least seventy-two of these public executions during 1555 and 1556, sometimes *en masse*.[2] With family members periodically under interrogation, and facing a situation of increasing danger, Anne Locke accepted the invitation of John Knox to escape into exile in Geneva with her two young children.†

By the time of Locke's arrival in 1557, Geneva was a hive of reformist activity. Her English neighbours and friends were involved in the massive task of writing the Geneva Bible, transcribing and publishing

* Anne Locke's name is spelled variously, as Lock, Locke and Lok; her dates are *c*.1534 to after 1590. Through Thomas Cromwell's patronage, her father later acquired extensive property outside the city walls, on Bishopsgate, close to the family of the later female poet, Aemilia Lanyer, née Bassano. See Suzanne Woods, 'Anne Locke and Aemilia Lanyer: A Tradition of Protestant Women Speaking' in Amy Boeski and Mary T. Crane (eds), *Form and Reform in Renaissance England: essays in Honor of Barbara Kiefer Lewalski* (London: Associated University Presses, 2000), pp. 171–83, p. 172.

† Knox is sometimes termed the 'Father of Presbyterianism' and jointly led the English Church in Geneva. The Locke and Vaughan families entertained him in 1552 and 1553, when he preached at court at Edward VI's invitation. They also assisted him prior to his exile upon Mary's accession. In 1554 he began a correspondence with Anne Locke, and initially her sister-in-law Rose Hickman, from Geneva.

John Calvin's sermons in different European languages, and preparing the Psalms for congregational use, in place of the earlier Latin Catholic models. The most profitable way that Locke could use her skills to aid the community, and the Calvinist cause, was to assist in this work and she is the only known female exile of this period to have done so. She translated from French four of Calvin's sermons on Isaiah 38, preached between 5 November and 16 November while she was in Geneva; to this she added a dedicatory letter to the Duchess of Suffolk and an original sonnet sequence. This takes the form of an introductory five sonnets, followed by the sequence of twenty-one sonnets based upon Psalm 51, entitled *A Meditation of a penitent sinner, upon the 51. psalme.*[*] The volume was published upon her return to England in January 1560, under the title of *Sermons of John Calvin, Upon the Songe that Ezechias made after he had been sicke, and afflicted by the hand of God.* By this time Elizabeth I had taken possession of the throne and the state religion had reverted to Protestantism.

Three 'Powers of the soul'

Perhaps surprisingly, despite the reformers' ardent desire to distance themselves from Catholicism, their devotional works are often founded upon or interact with the earlier works; and Locke's sequence evokes significant parallels with contemporary Catholic meditations.[3] Typically these used visual images to call upon the 'three powers of the soul', the memory, the understanding and the will, to assist immersion in a vividly-imagined recreation of a biblical scene. The process promoted a heartfelt affective response, remembrance of sins and understanding of personal guilt, finally inducing remorse and repentance. The gratitude for forgiveness then prompted determination to lead a better life. Protestant distrust of images, however, favoured the written biblical word rather than iconic images from Christ's life. Locke's sequence therefore explores themes of guilt, sin and desire for redemption, all predicated upon the theological doctrine of predestination rather than

* The sequence comprises of five prefatory sonnets before a main sequence of twenty-one sonnets based on Psalm 51.

imagined images of biblical events.* In this theory of deliverance abject belief in one's own corruption is necessary in order to begin the path to salvation and in the prefatory sonnets Locke lays bare the desperate psychological state of her penitent believer:

> The heinous gylt of my forsaken ghost
> So threates, alas, unto my febled sprite†
> Deserved death, and (that me greveth most)
> Still stand so fixt before my daseld sight
> The lothesome filthe of my disteined life,
> The mighty wrath of myne offended Lorde …
> (Pref. Sonnet 1: 1–6)

The heading to this section indicates that it expresses 'the passioned minde of the penitent sinner', meaning the impassioned, or unbalanced, state of mind. The severe spiritual self-examination demanded by Calvinism, compounded by the doctrine of predestination, led many devout Christians to believe that they were destined for Hell. The despair which frequently resulted from this dilemma was of itself a sin, however, as it indicated doubt that Christ's sacrifice was effective in its reparation for mankind's crimes, and therefore able to secure man's salvation.

Guilt and the 'Forsaken ghost'†

The 'heinous gylt' of the opening line of the prefatory sonnets links both the doctrine of Original Sin‡ and the reformers' theory of selective

* Predestination: John Calvin further developed St Augustine's teachings to conclude that some individuals were predestined for heaven, chosen by God to be his Elect; while others – the Reprobate – were equally predestined for Hell. In Catholic doctrine salvation was earned by living a good Christian life, performing good works and adhering to the teachings of the Church; under Protestantism there was nothing one could do to 'bargain' with God as his free gift of grace could not be earned.

† Here 'ghost' and 'sprite' both mean the soul or spirit.

‡ Christian doctrine holds that Original Sin was inherited from Adam as a consequence of his sin in Eden. The reformers considered mankind to be inherently sinful, corrupt and unable to assist itself in attaining salvation.

salvation, to reveal a speaker who is acutely aware of her sinful state.* Fear that she is abandoned by God is indicated in the reference to the 'forsaken ghost' (Pref. Sonnet 1: 1). The oppressive weight of guilt disables her 'enfeebled' spirit and she freely recognises that she deserves God's wrath and therefore death. This is an everlasting death, however, and the allusion is to damnation, echoed in the reference to the 'furnace' of the breast (Pref. Sonnet 1: 12) burning with grief in anticipation of the fiery pits of hell.

To the doctrinally-aware reader, acceptance of guilt and desire for re-instatement within God's care, ironically indicates that the speaker is already on the path to redemption. Acceptance of God's judgement also reveals that she is one of the 'godly', rather than the Hell-bound Reprobate. As the prefatory notice announced, the context of the soul-searching misery is the penitent's disordered mind, led astray by religious fervour. Dejection arises because she 'Can not enjoy the comfort of the light, / Nor finde the waye wherein to walke aright' (Pref. Sonnet 1: 13–14): the speaker has metaphorically lost her way and the sure guidance of the 'light' of the gospels. Realisation of her overwhelming guilt causes a paralysis of fear, as images of her sins 'stand so fix'd' before her mind's eye, in vivid endorsement of culpability (Pref. Sonnet 1: 4). Somewhat ironically, the self-loathing generated resounds with the sentiments of the [Catholic] Jesuit exercises of St Ignatius de Loyola: '[I] see all my corruption and foulness of body ... whence having sprung so many sins and many wickednesses and such most hideous venom'.[4]

Tears of Repentance: the 'Streames of the distilléd brine'

The first quatrain of the first sonnet introduces the conceit of 'dasled sight' (Pref. Sonnet 1: 4) and the linked metaphors of light and impaired vision are extended and developed throughout the sequence. Confused

* Although the feminine pronoun is used here in discussion of Locke's sonnets, the work remains steadfastly ungendered, indicating its application to all, male and female alike. The 'she' should not be confused with Locke herself who seems to have been convinced that she was one of the Elect, see her prefatory dedication.

and copious tears cause a literal blurring of sight, refiguring the 'holy' weeping of medieval mystics, whose meditations often prompted similar responses.* Sonnet 2 is a syntactical continuation of the first, returning to the same metaphor, as the voice designates herself a 'blinde wretch', lamenting that she cannot find 'the way that other[s] oft have found' (Pref. Sonnet 2: 1, 4, 6). Locke revitalises familiar imagery of lost paths in dangerous terrain, calling to mind the filthy Tudor alleys and open sewers, in her conceit that God's anger has thrown her into the 'mire', within which she flails, 'groap[ing] about in vaine' (Pref. Sonnet 2: 12). The couplet offers respite from a claustrophobic sense of enclosing, suffocating darkness and dirt, in the apostrophe† of the penitent seeking God's favour, as she repeatedly cries for mercy with 'fainting breath' (Pref. Sonnet 2: 13, 14).

Enter Demon Despair

The insistent calls for mercy develop into a 'shrieking crye' in the following sonnet which, rather than prompting divine intervention, alarmingly summons the demon 'despeir' (Pref. Sonnet 3: 3). Locke's familiarity with Sir Thomas Wyatt's *Certayne Psalms* is apparent throughout her sequence and this is a likely source for her inspiration for the personified Despair figure.‡ Wyatt's penitential Psalm 6 follows a similar trajectory of repentance and 'bymonyng' [bemoaning], stating: 'I open here and spred / my fawte to the[e]', which Locke further develops into: 'Even then despair before my ruthefull eye /

* Mary of Oignies (d. 1213), St Bridget of Sweden (1303–73), Dorothea of Montau (1347–94) and Margery Kempe (*c*.1373–*c*.1440) were all noted for 'frequent and sustained holy tears'. See *The Book of Margery Kempe,* translated by B. A. Windeatt (London: Penguin, 1985), pp. 17–22 and *passim*, p. 21.

† Apostrophe: a turning away from the matter in hand to address an absent person or thing, as in an address to God or Nature, for example.

‡ Wyatt's *Certayne Psalms* are, in fact, the seven penitential Psalms which are: 6, 32, 38, 51, 102, 130 and 143, of which Psalm 51 was the most significant to both Catholic and Protestant rituals of penitence. See Hannibal Hamlin, *Psalm Culture and Early Modern English Literature* (Cambridge: Cambridge University Press, 2004, repr. 2007), chapter 6, 'Psalm 51: Sin, Sacrifice, and the "Sobbes of a Sorrowfull Soule"', pp. 173–217.

Spredes forth my sinne and shame' (Pref. Sonnet 3: 3–4). Again, Wyatt's Psalm 6 may have provided the inspiration for the scalpel-sharp probing, as he writes of 'Inward remorce so sharp that it is like a knife'.[5] Despair encourages Locke's penitent to believe that she is abandoned, assuring her that she is 'refused' [Reprobate] and representing her cries as less than human ['brayest'] (Pref. Sonnet 3: 5–6). The sonnet foregrounds the doctrine of Predestination, already alluded to in the previous sonnet's 'I groape for *grace*' (Pref. Sonnet 2: 11, emphasis added). Despair's corrosive lies aim to convince the speaker that her pleas are 'bootlesse' [useless] because she is predestined for hell:

> Thy reprobate and foreordained sprite,
> For damned vessel of his heavie wrath …
> … Of his swete promises can claime no part:
> But thee, caytif, deserved curse doeth draw
> To hell, by justice, for offended law. (Pref. Sonnet 3: 8–14)

The Persecutory Imagination

Although alien to a modern secular society, the issue of salvation was of the gravest concern to many devout Protestants, even into the eighteenth century.*[6] Prominent religious figures addressed the overwhelming anxieties of their readers in publications which offered assurance and sometimes aids to determine one's state of grace [or lack]. These carried disturbing titles such as *A Treatise tending unto a declaration whether a man be in his estate of damnation or in the estate of grace* (1590) and *A plaine man's path-way to heaven, Wherin every man may clearly see, whether he shall be saved or damned* (1601).[7] Locke's work can be placed within this genre of popular religious writing, as an early spiritual guide. The purpose of the sonnet sequence is to encourage cathartic participation in the journey of her sinner, accepting one's own guilt and working through an affective penitence towards the promise of salvation. The

* See, for example, John Bunyan's *Grace Abounding To the Chief of Sinners* (1765).

lexical choices evoke the law courts, as Despair's judgement, upheld by the 'selfe witness of [her] beknowing hart', convinces the speaker that her punishment is just and the sentence is proclaimed: 'To hell, by justice, for offended law' (Pref. Sonnet 3: 14).

Sonnet 4 examines the speaker's reactions to Despair's judgement on her 'trembling soul' (Pref. Sonnet 4: 1). She takes as 'evidence' of her damned state the overwhelming number of her sins and, importantly, her earlier 'senselesse chere' in feeling that she was one of the 'saved'. Such paradoxical situations arise frequently in contemporary discussions of the signs of salvation. Initially individuals frequently consider themselves saved by simply living a pious life, but the state of false security belongs to the 'blind' soul which must experience a spiritual awakening to appreciate fully its sinfulness.[8] Spiritual pride in one's own piety is also especially condemned in the guides to salvation as Arthur Dent demoralisingly pronounces, 'But you are blind, and know not what is in you; but dimly imagine you shall be saved … And because this blindness maketh you bold, you will seem to be resolute in words … in truth you are deluded with a false light.'[9]

Brought to an imagined Morality Play 'hell's mouth'* by this terrifying chain of realisations, Locke's penitent 'quake[s] for feare' (Pref. Sonnet 4: 1–7), although the parentheses indicate that her conscience wishes to respond to the accusations. Locke relies upon the astute reader understanding that the conscience was considered to contain the last spark of divinity, given to mankind on its creation. Aligned with the soul, it was an arbitrator of God's purpose. The unspoken objection arises from the germ of knowledge, deep within the soul, that she cannot be abandoned: 'He is faithful that hath promised, though we cannot believe' (II Timothy 2:13). The end of the second quatrain presents the zenith of terror, as the speaker reels at 'the throte of hell' (Pref. Sonnet 4: 7). Henceforth, she recognises, her only hope is to throw herself upon God's mercy. As Calvin elucidates from the epistles of St Paul:

> … nothing stimulates us so strongly to place all our confidence

* The hell's mouth was a common prop of the morality drama, signifying the point of no return, when man would finally and inescapably be called upon to atone for his sins.

> and assurance in the Lord as self-diffidence, and the anxiety produced by a consciousness of our calamitous condition.[10]

The final poem of the prefatory series sees the speaker overcome by perceptions of divine 'everlastyng hate' (Pref. Sonnet 4: 4). So despairing is she that her earlier persistent cries for mercy are reduced to the 'woefull sound', of 'smoking sighs, and oft repeated groans' and 'confused crye[s]' (Pref. Sonnet 5: 7, 8, 3). The loss of speech indicates a state of utterly humbled contrition: she is so abased that she has relinquished God's gift of speech and is ready to emerge as a new person.* The repetition of participal adjectives such as 'foltring' [knee], 'yelding' [hand] and 'smoking' [sighs] and the present participles 'daring', 'bendyng' and 'dredyng' (Pref. Sonnet 5: 1–11) create both a sense of immediacy and propulsion towards judgement; unlike the previous pleading, however, this is before 'heavens throne'. The penitent craves the 'crummes of all sufficing grace' (Pref. Sonnet 5: 6, 4), emphasising that only through God's gift of grace can the speaker be saved. Locke crowds the final quatrain with figures of repetition and antithesis: 'Before the Lord, the Lord, whom synner I, / I cursed wretch, I have offended so …' (Pref. Sonnet 5: 9–10).

The pivotal point of this prefatory sequence is its final word. Despite being 'tost with panges and passions of despair', Locke seeks mercy with repentant '*chere*' (Pref. Sonnet 5: 13–14, added emphasis). The joy represents the hope of a path found and, hence, assurance of salvation as one of the Elect.

The prefatory sequence can be read as a 'preparation of place' device prior to full immersion in the main penitential *Meditation*, discussed in the Extended Commentary below, or as a short *memento mori*,† perhaps intended as part of a pious daily religious regime.‡ The three most common types of despair identified in religious guides are illustrated:

* St Ignatius Loyola instructs that in a meditation upon sins, the meditator must 'consider that [his] soul is imprisoned in this corruptible body, and [his] whole self in this vale of misery, as it were in exile among brute beasts,' *Spiritual Exercises*, p. 20, 21.

† A reminder of the inevitability of death.

‡ Catholic spiritual exercises commonly begin with this type of device; see, for example, *The Spiritual Exercises of St Ignatius Loyola*; Martz, pp. 25–32.

despair of God's mercy, of one's own sinful condition, and of the inadequacy of repentance. As such it also offers a pious model of acceptable Protestant penitence and the comfort of hope to those afflicted by religious despair.[11]

Mary (Sidney) Herbert, Countess of Pembroke, and the Sidney *Psalmes*

Although both women worked within the genres of translation and Psalm paraphrase, Mary Sidney's writing platform was markedly different to that of Anne Locke. Sidney was born into a noble family which had staunch Protestant affiliations and political influence at court.* Her education rivalled that of the best-educated young men of her day, including Italian, French, Latin, perhaps some Greek and even Hebrew and, unusually for a girl, training in rhetoric. She was born three years into Queen Elizabeth's reign, Protestantism was re-established as the state religion, and Anne Locke's volume had been published just a year before.

The Countess's most extensive literary project was the metrical paraphrase of all one hundred and fifty of the Psalms. The project to transpose the Psalms into metre was most probably envisaged as a joint project but was barely started at Sir Philip Sidney's death in 1586.[12] His sister completed the endeavour, re-working his forty-three finished Psalms and writing her own versions of the remaining hundred and seven. Although the *Psalmes of David* was widely circulated and admired by contemporary poets, the manuscript was not rediscovered and published until the nineteenth century. The innovatory collection, in which Gary Waller identified one hundred and sixty four different stanzaic forms and ninety-four metrical schemes,[13] is considered to have

* Mary Sidney lived from 1561 to 1621. The maternal side of her family were dangerously involved in the plot to put the Protestant Lady Jane Grey on the throne after the death of Edward VI, to avoid the state religion reverting to Catholicism as, in fact, happened under Mary I. Mary Sidney's uncle, Lord Guildford Dudley, married Lady Jane and was executed for his part in the conspiracy, as was his father, John Dudley, Duke of Cumberland.

influenced the work of poets John Donne, George Herbert and Aemilia Lanyer, among others. Hannibal Hamlin states that the collection was 'clearly the model' for George 'Herbert's *The Temple'* (and which then itself inspired works like [Henry] Vaughan's *Silex Scintillans* and [Christopher] Harvey's *The Synagogue*)'.[14]

Differences of social status, religious fervour, political climate, and authorial intention differentiate the Countess and Anne Locke's approaches to their Psalm paraphrases, despite the use of broadly similar sources. Whereas Locke's project was conceived in the heat of Calvinistic fervour and intended as a pious and practical tool, the Countess wrote from the centre of a thriving intellectual and literary milieu, from a privileged background and a stable state religion of moderate Protestantism. Her work was a landmark in religious lyricism and should be considered primarily from a literary, rather than theological perspective. There are no 'work in progress' versions of Locke's sonnets, so her working practice and literary development remain unclear. By contrast, different versions of the Countess's poems are preserved and provide insights into the crafting process, which clearly indicates their courtly aspect and a preoccupation with *literary* excellence. As Danielle Clark points out, the Countess's familial and political connections link back to the Genevan reformers[15] and her work can be seen as extending their psalmic foundation. The Sidney Psalms were written for an audience very familiar with the many differing English versions of the texts and an aspect of their popularity was this intertextuality; readers noting the differences between, and skilful interpretations of, the well-known verses.

'House-confinéd maids': Social and Political Implications

As with Locke's speaker, the voice of the Countess's *Psalmes* remains ungendered. In places, nonetheless, she adjusts her sources to emphasise women's life experience. Some of her earlier versions were edited in the 'finished' presentation copy, intended for the queen[16] – this may represent a diplomatic shrewdness, as they emphasise the typical sphere of Elizabethan wives: pregnancy, childbirth and children. Particularly noteworthy in this vein are the allusions to pregnancy found in Psalms 58 and 139. Psalm 58 speaks of destroying David's enemies, which to Protestant Elizabethans metaphorically denoted the overcoming of Catholicism. The Geneva version of the Psalm introduces the theme of conception stating that evil-doers 'are strangers from ye womb: even from the belly have they erred' (Psalm 58:3) and verse eight offers the striking imagery 'Let them consume like a snail that melteth, and like the untimely fruit of a woman, that hath not seen the sun' (Psalm 58:8). The Countess's rendition suggests experience of placental abruption, resulting in stillbirth:

> So make them melt as the dishowsed snail
> Or as the embrio, whose vitall band
> Breakes er it holdes and formlesse eyes do faile
> To see the sun, though brought to lightfull land. (Psalm 58: 22–5)

At a time of high infant mortality the imagery would have resonance for many women readers. For Queen Elizabeth the subject held significance, despite her virginal status, as stillbirth and the lack of male issue had enabled her own succession, and the inability to present Henry VIII with a live male heir was a contributive reason for her mother's execution.* The 'lightfull land' of line twenty-five may refer to the Reformation of the Church and the re-establishment of Protestantism in England, as Queen Elizabeth was hailed as a new David for returning the country to the faith after the reign of Mary I.

Psalm 68 is concerned with celebrating David's victories over his enemies and restoring the Ark of the Covenant to Jerusalem, which reformers also read metaphorically as restoring the 'true religion' to England. In an interesting link with the Countess's project, Calvin's *Commentary* states that in David's time women were responsible for the singing of the triumphal song. He points out therefore that the words

* Anne Boleyn's execution in 1536 was ostensibly as punishment for adultery but the evidence was, and is still, widely considered to have been fabricated in order to make way for a new wife who might produce a male heir. Jane Seymour, Henry's third wife, presented him with his son, Edward, but died as a complication of childbirth in 1537.

may be seen as David's or 'as forming the song of the women'.[17] Although the Countess's sources say relatively little about women, verse twelve of the Geneva Bible (1599 version), has 'she that remained in the house divided the spoil'. The Countess creates a more empathic and rustic, '*we* house-confinéd maids with distaffs* share the spoyle' (Psalm 68: 34, emphasis added) spoken, as Calvin suggests, by the women themselves.[18]

'Fearfully and wondrously made': Psalm 139

The Countess's Psalms frequently enliven and contemporise the biblical material for her readers, for example in the unusual imagery of carpentry and house-building, linked to the development of the foetus in her Psalm 139. The Geneva Bible version gives thanks for the miracle of mankind's creation, 'I will praise thee, for I am fearfully and wondrously made' (l. 14), whilst emphasising the omnipotence of God, 'My bones are not hid from thee, though I was made in a secret place' (l. 15). Themes of conception and pregnancy are also alluded to in God's covering the shapeless soul with skin in the mother's womb, giving it physical form (ll. 13, 16). Whilst frequently echoing her biblical source, the Countess develops intriguing imagery by combining dissimilar semantic fields, in typically metaphysical conceits:†

> Each inmost peece of me is thine:
> while yet I in my mother dwelt,
> all that me clad
> from thee I hadd.
> Thou in my frame hast strongly delt;
> needes in my praise thy workses must shine
> so inly them my thoughts have felt.

* A distaff is a spindle holding a clump of fleece or flax for spinning, and also a symbolic representation of woman at the time.

† Conceit: an unexpected metaphor combining divergent images.

Thou how my back was beam-wise laid,
and raftring of my ribs dost know:
know'st ev'ry point
of bone and joint,
how to this whole these partes did grow,
in brave embroidery faire araid,
though wrought in shop both dark and low.

(ll. 43–56)

Enhancing the concept of God as a great 'artificer', perhaps suggested by Calvin's *Commentary*,[19] Sidney develops the 'frame' trope of line 47, to incorporate the description of a timber-framed house under construction, the central roof beam supporting the rafters of the roof, presumably a common sight in her time. This startling image actually represents the spine and ribs of the unborn child within the womb, the 'secret place' of the Genevan version. The Psalm can be termed mimetopoetic,* as is apparent from the visual organisation of the poem on the page. Through the arrangement of her lines she creates a representation of the human spine, with graded short and long lines mimicking the vertebrae. In George Puttenham's terms this is 'Proportion in figure … so called because it yelds an ocular [visual] representation'.[20]

Again, probably relying on the *Commentary*'s references to fabric production, the Countess further develops the 'frame' imagery, moving from carpentry, typically male artisanship, to conventional female handicrafts. Sewing was a routine female occupation, while tapestry work and fine embroidery were considered genteel accomplishments. Both of the latter were executed on stretched fabric held in place in a frame. The complex layering, slashing, beading and embroidering of sumptuous formal Elizabethan garments is evoked in the Countess's imagery describing the layered bones, sinews and tissue of the body as 'in brave embroidery faire araid'† (l. 55). Her reference to the 'shop both dark and low' (l. 56) is inspired by the *Commentary* which calls attention

* Mimetopoetic poetry: verse forms which mimic the form of the subject.

† 'Araid': displayed or adorned.

to God's 'most perfect work of all' being created in darkness, but her use of 'shop' evokes a sense of the cramped and humble craft workshops of the capital which serviced the opulent lifestyle of the court. There are many such explorations of theme in the *Psalmes* which encourage her contemporary reader's imaginative engagement. The biblical Book of Psalms had retained a central place in Christian worship since the time of the Church Fathers,* but the reformers especially encouraged readers to take their guidance from it, applying the wisdom to everyday life. Contemporary estimation of its value is expressed in Richard Hooker's, '[for] What is there for man to know that the Psalms are not able to teach?'[21]

Mystery and 'Measure'

The most impressive aspects of the Sidney *Psalmes* are their originality and assured craftsmanship. The very short Psalm 117 is rendered in acrostic form, for example, reading 'PRAISTHELORD' in the capitalised first letters of each line, very much extending the two verses of the Geneva Bible version. Some of her innovation is actually prompted by biblical precedent, as in her twenty-two stanzas of Psalm 119, each of which is presented in a different stanzaic form and beginning with a different letter of the alphabet.[22] In the biblical source the letters correspond to the letters of the Hebrew alphabet and are a meditation on God's law. The Countess rendered her Psalms 120 to 127 in unrhymed form intended to imitate quantitative Hebrew verse,† her interest most probably arose as a result of her brother's experiments in transposing Hebrew poetics. Her interest in measure and proportion

* The Church Fathers were important early Christian theologians of the first centuries, such as Tertullian (160–225), St Jerome (354–430) and St Augustine (354–430). St Augustine's works were particularly valued in this era.

† Quantitative verse: verse which relies for effect upon length or brevity of the syllables, rather than rhyme or rhythm. Members of the Sidney circle including Philip Sidney, Gabriel Harvey and Edmund Spenser, among others, are known to have worked with this form. See Gary Waller, *English Poetry of the Sixteenth Century* (Harlow, Essex: Addison, Wesley, Longman Ltd, 1986, repr. 1993), pp. 54, 55.

can also be traced in the myriad of rhyme and stanzaic patterning evident in the collection.

To the Renaissance imagination, poetry was aligned with mathematics, geometry and music, all subjects relying on proportion and balance, quantifying and measuring. Scholars defined poetry as 'measurable speech' which emphasised 'number' and 'proportion'.[23] The counted syllables and rhyme patterns may be used to symbolise aesthetic concepts of symmetry, discordance, mysticism or perfection. Prominent courtiers, including members of the Sidney circle, were involved in the study of numerology, astrology and 'mystical sciences' and the Countess's interest in these areas is apparent in some of the *Psalmes,* which reveal schemes of numerical and alphabetical patterning in their structural organisation. Psalm 55, for example, contains complex correspondences representing the Trinity:* the structure of the poem centres on patterns of three, these are three rhymes presented in palindromes,† twelve lines to each stanza and six stanzas in total. The first stanza, for example rhymes: *abccbaacbbca*:

My god glad to look, most prone to heere, *a*
an open eare o lett my praier find, *b*
and from my plaint turne not thie face away. *c*
behold my jestures, harken what I say *c*
while uttering mones with most tormented mind, *b*
My body I no lesse torment and teare. *a*
for loe their fearfull threatnings wound mine eare, *a*
who griefs on griefs on me still heaping laie, *c*
a mark to wrath and hate and wrong assign'd, *b*
therefore my hart hath all his force resign'd *b*
to trembling pants, death terrors on me pray, *c*
I feare, nay shake, nay quiv'ring quake with feare. *a*
(ll. 1–12)

* The Trinity represents the threefold nature of the Christian God: Father, Son and Holy Ghost.

† A palindrome is section of verse or sentence which is the same backward as forward, in rhyme schemes, for example, *abccba*.

As with Psalm 139, the visual impact of the written word on the page was an important authorial consideration. The structure of Psalm 55 creates undulation in the block of text: the beginning positions of the first three lines form half of a curve, which is completed by the next three lines, the starting points of which mirror lines one to three, creating a complete concave curve [⊃]. The same format is repeated in the remaining six lines, thus forming a visual representation of the Arabic numeral three [3], so drawing attention to the patterning of triads within the rhyme scheme and the underlying theological implications.* As these two *Psalmes* indicate, the Countess often uses the structures of the poems to provide 'keys' to the hidden content. This embellishment is delineated by Puttenham, 'most times your occular proportion doeth declare the nature of the audible … this is by a natural *simpathie*, betweene the eare and the eye'.[24]

John Donne: The Sacred and Profane in Discordant Harmony

John Donne's imaginative engagement with religious doctrine is often surprising and can be confrontational, while the imagery and semantic field employed in his devotional poetry can also be disturbingly physical. As critics often remark, Donne intermixes the sacred and the profane within his poetry, promoting a sense of enhanced physicality alongside deeply-felt spiritual emotions. For this reason scholarly opinion is often divided regarding whether poems relate primarily to concupiscent or philosophical experiences.[25] Ultimately, however, he presents a notion of body and spirit held within the 'wrap' of human existence, much like the sentiment of Herbert's 'Coloss. 3.3', discussed below. Donne's short sonnet sequence, 'La Corona', like Anne Locke's devotional work, may seem at odds with its poetic form. During the early Renaissance, sonnets were most commonly associated with courtly love poetry of a more worldly perspective; nonetheless, they did often contain a more spiritual

* Of all Sidney's *Psalmes*, only eight poems are what would be termed 'left justified' today. These are Psalms 111, 117, the 'f' poem of Psalm 119, Psalms 121, 122, 126, 127 and 140.

element. The Petrarchan-inspired sonnet, for example, frequently retained traces of Neo-platonism,* which can quite easily be aligned with the Christian perspective of God as the source of love. In these terms the sentiment governing these religious works is merely diverted from Eros to Agape.†

'La Corona', '*a crown of prayer and praise*'

The 'La Corona' ['The Crown'] poems achieve their sequential pattern by using the final line of each sonnet as the first of the succeeding one, finally repeating the first line of the first sonnet as the last line of the final sonnet, creating the circlet of the title. Donne's '*crown of prayer and praise*' (Sonnet 7: 14), as he terms it, also has strong Catholic overtones, no doubt revealing sediments of theological doctrine from the earlier part of his life, prior to his conversion to the Anglican faith. Critics often read Donne's poetry as a site of conflict between his inherited Catholic loyalties and his own later Anglican conversion. John Carey's monograph *John Donne, Life, Mind and Art* is particularly illuminating in this respect.‡ To a greater or lesser degree, critics now tend to assume that Donne's own straitened familial circumstances were responsible for his rejection of Catholicism and his conversion, which enabled him to build a successful career in the Anglican ministry.

The impression of 'La Corona' is different to that evoked by Donne's controversial *Holy Sonnets* in that, although it is similarly devotional,

* Neo-platonism: Renaissance interpretation of Plato's philosophy, in this case his theory of love.

† Eros: erotic love; Agape: reciprocal love between God and mankind.

‡ Donne's grandmother was Thomas Heywood's wife and one of Sir Thomas More's nieces. More was martyred for his faith in the reign of Henry VIII and was subsequently canonised. See John Carey, *John Donne, Life, Mind and Art* (London: Faber and Faber, 1981). See also Carey, pp. 15–18, regarding anti-Catholic persecution in the late sixteenth century England of Donne's youth. He eloped and married secretly the ward of his employer, Sir Thomas Egerton. Her name was Ann More and she was about seventeen, at least twelve years his junior. Although the couple seem to have had a good marriage, the controversial union marred his career. Donne lost his job, was cast into prison, and for a number of years existed in poverty, dependent upon the charity of friends to support their ever-growing family.

there is an absence of the violent soul-searching urgency found in some of the latter. Helen Gardner and John Carey both draw attention to Donne's inspiration in the formal Catholic liturgy and doctrine. In Carey's words 'La Corona' is 'the work of a man who has renounced a religion to some manifestations of which he is still, on a profound level, attached'.[26] The sequence has been considered comparatively formal and detached, dominated as it is by its meditative structure of the stages of Christ's life: the 'Annunciation', the 'Nativity', the teaching at the 'Temple', his 'Crucifying', his 'Resurrection' and 'Ascension'. As is frequently remarked, the emphasis on liturgy, the rosary-like circle of sonnets, and the lingering praise of the Virgin Mary clearly demarcate the work as focused through the lens of Catholic devotions.

Interesting aspects of the work which are often missed, however, are the very many links with the visionary final book of the Bible, The Revelation of St John. Revelations has provoked controversy over the ages, mainly because of its extravagant allegorical nature, but it was understood in the Renaissance as metaphorically describing the struggle between Satan and the Church. As such it is eschatological, dealing with the end of the world, the final judgement, punishment of evildoers and the reward of the faithful.[*] Typically of Donne, seeming paradox and skilled linguistic play characterise the sonnets, the first of which alerts the reader to the underlying link with Revelations in the rhetorical figure of polyptoton[†] centring on 'end': 'The ends crown our works, but Thou crown'st our ends, / For at our ends begins our endless rest' (Sonnet 1: 8–9). Employing familiar imagery from *The Book of Common Prayer*'s Burial of the Dead, 'Resurrection', the sixth sonnet, also evokes the last judgement and the awakening of the dead from their graves, to join in everlasting life:

* During the interregnum a dissenting religious group, known as the Fifth Monarchists, read Revelations as a prophecy of the coming of a new age, expected in 1666, and Christ's return to earth to rule. See Revelation 20:4, 11–15.

† Polyptoton: a rhetorical figure of repetition in which the root of a word occurs in different forms.

> And life by this death abled shall control
> Death, whom Thy death slew; nor shall to me
> Fear of first or last death bring misery,
> If in thy life-book my name thou enroll.
> Flesh in that long sleep is not putrified,
> But made that there, of which, and for which it was;
> Nor can by other means be glorified. (Sonnet 6: 5–11)

Revelations 20 explicitly prophesises the gathering of the dead 'small and great' who stand before God's great white throne, waiting for the books to be opened which will reveal their past lives and upon which they will be judged, 'And whosoever was not found written in the book of life was cast into the fire' (Revelations 20:12, 14).

The italicised connecting last and first lines of consecutive sonnets have the appearance of a refrain, read in Donne's own terms as '*praise*'; these suggest a joyful hymn of celebration and twice resound with appropriately eschatological themes: '*Salvation to all that will is nigh*' (Sonnet 1: 14 and Sonnet 2: 1) and '*Salute the last and everlasting day*' (Sonnet 6: 14 and Sonnet 7: 1). The decision to write seven sonnets in the sequence strengthens the Revelations link, as the number appears frequently here in the seven Churches of Asia, the seven angels of punishment, the seven golden candlesticks, seven stars, the seven seals, seven trumpets and the seven plagues, for example.* In broader religious terms, the number was also associated with the seven cornices of hell and the seven penitential Psalms, both of which continue the 'last days' connotations, as the Psalms, particularly Psalm 51, were often used as a final prayer before death. As can be perceived, the sequence operates on many levels, relying on a knowledge of these allusions to interpret all its connotations.

* The number seven was frequently given ceremonial significance in royal or church processions or display, and was considered to have mystical significance. There are late sixteenth-century records of seventh sons of seventh sons and seventh daughters of seventh daughters claiming divinely-given healing powers, for example. See Keith Thomas, *Religion and the Decline of Magic* (London: Penguin, 1971, repr. 1991), pp. 237–9. Regarding interest in numerology as found in the literature of the time, see Alistair Fowler, *Triumphal Forms: structural patterns in Elizabethan poetry* (Cambridge: Cambridge University Press, 1970), *passim*.

Although Donne is considered to have been Arminian[*] in his later life, terminology and habits of thought arising from more severe Calvinism frequently erupt in the religious sonnets, both here in 'La Corona' and also in *Holy Sonnet* 14 for example. Sonnet 6 of the sequence focuses on the saving power of Christ's blood, reiterating the *sola fides*[†] doctrine of the religious reformers: only through sincere faith in the efficacy of Christ's sacrifice can an individual be saved.[‡] The personified soul is depicted as 'dry' and 'stony hard' and yet paradoxically also 'too fleshly' (ll. 1, 3), the repeated tongued 'l' sound suggesting a voluptuousness which contrasts sharply with the earlier imagery. 'Hardness of heart' was a loaded expression during the time of Donne's writing, denoting those who stubbornly resist God's grace, the Reprobate, according to the Calvinist doctrine of predestination. The concept arises in Marlowe's *Dr Faustus*: 'My heart's so hardened I cannot repent' (*Dr Faustus*, sc. 7:18), as does the preoccupation with Christ's blood, 'See, see where Christ's blood streams in the firmament / One drop would save my soul, half a drop' (*Dr Faustus*, sc. 14: 18, 75, 76). Donne's conceit is that the soul is too wrapped in worldly concerns, the world of the flesh, rather than the spirit and is thus hardened to the call of the Holy Ghost.

The 'hardness' imagery is extended in the first quatrain, calling upon the parable of the seed which falls upon the stony ground, which 'withered away, because it lacked moisture' (John 8:6), although Donne's craved 'drop' of moisture is not rain, but Christ's blood. In a visual rhyme 'foul', is teamed with 'soul', in the *abba* rhyme scheme, leading to further visual play in the use of 'able' as a transitive verb:[§]

* Arminians rejected the Calvinist doctrine of Predestination, in favour of a conviction that God *knew* that some would refuse Christ, rather than God *decreeing* who would believe and therefore be saved.

† Latin: 'only faith'.

‡ See Part Four: 'Religious Works and Controversy' for a discussion of the religious background to the period.

§ Used in the sense of 'to [en]able someone'.

Moist with one drop of Thy blood, my dry soul
Shall—though she now be in extreme degree
Too stony hard, and yet too fleshly—be
Freed by that drop, from being starved, hard or foul,
And life by this death abled shall control
Death, whom Thy death slew; nor shall to me
Fear of first or last death bring misery,
If in thy life-book my name thou enrol.
(Sonnet 1: 1–8, added emphasis)

This has the effect of linking the first and second quatrains by re-introducing the sanguine imagery evoked by 'bled' and also linking it to the victory over death. Despite Donne's reputation for ambiguity and witty wordplay, the seemingly paradoxical reasoning is in fact found within his liturgical and biblical sources. This second quatrain emphasises that death, both actual and metaphorical, is empowering, or '[en]abling', rather than representing disempowerment or loss of control. The mystery of death's victory over death has its roots in the biblical account of the Resurrection but commonly found its way into other religious works. The Genevan Book of Psalms (1557) bore a device representing 'Death of Death' and the axiom 'Death is death's cure and conqueror', for example,[27] and the Collect for the Easter Day service employed similar ambiguous phrasing, 'Christ rising from the dead, dieth not'.[28] The blending of contraries, life and death and first and last (ll. 5, 7), and the implied seasonal cycle of plant growth embedded within the linked Christian discourse, amplify the sense of rebirth, appropriate to a poem figuring the mystery of the Resurrection. The cyclical effect of the linked rhymes leads back to the original refrain of the first sonnet, and mimics God's decree in Revelations 1: 11–17, 'I am Alpha and Omega, the First and the Last'.

As Helen Gardner observed, the sonnets' rhyme scheme uses the *abbaabba* octave favoured by Philip Sidney, but thereafter employs two patterns. The first sonnet has a 'closed' scheme, rhyming *cdcd* before the couplet. The third and fifth sonnets follow this same pattern, while the second, fourth, sixth and seventh adopt an 'open' [or mirror] scheme of *cddc*.[29] This forms an ebbing and flowing pattern of closed and open [repeated twice], ending with a repeated 'open' which further enhances the sequence's metaphysical aspects. The device illustrates fluctuating commitment and a speaker torn between the polarities of the flesh and spirit, assured faith and doubt, life and death. Significantly, in the final movement, the form remains 'open' to the faith, ensuring salvation.

In many respects the pious poetry of Anne Locke and the Countess of Pembroke, in their different ways, can be considered important predecessors to the better-known and more frequently studied work of male poets, such as Donne and Herbert. Some of Donne's verse, for example, demonstrates similar complex numerical patterning in metre and stanzaic as found in the Countess's experiments.[30] His complex theological background, which especially erupts in his *Holy Sonnets*, seems to point to deep religious uncertainty and has obvious links with the Calvinistic despair depicted in Locke's *Meditation*. Although Protestant, Herbert's interest in the material aspects of devotional practice is influenced by Catholic practice, as is Locke's verse, and his 'aesthetic pleasure in complexity' and 'interwoven intricacies' are very much in concordance with the Countess's poetic stance.[31]

George Herbert: Conceit and Devotion

George Herbert's personal connections with the elder poet John Donne no doubt influenced his poetic development, but his work also demonstrates shared interests with Mary Sidney's *Psalms*.* Herbert's mother was a patron of Donne and the dedicatee of his major work, the *Holy Sonnets*. Despite a promising career within the University of Cambridge and a notable gift of oration, Herbert took religious orders in his late thirties. His poetry is characterised by intense religious sentiment alongside a fascination with poetical representation, whether in elaborate metaphysical conceit or the arrangement of the poem on the printed page. Herbert's preoccupation with ornamental and architectural features of the church is evident in his exploration in the

* Herbert lived from 1593 to 1633. Donne from 1572 to 1631.

collection published under the title *The Temple* (1633). The collection moves from 'The Church-porch', to 'The Altar', noting 'Church-monuments', 'Church-music', 'The Church-floor' and 'The Windows', guiding the reader through the material presence of the building, whilst promoting his/her spiritual welfare. Similarly to the Countess, Herbert uses the 'Proportion in figure' device, in the 'The Altar', 'Easter Wings (1)' and 'Easter Wings (2)', in that their printed shapes on the page replicate the form of their subject matter. 'Paradise' also employs witty intellectual games something akin to the Countess's linguistic and proportional experiments. As in Marvell's 'The Garden', horticultural imagery figures God as a divine gardener, in this case pruning not only the growth of plant and man, but also the lines of poetry:

> I bless thee, Lord, because I GROW
> Among thy trees, which in a ROW
> To thee both fruit and order OW. (ll. 1–3)

After deliberation regarding God's sharp – and not always welcome – intervention in man's life, the droll exercise culminates in:

> Such sharpness shows the sweetest FREND
> Such cuttings rather heal than REND
> And such beginnings touch their END. (ll. 13–15)[32]

As the Countess embedded hidden thematic links in her patterning and experimented with acrostics, so Herbert played similar intellectual games with his readers. In 'Coloss. 3.3',* he creates a diagonal acrostic, based upon the biblical verse: 'For ye are dead and your life is hid with Christ in God':†

> *My* words and thoughts do both express this notion,
> That *Life* hath with the sun a double motion.

* St Paul's epistle to the Colossians 3:3.

† This patterning is also known as *carmen figuratum:* a poem or other text in which some words are positioned to stand out from the rest and give a different reading.

> The first *Is* straight, and our diurnal friend,
> The other *Hid*, and doth obliquely bend.
> One life is wrapt *In* flesh, and tends the earth.
> The other winds towards *Him*, whose happy birth
> Taught me to live here so, *That* still one eye
> Should aim and shoot at that which *Is* on high:
> Quitting with daily labour all *My* pleasure,
> To gain at harvest an eternal *Treasure*.
> ('Coloss. 3.3': 1–10, emphasis added)

In the second line's 'double motion', Herbert draws upon discourse of seventeenth-century scientific discovery to provide an ingenious conceit relating to the laws of planetary motion. The Keplerian theory of the elliptical course of the planets is used in lyrical fashion to yoke together concepts of the infinite and the nature of mankind.[33] The 'straight' (l. 3) lines of the ellipse continue the notion of parallelism suggested in the division between 'words and thoughts' (l. 1), while the 'bend' (l. 4) represents the loop at either end of the course. This hidden aspect of the planetary orbit is used to represent the spiritual, while the life which is 'wrapt in flesh' (l. 5) denotes mankind's daily, seen, existence on earth.

The principal underlying themes are the biblical creation and judgement of mankind, as written in Genesis. The concept of mankind's 'dual nature' arises from this account, as Adam was created from the 'dust of the ground' and animated by God's breath which provided the spirit, or soul (Genesis 2:6). The two aspects of man's nature were considered to be in uneasy tension: the spiritual aligned with the aspirational and elevated, striving towards heaven, and the corporeal associated with human appetites and base animal instincts. Man's post-lapsarian punishment, e.g. after the Fall from Eden, was that he must earn his food 'by the sweat of his brow' and the voice of the poem accepts the judgement willingly, aware that through this daily toil he earns the 'harvest' (l. 10) of everlasting life beyond death. Importantly, the poem presents scientific and religious discourse in alignment, as complimentary facets of a providential outlook.

Extended Commentary: Locke, *A Meditation* (1560)

Authorial Anxieties

Anne Locke's sincere desire to avoid spiritual pride found expression in a well-defined strategy. The distraction of the imagination was often considered a threat to heartfelt engagement with the sacred texts, to both orthodox and reformist ministers. As a hedge against this Locke used just one poetic model, the tightly-structured English sonnet form. At the time of writing, this was not widely known, although Locke may have encountered the form in the introductory sonnet of Sir Thomas Wyatt's *Certayn Psalmes* (1549).* Nonetheless, her *Meditation* of 1560 is the earliest known published sequence of English sonnets.[34] A further method of maintaining focus and providing parameters for her imagination involved keying the sonnets into the verses of Psalm 51, which appeared italicised in the right hand side margin of each sonnet. Despite this limiting strategy, however, the nineteen verses of the Psalm are rendered into twenty-one sonnets.† The marginal version of the Psalm also demonstrates Locke's humility. Rather than writing her own paraphrase, Locke created an intertexual compilation from the work of respected co-religionists, acknowledging their scholarship and veracity.‡ Her tactics perhaps indicate anxiety of authorship, exacerbated because of her gender, but more likely arising from a concern to distance herself from accusations of literary ambition. Queen Katherine Parr similarly

* The earliest published English sonnet was the introductory poem by Henry Howard, Earl of Surrey, in Sir Thomas Wyatt's *Certayn Psalmes* of 1549. Surrey's work reached a wider audience when Richard Tottel published a particularly successful anthology of popular verse in London in June 1557, which included thirteen 'English' sonnets by Surrey. Although the title was *Songes and Sonnettes*, it was known as *Tottel's Miscellany*.

† The first and second sonnets are devoted to verse one and sonnets five and six explicate verse four.

‡ Locke's main sources are the Matthew's Bible, Myles Coverdale's two versions and the Geneva Bible versions, but she was also influenced by Théodore Bézé, Richard Taverner, Zwingli and Martin Bucer's versions and Sir Thomas Wyatt's *Certayn Psalmes*.

prefaced her *lamentacion of a synner* (1547) with, 'I trust no bodye will judge I have doon it for prayse'.[35]

The Main Sequence, 'Hidden and secrete thinges'

The sonnets of the main *Meditation* revisit the themes of the prefatory sequence.* In the earlier section, for example, loss of speech was represented as 'smoking sighs' and 'grone[s]' (Pref. Sonnet 5: 8) and in the *Meditation* the theme evolves, in the recognition that failed speech requires God's help to articulate not only moans of misery, but also praise for his mercy:

And loose my speche and make me call to thee.
Lord open thou my lippes to shew my case …
Lord loose my lippes, I may express my mone,
And finding grace with open mouth I may
Thy mercies praise, and holy name display.
(Sonnet 17: 6–7, 12–14)

Despair, the callous and scornful adversary who spreads the sinner's faults before her 'ruthefull eye' (Pref. Sonnet 3: 3, 4), here in the main sequence works in partnership with Conscience, who adopts the role of a sadistic surgeon, and is graphically rendered in violent imagery:

My cruell conscience with sharpned knife
Doth splat my rippéd hert, and layes abrode
The loathsome secrets of my filthy life,
And spredes them forth before the face of God …
(Sonnet 5: 9–12)†

* The heading to this section ambiguously claims that the sonnets were 'delivered [her] by a friend', rather than being written by Locke herself. Using evidence from lexical analysis, parallels within the translations and her later volume *Of the Markes of the Children of God* (1590), however, modern criticism now accepts that the denial can be attributed to a reluctance to claim literary or spiritual credit. See Felch, pp. liii, liv.

† See Wyatt's *Certayne Psalmes*, Psalm Six: 'I open here and spred / My fawte to the' for similarities.

Psalm 51:6 states God's love of truth, but Locke's approach is from a contrary perspective, denigrating the 'hidden face' and 'trutheles visour' (Sonnet 8: 1, 2) of the hypocrite, perhaps referring to those who abandoned the reformed faith when Catholicism was reinstated in England. Most of the sonnets of both the prefatory section and the *Meditation* proper follow a regular *abab cdcd efef gg* rhyme pattern. This sonnet, however, introduces a variation after the first quatrain, adopting a scheme which falters forward yet procrastinates in the return to the '*b*' rhyme: *abab cbcb dcdc ee*.

Illustrating the 'three powers of the soul', this middle quatrain depicts the effect of grace on the spirit: working on the memory it fires the understanding and inspires the will to change. The central confusion in the rhyme replicates the speaker's conflicting emotions: the gift of grace is of inestimable value but also facilitates understanding of the teeming proliferation of sins. Locke creates an effect of movement and repetition with the rhetorical figure of isocolon,* which uses paralleled structures. The first three lines quoted here are end-stopped and return to a similar starting point but the enjambment of the fourth signals a breakthrough, illustrating the action of God's gift:

> This secrete wisedom hast thou granted me,
> To se my sinnes, and whence my sinnes do growe:
> This hidden knowledge have I learned of thee,
> To fele my sinnes, and how my sinnes do flowe
> With such excesse … (Sonnet 8: 4–9)

The focus progresses from sight to feeling, gathering stress with the repetition of 'sinnes', and plunging into the final quatrain without pause until the caesura of 'excesse'. The pleonastic† proliferance of phrases of dread exemplify the 'excesse' and amplify the headlong progression, which is only relieved by the hope of God's intervention. This forward thrust coupled with the backward-looking rhyme pattern generates

* Isocolon: a series of paralleled elements of a sentence or verse having similar structure.

† Pleonasm: a piling up of words for emphasis.

tension, imitating the speaker's racing comprehension and simultaneous riveting fear.

'Plentious streames of clensing grace'

Sonnet 3 and Sonnet 9 are linked. The first elaborates the psalmic verse, 'Wash me yet more from my wickedness, and clense me from my sinne' and Locke's focus revolves around concepts of pollution, sin and cleansing. The unrelenting probing of terrifying concepts illustrates the acute sensitivity of the sinner, and her melancholic frame of mind is obvious from the anaphorical* repetition of 'So foule', which persistently returns to her perceived contamination:

> So foule is sinne and lothesome in thy sighte,
> So foule with sinne I see myself to be,
> That till from sinne I may be washed white,
> So foule I dare not, Lord, approche to thee. (Sonnet 3: 1–4)

Initially foulness and sin are paired, seemingly inevitably, but sin is jettisoned by the third line, permitting 'foule' to appear alone on the fourth. This anticipates progression to a solution in the second quatrain which moves forward to the core of the psalmic verse: the craved purging to remove sin. Focus on the repeated 'washe' does not indicate a hopeless contamination, however, as the 'Oft hath thy mercie washed me before' (Sonnet 3: 5) points to her recoverable position.

Locke's use of the powerful adjective 'leprous' to articulate the horror and pollution of sin (Sonnet 3: 12), was most probably suggested by Wyatt's *Certayne Psalmes* version of Psalm 51: 'as the [Jews] do hele the liepre sore / With hysope clense, clense me'.[36] This link is developed in Sonnet 9, which enlarges upon the seventh verse of the Psalm, 'Purge me with hyssope, and I shall be cleane: washe me, & I shall be whiter then snowe'.[37] Old Testament Hebrew purification rituals frequently used hyssop, but Calvin's *Commentary* on the Psalm draws attention to Leviticus 14, which pertains specifically to the ritual cleansing of those suffering the

* Anaphora: the repetition of a word at the beginning of subsequent phrases.

'plague' of leprosy.[38] In Locke's time the herb was still used medicinally, appearing in the newly-popular medical handbooks as a purge.

Sonnet 9 returns to the leprosy and hyssop theme of the sonnet's marginalia, dilating further to include implied criticism of Catholic doctrine. As in Sonnet 8, the rhyme patterns are unusual and indicate Locke's emphasis on important points of reformist doctrine. The first quatrain launches immediately into distinction between the Old Testament Laws of Moses* and the new reformed understanding of the Scripture:

> With swete Hysope besprinkle thou my sprite:
> Not such hysope, nor so besprinkle me
> As law unperfect shade of perfect light
> Did use as an appointed signe to be
> Foreshewing figure of thy grace behight.† (Sonnet 9: 1–5)

The *abab* rhyme scheme again spills over into the second quatrain in 'behight' ['*a*' rhyme], the unexpected rhyme drawing attention to the vitally important content: the Mosaic Laws were for guidance, as 'appointed signe[s]', prior to Christ's ministry. Reformers considered the Old Testament to be 'unperfect', prefiguring of Christ's teaching, his sacrifice and the New Testament Gospels. Locke's resolute rejection of the old methods of absolution points to Roman Catholic rituals and ceremonies, fiercely denunciated by the reformers as having deviated from the 'true' religion. The rhyme run-on above may prompt anticipation of a '*b*' rhyme to readers familiar with the popular *strombotto*‡ form, but Locke introduces an abrupt '*c*' rhyme, to focus emphasis on Christ's death; in her terms, the only efficacious sacrifice. Underlining the point, her Christ is synonymous with the cleansing herb: 'With death and bloodshed of thine only sonne, ['*c*' rhyme] / The swete hysope, cleanse me defyled wyght' ['*a*' rhyme] (Sonnet 9: 5–6). Locke's

* Mosaic Law: the first five books of the Bible are considered to contain the Law of Moses.

† 'Behight': named, determined or promised.

‡ The *strombotto* uses the rhyme scheme *abababcc*. See Part Three: 'The Sonnet and Amatory Verse'.

enjambed colloquial sentences are contrasted with short, simple structures, chiasmus* and caesura, heightening the impact of the heartfelt apostrophes. The first section of the broken line 8, for example, simply asks 'Sprinkle my soul'. The significant point of the final section of the poem is the plea, 'wash me well *within*' (Sonnet 9: 12, emphasis added). Her subtextual reference is to inward and heartfelt contrition, rather than the outward show of ceremony and ritual: shorthand among the reformers for Catholic pomp.

The offering of the 'Humbled hart'

The new religion endorsed a personal interaction with God and interpreted misfortunes of all types as divine correction. As Sonnet 3 inferred, the 'sinnes' and despair of Locke's speaker are understood as a plague, with the implication that they are God's castigation. In order to recover a place in God's favour, as one of the Elect, the sinner must therefore atone for past offences, but Locke distinguishes between reformed and orthodox Catholic practice. The sacrifice demanded is that of a personal 'broken humbled hart' (Sonnet 19: 14), rather than empty rituals of repentance. The closing section of the sequence opens out the plea for forgiveness to include all of 'Sion', petitioning its protection and continuance:

> To spread thy bountie and thy grace upon
> Sion, for Sion is thy holly hyll:
> That thy Hierusalem with mighty wall
> May be enclosed under thy defense,
> And bylded so that it may never fall
> By myning fraude or mighty violence. (Sonnet 20: 2–8)

To the English exiles of her community, the walled city and holy hill of the sonnet denoted the cramped city of Geneva, overflowing with religious refugees, with St Peter's Cathedral high above the lake. Although the poem is based upon David's Psalm, Locke's elaboration

* Chiasmus: two sets of corresponding terms 'back to back' in inverted order (*ab* – *ba*).

clearly points to the struggle of emerging Protestantism, embattled, persecuted and undermined throughout Europe.

The final sonnet again alludes to the reformers' 'City of God', Calvin's theocracy, pledging the yielded hearts of the community. Emphasis has moved from the despairing individual, undermined and marginalised by self-doubt and despair, to focus on the united godly community of co-religionists. Even so, Locke is determined to distinguish between the God of this society and an implied other god:

> And round about then shall thy people crye;
> We praise thee, God, our God: thou onely art
> The God of might, of mercie and of grace.
>
> (Sonnet 21: 7–9)

The three-fold identification of God echoes the Trinity, significantly ending on 'grace', God's gift which enables salvation, according to the doctrine of Justification by Faith.[*] The repetition of the alliterative 'm' in the final quatrain anticipates the final 'me' of line 12, 'Be, Lord of mercie, mercifull to me' (Sonnet 21: 12). The one line is loaded with rhetorical device, utilising ploche,[†] antithesis and chiasmus polyptoton[‡] which all lead to the simple 'me', drawing focus back to the individual after the earlier universalising impulse. The plea itself is that God imputes the speaker righteous,[§] eradicating sins, in order that she may feel the presence of grace at work within her.

Notes

1 See J. S. Brewer, James Gairdner and R. H. Brodie (eds), *Letters and Papers, Foreign and Domestic*, *of the Reign of Henry VIII*, 1509–47, 21 vols (London: Longmans, Green, Read and Dyer, 1862–1910), vol. 21, part 2,

* See Part Four: 'Religious Works and Controversy'.

† Ploche: the repetition of the same word in a short span of text.

‡ Polyptoton: the use of the same word in different cases.

§ 'Impute righteous' is a reformed theological term meaning that, although sinful, through God's mercy the believer was judged as being righteous.

1546, 8 Sept., letter no. 52, Vaughan to Paget, Also cited Susan M. Felch (ed.), *The Collected Works of Anne Vaughan Lock* (Arizona Center for Medieval and Renaissance Studies in conjunction with Renaissance Text Society: Tempe, Arizona, 1999), p. xxi n25.

2 John Gough Nichols (ed.), *The Diary of Henry Machyn, A London Citizen, 1550 to 1563*, for the Camden Society (London: J. B. Nicholson and Son, 1848), vol. 42, pp. 82–98, 108. W. R. D. Jones suggests that approximately 280 individuals were martyred during Mary's reign and a further '800 or so went into exile': *The Mid-Tudor Crisis, 1539–1563* (London: Macmillan, 1973), p. 100.

3 See Louis Martz, *The Poetry of Meditation: A Study of English Religious Literature of the Seventeenth Century* (New Haven and London: Yale University Press, 1962), p. 7; also *The Spiritual Exercises of St Ignatius de Loyola*, translated and edited by Joseph Rickaby (London: Burns, Oates and Washbourne, 1923).

4 Loyola, *Spiritual Exercises*, pp. 33, 34.

5 Wyatt, Psalm 6:123, *Collected Poems,* p. 102.

6 The heading is taken from the title of John Stachniewsky's excellent book on the agonising self-doubt and despair often caused by devout Protestant belief. John Stachniewsky, *The Persecutory Imagination: English Puritanism and the Literature of Religious Despair* (Oxford: Clarendon Press, 1991).

7 William Perkins, *A Treatise tending unto a declaration whether a man be in his estate of damnation or in the estate of grace* (1590); Arthur Dent, *A plaine man's path-way* (1601). See also John Taffin's *Of the Markes of the children of God,* translated by Anne Locke (1590), STC 23652; William Perkins's Latin *Armilla aurea* (1590) including Theodore de Bèze's *An excellent treatise of comforting such as are troubled about their predestination,* STC 19655, translated by Robert Hall as: *A golden chain, or the description of theologie containing the order and causes of salvation and damnation* (1591), STC 19568, note especially Chapter 42 'Of the Second Assault [of the devil]'.

8 Dean Ebner, *Autobiography in Seventeenth-Century England* (Paris: Moulton, 1971), pp. 42–8. See also John Calvin, 'One Hundred Aphorisms' in *Institutes of the Christian Religion* (1536 edn), translated by Henry Beveridge (1845) (Grand Rapids, Michigan: Wm. B. Eerdmans Publishing Co., 1993), Book III: 48.

9 Arthur Dent, *A plaine man's path-way,* facsimile of 1860 edn (Pittsburgh: Soli Deo Gloria Publications, no date), p. 24. Calvin himself also pointed to the 'very large mixture of hypocrites, who have nothing of Christ but the name and outward appearance', Calvin, *Institutes*, III: iv, 9.

10 Calvin, *Institutes* III: ii, 23.

11 Dent, *A plaine man's path-way*, p. 195.

12 Margaret Hannay draws attention to the poem 'to the 'Angell spirit' of Philip Sidney in which Mary Sidney writes '[the Senders] which once in two, now in one Subject goe' (l. 21). This appears in the copy of the Psalms intended for presentation to Queen Elizabeth. 'Mary Sidney and Admonitory dedication' in M. P. Hannay (ed.), *Silent But For The Word: Tudor Women as Patrons, Translators, and Writers of Religious Works* (Ohio: Kent State University Press, 1985), p. 152.

13 Gary F. Waller, 'The text and Manuscript Variants of the Countess of Pembroke's Psalms', *Review of English Studies* 26 (1975), pp. 1–18.

14 Hannibal Hamlin, *Psalm Culture and Early Modern English Literature* (Cambridge: Cambridge University Press, 2004), p. 181.

15 Danielle Clark, *The Politics of Early Modern Women's Writing* (Harlow: Pearson Education, 2001), pp. 138, 139.

16 Hannay, p. 52.

17 John Calvin, *Commentaries*, vol. 10, part III, Psalm 68, translated by John King [1847–50], available online through http://sacred-texts.com.

18 *The Collected Works of Mary Sidney Herbert, Countess of Pembroke*, Margaret P. Hannay, Noel J. Kinnamon and Michael G. Brennan (eds), vol. 2, *The Psalmes of David*, 'Variant Psalmes', MSS B, 1 (Oxford: Clarendon Press, 1998), pp. 268, 269. The presentation copy version was altered to '[we] that weak in howse did lye' (l. 28).

19 Beth Wynne Fisken, among others, draws attention to this source as one of Mary Sidney's sources, 'Mary Sidney's Psalmes' in *Silent But For The Word*, pp. 166–83, p. 178. All Calvin's biblical *Commentaries* are available online.

20 George Puttenham, *The Arte of English Poesie* (Cambridge: Cambridge University Press, 1936, repr. 1970), pp. 91–101, p. 91.

21 Richard Hooker, *Of the Laws of Ecclesiasticall Polity, Book V,* in *The Works of Richard Hooker,* vol. 2, W. Speed Hill (Cambridge Mass. and London, 1977), p. 150, cited Hamlin, p. 2.

22 *The Collected Works of Mary Sidney,* vol. 2, 192–212, 425–31. The Hebrew alphabet is transliterated in the Geneva Bible Psalm as: ALEPH, BETH, GIMEL, DALETH, HE, VAU, ZAIN, CHETH, TETH, JOD, CAPH, LAMED, MEM, NUN, SAMECH, AIN, PE, TZADDI, KOPH, RESH, SCHIN and TAU. The Countess's version omits J, U, X and Z of the English alphabet, hence the sequence is 22 poems in length, matching the Hebrew version, rather than 26.

23 William Webb, *Discourse of English Poetry*, in *Elizabethan Critical Essays* (Oxford: Oxford University Press, 1948), vol. 1, p. 248, cited by Clark Hulse, 'Tudor Aesthetics' in A. F. Kinney (ed.), *The Cambridge Companion*

to English Literature 1500–1600 (Cambridge: Cambridge University Press, 1999), pp. 29–63, p. 42.

24 Puttenham, p. 85.

25 See Martz, pp. 212, 213.

26 Carey, p. 51; Helen Gardner, 'The Religious Poetry of John Donne', in *John Donne: A Collection of Critical Essays* (Englewood Cliffs, N.J.: Prentice-Hall, 1962), pp. 123–36, pp. 124, 125.

27 Translation of '*MORS MORTIS MEDICIA ET VICTORIA*' in Felch, p. xxxix, citing Lewis Lupton, *A History of the Geneva Bible,* 25 vols (London: Olive Tree, 1966–94), vol. 4, p. 74.

28 *The Two Liturgies, A.D. 1549 and A.D. 155 set forth with authority in the Reign of Edward VI,* J. Ketley (ed.) for the Parker Society (1844), p. 248, digitalised version from the University of Toronto Collection.

29 Gardner, p. 124.

30 Alistair Fowler points out that 'The Ecstasy' falls into a 7/5/7 pattern of nineteen stanzas, in which the central section represents the combination of the two souls of the lovers and 5 is the 'nuptual number combining the first masculine [odd] and the first feminine [even] numbers, but also denote[ing] the fifth, purer, quintessential element. Alistair Fowler, *Triumphal Forms: structural patterns in Elizabethan poetry* (Cambridge: Cambridge University Press, 1970), p. 74.

31 Ann Pasternak Slater (ed.), introduction to *George Herbert: The Complete Works,* (London: David Campbell Publishers Ltd, 1995), p. xviii.

32 All quotations from *George Herbert: The Complete Works.*

33 Johannes Kepler (1571–1630) helped to promote acceptance of the Copernican theory that planets orbited around the sun, rather than the earth, in *Epitome Astronomia Copernicanae* (Epitome of Copernican Astronomy) books i-iii (1618–21). His elliptical theories of planetary motion were published in *Astronomia Nova* (New Astronomy) (1609) and *Epitome Astronomia Copernicanae*. See Lisa Jardine, *Ingenious Pursuits: Building the Scientific Revolution,* for a lively discussion of the scientific advances of the seventeenth and early eighteenth centuries.

34 'The achievement of the sonnets of the *Meditation* is astonishing – they were brilliantly written for their date, and at least very competently written for any date …', Michael Spiller, 'A Literary "First": the Sonnet Sequence of Anne Locke (1560)', in *Renaissance Studies* (1997), vol. 11, no. 1, pp. 41–55, p. 45.

35 Katherine Parr, *The lamentacion of a synner, made by ye most virtuous Ladie, Quene Caterin* (1547) STC 4827 (unnumbered); also available in *Early Modern Englishwomen, A Facsimile Library of Essential Works*, Betty Travitsky and Patrick Cullen (general eds), vol. 3, part 1, *Printed Writings, 1500–*

1640; Katherine Parr, edited by Janel Mueller (Aldershot: Scolar Press, 1996).

36 Muir and Thomson (eds), *Collected Poems of Sir Thomas Wyatt*, p. 114, ll. 469–70.

37 Geneva Bible version.

38 Geneva Bible, Leviticus 14:8, 9, 10 and Calvin's *Commentary* on Psalm 51, available online.

Humanist Prose and Rhetoric: More, Philip Sidney, Wilson and Puttenham

Sir Thomas More is recognised today as England's foremost humanist scholar of his time. His extensive reading of philosophical and political classical works surfaces in his solutions to the ethical and social problems of society embedded in his prose work, *Utopia* (1516). His intellectual circle encompassed not only prominent contemporaries in England but also the wider social network of humanist scholars in Europe, of which Erasmus of Rotterdam was the outstanding central figure. Peter Giles, whose fictional representation appears in *Utopia*, Jerome Busleiden, Guillaume Budé and Thomas Lupset were part of this group and actively participated in promoting the idea of Utopia as a newly-discovered island, which was not as implausible a hypothesis then as it seems now.*

More's original intention may have been simply to write a scholarly entertainment for his circle of European humanist friends and associates. The name of the island has entered into the English language, however, used to describe an ideal place, although with nuances of the impossible and implausible. More's text is a response to the classical deliberations on ideal forms of government and social systems, such as Plato's fictional

* English scholars of his circle included John Colet, Thomas Linacre and Sir Thomas Elyot. The letters circulated between the European humanists, perpetrating the notion of Utopia as a reality, are sometimes reproduced with the text. See, for example, the Norton Critical Edition and *The Complete Works of Sir Thomas More*.

commonwealth, *The Republic* (*c.* 360 B.C.). It is similarly hierarchical and depends upon individual commitment and sacrifice for the benefit of the entire society. As with other examples of the genre, the fulsome praise of the idealised commonwealth forms a critique of the author or central character's home society. Whole literary genres of utopic and dystopic fiction have grown around the concept, the latter particularly often contrasting and exploring the political functioning of a society contrasted with the need for personal expression and liberty.

From its first publication in Latin in 1516, *Utopia*'s multivalent aspects have generated an equal variety of readings, claiming it for widely divergent schools of thought. These are further complicated by More's playful misdirections and his vested interest in obscuring his intentions. Additional questions are raised by the inconsistencies of tone between the two books, which even a casual reader cannot fail to notice; the engaging and lively narrative of Book I, written later, contrasts with the dry factual delivery of Book II. Book I is in the form of a Platonic dialogue, a question and answer format, and provides the rationale for introducing the 'perfect' commonwealth of Utopia.

A brief survey of some of the critical approaches to the work reveals a number of diverse objectives. These include: a sixteenth-century vision based on Plato's *Republic*; a model of an ideal society modelled on early Christian precepts; a social and political critique of More's times; a proto-Marxist manifesto; a design for a communal colony inspired by voyages to the New World; or a playful argument by antithesis, proving the impossibility of such an idealised society.[1]

In this age of expansion the margins of the known world were being stretched to admit alien terrains, new races and social organisations. The explorations and discoveries of John Cabot, Christopher Columbus and Amerigo Vespucci seemed no less fantastical to contemporary Europe in the early sixteenth century than those described by More. Written accounts and detailed engravings of exotic locations, even into the seventeenth century, routinely described mythical beasts and monsters, such as 'dog-headed men', unicorns and headless men whose faces were on their chests.[2] Early cartographers, meanwhile, were frequently compelled to 'patch' known and charted coastlines with unverified observations or speculative guesswork.* The heroic navigators' accounts of distant provinces provided a wealth of detail about the races and customs of the new lands, often in a similarly dry mode as *Utopia*'s Book II. More would have been familiar with at least some of these accounts, such as Columbus's *Letter*, published in Latin in 1494 and Vespucci's *Mundus Novus* (1507).†

Starting with More's misleading allusion to the 'New Island of Utopia', on the title page, his authorial strategies are intended to enhance the realism of the narrative. He introduces actual historical figures, for example, including his own persona 'More', and the humanist scholars Peter Giles and Cuthbert Tunstall, both of whom he spent time with on a trade mission of 1515. The inspired linking of one of the book's central characters, the fictional traveller Ralph Hythloday, with the voyages of a contemporary explorer in documented geographical locations increases this verisimilitude: 'He accompanied Vespucci on the last three of his four voyages, accounts of which are now common reading everywhere' (Book I: 5). The narrative is also rendered plausible in the chain of personal acquaintance, as Hythloday is said to be contactable by Giles in the accompanying letter, whilst a helpful degree of ambiguity is achieved by his being a traveller and not available for questioning.[3] In a similar sleight of hand, but which works in reverse, More creates instability within the narrative by his use of his fictional self 'More'; this convenient persona distances himself from allegations of subscribing to subversive opinions.‡ This complicated chain of narration, from the author, his fictional persona, representations of actual historical personages to an entirely fictional character, presented

* Henricus Martellus Germanicus's map of Africa of 1489, for example, could only be completed as far as Diaz's expedition of 1487 had ventured. The westerly side is cluttered with detail and place names, whereas the side depicting the western coast and Asia is speculative and seems uninhabited because he had no verifiable information.

† More is also believed to have had an interest in discovery through his brother-in-law, John Rastell, who undertook a voyage to the New World just a year after the publication of *Utopia*. See Hexter, *The Complete Works of Sir Thomas More*, volume 4, p. xxxi.

‡ The author and character should not be confused. In this guide 'More' denotes the fictional character.

as a contemporary, may be termed 'skaz'. Russian Formalism uses the term to describe this narrative strategy, which emphasises spoken language, often features humorous embedded anecdotes, and distances the author.[4] More's playful humour also surfaces in his deliberate false trails and inconsistencies, which compel the reader to sift through both sides of a debate in an attempt to understand his position.

Book I, Prelude and Social Critique

The structure of the narrative in Book I is relatively fragmented and more complex than that of the second book. The first section introduces Ralph Hythloday as a Portugese traveller recently returned from the newly-discovered island of Utopia. His portrait recommends him as a ship's captain, mature, intelligent, learned in classical languages, and widely-travelled in both the Americas and the Far East. Hythloday's accounts of his travels, punctuated by shrewd comments 'about the manners and governments of each place', elicit the admiration of both 'More' and Peter Giles. To his audience, Hythloday's academic learning, wide knowledge, and valuable experiences of other cultures distinguish him as pre-eminently qualified for an advisory role at court in the service of a ruler. These observations lead into the important section known as the 'Dialogue of the Counsel', in which the advantages and disadvantages of such a role are debated from a personal perspective. Beneath this superficial level, however, there are also much wider humanist debates about the creation and maintenance of the optimum form of commonwealth and the individual's role within it.

Arguments for entering public service include the opportunity for personal gain, whether wealth, power or public recognition, and the ability to benefit one's family through association and patronage. Hythloday's response is pragmatic, and may seem surprising, given More's own Christian humanist background. He feels no debt to his family, having already distributed his possessions among them, and the idea of service is 'absolutely repellent to [his] spirit' (Book I: 7). He wryly points out that 'only one syllable' (Book I: 7) distinguishes 'service' and 'servitude', a state that he deplores. As, paradoxically, he has no ambition towards personal gain or prestige, he identifies himself to 'More' as precisely the type of individual to take up such a position:

> It is clear ... that you want neither wealth nor power, and indeed I value and revere a man of such a disposition as I do the greatest persons in the world. (Book I: 8)[5]

Following the Platonic model, 'More' equates public service with happiness and, when rebutted, urges participation as being worthy in its outcome by positively influencing the welfare of the people, and as an inspiration to others to perform 'noble and just actions' (Book I: 8). Themes addressed in Plato's *Republic* form an undercurrent to the work and this section engages with the concept of 'Philosopher Kings', expounded by Socrates, 'Unless communities have philosophers and kings ... or people who are currently called kings and rulers practice philosophy with enough integrity ... there can be no end to political troubles'.[6]

The ensuing intense censure of current political systems, which illustrate these 'troubles', no doubt contributes to the author's wish to distance himself from the opinions expressed by his characters. The fundamental problem highlighted by Hythloday is that the high-flown philosophical theories, suggested as benefiting the Commonwealth, have no place in reality. The court is not the fount of enlightened leadership and compassion; it is populated by self-seeking flatterers who fawn upon the ruler, pursuing strategies of preferment. It is to their benefit to promote the interests of the Prince, whether ethically sound or corrupt. Hythloday also points out that an honourable man could not change the system, nor could he exist within it; he would be either disregarded, be used as a screen for dishonest transactions, or become corrupted himself. This is the stoical view that an evil and corrupted state will not be changed by the action of a wise man. According to Seneca he should not 'struggle to no purpose, nor spend himself when nothing is to be gained'.[7] It is quite contrary to More's own humanist outlook.

Poverty, Crime and Capitalism

Hythloday's heated response to political manoeuvres in Europe maligns rulers whose prime interest is war and the acquisition of new territory, rather than the proper government of their own kingdoms. More – a lawyer by training – also denigrates the English judicial practice, in Hythloday's disparagement of the 'proud, obstinate, ridiculous judgments [he has] heard, *even* in England' (Book I: 8, 9, added emphasis). The 'Cardinal Morton' episode is central to this discussion, as Hythloday reveals the grave mismanagement of fundamental social problems and the brutal state responses to petty crimes. An astute sense of self-preservation was no doubt at play when More chose to set this exchange just over a decade before his own king acceded to the throne.* The purpose of this first book is to underscore all of the perceived failings of contemporary life which may be corrected in an ideal commonwealth, which is then presented in Book II.

Hythloday's account vividly describes the spiralling state of despair, disorder and crime set in motion through the unchecked voracity and lack of charity of wealthy landowners. The pervasive influence of ruthless capitalism is identified with dangerous decay, which systemically undermines civilised society, leading to a discussion of goods held in common ownership. Again, More is working with classical themes; Plato's prescription for the ruling class in his *Republic* is the inspiration for Hythloday's pronouncement, although More's own solution is more radical:

> Thus I am wholly convinced that unless private property is entirely done away with, there can be no fair or just distribution of goods, nor can mankind be happily governed. As long as private property remains by far the largest and best part of mankind will be oppressed by a heavy and inescapable burden of cares and anxieties. (Book I: 28)

* Hythloday sets the visit shortly after the Cornish revolt of 1497, which was against the over-zealous taxation of Henry VII, see Book I: 9.

As J. H. Hexter notes, Plato's superior race, the Guardians, do not possess any personal property 'except what is absolutely indispensible' as it endangers themselves and the community over which they rule.[8] He points out that More extends *The Republic*'s partial communalism to include all members of society, linking mechanisms of justice and the fair distribution of commodities with Platonic theories.[9] An astute reader will remember that, ironically, at the beginning of this section Hythloday argued that there was no place for reason or philosophy in the government of the commonwealth. The work in its entirety is replete with similar contradictions and theories, which seem to be quite the converse of More's own philosophy. The reader is therefore constantly required to examine the subtler implications of the text and draw reasoned judgement from the evidence presented. This is the lawyer More at play.

Linguistic Play and Slippage

As Travis Decook so appositely remarks, conflicting ideas about communication characterised Reformation debates about man's relationship with God and God's expectations of his creation.[10] Although later discussions of ecclesiastical terminology are treated with great gravitas, More's enjoyment of the slipperiness of language is evident in *Utopia*. He is aware of the rift between language and signification; the inability to fix 'truth' in words.* For example, in an ambiguous blending of Greek and Latin, the name of Utopia can be interpreted as 'Good Place' but can also mean 'No Place' and 'Hythloday' means 'Learned in [or peddler of] nonsense'. Hythloday is certainly learned and earnest in the extreme, to the extent that his descriptions are clouded by admiration of the 'wonderfully wise and sacred institutions of the Utopians' (Book I: 28). Moreover, as critics have pointed out, the nouns which describe places and official positions often succeed in negating the denoted: Eric Nelson's study suggests that the

* See, for example, More's vehement condemnation of William Tyndale's translation of the New Testament in *A Dialogue Concerning Heresies* (1528–9) (sometimes known as *A Dialogue Concerning Tyndale*) and *The Confutation of Tyndale's Answer* (1532).

Greek constructions 'connot[e] "nonsense" or "non-existence"', this includes the half-way communities of the Polylerites ('much nonsense') and the Achorians ('no country').[11] More's puckish sense of humour no doubt lurks beneath the surface here, entertaining his first readers with etymological puzzles. More's letter to Peter Giles, published with *Utopia*, humorously protests that if he wished to indicate to learned readers that the island was fictional he could have affixed nonsensical names indicating that the place was 'nowhere', the river 'without water, and the ruler had no people'.[12] This, of course, is exactly what he did. In Decook's terms, More considered that the message changed according to the needs and circumstances of the reader. This outlook aligns with twentieth-century semiotic theories, such as Saussure's and Barthes's,* which emphasise the constructed and changing nature of language. Similar anxieties of representation and interpretation predominate in discussion of language during this time, especially in the religious domain, but also in the wider field of 'literature'.

The Moral Purpose of Literature

The debate regarding the relative value and purpose of different types of literature in the Renaissance was inherited from classical authors. The humanist educational endeavour, associated with scholars and educators such as Thomas Linacre, Roger Ascham and Richard Mulcaster, established numerous grammar schools which taught very similar curricula, ensuring that all educated young men shared a wide knowledge of the classics and were extensively trained in the art of rhetoric. Christian humanists such as Sir Thomas More considered that education should be used in the service of the community, as is apparent from the Dialogue of the Counsel section of *Utopia*. The effects of rhetorical techniques in oration and literature and the possibility of

* Ferdinand de Saussure (1857–1913): Swiss linguistic theorist particularly associated with the development of the theory of semiotics, the system of signification within language. Roland Barthes (1915–80): French literary theorist particularly remembered for his seminal essay 'Death of the Author' (1968).

curbing its power were subjects of heated debate in the Renaissance as they could be used for beneficial or devious ends. In his *Republic*, Plato had decided against literary arts altogether, except the 'harsher, less entertaining poets and storytellers'. Their field was restricted, however, to representing the 'good man' and their works were to promote 'principles […] originally established as lawful'.[13] Plato's main concern is with misrepresentation and deceit, and he is particularly suspicious of 'representational' works which impersonate characters, adopt idiom and represent emotion. He considers these 'dishonest' because of the corrupting possibilities of promoting undesirable characteristics and principles.[14] The subversive tendency of unregulated language in its emotional appeal is at the core of this apprehension.

The underlying moral purpose of literature, and the extent of permissible artistry by which to achieve this, is the subject of numerous Renaissance works. Some works of literary theory, such as Thomas Wilson's *Arte of Rhetorique* (1553) and George Puttenham's *Arte of English Poesie* (1589), were undoubtedly used as handbooks by aspiring poets, courtiers, or diplomats. Their moral purpose may be considered questionable in these terms, as they teach the individual to exploit language for their own purposes for preferment and tangible gain. The debate about language is particularly complex in evaluating the role of eloquently persuasive language which aims to sway the hearer, as it may be used for ethical or iniquitous purposes. As Neil Rhodes observes, much Elizabethan literature questions rhetoric and its moral value.[15]

The early part of the sixteenth century struggled with the idea of creating literature in English, as it was often considered 'vulgar' and too sparse to accommodate the copious eloquence taught in Latin in grammar schools and universities. Sir Thomas More's *Utopia*, for example, was published in Latin and did not appear in English translation until 1551. Many prominent and classically-educated figures found it more difficult to express themselves eloquently in English than in Latin. Due to the perceived paucity of the vernacular tongue, some educators urged the adoption of foreign words and a creative approach to Latinate adaptations and neologisms. Thomas Wilson and George Puttenham were both opposed to this eclectic approach, despite their shared interest in elaboration of expression, scathingly dubbing obscure Latinisms 'inkhorn terms' to be avoided by the novice writer.

Wilson's explanation of mankind's gift of persuasion is couched in religious and specifically Protestant terms: despite the state of gross brutality to which men descended after the Fall, God was moved to pity and gave the gift of eloquence to those few who remained rational and faithful to His word. Hence, Wilson's concept of rhetoric is as wholly beneficial, despite the reformers' general distrust of elaborate representation. In his Preface he attributes the civilising process to reason and rhetoric, pointing out that the co-operation necessary in a commonwealth can only be achieved through language which engages the emotions.[16] Setting out his aims, he states the didactic purpose of eloquence clearly: the orator's purpose is primarily to teach, which he does by stealth, delighting and persuading: 'delight them, and win them, weary them and you will lose them forever'.[17]

Self-help and Personal Responsibility: The Protestant Outlook

Wilson's influential and innovative guide can be located within the popular genre of self-help guidebooks of the sixteenth and seventeenth centuries. Its very practical purpose was the training of individuals in the art of persuasive and eloquent speech, whether verbal or written. The volume is divided into three books which give detailed directions for the ordering and embellishing of orations for different purposes. The first introduces the aims of rhetorical address and defines customary schema for given circumstances. The practical and plain style of the models aligns it with the teaching texts of the grammar schools in its accessibility, although Wilson's intention is to place rhetoric at the disposal of the untutored adult. His Preface articulates his purpose as revealing the wisdom of the classical authors to 'the unlearned [who] by seeing the practise of others, maie have some knowledge themselves'.[18] George Puttenham similarly draws attention to his civilising process in his *Arte of English Poesie* (1589). Using 'English poesie' as a persona for the Everyman reader, he claims that his volume succeeds in:

> ... pulling him first from the carte to the schoole, and from thence to the Court, and preferred him to your Majesties service in that place of great honour and magnificence to geve entertainment to Princes, Ladies of honour, gentlewomen and Gentlemen ...[19]

This egalitarian inclination can be identified in many Protestant works of the time, which emphatically link the individual's spiritual accountability with responsibility for personal health and circumstances.* Wilson's extended prefatorial notices to the reader patently identify his religious outlook, in sentences peppered with the terminology of Protestantism. In the 1560 edition, for example, he writes at length of his imprisonment in Rome and interrogation by the Inquisition, dwells on man's fallen state and corruption – a typically Protestant preoccupation – and reminds his readers of God's free gift of 'heavenly grace' to those who 'call unto him with stretched hands and humble heart'.[20]† In his 'oration deliberative' elaborating on the theme of 'Justice', a subdivision on religion subverts the section on 'custome' to deliver a sidelong swipe at Catholicism, complaining that Christ is not worshipped in spirit but:

> In Copes, in Candelsticks, in Belles, in Tapers, and in Censers, in Crosses, in Banners, in shaven Crownes, and long Gownes, and many good morrows els ...[21]

Ryan J. Stark identifies an urgent sense of impending Apocalypse in the work, stating that Wilson's reason for writing is, 'primarily so that students might defend themselves against the Devil's [and Rome's] eloquence before the world ends – for the sake of their own redemption

* Several Protestant divines, for example, wrote medical handbooks for the lay person, linking spiritual and physical health and personal responsibility for both, without relying on the intervention of ecclesiastical or medical mediators.

† According to the Protestant outlook, salvation was only possible through God's gift of grace, which could not be earned or negotiated through the performance of penance or good works. The term 'grace', therefore, is loaded and often denotes this theological perspective. Compare the language with Anne Locke's religious sonnets in Part Three: 'Religious Verse'.

as well as England's'.[22] Stark's argument cites the overtly Protestant tenor of Wilson's examples provided to illustrate his rhetorical figures. In particular, he highlights similarities with apocalyptic references in several texts of the time, including John Cheke's *The Hurt of Sedition* (1549). In common with many other examples of contemporary reformist polemics, Cheke's text identifies the Pope with the Antichrist.[23]

In Book III, Wilson does employ anti-Catholic terms, but perhaps not as habitually as suggested by Stark. In his explanation of the uses of repetition, however, Wilson creates a litany effect based upon the name of the young king, Edward VI, who introduced full-scale Protestantism as the state religion:

> King Edward hath overthrowen Idolatrie, King Edward hath banished Superstition, King Edward hath by God's help brought us to the true knowledge of our creation ...[24]

It was such sentiments that impelled Wilson to seek refuge abroad during Mary I's reign and were responsible for his papal interrogation between the first publication of the book and the 1560 reprint.

'Poesie' and Nationalism

Both Wilson's *Arte of Rhetorique* and George Puttenham's *The Arte of English Poesie* employ similar structures, and Puttenham's content was, no doubt, also influenced by the earlier text.* The intersection between them is inevitable as the eloquent embellishments of rhetoric are used extensively in poetry ('poesie'). Their roles as practical guides are only part of their value, however; their own literary aspects should not be overlooked. Andrew Hadfield's close examination of the exemplars in the two texts, for example, finds an underlying and unifying agenda of nationalism.[25] This is evident not only in the larger purpose of creating a fittingly impressive national literature through their didactic element,

* Puttenham's text also seems to have been heavily influenced by Sidney's *Defence*, see the next section of this same discussion.

but also in the anecdotes and insights which they use as examples of individual literary strategies. In his exercise entitled 'praysing a noble personage', for example, Wilson's subdivisions begin with the subject's 'birthe and infancie'. Discussing how these topics may be 'opened' and contribute to the praise, he defines a complicated hierarchy of status, which clearly indicates that being born as an English *man* places the individual at the highest social pinnacle, above an Irish man, a French noble and a Scots man, for example.* Outlining the range of poetic genres, meanwhile, Puttenham pays tribute to the English writers who have 'so much beautified our English tongue as at this day it will be found our nation is in nothing inferior to the French or Italian'.[26] He is also concerned to establish a refined and standardised English which emulates the language of the court and 'the shires lying about London within lx. [60] myles', in order to avoid 'abuse [of] good speeches by strange accents or illshapen soundes, and false ortographie' [orthography] (pp. 144, 145).† Puttenham's vision of an elevated lexicon, liberated from the vulgarity of unorthodox pronunciation, orthography and regional dialect, can be read as elitist, but his intention is to create a great national literary culture to rival the *belles-lettres* ‡ of both contemporary and classical nations.

Sidney's *Defence* or 'Apologie'

Puttenham's *Arte of English Poesie* and Sir Philip Sidney's *Defence of Poesy* (*c.* 1580) illustrate the Renaissance interest in literary theory and specifically the roles of poetry and the poet. Sidney's *Defence*, however, is in the form of a classical oration, ostensibly arguing the value of poetry, rather than being a practical manual of instruction. The *Defence*

* Wilson wrote, 'To be born a "manchilde" denotes "courage, gravity and constancie", while being born female "declares weaknesse of spirit, neshness [coldness] of body, and fickleness of mind"' (*The Art of Rhetorique*, Book I, p. 12).

† Orthography: a system of writing.

‡ French: literally, 'Fine Letters', meaning sophisticated and eloquent writing valued for its form as much as content. The classical equivalent is *bonae litterae*, but refers specifically to Latin and Greek literature.

was also published, with slight variations, under the title of *An Apologie for Poetrie* in 1595, nine years after Sidney's death.* It is likely that he was working simultaneously on this and his sonnet sequence, *Astrophil and Stella*, between 1580 and 1582, although it is often read as a direct response to Stephen Gosson's attack on the theatre and poetic arts, *The School of Abuse*, which was dedicated to Sidney in 1579. Gosson quite expected that Sidney would endorse his work, most probably due to their shared staunch Protestant outlook. Sidney, it seems, was keen to distance himself from Gosson's attack, no doubt because the tirade lacks subtlety and has the invective air of popular pamphlets such as Joseph Swetnam's later contribution to the 'Woman Debate'.† Gosson's title, in fact, sets out his intention in a similar fashion to Swetnam, suggesting that the work should not be taken seriously: 'Conteining a plesaunt invective against Poets, Pipers, Plaiers, Jesters and such like Caterpillers of a commonwealth; Setting up the Flagge of Defiance to their mischievous exercise'.[27] As is often pointed out by Sidney scholars, although Sidney deals in similar material and rehearses commonly-held beliefs, arising from the Renaissance humanist education programme, he does not interrogate Gosson's claims explicitly. In fact, the wide range and eclecticism of the *Defence* makes it a useful contemporary survey of perceptions of the role of poetry during the era.[28]

'An artificiall declaration of the mynde'

One way of approaching Sidney's *Defence* is as an adept formal oration which follows the very precise guidelines of classical and contemporary works of rhetoric. Some of the recognisable influences are from Cicero's *De Oratore*, Quintilian's *Institutes*, Horace's *Ars Poetica* and Platonic theories of the Idea and Form, found in *The Republic*, *Meno* and other dialogues.[29] The *Defence* is presented within the formal framework of

* William Ponsonby as the authorised publisher of Sidney's works printed *The Defence of Poesy* first but the execution was careless; Henry Olney published the work as *An Apologie for Poetrie* in a more precise version, but without permission and was obliged to withdraw it. Manuscript copies also circulated during Sidney's lifetime.

† See 'The Woman Debate' (or *Querelle des Femmes*) chapter in Part Four of this volume.

oration suggested in such sources, and in contemporary handbooks, such as Thomas Wilson's, which were Renaissance compilations of these theories. Hence, it should perhaps be read as a self-conscious exercise in oration. Catherine Barnes points out that Sidney's work is primarily concerned with form and persuasion, rather than a logical counterpointing of the negative claims against the art outlined in Gosson's and other attacks.[30] Arguing the lack of cohesive argument, for example, Barnes draws the conclusion that its force is due to its 'sophisticated exercises in audience psychology rather than by intellectually cogent argumentation'.[31] Sidney uses the arts of rhetoric and persuasion to manipulate the reader to his line of thought. This witty exercise is what rhetoric is all about, and why it earned its dubious reputation with critics like Gosson, and therein lies the humour.

Sidney's rhetorical template is helpfully delineated in the version produced in *The Miscellaneous Prose of Sir Philip Sidney*, which clearly indicates the oration's formal divisions: Exordium, Narration, Proposition, Divisions, Examination [1 and 2], Refutation, Digression and Peroration, as discussed below.[32] As Kenneth Myrick noted more than seventy years ago, in its engaging nature and modesty, Sidney's opening in the *Defence* is a typical example of classical and contemporary directives for persuasive Exordia.[33] Wilson's *Arte of Rhetorique*, for example, advises that the first task of the orator [in the Exordium] is to elicit the indulgence of the listener, 'to win the chief hearers' good willes, and perswade them to our purpose', in order to move affections and 'get the overhand'.[34] Sidney fulfils the directive by generating personal interest and engaging the sympathies of his audience, by relating a humorous anecdote about horse-riding lessons shared with a friend in Italy.

Wilson's second section of the 'Demonstrative' oration follows Quintilian's outline in praising the subject's 'worthinesse', in a detailed example of a noble *person*'s ancestry, great deeds and the inspiration that he presents to those who follow.[35] Sidney's response is the encomium to poetry, which we recognise as the major part of his *Defence*, based on the same divisions. For example, where the classical oration deals with the noble personage's 'birth and infancie', Sidney defines the ancient foundations of the art of poetry in Greece and Rome. Sidney's witty narrative ranges through a history of poetry and its moral and didactic dimensions by recording the 'life stages' of his subject.

This second part of Sidney's *Defence* contains interesting insights into Sidney's attitude to the function and status of poetry and the poet, providing some useful points of comparison for his own poetic work. At times it can be difficult to divide the parodic from the sincere, however. The argument of the *Defence* is based upon commonly-held beliefs derived from the classical authors, shared by Sidney's generation, although largely unattributed. For example, his discussion of the poet's divine inspiration and civic usefulness also appears in Puttenham's *Arte of English Poesie* (1589), in more direct and condensed form. This may, in fact, have been based upon Sidney's *Defence* which could have been in manuscript circulation as early as 1581. Puttenham terms the early poets as 'first prophets or seears, *Videntes*', outlining their role in establishing and maintaining social structures as:

> First lawmakers to the people, and the first polititiens, devising all expedient meanes for th'establishment of Common wealth, to hold and containe the people in order and duety by force and virtue of good and wholesome laws, made for the preservation of public peace and tranquillitie.[36]

Sidney's more embellished and denser argument covers a similar field, recalling the debt that ancient and modern societies owe poetry, through its inspiration of philosophers, historians and 'law-giving devines'.[37] His wide-ranging review embraces Ireland, Turkey, Italy and the classical civilisations, culminating in the observation that in Ancient Rome poets held the title of '*Vates*', which he identifies as 'forseer, or prophet'.[38] Sidney's combination of Christian and pagan concepts of divine inspiration are complex and generate ambivalences and tensions. Illustrations provided set the 'heavenly poesie' of the biblical Psalms, against the 'godless superstition' of Roman poets, for example, seeming undecided whether the versified oracles of Delphos and Sibilla should be condemned to the same degree, due to the reverence in which they were held.[39] The obliqueness intensifies as Platonic theories of pre-existing Forms are brought into play, which Sidney claims the poet's elevated sensitivity is able to perceive and utilise in the creation of poetry, naming him a type of heavenly 'maker'.

The 'Heavenly maker'

The claim that mankind's 'making' is achieved by harnessing 'the force of a divine breath' is controversial and Sidney's recognition is wrapped in the claim that it should not be 'deemed too saucy'.[40] The intertwined concept of divine inspiration allied with God-like creation of poetic forms is rendered more problematical by Sidney's claim that poetry is not merely the mimetic, e.g. exact, reflection of what already exists in nature, but surpasses nature in the poet's 'delivering [ideas] forth in such excellency as he imagined them'. The claim is for a type of free conception, soaring above worldly concerns. In this era, however, the imagination itself was suspect due to its unavoidable reflection of mankind's fallen nature; Sidney's 'infected will', in fact.[41]

Ronald Levao's astute reading of *A Defence* reveals many contradictions in Sidney's discourse, as he negotiates tortuous lines of argument which seem in places to negate themselves. Sidney's formula by which the persuasive force of poetry may achieve its moral aim is the commonplace to 'teach and delight', percolated through numerous classical and contemporary sources from at least Horace onward.[42] Sidney's solution emphasises the moral purpose of poetry which, as Levao points out, ultimately returns to the humanist response to rhetoric and learning with its specific aim to rehabilitate, reform and create a perfected 'common weal'.[43]

In what has been described as a flash of courtly *sprezzatura*, the concluding part of Sidney's *Defence*, the Peroration, lightly revisits the wide range of theories and critical debates about poetry contained in the complex and contradictory oration. Levao reads Sidney's tone as playful, suggesting that the complex arguments are summoned 'like actors at the end of the play, taking their bows'.[44] In this case it is the voice of the *Defence*, rather than the work itself, which remains with the reader; the persuasive and manipulative voice of a consummate rhetorician, enjoying the spectacle of his own engrossed audience.

Sidney's *Defence* reiterates classical theories of poetry and the role of the poet using citation and example which would have been familiar to his contemporaries, trained in early modern grammar schools. The didactic purpose of literature described was a commonplace by the time of writing, as was its ability to promote good works. Sidney maintains, however, that the art of the poet is found not only in reflecting the world as God created it, but in the God-given power to create. As he terms it, others deal in metaphors but the poet alone, due to his prophetic gifts, has the visionary abilities to create the metaphors.[45] The influence of the *Defence* can be traced in the works of later writers, including those of the Romantic school, particularly Shelley, who wrote his own *Defence of Poetry*, Coleridge and Wordsworth, in their attitudes to poetic inspiration. Sidney's argument that poetry does not imitate what already has existence, but creates from the poet's mind, seems to contradict the concept of the *pictura poesis*[*] which he delineates. The imitation which Sidney suggests the 'right poet' creates is not related to the nature of material things, but rather to the shapes of the divine mind, referring, in fact, to Neo-platonic concepts of the Forms.[†] Modern literary theory has associated these concepts of poetry with twentieth-century theories of semiotics, in its discussion of the metaphoric nature of poetry.[46]

Extended Commentary: More, *Utopia* (1516), Book II

As J. H. Hexter persuasively argues, Book II of *Utopia* seems to have been written during a protracted diplomatic mission to the Netherlands in the service of Henry VIII.[47] It may be imagined that conversations

* *Pictura poesis*: literally, a poetic picture. Horace used the phrase '*ut pictura poesis*' in his *Ars Poetica* (*c*. 20 B.C.), which translates as 'as is painting, so is poetry'.

† Plato developed the theory that all things which had their existence on earth, and were discernible by the senses, were in fact reflections of their pure and abstract Forms, which existed outside time and space.

within More's humanist circle of acquaintances during this time, regarding problems of governance, and political and social evils of their times may have prompted More to begin the work. As indicated above, it introduces an 'ideal' society which, despite benefiting from numerous social advantages, nonetheless, raises important questions about the nature of citizenship and the role of personal rights within a moral commonwealth.

The social organisation of *Utopia* is founded upon the provision of a stable and adequate standard of living for all members of society, in return for productive output and the co-operation of all members towards the benefit of the commonwealth. As a result of their admirable organisational skills, a temperate climate, and an equitable attitude to work, the people are never without food and all contribute to its production: 'Agriculture is the one occupation at which everyone works, men and women alike, with no exceptions' (Book II: 36). No individual is in a position to benefit from the system without contributing to it, contrasting with the evils of a hierarchical class system, based on wealth and personal possessions, identified in Book I. The work ethic is so strictly-endorsed, in fact, that any Utopian who wishes to travel away from home must not only obtain permission to leave her or his own area and tasks, but must undertake work at their destination if they stay anywhere for longer than a day:

> ... he gets no food until he has completed either a morning's or afternoon's stint of work. On these terms he may go where he pleases within his own district, yet be just as useful to the community as if he were at home. (Book II: 45)

As Hythloday points out, there is no opportunity to indulge in fruitless activities or idleness and the community necessarily benefits from the continuity of production. As the fruits of their labour are divided amongst all 'such a life style must necessarily result in plenty of life's good things' (Book II: 45). The conversational style of presentation masks the underlying deeply philosophical precepts that lie beneath. As George Logan persuasively argues, *Utopia* mirrors the 'inveterate Greek practice of comparing polities'.[48] Apart from the Platonic concepts of *The Republic* and *Laws* alluded to in *Utopia*, Logan suggests that More also engages with Aristotelian theory as presented in the *Politics*.

Fundamental concepts of well-being for the individual form the basis for More's social and political organisation, as illustrated above, which align with Aristotle's explicit announcement that the determining of an ideal constitution relies upon discovering the 'the most desirable way of life'.[49] Hythloday's learning, called to attention by the character 'More' in Book I, is evident here as the author More has him articulate his view of Utopia through recognisable classical theories of the ideal commonwealth. Although relatively obscure to most modern-day readers, these were familiar to his readership due to Renaissance humanist educational practice.

Rational Organisation versus Human Emotion

Although the description of Utopia is narrated by Hythloday uninterrupted, 'More' had already introduced a note of scepticism when its principal tenets were introduced in Book I, thus priming the reader to maintain a critical distance from the account of the exemplary society of Book II. 'More' supplied objections to the commonality of goods, for example, citing loss of ambition, induced indolence and increased bloodshed if individuals were denied legal protection of their own gains. Hythloday is unable to apprehend the human anomalies created within the constraints of an inflexible social contract.

Aside from their expedient attitude to population control which deploys individuals to locations as necessity requires, perhaps the most disturbing and inhumane aspect of *Utopia*'s constitution is its dependence upon slaves. Slavery is considered a practical and just punishment for Utopians who commit severe crimes. Compared with the transitory spectacles of capital punishment, used for deterrence in Europe, these individuals serve as perpetual living examples, whilst benefiting the state by their labour. A second type of slave is the condemned men of other nations, who the Utopians either buy 'at a very modest rate' or acquire *gratis* (Book II: 59), specifically for this purpose. The final class is unusual in that they are non-Utopians who choose to endure a life of slavery on the island in preference to freedom in their home land. Even within the institution of slavery there is a hierarchy, however, as these people are treated 'almost as citizens' and are free to return home if they wish, with a parting gift (Book II: 59). Slaves do all the heavy, dirty work and anything deemed unsuitable for citizens, including the slaughtering of animals. They are always fettered, albeit with manacles of gold and silver, and if they rebel are put to death. Although it is difficult for a modern reader to align the Utopian judicial practice with Christian or humanitarian principles, it must be remembered that slavery was commonplace at the time of writing and More's policy would be seen as being led by political necessity and the greater benefit of the commonwealth.

As required in numerous contemporary and inherited theories of social order, each individual has their own trade, to which they must adhere.* Underlining the general lack of accommodation of human emotion, however, in Utopia the rationalisation of this precept declares that a child who does not wish to follow his father's [*sic*] trade must be adopted into a family which practises the trade of choice (Book II: 37), regardless of personal ties. Other denials of individualism include all homes being exactly the same and exchanged frequently; enforced participation in communal activity, overseen by elders; and a dress code which decrees that all dress alike in plain undyed and unadorned garments.

Women's Roles and Working Conditions

Besides the general training in agriculture, all women are instructed in a trade, although they engage in the 'lighter' crafts, such as cloth production. There does not seem to be provision for girls to move families and trades, as their brothers do, and women are responsible for all family-related chores, in addition to their trade. These include the

* *The Republic* similarly makes this proviso. Robert Adams (ed.) draws attention to the trades missing from the list which More provides, suggesting that there seem to be no producers of books, glassware, armour, ships and many other articles in use on the island. *Utopia*, Norton Critical Edition, p. 36 n6.

meal organisation and production for the extended family of up to 390 people, by rota, and the more mundane cleaning, child care, laundry, and of family garment production.[50] A further inequality is enshrined in the 'Last Feast' rituals of each month, when women are required to kneel before their husbands 'to confess their various failings and negligences, and beg forgiveness for their failings' (Book II: 80). Utopia is palpably hierarchical and paternalistic in this and other requirements but, nonetheless, is presented as an equal society.

Working conditions are immeasurably better for the Utopians than their English counterparts, as they benefit from a highly-organised system of production. It requires only six hours' work each day from the able-bodied, which is rendered less taxing by being divided into two stretches, separated by a period of rest. As they rise early, there is ample time before work to attend public lectures, a particularly popular pastime, but not obligatory. After the evening's communal meal Utopians amuse themselves for an hour in conversation, playing music, doing mathematical puzzles or playing board games modelled on medieval morality themes, before their eight o'clock bedtime. How seriously More intended this to be taken is open to question, but the 'vices' of laziness and idleness preoccupy him as a drain on society's resources. Via Hythloday he condemns the 'idlers' who contribute nothing but consume twice as much as the workers, suggesting that re-distribution of labour would create a labour system which made only reasonable demands on all (Book II: 39).

Many of More's innovations in Utopia were radical to his contemporaries, and while some are no doubt intended to amuse, as in the naked inspection of proposed marriage partners, they often have respectable classical provenance. The modern reader is often at a disadvantage in not recognising these, but even a contemporary of More's could expect little help in unravelling his intentions. Reviewing the conflicting critical reponses to *Utopia*, David Halpin concludes that no matter whether More's proposals are serious, or primarily satirical, 'Utopia draws us into an imaginary perfected world, the comprehension of which helps one to think differently and critically about existing reality'.[51]

Notes

1 Edward L. Surtz discusses the religious implications of the text in detail in his 'Humanism and Communism', an extract from *The Praise of Pleasure* (Cambridge, Mass.: Harvard University Press, 1957) reprinted in Sir Thomas More, *Utopia*, Norton Critical Edition, translated and edited by Robert M. Adams (New York and London: W. W. Norton and Company, 1957, 2nd edn 1975), pp. 169–81. See also J. H. Hexter (ed.), *The Complete Works of Sir Thomas More* (New Haven: Yale University Press, 1965).

2 John Hale, 'A World Elsewhere' in *The Age of the Renaissance* (London: Thames and Hudson, 1967), pp. 338, 339.

3 'Therefore, I beg you my dear Peter, to get in touch with Hythloday – in person if you can, or by letters if he's gone,' Thomas More to Peter Giles, the prefatory letter to the volume, reproduced in 'The Humanist Circle: Letters', Thomas More, *Utopia*, Norton Critical Edition, pp. 108–33, p. 111.

4 See Neil Cornwall's definition in the online *Literary Encyclopedia*.

5 For discussion of the individuals' fitness to advise, see Plato, *Republic*, translated by Robin Waterfield (Oxford: Oxford University Press, 1993, World's Classics edn, 1994), p. xxxiv.

6 Plato, *Republic*, 8: 473d.

7 Seneca, *De otio* III: 3, quoted in George M. Logan, *The Meaning of More's 'Utopia'* (Princeton: Princeton University Press, 1983), p. 103.

8 Plato, *Republic*, 5: 416e, 417b.

9 *Complete Works of Sir Thomas More*, 'Sources, Parallels and Influences', p. cliv.

10 Travis Decook, 'Utopian Communcation', *English Language Studies*, 48:1 (2008), pp. 1–22.

11 Eric Nelson, 'Greek nonsense in More's *Utopia*', *Historical Journal*, 44 (2001), pp. 889–918, pp. 890, 891. See also James Romm, 'More's Strategy of Naming in the Utopia', *The Sixteenth Century Journal*, 22:2 (1991), pp. 173–83.

12 Letter 'More to Giles', cited by J. H. Hexter, 'The Composition of *Utopia*' in *The Complete Works of Sir Thomas More*, vol. 4, p. cxlviii.

13 Plato, *Republic,* 4: 398a, 398b.

14 Plato, *Republic*, 4: 392c, 392d.

15 Neil Rhodes, *The Power of Rhetoric and English Literature* (Hemel Hempstead: Harvester Wheatsheaf, 1992), p. 59.

16 Thomas Wilson, *An English Rhetoric* (1560 extended version) excerpt in Brian Vickers (ed.), *English Renaissance Literary Criticism* (Oxford: Clarendon Press, 1999), pp. 73–124, p. 75. *The Arte of Rhetorique* is available through Early English Books Online (EEBO) electronic resource, Short Title Catalogue number (STC) 25799. See also Andrew Hadfield, *Literature, Politics and National Identity, Reformation to Renaissance* (Cambridge: Cambridge University Press, 1994), p. 109.

17 Wilson in Vickers, p. 77. As Vickers points out, Wilson's 'affective triad' is attributed to Cicero in *Brutus*, re-appears in Horace's *Ars Poetica* and Quintilian's *Institutes*, and subsequently arising in numerous Renaissance discussions of rhetoric: Vickers p. 77 n7.

18 Wilson, 'Preface', in Vickers, p. 76.

19 George Puttenham, *Arte of English Poesie*, ed. by Gladys Doidge Willcock and Alice Walker (Cambridge: Cambridge University Press, 1936 repr. 1970), pp. 289, 299.

20 Wilson, 'Preface', in Vickers, p. 76.

21 Thomas Wilson, *The Arte of Rhetorique* (1560), G. H. Mair (ed.) (Oxford: Benedictine Classics, 1909 repr. 2008), Book I, p. 29.

22 Ryan J. Stark, 'Thomas Wilson's Apocalyptic Rhetoric', *Studies in Philology* 106 (3), pp. 341–53, pp. 341, 342.

23 In this context, see also Nicholas Ridley, *A piteous lamentation of the miserable estate of the churche of Christ in England* (1566) STC 21052 and *Certe[n] godly, learned, and comfortable conferences* (1556) STC 21048; John Aylmer, *A harborowe for faithfull and true subjects* (1559) STC 1005; Thomas Becon, *The actes of Christe and of Antichriste* (1577) STC 1711 and *The displaying of the Popish masse* (misleadingly claims 'published in the dayes of Queene Mary', but it was 1637), STC 1719.

24 The sentence continues in like fashion. Wilson in G. H. Mair (ed.), Book III, pp. 165, 166.

25 See Andrew Hadfield, *Literature, Politics and National Identity, Reformation to Renaissance* (Cambridge: Cambridge University Press, 1994), pp. 108–31.

26 George Puttenham, *Arte of English Poesie* in Vickers, pp. 191–296, pp. 209, 210.

27 Stephen Gosson, *The School of Abuse* (extended title) (1579), available via the University of Oregon's *Renascence Editions*: http://www.uoregon.edu/.

28 See Katherine Duncan-Jones and Jan van Dorsten (eds), *Miscellaneous Prose of Sir Philip Sidney* (Oxford: Clarendon Press, 1973), p. 62. The editors link

Sidney to prominent European writers and their theories of literature, such as Hubert Languet and Henri Estiene, p. 63, but the work also contains summaries of classical authors' thoughts on poetry from a variety of sources.

29 See *The Republic*, III and IV–VII; *Meno* 71–80.

30 Sidney terms these 'poet-haters', who 'seek praise by dispraising others', *A Defence of Poesy* in Duncan-Jones and van Dorsten (eds), pp. 59–121, p. 99.

31 Catherine Barnes, 'The Hidden Persuader: The Complex Speaking Voice of Sidney's *Defence of Poetry*', *PMLA* 86:3 (1971), pp. 422–7, p. 422.

32 Katherine Duncan-Jones and Jan van Dorsten (eds), *The Miscellaneous Prose of Sir Philip Sidney* (Oxford: Clarendon Press, 1973), pp. 59–121, pp. 71, 72. The version of *A Defence*, reproduced in *English Renaissance Literary Criticism*, Brian Vickers (ed.), pp. 336–91 also has the rhetorical divisions.

33 See Kenneth Myrick, *Sir Philip Sidney as a Literary Craftsman* (Lincoln, Nebraska: University of Nebraska Press, 1935 repr. 1965), pp. 46–83 for contemporary and classical resonances.

34 Wilson, G. H. Mair (ed.), Book I, pp. 7, 8.

35 Wilson, G. H. Mair (ed.), Book I, p. 10. See Myrick, p. 58.

36 George Puttenham, *The Arte of English Poesie* (1589), ed. by G. D. Willcock and A. Walker (Cambridge: Cambridge University Press, 1936, repr. 1970), p. 7.

37 *Miscellaneous Prose*, pp. 74–6.

38 *Miscellaneous Prose*, p. 76.

39 *Miscellaneous Prose*, p. 77.

40 *Miscellaneous Prose*, p. 79.

41 *Miscellaneous Prose*, p. 79.

42 *Miscellaneous Prose*, p. 80.

43 Ronald Levao, 'Sidney's Feigned Apology', *PMLA 94:2,* pp. 223–33, p. 227, 228.

44 Levao, p. 231.

45 See R. S. Bear's excellent introduction and discussion in the Renascence edition of Sidney's *Defence*, hosted by the University of Oregon.

46 See 'Sir Philip Sidney: An Apology for Poetry' in the *Norton Anthology of Theory and Criticism*, ed. by William Cain, Laurie Finke *et al* (New York and London: W. W. Norton and Company, 2002), p. 325. For theories of semiotics see Ferdinand de Saussure, 'The Nature of the Linguistic Sign' in David Lodge (ed.), *Modern Criticism and Theory: A Reader* (Harlow, Essex: Addison Wesley Longman Ltd., 1988), p. 10–14.

47 Hexter, pp. xvi–xli.
48 Logan, p. 131.
49 Aristotle, *Politics* (VII: 1323a), cited in Logan, p. 133.
50 Adams, *Utopia*, Norton Critical Edition, p. 43 n1 and p. 38 n9.
51 David Halpin, 'Utopianism and Education: The Legacy of Thomas More', *British Journal of Educational Studies*, 49: 3 (2001), pp. 299–315, p. 308.

Life Guides, Mother's Advice and Conduct Books: Castiglione, Hoby and Whately

Medieval 'courtesy books' were mainly concerned with the domestic courtesy associated with hospitality and manners within the noble household. The Conduct Books of the Renaissance period, by comparison, dealt with almost every aspect of contemporary life. In a social climate of changing roles and expectations, with printed books becoming increasingly available to the more literate general public, handbooks of guidance to assist individuals negotiate their path through life, and even death, became popular. These ranged from academic and scholarly texts to assist professional development, on subjects such as rhetoric and logic; medical texts for a lay readership; spiritual guides; manuals of domestic affairs, including marriage guides; and from the early seventeenth century, Mother's Advice books, often written by pregnant women to their children in case they did not survive the birth.

Imitation and Self-fashioning in Castiglione's *Cortegiano*

One of the most influential of these Conduct Books was Count Baldassare Castiglione's *Il Libro del Cortegiano* of 1528, which was translated and disseminated throughout Europe. Sir Thomas Hoby's English version was probably begun during his retreat to Padua during the reign of Mary I[1] and it was published in England in 1561 as *The Book of the Courtier*. Although it is considered the consummate guide to 'self-fashioning'[2] for the aspiring courtier, close reading reveals underlying social tensions which may seem at odds with its perceived purpose.

The text takes the form of a series of fictional dialogues between members of the court of Urbino in Italy in 1507. Castiglione was based at this court between 1504 and 1508, enjoying the friendship of the named characters and other leading intellectuals of the day, and as Amedeo Quondam points out he and these contemporaries were very familiar with the conflicting demands of court life.[3] The framework for the conversations is the evening gatherings overseen by the Duchess, Elisabetta Gonzaga, after her ailing husband has retired for the night. In an atmosphere of a literary or philosophical salon, verbal entertainments are devised on a nightly basis, to which individuals contribute witty and diverting opinions.

In the prefatory letter addressed to the Bishop of Viseu, Castiglione defends his decision to write in his own Lombardy idiom and refuses to participate in the contemporary debate about appropriate linguistic form for *belles-lettres*.* Ironically, the use of plain regional dialect does make a political point, however, aligning the text with the work of other humanist writers who wrote in vernacular languages, rather than more usual Latin of 'high' literature. He also pre-empts criticism for not emulating the admired prose of Boccaccio (1313–75), claiming that his is a new literary form for which there are no suitable models.† This highlights the importance of imitation to the Renaissance scholar, relevant both to the composition of the text and its content. The educational training of young men throughout Europe was based on this precept and, as Daniel Javitch points out, there is an idealism embedded within the concept in the striving towards a possibility of perfection: 'Indeed, the challenge was to try to attain the greatest

* French: 'fine literature', especially aesthetically pleasing and embellished works.

† Giovanni Boccaccio was an Italian humanist poet and author and a contemporary of Petrarch. His most famous works are *The Decameron* (*c.* 1349–51) and *De Mulieribus Claris* (Of Famous Women) (*c.* 1369).

similarity to the model, and even if one could not equal its perfection, to come as close as one's capacity allowed.'[4]

Castiglione's claim is to provide as complete a guide as possible to the required skills of the profession, firmly setting the book within the parameters of the didactic Conduct Book genre. The implied outcome is that, through conscientious application, it is possible to acquire proficiency and the flair of a consummate courtier, learned by imitation with expert guidance. Modern day criticism often tends towards deconstruction of the precept, however, focusing on anomalies within this premise.

Class Tensions: Reliable Narrator or *Agent Provocateur*?

In Book I, Count Ludovico da Canossa, one of the Duchess's circle, seems to state uncompromisingly that the perfect courtier should be of noble birth, as the 'lustre of nobility' which guides him to virtue and great acts 'for fear of dishonour' does not inspire those of lowly birth (Book I: 14). He intimates that a natural essence of virtue and honour, '*grazia*' (grace), is inherited by the sons of the nobility. In a seeming contradiction, however, 'those that are not so perfectly endowed by nature can, with care and effort, polish and in great part correct their natural defects' (Book I: 14). Reverting back to the natural superiority of the highest social classes, he maintains that noble birth 'is always honoured … because it stands to reason that good should beget good' (Book I: 16). If the book is intended as a guide to the *achievement* of courtly skills, it seems to be self-defeating in Canossa's terms. Read literally, the ideology propounded within these arguments represents the hegemony of the ruling classes throughout Europe. In Raymond Williams's terms, 'the whole lived social process as practically organised by specific and dominant meanings, values and beliefs of a kind that can be abstracted as a "world-view" or "class outlook"'.[5]

Against this claim, however, Jennifer Richards suggests that Castiglione deliberately places untenable or paradoxical arguments within the text to encourage his readers to question them. She asserts that both sides of the argument are gradually revealed, requiring active readership to evaluate and draw independent conclusions.[6] As Canossa protests that he is not qualified to instruct on this subject, for example, his pronouncements might be expected to be faulty. Conversely, his light rejection of his expertise may be an example of *sprezzatura* (discussed below). Richards identifies imitation of Cicero's *De oratore* in this rhetorical game of *dissimulatio.*[*] As she points out, in response to the interventions by Fregoso, another courtier, Canossa gradually adjusts his perspective, going on to suggest that his original claims were actually intended to be controversial and prompt dissent:

> Throughout the discussion, Canossa is committed to the idea that all we need is talent and a willingness to adopt the contemporary linguistic idiom, but he needs to defend his position against an interlocutor, Fregoso, who champions the need for imitation.[7]

Such contradictions arise frequently within the text. Initially, for example, Fregoso declares that the courtier's devotion to his prince demands 'all his thought and strength of spirit' conditioning his 'every desire and habit and manner' in concerted effort to please (Book II: 18). This idealistic aim is compromised by the later suggestion that situations should be managed to gain maximum recognition for one's service. Similarly, the suggestion that good service gains recognition and favour is also undermined in this section when the discussion moves to the powers of a ruler to accept or reject a courtier's suit at will:

> … although he may be quick at repartee and may cut a good figure by his gestures, manners, words, and all else that is needful, [sometimes] … a prince will show that he esteems him little, nay, will be the readier to offend him in some way … so that he can be the worthiest man in the world and still be put down and derided. (Book II: 32)[8]

* Latin: dissemblance, the concealment of truth, especially in a didactic or oratorical context.

Similar objections are raised in Sir Thomas More's *Utopia* in the famous 'Dialogue of the Counsel' section, which suggests the precariousness of life at court and the difficulties of a man of honour in a corrupt environment.*

'*Sprezzatura*': Nature versus Artifice

One of the most cited sections of *The Courtier* is the discussion of the sophisticated nonchalance cultivated by the courtier to enhance his profile. The neologism used to express this is '*sprezzatura*', meaning the casual detachment and deprecation with which he performs artful feats, whether conversational, poetic, musical or of any other admired talent. In Canossa's terms, the *sprezzatura* is to be prized above the accomplishments, he paradoxically claims: 'we may call that art true art which does not seem to be art' (Book I: 26). The resemblance between self-conscious performance and the overt display of Renaissance art and literature often draws critical comment: this is self-presentation as a dexterous tableau. Just as scholars appropriated impressive verbal flourishes to introduce them into their own works, the courtier is urged to emulate the desirable traits of his companions, becoming a composite living image of Renaissance manners and good taste. Jean Baudrillard's† theories of the 'loss of the real' might question whether the courtier's superficial persona bears any relation to the 'real' person below. In post-modern terms, the representation, or simulacra, takes the place of the article it is intended to represent and the 'game' of representation then becomes itself 'self-validating', providing the desired social identity.[9]

Count Canossa suggests that, in order to preserve the notion of *grazia*, the artfulness of the performance must be concealed by a manner which suggests ease of accomplishment. This duplicitous environment is termed by Harry Berger Jr 'a self-fulfilling culture of suspicion', where nothing is quite as represented. As he goes on to cite, Eduardo Saccone has argued

* See Part Three: 'Humanist Prose and Rhetoric' and Part Four: 'City, Court and Country'.

† Jean Baudrillard: French sociologist and post-modern theorist, his *The Perfect Crime* (1996), investigates the 'loss of the real' in modern society.

that this effectively creates two audiences: the initiated who understand the artificiality of the performance and the naïve who are duped by the deception.[10] The vested interests of the nobility are revealed in this situation, in what amounts to coded behaviour. Their 'insider' status ensures understanding of the situation and they are able to indicate to the rulers awareness of the duplicitous nature of court life, demanding maintenance of appearance and ceremony in even the most adverse of situations. By contrast, the 'upstart' newcomers misread the elitist signals, which intend to exclude them.[11]

Love that brings 'Neither blame nor Displeasure'

At the Duchess's request the discussion of the last evening eventually turns to love (Book IV: 50). The vision that Pietro Bembo describes as desirable for a mature courtier is derived from Plato's *Symposium* and negotiates a *scala*, or ladder, of appreciation, beginning with the sensual love of one beautiful individual and gradually ascending to the source of all beauty and goodness, God. A modern outlook has difficulty accepting the Renaissance commonplaces which Bembo articulates to reach this point, however:

> Beauty springs from God and is like a circle, the centre of which is goodness. And hence, as there can be no circle without a centre, there can be no beauty without goodness. Thus a wicked soul rarely inhabits a beautiful body, and for that reason outward beauty is a true sign of inner goodness … Hence, the wicked are also ugly, for the most part, and the beautiful are good … (Book IV: 57, 58)

Bembo reveals that the limiting effects of sensual love can only be overcome when the courtier is capable of appreciating the universal concept of beauty. The chain leads to appreciation of the beauty of the intellect and on to the 'universal intellect', which works upon the soul until, 'aflame with the most holy fire of true divine love, [it] flies to unite itself with the angelic nature' (Book IV: 68). Although readers frequently find this metaphysical dialogue at odds with the worldly and political tone of the first three books, Lawrence Ryan suggests that the discussion of ideal love is in keeping with the earlier books, providing a 'proper climax to the whole', in that the Neo-platonic theory of love provides an underpinning vision of a moral society.[12]

Since the sixteenth century the 'structural break'[13] of Book IV has provoked speculation, owing to its contrast with the ideals of the previous three sections. J. R. Woodhouse convincingly argues that the altered focus is predicated upon the protracted production time and subsequent revisions of the text. Highlighting Castiglione's own changed circumstances between 1508 and the mid 1520s, when he became Papal Nuncio, he raises the possibility that Castiglione may have wished to disassociate himself from the trivial and lavish life of the court. Woodhouse suggests that sections published by Vittoria Colonna,* without Castiglione's assent, may have threatened his prospects of career advancement, particularly as the courtier depicted was quite widely considered to be a self-portrait.[14] Castiglione's 1528 revision of the text adjusted the earlier books to compliment the more moralistic tone of the fourth book. In places, for example, he justifies courtly accomplishments, provided that they inspire and guide the ruler to positive acts.[15]

Thomas Hoby's *The Courtier*

Thomas Hoby's translation of the text (1561) generated both effusive praise and scathing assessment in almost equal measure. It was a very influential and prized text during its own time, but later commentators have remarked upon the 'poor' quality of translation and prose, prompting one translator to comment, 'It is certain however, that Sir Thomas did not understand his Author'.[16] However, as Richards notes, what some critics miss is the sympathy which Hoby demonstrates with

* Vittoria Colonna (1480–1547): a gifted poet especially remembered for her Petrarchan-style sonnets, as documented in Castiglione's own preface. She was responsible for the initial unauthorised circulation of *Il Libro del Cortegiano.*

Castiglione's stated preference for vernacular speech.[17] Hence, the complaints of 'rough' or 'unpolished' language should rather be appreciated as artistic effect, rather than denigrated as impaired knowledge of Italian. Most interesting, within this context of linguistic proficiency, is the observation that the 1588 edition seems to have been intended as a self-help text for foreign language study. [18] This volume presented the original Italian text, side by side with Hoby's English translation, and also a French version, presumably also prepared by Hoby.

Fluid grace in modern foreign languages, especially French and Italian, was a necessity to the courtier, in order to entertain and demonstrate his learning, but also to accomplish diplomatic tasks at home or abroad. Hoby most probably used John Palsgrave's *Lesclarcissement de la langue francoyse* (1530) for his own study, and it is likely that his 1588 edition of *The Courtier* was used in a similar fashion, especially as it was multi-lingual.

The format of Hoby's 1588 edition clearly indicates its place within the genre of Protestant 'self-help' manuals, in its annotations for ease of use, with headings and important points highlighted for quick reference.* These later editorial additions align it with the reformers' religious texts, such as the Tyndale and Geneva Bibles, which encouraged study via their useful marginalia, summarising points, and directions to linked verses. Just as the new religion gave individuals personal responsibility for their own spiritual development, the advice manuals encouraged active participation in personal matters of social advancement, healing and health.

Family Values and Domestic Guides

Although some self-help guides were prompted by a philanthropic outlook, intended to equip individuals with skills to influence their own

* Jennifer Richards draws attention to Peter Burke's study which identifies in the 1561 edition '38 aids … [and] marginal glosses for use as an index and an appended summary of the chief qualities desirable in the male courtier', p. 478.

destinies, the popular marriage guides were mostly concerned with maintaining the status quo of a patriarchal hierarchy. The thorny questions of authority and subservience with which they dealt had their roots in complex ideological controversies about early modern gender roles and the role of marriage in post-Reformation society.* According to Protestant doctrine, marriage was no longer a sacrament, in that it was not a requirement for salvation, although it was ennobled as 'pleasing to God' and desirable for all members of society. A celibate life was considered undesirable and unattainable for most, as it required a special and rare gift. It was far better to honour God from within the confines of a godly marriage. Although the term 'companionate marriage' is often used in discussion of the period, the extent to which it was achieved in reality is questionable, as women were completely subject to their husbands. It is for this reason that scholarly opinion differs as to whether women were empowered or further restricted by the new reformed focus on the family.

The family unit was considered to mirror the larger overarching social hierarchy and was responsible for inculcating religious and moral values. Robert Cleaver's opening lines of *A godly forme of household government* (1598) encapsulated contemporary opinion: 'A household is as it were a little commonwealth, by good government whereof God's glorie may be advanced'.[19] Attempts to control and repress, so characteristic of the authoritarian regulation of the era, can be understood as responses to contemporary religious, political and social tensions. As is often pointed out, conflicting attitudes and practices often seem to co-exist in the era and it is impossible to discover how far the published prescriptive texts on marriage reflected or modelled actual relationships between spouses. The more repressive Puritan tracts seem to outline a state of permanent near-warfare, while extant letters and diaries and some Mothers' Legacies (see below) give evidence of warmer reciprocal affections than might be expected.[20]

* See Part Four: 'The Woman Debate'.

'Holy matrimonie' versus 'a trap set for flies'

As Sara Mendelson and Patricia Crawford note, although there is a wealth of material describing married life for this period, 'Nearly all of it was written by men, who focused on the relationship between husband and wife from the husband's perspective'.[21] Although the female encomia,* which overlap somewhat with marriage advice texts, do sometimes emphasise the comfort of a 'good' wife, to a great degree the latter tend to emphasise the negative aspects of married life or adopt an adversarial position. Embedded attitudes towards female inferiority emphasise, for example, the necessity of a husband's maintaining authority over his wife, asserting his divinely-ordained right, as a matter of male dignity but also for the sake of social order. Because the family was a basic foundation upon which all of society depended, it was imperative that all members accepted their duties and limitations within the edifice. During Henry VIII's reign a set of homilies (sermons) was produced to reinforce theories of social order. On a regular and recurring basis notions of pious and civic obedience were in this way intertwined and delivered from the pulpit; a woman's disobedience towards her husband therefore had legal and religious significance. Emphasising the 'filthiness' of the lusts of the flesh, the 'Homily on the State of Matrimonie' presents the function of marriage as a necessary strategy of avoidance:

> … to bring foorth fruite, and to auoide Fornication. By which meane a good conscience might bee preserued on both parties, in brideling the corrupt inclinations of the flesh, within the limites of honestie.[22]

Unsurprisingly, the emphasis in this sermon is on Christian duty, rather than pleasure, but the view is generally negative, pointing out that strife is inevitable: 'few Matrimonies there be without chidings, brawlings, tauntings, repentings, bitter cursings, and fightings … [leading to] the

* Encomia: a formal expression of praise such as a eulogy or panegyric.

provocation of wrath, which stirreth them either to such rough and sharpe words, or stripes [whipping]'. The insoluble link of marriage clearly for many was a state of unholy misery.

As might be expected, marriage guides, therefore, often dwell upon the criteria by which to select a 'good' wife and warnings against being led astray by beauty, youth or the 'foolish flames' of love. Francis Osborne's *Advice to a Son* (1656) devotes an entire cautionary section to 'Love and Marriage'.[23] The casual misogyny gathers momentum as it progresses, mixing metaphors in its spleen. Osborne initially describes women as refreshing beverages during the heat of passion, but shortly after as 'painted boxes' which hide their poison from the naïve (p. 59). Returning to the same imagery later, he declares that once the fruits of love are enjoyed, 'children and time will empty [the box] of delight, leaving diseases behind and, at best, incurable antiquity' (p. 62). Osborne's tenor intensifies as he warms to his subject, advising 'Marriage, like a trap set for flies, may possibly be anointed at the entrance with a little voluptuousness'. The subsequent sections progress from biblical citation 'proving' that all women inherit Eve's inability to resist the 'heat of lust and pride', to warnings that if his wife is 'impotent or infected, as not a few are' he has no recourse to law or religion by which to sever himself from her (pp. 63, 64). His virulent imagination darkly outlines the cuckolding of a new husband by a calculating wife, aided by female members of the family for rewards of new gowns. Protesting against English customs which prevent women's isolation in the home, he warns that without care it may become as 'populous as a confectioner's shop' lewdly suggesting that 'gaudy wasps no less than lickerish flies make it their business to resort [there] in hope of obtaining a lick at you[r] honeypot' (p. 64).

The cynical sentiments expressed are based on an underlying misogyny, predicated upon *a priori** beliefs about women's nature.† These same attitudes inform not only supposedly humorous jokes, ballads and 'Woman Debate' pamphlets, but also more serious genres such as legal, religious and courtesy literature. Osborne's bitter

* *A priori*: pre-existing.

† See Part Four: 'The Woman Debate'.

denigration of women's supposed immorality is not only a caustic warning against marriage, but also a biting polemic against women generally and married women in particular. The editor points out, however, that the work was not intended for Osborne's son's private perusal and, as a satire on women, may be a bid for commercial success, intended to appeal to the tastes of a young male readership.*

'The web of all miseries, and sorrowes'

Despite the unmitigated male suffering depicted by Osborne, he does not detail the precise duties of either spouse, nor comment upon the chastisement of erring wives. William Gouge's earlier *Of Domesticall Duties* (1622) very precisely delineates the attitudes and correct demeanour of spouses towards each other, based on the Scriptures and helpfully divided under sub-headings for ease of consultation. In the 'Third Treatise', a lengthy section entitled 'Of the duties of Wives', for example, he lists and extemporises on such topics as 'Of a wife's acknowledgement of her own husband's superiority' and 'Of wives denying honour to [their] own husbands'. The volume also has wide margins on each page, which contain a plethora of cross-references, helpful summaries and biblical references, all of which give it the gravitas of similarly-annotated religious works. Explicitly noting the divine pleasure which decrees a wife's subordination, Gouge lists the precise reasons why women should accept their inferiority. These include linguistic customs, the primacy of creation in Genesis, and biblical endorsement, in for example, St Paul's 'an husband representeth Christ' (Ephesians 5:23).[24] Should a woman be mistreated in marriage, Gouge insists that she must endure her lot:

> Though an husband in regard of evill qualities may carrie the Image of the devil, yet in regard of his place and office he beareth the image of God. (pp. 272, 273)

* Louis B. Wright (ed.), *Advice for a Son,* pp. xxiv, xxv. Wright draws attention to its massive popularity with Oxford University undergraduates, which in 1658 prompted the Vice-Chancellor to forbid any further sales in the town, p. xxv. By 1689 it had gone into nine editions.

Although he maintains that a woman has honour in marriage, Gouge's main concern is the establishment and maintenance of order within the household, which is predicated upon a wife's willing acceptance and internalisation of her inferiority. To those women who complain that the decreed 'servitude' is slavery, he acknowledges that this is a bitter pill but nonetheless is a duty, comparable to the husband's different responsibilities within matrimony. In similar publications the training of a wife is often compared to the 'breaking' of a horse and Gouge demonstrates a like attitude. He emphasises the psychological adjustment necessary, stating that it is not enough that a wife performs the outward rituals of honouring her husband's status, voluntary acquiescence and belief in her inferior status is vital:

> [Subjection] may be forced, as one King conquered in battell by another, may be compelled to yield homage to the conquerer, but yet because he still thinketh with himselfe, that he is no whit inferior … but rather expect a time when he may free himselfe and take revenge of the conqueror. (p. 270)

The unexpectedly military semantic field underlines anxiety of female insubordination and rebellion. Although often limited to single sentences, a surprising number of the manuals do discreetly draw attention to the dangers of allowing hatred to ferment. Robert Cleaver, alert to the destructive possibilities of a wife's revenge, stresses 'his goodes are in danger, his house in suspition, his credit in balance and also sometimes his life in peril'.[25] Seventy years later, Edward Tilney similarly warned 'the man that is not lyked, and loved by his mate, holdeth his lyfe in continuall peril, his goods in great jeopardie, his good name is suspect and his whole house in perdition'.[26] Although Tilney's 'perill' may be read metaphorically, Cleaver feels compelled to face the unspoken obvious: 'it is easie to believe that she desireth not long life unto her husband, with whom she passeth a time so tedious and irksome'.[27] Catherine Belsey notes that husbands' fear of murder by their wives seems to have far out-weighed the documentary evidence of actual crimes perpetrated during the late Elizabethan period.[28] The husband murders that were documented in gory trial pamphlets, chronicles and even popular plays and ballads, emphasise the 'monstrousness' of the women, as the crime symbolised the subversive overturning of male authority.[29]

Diagrams of Duty: William Whately

William Whately's *A Bride-Bush* (1617) presents itself as a self-help manual to avoid the common 'woes', 'discontentment' and 'annoyance' of married life, claiming to 'pleade the case of marriage' by directing the couple to their duties. Despite his somewhat truculent tone in the prefatory letter, in which he urges the reader to take notice of his advice or 'be ignorant still', Whately seems to be more conciliatory than similar manuals – five chapters are devoted to love between the couple.[30] In a splendidly formatted diagrammatic contents list he articulates the interrelated and dependent aspects of love, which are then subdivided and divided again, illustrating his hierarchical and orderly rationale. The resulting theory is solidly pragmatic, however, listing under 'The means of attaining [love]', the dual header 'pleasingnesse and faithfulnesse', which is revealed to mean a woman's appropriate attitude to the man's 'name' and 'goods' amongst other things. The duties of husband and wife are presented in this same branched configuration, which replicates the format of rhetorical orations or sermons, the coherent structure of which aided memorisation. One can imagine a wayward wife being set sections to learn by rote as training or punishment.

'Whether a man may beat his wife; yea or no'

The main duty of the husband, unsurprisingly, is 'To governe or rule', which is sub-divided into 'To keep his authority' and 'To use his authority'. The latter divides into 'The parts of authority', 'The end of authority' and 'The manner, by practicing three virtues'. These are defined as 'Justice', 'Wisdom' and 'Mildness', all of which have notes regarding which parts of the text deal with these responsibilities (second contents page). Gina Hausknecht draws attention to these fundamental difficulties revealed in the text in its attempts to balance authority with mutual responsibility and love.[31]

In chapter 9 the duties of a 'governor' are discussed generally with the addition of a sentence allowing the husband to use reproaches upon his wife, including punishment. This is defined as 'withdrawing from her the plentifull demonstrations of kindnesse and the fruits of his liberalitie', including restrictions on her liberty and the 'enjoyment of many things delightful' (p. 106). The controversial subject of how far a man is entitled to physically punish his wife is embedded within the lexis of care and duty.[32] In common with most guides, Whately emphasises strongly the wife's need to internalise belief in her inferiority and the prevailing attitude is that, if she does not do so, she is at fault and this will bring upon herself deserved punishment.

Although he takes pains to stress that to resort to blows 'seemeth too impious in him to doe it, and too servile in her to suffer it' Whately struggles to align idealistic rhetoric with common practice. Offering chilling insights, he asks whether it is 'to err in love' to 'smite her on the face or to fetch bloud or blewness to the flesh' and if a man could bring himself to kiss the face that 'he hath laid upon with his fist, or with a cudgel'. Despite prompting the conscience to repudiate the barbarity, he does not offer outright condemnation, however, and allows that if a wife were to act in a foolish, childish or 'slavish' manner he sees no reason why the 'rod, staffe, or wand, should not be for the fooles back' (pp. 106–7).

The miserable state of the abused wife is revealed in chapter 14 of the guide. The wife is cautioned that even if she is struck without cause, she must accept the blow with humility, never rebelling against her husband's authority in word or gesture. If she is in mortal danger she may call upon the protection of the Magistrate, but in all cases must return to her husband without complaint. Observing that 'some men are so violent, as the wife may be in danger to have her braines knocked out', Whately eulogises those who keep the place that God has ordained for them, like good soldiers who know that 'in loosing his life, hee shall find it, because he chuseth rather to loose it doing his dutie, than save it by omission thereof' (p. 214).

Mother's Legacies

Death was a constant companion in this era from recurring outbreaks of disease such as smallpox, 'consumption' (tuberculosis), 'sweating sickness', 'the flux', 'tertian fever' and the bubonic plague.[33] As Lawrence Stone so aptly puts it, 'Death was at the centre of life, as the cemetery was at the centre of the village'.[34] For women in the first decade of marriage particularly, the threat was particularly felt, not primarily as a result of the violence outlined above, but in the grave dangers of childbirth. Diaries and letters poignantly record literate women's fears for their unborn children and of dying in childbed, although recent research suggests that maternal mortality figures were not as high as the women believed.[35] Thomas Forbes's research indicates, for example, that in the years 1583 to 1599, one London parish recorded deaths of seventy-six mothers in childbirth, equating a 2.35 per cent likelihood of dying. For the same parish he calculates that only seventy per cent of babies might be expected to survive until their first birthday and after weaning exposure to contaminated food and drink worsened the survival statistics.[36] Although this can only provide a snapshot of mortalities in one place in particular circumstances, it does underline the close proximity with death under which families existed.[37]

Childbearing and Salvation: Dorothy Leigh's *Mother's Blessing*

Within the animated debates about women's role in society, and marriage in particular, one fact remained indisputable: her biology determined both her perceived weaknesses and her value. Woman was a discordant union; aligned on the one hand with Eve, symbolising man's downfall, and on the other the Virgin Mary, representing his salvation. To the Renaissance imagination the common factor was motherhood. Eve, mother of all human life, was condemned to pain in childbirth when she was cast from Eden, and through the multiplying of mankind, the Virgin Mary eventually gave birth to Jesus Christ, mankind's saviour. Defined through Eve's 'inherited' wayward tendencies, contemporary woman expected to bear the travails of birth as punishment for her own and inherited sins. Anticipating an early death, Dorothy Leigh* wrote a manual of guidance for her sons, in the genre now recognised as 'Mother's Advice Books'. In this she states her belief that by atoning for Eve's sin in their suffering, women participate in the Virgin's redeeming act, regaining pre-lapsarian blamelessness:

> … what a blessing God hath sent to us women through the gracious Virgin, by whom it pleased God to take away the shame, which Eve our Grandmother had brought us to … Here is this great and woful shame taken from women by God, working in women; man can claime no part in it …[38†]

The maternal authority that Leigh claims for educating and guiding her sons in a godly life lies well within contemporary marriage guides' principles and the requirements of a good wife's duties. In the opening chapters of her *Mother's Blessing* (1616), nonetheless, she feels the necessity to explain her reasons for actually writing and publishing the work. Her bold statement 'neither care I what you [her sons] nor any shall thinke of mee' involuntarily acknowledges that within early seventeenth-century English society a woman appearing in print was considered immodest.

As becomes apparent as Leigh's guide progresses, she was a widow with three young sons and expected to die shortly. Her resolute aim to raise the children within her ardent Puritan faith gives her the courage to write in order to persuade them to 'labour for the spirituall food of the soule' from her grave.[39] As she states on the opening page, she considers the work to be a legacy, placing greater value on moral and spiritual guidance than on enriching them 'with transitory goods', despite her gentry background and the family's obvious landholding

* Dorothy [Kempe] Leigh (birth date unknown, died 1616): a Puritan mother of gentlewoman status whose maternal advice book for her sons was, nonetheless, dedicated to King James's daughter, Princess Elizabeth of Bohemia.

† Aemila Lanyer similarly links women's suffering in childbirth with their innocence, although the association is explicitly with Christ's suffering, rather than Mary's. See discussion of Lanyer's *Salve Deus* (1611) in Part Four: 'The Woman Debate'.

status. Chapter 44, for example, focuses on ethical business dealings, one section most insistently demanding that nothing be sold nor let to the ungodly, and especially that farms not be let to 'ani that thou doest not think to bee a true servant of God'. Frequently adopting a didactic and liturgical tone, in the repeated 'It is a sin', this entire chapter emphasises keenly the necessity to support and fraternise with 'the brethren' of believers and to disassociate oneself from the 'Enemy of God'. Leigh presents an embattled perspective, pointing out that reciprocity of kindly interest and preservation will not be found outside of the godly community, 'He will not bee liberal to the poore children of God, considering their wants as if they were his owne: for he hath no naturall affection towards them, because they are not his brethren'.[40] Concerned to avoid usurping God's office of judging the misdirected, she nonetheless advises that her sons use the 'discerning eye of faith' in order to know 'the child of God from a civill man' and, whilst praying for the latter, to favour their co-religionists. Leigh's belief system points to a closed system of circulating wealth and opportunity as, in her eyes, material gains are the gift of God and it is sinful to pass them on to unbelievers: 'Thou mai not impart the benefits of God ... but to those who[m] thou knowest be the lords true servants'.[41]

The work actually addresses a dual audience, as it was not written in manuscript for Leigh's sons' private use, but was published for general dissemination and, in fact, achieved great popularity. Her fifth chapter seems to indicate that she aims for a wide female readership, in that she specifically addresses women, to encourage them not to be ashamed by their 'infirmities'. She predictably associates these with inherited sin through Eve's transgression, but maintains that women therefore need to show how ardently they seek Christ to 'cast it out' and guide children in piety.[42] Leigh's own godly guidance is, of course, the text, and it is considered to have persuaded other women to write in the genre.

Whether looking to the distant future or consciously pitching the work to this wider adult readership, Leigh's tone often addresses matters which seem far from the experience of pre-pubescent grammar school boys, such as discussion of trials of a woman's chastity and instructions on how to deal with servants and choose a wife. Nonetheless, some of the engaging allegorical passages seem intended to capture the imagination of her children. Warning of the devil's wiles, for example, she animates her dialogue with rural imagery pertaining to fowling and fishing, familiar to boys of her time. In an interesting reversal of the familiar 'Fisher of Men' imagery associated with Christ, for example, she figures the devil as a wily fisherman, skilled in the preparation of a variety of poisonous baits to suit each soul that he desires to draw into hell. Her lively imagery speaks to the boys' experience, describing the lures that the devil uses to capture mankind:

> Some [hooks] he covereth with gold, some with silver, some with earth, some with clay, some with honour, some with beautie, some with one thing, some with another. Hee will not lay all bait alike … he knoweth that a little bait, will serve for little fish, and a great bait for a great fish … And besides this he must have alteration of baits as the cunning fisher.[43]

The cautionary tale outlines the unsuspecting swallowing of bait and near escape, before the devil's long line reels in the unfortunate victim from 'the sweete stream of the waters of life' to be thrown into 'a pan of boyling liquor'.[44] In the opening of the text Leigh's warm address to her sons remarks that her 'motherly affection … (as it often hath done)' causes her to 'forget' herself.[45] The creation of this engaging and detailed allegory may be an incidence of her 'forgetting', in which her close relationship with the boys surfaces. It does, nonetheless, have the serious aim of inculcating moral values and a fear of corruption in her sons.

Elizabeth Joscelin's 'Little legacy'[46]

Elizabeth Joscelin's *A Mother's Legacy to her unborne childe* (1624) is considered to have been influenced by Leigh's popular manual.[47] It is a poignant text, written by a young woman of twenty-seven who was convinced that she would not survive the birth of her first child. She did, in fact, die from puerperal fever, nine days after the birth of her daughter in October 1622. She had written the manuscript from the discovery of her pregnancy until a month before her delivery, leaving it in a drawer to be discovered after her death. The 'Approbation', written by Thomas Goad, and the prefatory letter addressed to Joscelin's husband, Taurell, give an extraordinary insight into her frame of mind as she prepared for what she saw as almost inevitable death.* Her manner throughout is of devout preparedness, even to the extent of ordering her 'winding sheet', or shroud, when she felt the first movement of the child. Her tenderness towards her husband is evident in her addresses ('most Dearly loved', 'Myne own dear love'), the reference to 'continually unclaspinge of our harts one to another' and the gentle reminder that she found it impossible to discuss these matters for fear of distressing him, 'dear remember how greevos it was to thee but to hear me say I may dy'.[48] As Sylvia Brown remarks, the Joscelins' relationship seems to have been the truly companionate marriage advocated in the less austere marriage guides of the period.[49]

Joscelin is concerned that her child is raised within moral and godly surroundings and especially anxious that he or she is respectful and of a humble demeanour. She urgently requests her husband not to be over-indulgent, warning that it encourages childish precocity which will develop into boldness and lack of humility. To the same end she implores that he does not encourage pride by dressing the child lavishly, fretting, 'in a daughter I more feare that vice pride'.[50] Despite her own prodigious aptitude for more 'masculine' academic subjects, she nonetheless expresses a strong desire that a daughter be trained in the traditional housewifely skills and religious works.[51] Justifying this by fear for her daughter's possible loss of modesty and lack of discretion in the use of her knowledge, she underlines the inappropriateness of learning in a wife. Despite the resolute tone, and the sharing of responsibilities to which she has alluded earlier, Joscelin acknowledges her husband's final authority in the raising of the child, however, adding

* Goad was an Anglican minister and claims to have known Joscelin when she was a child. He obtained the licence to publish her work after her death and was probably responsible for the editorial adjustments which appeared in the published edition. See Brown, p. 101.

the caveat that, if he does desire a learned daughter, she prays that she also be granted 'a wise and religious hart to use it for his glorie thy comfort and her own Salvatyon'.

Joscelin's apprehensions surrounding the problem of feminine intellectual activity, as a threat to integrity, is particularly paradoxical, given her own background. Joscelin's atypical education was devised by her grandfather, Bishop Chaderton of Lincoln, and far excelled that of many boys of her social status and time. Unresolved tensions are evident in her trepidation when first deciding to write the *Legacy*: 'my own weaknes appeared so manifestly that I was ashamed and dare not undertake it.' [52] Although this may be read as the conventional 'modesty topos', which understates actual proficiency, found in so many women's texts of this era, this does not seem to be Joscelin's aim. Whether her embarrassment is due to the 'unpolished' prose, as she suggests, or her vulnerability in assuming an authoritative voice, is open to question. This text, unlike Leigh's, was not intended for the public domain, despite going through six editions. As she makes quite clear, she expects that her only readers will be her children and husband, and it is upon this assumption that she is emboldened to write. The modern reader is left to construe Joscelin's own experiences as an educated woman, given her ardent desire to preserve her daughter from the self-conceit and immodesty of bearing associated with female education. She infers that a strict religious training, although of vital importance of itself, is also to be advocated as a corrective to misguided self-esteem.

The literary 'self' which Joscelin creates is compromised by the inconsistent portrait presented in her 'looking glasse'. That she was a paragon of piety is not in doubt; she was in the habit of memorising sermons and her frequent personalised biblical references bear witness to an easy familiarity with her scriptural sources.* In her concern to educate her child in religion, morality and gender-determined usefulness, she also conforms to the socially-condoned construction of femininity. Conversely, however, she is also a highly talented and

* Note Brown's interesting discussion of the slight misquoting and adapting of biblical sources, seeming to indicate writing from memory, rather than deliberate transcription from published texts in discussion of Leigh's work. Brown, p. 98.

educated woman, self-consciously adopting parental authority to write a conduct manual. Her awareness of these conflicting subject positions surfaces in the preamble, as she intimates in her reservations, aware that her integrity may be questioned. Joscelin's negotiations of these complexities highlight the proliferation of often conflicting discourses at play in the domestic advice books of the time. As Gina Hausknecht observes, 'bourgeois advice literature … presented ordinary men and women with a figuratively and ideologically complex set of ways to understand themselves as husbands and wives'.[53]

Protestant Ideals and Lived Experience

Critical trends have both contested and upheld the late sixteenth and seventeenth centuries' concepts of ideal marriage, as prescribed in domestic advice books; while the strategy of interpreting social practice through literary texts is often undermined by evidence revealed in personal correspondence, ecclesiastical records and judicial proceedings. Notions of a changed, more companionate, marriage are severely weakened by prescriptions in the austere Puritan tracts, although continuity of major themes can be identified throughout the sixteenth and seventeenth centuries.[54] Moreover, during the period, the relatively misogynistic authoritarian manuals and the milder and more compassionate texts do seem to co-exist, perhaps indicative of the authors' differing theological perspectives. All the guides express the importance of a mother's role in training her children in civility, morality and religion in their early years, while some also define a sharing of familial responsibilities, if weighted towards the husband's supposed greater expertise. The defining factor of most of the works is their scriptural foundation, whether overt and sermonising or as marginal endorsement. This provides the pivotal point where a mother can assume a greater degree of authority; as deputed guardian of familial spirituality and salvation she is given a voice, albeit qualified. As Valerie Wayne points out in the case of the Mother's Advice literature, most ironically, this speech is 'predicated on their erasure', as the texts often became the women's last will and testament.[55]

Extended Commentary: Castiglione, *The Book of the Courtier* (1528), Book III

During the Renaissance the concept of a female courtier was anomalous with the tightly-monitored parameters of accepted female conduct. Propriety and an untarnished reputation is continually required of women in the prescriptive texts of the day, not only in the performance of everyday tasks, but in dress, speech and even thought. In all respects, these were threatened by the self-display and social intercourse which the role demanded.

Nonetheless, the possibilities of advantageous connections and marriage prospects were tempting enough to encourage parents to lobby fiercely for positions at court for their daughters. Shortly after Anne Boleyn's execution, for example, Lady Lisle put in train a series of requests to influential kin and acquaintances to acquire posts for her daughters, Katherine and her own Anne, amplified by gifts of fattened quails for the king and his new queen.[56] At the time Anne Lisle was only sixteen and it is clear that her success was due to her beauty and wit, which ignited Henry VII's interest shortly before the death of Jane Seymour.[57] The court was a magnet for power-brokers, favour-seekers and social climbers creating a highly-charged atmosphere of compliance and complex power-relations, ripe for exploitation. Such an environment was particularly dangerous for young women, or the 'nymphs' as they were termed by admirers.[*]

* 'Praised be her nymphs, with whom she decks the woods; / Praised be her knights, in whom true honor lives' (lines 5–6), in Sir Walter Ralegh's 'Praised be Diana's Fair and Harmless Light' of Elizabeth I's court, published in *The Phoenix Nest* (1593), 'Set forth by R. S. of the Inner Temple, Gentleman' in *Renasance Editions*, available: http://www.uoregon.edu/.

The Role of the Female Courtier

Female courtiers and higher-ranking female 'Ladies of the Court' had to negotiate a contradictory path which demanded participation in courtly activities whilst still maintaining a virtuous reputation that was above suspicion. In Book III of *The Courtier* Guiliano de'Medici, the Magnifico, is prevailed upon to describe the perfect female courtier. Despite his seeming sincerity, contradictions lie just beneath the surface of his vision. Rather than curbing her speech and avoiding social intercourse with men outside her family, he requires the female courtier to 'entertain graciously every kind of man with agreeable and comely conversation' and, most specifically, she must be vivacious in lively company and not shy away from 'talk that is a little loose', for fear that she is thought to be assuming a false modesty (Book III: 5, 6, pp. 151, 153). In any other circumstance, the loquacious woman is considered to be of loose morals and the stigma lurks beneath the Magnifico's depiction. His pronouncements struggle with the underlying contradiction, needing constant qualification by contrary conjunctions and the negations of numerous 'buts', 'yets' and 'nots'. At length he is forced to acknowledge the untenable nature of her role:

> … [she will have] a kind manner as to cause her to be thought no less chaste, prudent, and gentle than she is agreeable, witty and discreet: thus she must observe a certain mean (difficult to achieve and, as it were, composed of contraries) and must strictly observe certain limits and not exceed them.
> (Book III: 5)

Joan Kelly-Gadol's seminal essay points out the limited, 'indirect and provisional' access to power permitted to even high-born women in the Italian states, despite the political and even military involvement of some spirited daughters of clashing powerful families.[58] She sees this as an inevitable situation when authority is crucially reliant upon military force which, as is made abundantly clear in *The Courtier*, is anathema to the training of ladies of the court. [59] As no distinction is made between the ruling nobility and the gentlewomen who serve, the portrait of the ideal female courtier also subtly shapes the configuration of the perfect 'Court Lady'. The Magnifico follows classical precedents in permitting men and women some virtues and abilities in common, such as learning, 'prudence [and] magnanimity'. Nonetheless, his construction of the female courtier is essentially decorative, accommodating and only as physically active as can be allowed within the term 'graceful' (Book III: 7, 8). David Quint's thesis is that she acts as a taming influence on the otherwise disorderly impulses of male members of court and society, which affords her importance, if of an effacing nature.[60] Apart from not participating in activities considered to be 'robust and strenuous manly exercises', the female courtier should monitor her performance of even condoned pastimes, such as singing or lute-playing, to ensure that they are measured and performed with 'gentle delicacy' (Book III: 8). She is urged to take the most profound care in her personal presentation, including the disguise of less desirable features, but to 'appear to have no care or concern for this' (Book III: 8, 9). This female version of '*sprezzatura*', rather than encoding the physical prowess, agility of mind or intellectual capabilities of the male courtier, then, is intended to denote that, despite her social accomplishments, she is virtuous, honourable – and has good dress sense. Although the encapsulated significance is different between the male and female's performance of indifference, nevertheless, both are required to exhibit the rehearsed disregard of well-practised behaviours.

'Pleasing and lovable to all': Courtship and Courtiership

There are, in fact numerous parallels between the status of the ladies of the court and the attention-seeking, subservient status of the male courtier, both of whom are dependent on the literal courting of favour from powerful patrons. Indeed, his self-display can be read as effeminising, recognised by Count Ludovico in the vivid likeness of the gloriously effete young men that he does not wish to endorse:

> I would not have our Courtier's face so soft and feminine as many attempt to have who not only curl their hair and pluck their eyebrows, but preen themselves in all those ways that the most wanton and dissolute women in the world adopt; and … appear so tender and languid that their limbs seem to be at the verge of falling apart … [and] the more they find themselves in the company of men of rank, the more they make of a show of such manners. (Book I: 19)

David Quint goes further in aligning the devotion expected of a courtier to his prince with the formal play of courtly love between the lady and her follower. As he points out, in this situation, the posturing and display of the courtier may be as much for the lady as the prince, and the 'favour' which he hopes to gain reaches from preferment to sexual gratification, with possible blurring of boundaries in each case.[61]

One of Gasparo Pallavicino's many misogynistic contributions to the discussion misrepresents classical theories of love, to explain why women remain in love with their first sexual partners, whilst 'a man commonly hate[s] the woman he first enjoyed' (Book III: 15). Platonic concepts of the soul's desire to ascend to perfection and Aristophanes's theory of divided lovers from *The Symposium* are alluded to in this witty, if hostile, reworking. According to Aristophanes, in their origins humans were doubled, having two heads, four arms, and so on. Attempting to counteract their unruliness, Zeus divided them, so that each was condemned to seek his or her partner for eternity in order to become whole again.[*] Gasparo's oblique allusion to 'the opinion of very wise men' is an example of the courtly nonchalance of *sprezzatura*, it is

* See Plato, *The Symposium*, translated by Walter Hamilton (Harmondsworth: Penguin Books, Ltd, 1951 repr. 1980), pp. 59–64 or online. Note there were originally three sexes: male, female, and hermaphrodite. Arisophanes uses this description to explain why some people prefer relationships with their own sex.

decidedly lacking in grace (*grazia*), however. He uses classical 'endorsement' to claim that women parasitically absorb perfection from men in sexual union, whilst they in turn permeate their partners with imperfection (Book III: 15). The culmination of his speech is the claim that 'all women without exception desire to be men' as, in this society, the pursuit of perfection equates desire to be male. The Magnifico's objection is interesting in that he recognises that women's aim is not the pursuit of perfection *per se*, but rather to escape their subservient role in a patriarchal society:

> … the poor creatures do not desire to be men in order to become more perfect, but in order to escape that rule over them which man has arrogated to himself by his own authority.
> (Book III: 16)

Noticeably, there is no recourse to the biblical ratification usual for the period, but the power relationship between the sexes is acknowledged as being simply claimed by man 'by his own authority'. Castiglione's apparently liberal outlook is somewhat undermined, however, when the Magnifico offers an alternative explanation to Gasparo's problem of different attitudes to love. This interacts with classical medical theories of the four humours which were considered to explain differences between peoples' characters and essential differences between men and women's 'nature'. The Magnifico identifies woman's 'firmness and constancy' as being a result of her cool physiology, compared with man's heat 'lightness, movement and inconstancy' (Book III: 16).* Although the ostensible intention is to defend and flatter women, the theory is based upon biological determinism and as such is essentialistic and limiting for both sexes. Moreover, it detracts from any moral explanation as it avoids the question of volition in both cases.

* Classical theories of medicine were based on the theory of humoral balance related to the four elements, earth, fire, water and air and the humours were black bile, yellow bile, phlegm and blood. Imbalances were thought to denote character and also contribute to ill-health. Women were associated with moisture and coolness, hence, the Magnifico's reference to 'frigidity' (Book III: 16).

Despite the presence of the Duchess Elisabetta and her companion Emilia Pia, Gasparo undermines each of the Magnifico's (apparently) liberal pronouncements, reiterating well-worn misogynistic opinions about women. The resulting shared dialogue has all of the elements of the later English 'Woman Debate' literature of the sixteenth and seventeenth centuries, whilst the Magnifico's expansive encomium of women lies within the conventions of the 'defence of womankind' texts, such as Boccaccio's *De mulierbus claris*[*] (1374).[†] Included in the Magnifico's eulogy are the unsung wives, sisters and daughters of prominent Romans, present-day female rulers of Spain and Italian sovereign states, and the contemporary victim of rape who committed suicide, in the time-honoured mode of Lucretia.[‡] Apart from the dubious ethics of celebrating the death of a *victim*, forced to die to avoid disgrace, the embedded discourse seems to be successful in overcoming Gasparo's ill-natured jibes. It is, however, flawed in its conflict with its framing scenario.

Female Authority and the Burden of Participation

The framing narrative presents Elisabetta Gonzaga as the leader of the evening gathering and as an ostensibly authoritative figure. As critics frequently observe, however, her position is undermined by her abrogation of authority to Emilia Pia, whose role, even so, is little more

* Latin: *Concerning Famous Women*.

† For 'Defences' see, for example, Geoffrey Chaucer's *Legend of Good Women* (pre. 1385), Thomas Elyot's *Defence of Good Women* (1540), Henricus Cornelius Agrippa's *A Treatise of the Nobility of Women* (1542), Edward Gosynhyll's *The Praise of all Women* (1542), Thomas Heywood's *The General History of Women* (1657) and Nahum Tate's *A Present for the Ladies* (1693). For the English seventeenth-century 'Woman Debate', see Part Four.

‡ According to the Roman Historian, Livy, Sextus Tarquinius, the son of the last King of Rome, raped Lucrece [Lucretia], the virtuous wife of Tarquinius Collatinus in 509 B.C. The desire to protect the name of her family compelled her to commit suicide and the revolt against the ruling family which ensued resulted in the founding of the Republic. The familiar story provided inspiration for numerous works of art and literature during the Renaissance, such as Shakespeare's *The Rape of Lucrece* (1594) and paintings by the great Italian Masters.

than marginal in the discussions. The duchess, in fact, then relieves her and the other women of the '*burden* of participation' (Book I: 7, added emphasis). As Pamela Joseph Benson notes, Pia's later entry into the dialogue fails when she attempts to direct the debate from esoteric theories to less abstract defences of women. Her lack of authority is evident here and elsewhere, despite the duchess' endorsement.[62] Benson also reads Pia's discomfort with classical philosophy as Castiglione's confirmation of Gasparo's earlier statement that the women are incapable of following 'subtleties' (Book III: 15). The point demarcates the male and female spheres of experience, as male courtiers would have benefited from a sound classical education, whereas, although some women of the nobility were highly educated, women's training was more usually directed towards practical skills and the inspiration of piety.

Renaissance educators diverged regarding the precise parameters of curricula desirable for women, but some approved the study of modern and classical languages for noblewomen, along with accomplishments such as drawing, singing and musical performance, to make them agreeable companions for their husbands.[63] Female participation in court life demanded enhanced levels of the types of accomplishments designated as fitting entertainment in private for spouse and family, but could severely compromise a woman's public persona. Recognising these dangers, Richard Braithwaite's *The English Gentlewoman* (1631) warns his female readers to remain focused on their piety even in such circumstances. In a section on the hypocrisy of court life he extols the lasting benefit of heavenly rewards, as opposed to material advantages, directing his readers to 'bee endenizened in heaven … naturall Citizens, angelicall Courtiers'.[64]

Notes

1 See Christina Garrett, *The Marian Exiles, A Study of Elizabethan Protestantism* (Cambridge: Cambridge University Press, 1939, repr. 1966), pp. 184–6.

2 'Self-fashioning' is Stephen Greenblatt's term, borrowed from *Renaissance Self-Fashioning: from More to Shakespeare* (Chicago and London: University of Chicago Press, 1980).

3 See Amedeo Quondam, 'On the Genesis of *The Book of the Courtier*' in Daniel Javitch (ed.), *The Courtier*, The Norton Critical Edition (New York and London: W. W. Norton and Company, 2002), pp. 283–95, p. 284. All quotations are from this edition.

4 Javitch, p. x.

5 Raymond Williams, *Marxism and Literature* (Oxford University Press, 1977), p. 101, cited Peter Barry, *Beginning Theory: an Introduction to Literary and Cultural Theory* (Manchester and New York: Manchester University Press, 1995, repr. 2002), p. 164.

6 Jennifer Richards, 'Assumed Simplicity and the Critique of Nobility: Or, How Castiglione Read Cicero', *Renaissance Quarterly*, 54: 2 (2001), p. 472.

7 Richards, p. 472.

8 See Virginia Cox's 'Castiglione's *Cortegiano*: The Dialogue of Doubt' in Javitch, pp. 303–19, pp. 316, 317.

9 Peter Barry, 'Postmodernism', p. 92. The section actually refers to language games but is equally applicable to the play of self-representation.

10 Eduardo Saccone, 'Grazia, Sprezzatura, Affettazione' in 'The portrait of the Courtier in Castiglione', *Italica* 64 (1987), pp. 1–18, cited Harry Berger Jr, 'Sprezzatura and the absence of grace', in Javitch, pp. 295–307, pp. 301, 302.

11 See Javitch's interesting discussion on the political considerations of the role in '*Il Cortegiano* and the Constraints of Despotism' in *Castiglione: The Ideal and the Real in Renaissance Culture*, ed. by Robert W. Hanning and David Rosand (New York and London: Yale University Press, 1983), pp. 17–28, also reproduced in Javitch, pp. 319–28.

12 Lawrence V. Ryan, 'Book Four of Castiglione's Courtier: Climax or Afterthought?', *Studies in the Renaissance*, 19 (1972), pp. 156–79, p. 157.

13 J. R. Woodhouse, 'Book Four of Castiglione's *Cortegiano*. A Pragmatic Approach', *The Modern Language Review*, 73 (1978), pp. 62–8, p. 62.

14 Woodhouse, p. 67.

15 Woodhouse, p. 67.

16 Robert Samber in his translation of 1724, Book I, pp. v–vi, cited in Julius A. Molinaro, 'Castiglione and His English Translators', *Italica*, 36: 4 (1959), pp. 262–78, p. 265. See also Peter Burke's discussion of the difficulties of translating Castiglione's terms in 'The Courtier Abroad: Or, The Uses of Italy' in Javitch, pp. 388–400, p. 394.

17 Richards, pp. 460–86, p. 478.

18 Richards, p. 478.

19 Robert Cleaver, *A godly forme of household government for the ordering of private families, according to the direction of God's word* (1598), p. 1, available via Early English Books Online (EEBO), STC 5382. Both this and Tilney's guides both do genuinely seem to be less authoritarian and more conciliatory than Gouge or Whately's.

20 Patricia Crawford and Laura Gowing (eds), *Women's Worlds in Seventeenth-Century England* (London and New York: Routledge, 2000), pp. 169, 176, 177.

21 Sara Mendelson and Patricia Crawford, *Women in Early Modern England* (Oxford: Oxford University Press, 1998), pp. 126–48, p. 126.

22 'Homily on the State of Matrimonie'. The two books of homilies, digitalised by the University of Toronto, are available on its website.

23 Francis Osborne's *Advice to a son*, in Louis B. Wright (ed.), *Advice to a Son, Precepts of Lord Burghley, Sir Walter Raleigh and Francis Osborne* (Ithaca, New York: Cornell University Press, 1962), p. 62.

24 William Gouge, *Of Domesticall Duties*, p. 270, available via EEBO, STC 12119.

25 Cleaver, p. 167.

26 Edward Tilney, *A brief and pleasant discourse of duties in marriage called the flower of friendship* (1568) available via EEBO, STC 552.1.

27 Cleaver, p. 167.

28 Catherine Belsey, 'Alice Arden's Crime', in *The Subject of Tragedy: Identity and Difference in Renaissance Drama* (London and New York: Methuen, 1985), pp. 135–48, p. 135.

29 See Garthine Walker, '"Demons in female form": representations of women and gender in murder pamphlets of the late sixteenth and early seventeenth centuries' in William Zunder and Suzanne Trill (eds), *Writing and the English Renaissance* (London and New York: Longman, 1996), pp. 123–39.

30 William Whately, *A Bride-Bush: or, a direction for married persons Plainly describing the duties common to both, and peculiar to each of them*, available via EEBO, STC 25296.

31 Gina Hausknecht, '"So Many Shipwracke for Want of Better Knowledge": The Imaginary Husband in Stuart Marriage Advice', *The Huntington Library Quarterly*, 64:1/2 (2001), pp. 81–106, p. 82.

32 The heading, 'whether a man may beat his wife; yea or no', is a side note to the paragraph discussed below, Whately, p. 106.

33 See Paul Slack, 'Mortality crises and epidemics 1485–1610' in Charles Webster, *Health, Medicine and Mortality in the Sixteenth Century* (Cambridge: Cambridge University Press, 1979), pp. 1–8. Although it is

not possible positively to identify some of these fevers from their colloquial names, it is likely that they included typhoid and influenza.

34 Lawrence Stone, *The Family, Sex and Marriage in England 1500–1800* (Harmondsworth: Penguin, 1977 repr. 1985), p. 54.

35 See Thomas R. Forbes, 'By what disease or casualty: the changing Face of Death in London', in *Health, Medicine and Mortality in the Sixteenth Century*, ed. by Charles Webster (Cambridge: Cambridge University Press, 1979), pp. 116–39, p. 127. In one survey comparing records for five London parishes for the same period, he notes that only St Botolph's without Aldgate recorded any deaths resulting from childbirth (1.5%), which were far outnumbered in the same parish by those caused by plague, consumption and/or convulsions (45.8%), p. 127.

36 Forbes notes that St Botolph's was unusual in recording these deaths, but also that they most probably include foetal deaths and babies carried to full term. Forbes, p. 123, 139.

37 See R. Schofield, 'Did Mothers Really Die?' in *The World We Have Gained: Histories of Population and Social Structure*, ed. by L. Bonfield *et al.* (Oxford: Basil Blackwell, 1986), pp. 255, 259, cited in *Women's Writing in Stuart England*, Brown (ed.), p. 91.

38 Dorothy Leigh, *A Mother's Blessing* (1616), available via EEBO, STC 15402. Also reproduced in *Women's Writing in Stuart England: The Mother's Legacies of Dorothy Leigh, Elizabeth Joscelin, and Elizabeth Richardson*, ed. by Sylvia Brown (Stroud, Gloucestershire: Sutton Publishing, 1999), pp. 3–87, chapter 3, p. 23.

39 Leigh in Brown (ed.), chapter 2, p. 22; STC 15402, chapter 2, p. 4. (The first reference is to Sylvia Brown's *Writing in Stuart England* and the second is the original EEBO text.)

40 Leigh in Brown (ed.), chapter 44, p. 71; STC 15402, chapter 44, pp. 243, 244.

41 Leigh in Brown (ed.), chapter 44, pp. 71, 72; STC 15402, chapter 44, p. 248.

42 Leigh in Brown (ed.), chapter 5, p. 24; STC 15402, chapter 5, p.17.

43 Leigh in Brown (ed.), chapter 38, pp. 60, 61; STC 15402, chapter 38, pp. 193,194.

44 Leigh in Brown (ed.), chapter 38, pp. 60, 61; STC 15402, chapter 38, pp. 193,194.

45 Leigh in Brown (ed.), chapter 2, p. 22; STC 15402, chapter 2, p. 4.

46 The quotation in the heading to the section is from Elizabeth Joscelin's prefatory letter to her husband, Joscelin in Brown (ed.), 'Elizabeth Joscelin's Manuscript Mother's Legacy', pp. 106–39, p. 106; available as the 1624 published edition of *A Mother's Legacy to her unborne childe* via

EEBO, STC 745.05, prefatory letter, 'To my truly lovinge and most Dearly loved husband Taurell Joscelin', unnumbered page.

47 Note, as spelling was not standardised, names and other words were spelled variously. Modern spelling of her name often substitutes a single for the double 'n' but Joscelin herself uses it in her dedication. Joscelin, in Brown (ed.), p. 107; STC 745.05, prefatory letter, unnumbered.

48 Joscelin in Brown (ed.), p. 108; STC 745.05, prefatory letter, unnumbered.

49 Brown (ed.), p. 99.

50 Joscelin in Brown (ed.), p. 108; STC 745.05, prefatory letter, unnumbered.

51 See Valerie Wayne, 'Advice from mothers and patriarchs' in *Women and Literature in Britain 1500–1700*, Helen Wilcox (ed.) (New York and Cambridge: Cambridge University Press, 1996), pp. 56–79, p. 64; Brown, pp. 93, 94.

52 Joscelin, in Brown (ed.), p. 106; STC 745.05, prefatory letter, unnumbered.

53 Hausknecht, p. 84.

54 See Kathleen M. Davies, 'The Sacred Condition of Equality: How Original Were Puritan Doctrines of Marriage?' in *Social History*, vol. 2, no. 5 (May 1977), pp. 563–80.

55 Wayne, p. 71. Wayne's discussion centres on the women's 'portraits' within the texts, but is equally applicable to their voices.

56 Muriel St Clare Byrne and Bridget Boland (eds), 'Katherine and Anne Bassett' in *The Lisle Letters: An Abridgement* (London: Secker and Warburg, 1981, repr. 1983), pp. 201–11.

57 St Clare Byrne and Boland, p. 201.

58 Joan Kelly-Gadol, 'Did Women Have a Renaissance?' in Javitch, pp. 340–52, pp. 340, 341.

59 Kelly-Gadol, pp. 340, 341.

60 David Quint, 'Courtier, Prince, Lady: The Design of *The Book of the Courtier*', *Italian Quarterly* 37 (2000), pp. 143–46, reprinted in Javitch, pp. 352–65, pp. 353, 354.

61 Quint, p. 355.

62 Pamela Joseph Benson, *The Invention of the Renaissance Woman* (Pennysylvania: Pennsylvania State University Press, 1992), p. 85.

63 See Juan Luis Vives's influential *Instruction of a Christen Woman* (1523), English translation by Richard Hyrde (1529), discussed in Elaine Beilin's *Redeeming Eve: Women Writers of the English Renaissance* (Princeton, New Jersey: Princeton University Press, 1987), pp. 4–15; Richard Mulcaster's

Positions wherin those primitive circumstances be examined which are necessary for the training up of Children (1581), STC 18253, pp. 176–82.

64 Richard Braithwaite, *The English Gentlewoman* (1631), available via EEBO, STC 3565, p. 314.

Part Four
Critical Theories and Debates

City, Court and Country

Despite the lure of financial gain and relief from the hardships of rural existence, life in town, and especially the capital, was recognised as harmful to the health – 'With Famine, Wants, and Sorrows many a Dosen, / The least of which was to the Plague a Cosen'.[1] Ben Jonson's lurid epigram 'On the famous Voyage' envisages a journey down London's Fleet ditch in mock-heroic style as two 'horrid knaves' encounter the stench, filth and nauseous effluvia of contemporary London life:

> … How dare
> Your dainty Nostrils (in so hot a Season,
> When every Clerk eats Artichokes and Peason,
> Laxative Lettuce, and such windy Meat)
> Tempt such a passage? when each Privies Seat
> Is fill'd with Buttock? And the Walls do sweat
> Urine, and Plasters? (*Epigrams* 134: 144–50)

Letters sent between family members and literary works alike deplore the poor accommodation, exposure to pestilence, but also the inferior quality of food and drink. The abundant fresh food available to Lady Lisle at her home in Calais was therefore a valuable resource when cementing relationships or seeking favour at court. She provided venison, mews and wine as a settlement on her young son's accommodation in London, gifts of dottrels* and quails to Queen Anne Boleyn, and herrings to help with the Lenten requirements of her brother-in-law.[2]

Despite the assistance of country 'cousins' and the exertions of farmers and traders of the surrounding countryside, reliable access to fresh and nourishing produce in the capital was limited. Sir Francis Bryant, a courtier of Henry VIII's reign, noted 'In town there is not good corn, often bread is unleavened and evil baked' and the lack of 'wholesome water'.[3] Around sixty years later, Ben Jonson still had reservations about the level of hygiene – and the contents of pies – in taverns and bakeries:

> The Sinks ran Grease, and Hair of meazled Hogs,
> The Heads, Houghs,† Entrails, and the Hydes of Dogs:
> For, to say truth, what Scullion is so nasty,
> To put the Skins, and Offal in a Pasty?
> Cats there lay divers had been flead and rosted,
> And, after mouldy grown, again were tosted,
> Then selling not, a Dish was ta'ne to mince 'em,
> But still, it seem'd, the rankness did convince 'em.
>
> (*Epigrams* 134: 125–32)

Notwithstanding the physical dangers, city life was considered to be a threat to public morality, if not the soul itself. As young people were attracted to urban life, they broke – or significantly loosened – family connections in an era which defined itself largely through the ties of kith and kin. Local affinities and loyalties towards the ruling squirarchy were also weakened if not lost, often leaving vulnerable young adults to make their way without traditional protection or preferment.

* Mew was a common name for a seagull and dottrels are coastal birds.

† Hough, or hock, is the ankle joint of the hind leg of an animal.

'Neither householders nor citizens': Apprentices, Subjection and Retaliation

Boys apprenticed to tradesmen of the towns were in a liminal position and perhaps in no better situation than youths forced to make their own way, as records of law courts reveal in cases of gross mistreatment and neglect.[4] Long apprenticeships, typically of six years' duration, requiring the trainee to live with the family of the master tradesman, could be misery for the youth or his hosts. Paul Seaver makes the valid point that in times of hardship, younger sons of even gentry status were sometimes in this straightened position, as the family inheritance was protected from subdivision and bequeathed to the eldest son.[5] He cites Thomas Powell's interesting guide written for the luckless father of six boys and three daughters, instructing him how best to assist their advancement with no expenditure. *Tom of all Trades* (1631) contains very detailed information about schools and colleges which have associated funding and scholarships, how to progress in the Church and court, and how best to ensnare a solid, well-appointed husband. As Seaver remarks, the author also very pragmatically advises setting the young men to apprenticeships early, to ensure that they are less resentful of losing home comforts.

Miho Suzuki's research on London apprentice riots of the 1590s reveals a succession of royal proclamations aimed at quelling apprentices' outrageous 'lewd' and dangerous behaviour. From initially demanding a curfew on their movements after nine in the evening, these escalate to decree that culprits be imprisoned at Bridewell Prison and even executed on the gallows. The overriding impression is that the late night city streets were the domain of marauding violent gangs of disgruntled youths. As Suzuki points out, in these documents apprentices were likened to masterless vagabonds, much as were the players* of the time, as they occupied marginal positions, and were not fully integrated into concepts of social hierarchy. Although unlawful and aggressive in expression, however, their motivation was often in the interest of the

* Player: term used for a dramatic performer at the time.

poorer citizens, as in the direct action they took against over-pricing and the profiteering on daily commodities.[6]

Rogues' galleries: 'Coney-Catchers and Bawdy Baskets'

New Historicist critics read the royal proclamations and court records of such public disorder against the innovatory city comedies by Ben Jonson, Thomas Dekker and Thomas Middleton, which humorously portrayed the activities of this sector of London life. In their schemes, scrapes and mishaps, the plays often feature characters from the underbelly of society: confidence tricksters, corrupt figures of authority, opportunists intending to marry to procure a fortune, and even a female cross-dressing pick-pocket.* City or civic comedies share a carnivalesque celebration of diversity and a pragmatic approach to survival with the popular genre of underworld literature. Tracts and pamphlets aimed at the common reader and written in colloquial language proliferated as cheap printed works became more easily available. The anonymous *Coney-Catchers and Bawdy Baskets*† pamphlets (1592 and 1593) served as a guide to all known types of criminal, furnished with names and locations of those to avoid, while the title page of Dekker's *The Bellman of London* (1608) states its purpose as '*Bringing to Light the Most Notorious Villanies that are now Practised in the Kingdom*'. Clearly, London supported numerous sub-cultures at odds with established order and feared by upright citizens.

The Malcontent‡ of the Jacobean Revenge Tragedy reflects the position of many young men of the era, educated beyond the status or

* *The Roaring Girl*, by Middleton and Dekker (*c.*1607–10), features a cross-dressing thief named 'Moll Cut-Purse' who was based on an historical figure named Mary Frith, who went under the same name.

† Coney-Catcher: literally a rabbit catcher, but used to mean a poacher or other petty criminal; Bawdy-Basket: woman of loose morals who sells items in the streets, including lewd literature. See also John Awdeley's *The Fraternity of Vagabonds* (1561) and Thomas Harman's *A Caveat for Common Cursitors* (1566). Critical opinion debates the balance of veracity and fiction in all such guides, however.

‡ Malcontent: marginalised male stock character in Jacobean Revenge Tragedy, who becomes involved in transgressive acts as a result of the failure of the judicial system to avenge his grievances.

means of their families and unable to find honest employment in town society. As the young men became easy prey to dishonest or dishonourable patrons, similarly young women's virtue might be seriously exploited in the struggle for independent existence. In a society caught between a model of hierarchical ties of interdependence and one which rested on personal ambition and commercial exchange, it could be difficult to draw acceptable parameters of behaviour. Reliant on favour and patronage for economic survival, the dependent individual may not be in a position to set the tariff or decide what can be bartered.

Young 'Gentilwomen' in Town

The experiences of Isabella Whitney and Aemilia Lanyer, young women of respectable middle-class backgrounds, have similarities, in that both were exiled from their chosen life in the capital and lamented their changed circumstances in published verse form. Assuming that the voice of her poems is not a fictional persona, Whitney's two volumes provide insights into her family connections and her social status, revealing that she, her brother and her sisters were in all service in London. *A Copy of a Letter, lately written in meeter by a yonge gentilwoman to her unconstant lover* (1567) breaks numerous cultural prohibitions. The genre itself, as original poetry written by an unmarried young woman, was reprehensible to prevailing notions of morality, but the candid letters and responses, which form the subject matter, could be said to indicate degeneracy in that Whitney (or her persona) admits, and provides insight into an amorous liaison. Publishing compounds these difficulties as the prurient evidence is made available to the gaze of all-comers for a price. Much like Rachel Speght and the female-voiced pamphlets as discussed in Part Four: 'The Woman Debate', however, Whitney's stated aim is to protect women from exploitation, as the sub-title of her first volume indicates in the 'Admonition to al yong gentilwomen, and to al other mayds in general to beware of mennes flattery'.[7] An obvious influence on her work is Ovid's *Heroides*, especially letter VII from Dido to Anaeas and letter XII from Medea to Jason, although there are other classical references in the examples she gives of negative or loyal love.

Internal evidence also reveals a familiarity with Ovid's *Metamorphoses* (Transformations) and the humorous *Ars Amatoria* (Arts of Love), both very popular and influential works, neither of which were considered appropriate reading material for modest young women in the late sixteenth century.

Whitney's second volume, *A Sweet Nosegay* (1573), seems to have been written when she had fallen upon difficult times in London. Written in December from Alchurch Street in the city, the prefatory letter, 'The Aucthor to the Reader', reveals that she had been sick since the autumn and so had lost her place in service, 'This harvestyme, I harvestlesse, / and serviceless also'.[8] Continuing her justification for writing, she explains that the work was written after becoming frustrated or disillusioned with the different areas of self-directed studies that she imposed upon herself during this enforced leisure time. Rather than the idle and welcome freedom of the moneyed classes, however, her inactivity was threatening to her livelihood, glimpsed in references to her 'lucklesse life' here and financial hardship intimated in her wry 'Wyll and Testament', addressed to London as she is obliged to leave the city. From circumstantial evidence, it would seem that Whitney was inspired to write the text during the walks of her convalescence down Bishopsgate and into the countryside near Spitalfields, while friends and relatives sought her new employment. The introductory section of the volume indicates that by December this was arranged and she was obliged to leave London. The poem takes the form of a faux last will and testament upon the pretence that leaving London implies death to her: 'The Aucthour (though loth to leave the Citte) upon her Friendes procurement is constrained to departe: wherefore she fayneth as she would die)' (*E ii verso*). It is remarkable for its lively depiction of contemporary London life, its named locations and practical detail of stores and commodities, providing a guide from the River Thames to the central merchant district around St Paul's Cathedral:

> By Thames you shall have brewers' store,
>   and bakers at your will.
> And such as orders do observe,

and eat fish thrice a week,
I leave two streets, full fraught therewith,
they need not far to seek.
Watling Street, and Canwick Street,
I full of woolen leave;
And linen store in Friday Street,
if they me not deceive.
And those which are of calling such,
that costlier they require,
I mercers leave, with silk so rich,
as any would desire.
In Cheap of them, they store shall find,
and likewise in that street,
I goldsmiths leave, with jewels such,
as are for ladies meet. (ll. 35–52)*

Continuing the 'unconstant lover' theme of her earlier volume, Whitney unusually figures London as the masculine and unsympathetic cause of her and other women's suffering. Her litany of cruelties and failed responsibilities that might reasonably be expected from a male paramour or patron include that 'he' never tried to alleviate her financial distress, would not stand credit for her year's board, nor help with the costs of providing her clothing (*E ii verso*). Beneath the humour, the narrative demonstrates an acute awareness of the precarious finances of the young inhabitants of the capital, beginning with the introductory insights into the budgetary difficulties of a young independent woman of the town detailed above. The theme hovers insistently in the declaration that she herself is 'light of purse' and the will's considerate provision of rich widowers for 'maidens poor'† to 'set them afloat', and the corresponding wealthy widows to 'help young gentilmen' (ll. 2, 77, 80).

* All of these locations can be found on the Agas Map, available: http://mapoflondon.uvic.ca/

† As she has no tangible assets, the 'wyll' humorously bestows upon the named inhabitants London itself – the streets, the shops and products – rather than material wealth.

Making a Sort of Path to One's Own Preferment*

The records of the astronomer Simon Foreman reveal Aemila Lanyer's similar preoccupations, as she anxiously consulted him regarding the possibilities of her being called back to court and her husband's prospects of advancement. Born into a family of Italian court musicians, she became accustomed to a luxurious life as the young mistress of the most powerful male member of the court, Henry Hunsden, cousin of the queen. To modern concepts of morality the relationship may seem unseemly at best, if not exploitative, in that Lord Hunsden was at least forty years her senior. Well-documented incidences of political manoeuvring by leading families in the realm throughout the Tudor period indicate that such arrangements were actively sought, however, providing the liaison was lucrative enough.[†] As Martin Wiggins observes, the trade in women's bodies in such circumstances mirrors the legitimate marital bargaining among noble families of the day.[‡] In Lanyer's case, the affair facilitated her social advancement and acceptance in the highest society of the realm, at least until her pregnancy resulted in a hasty retirement with a handsome dowry and an arranged marriage to another musician.

As the extensive list of dedications to Lanyer's 1611 volume of poetry, *Salve Deus Rex Judeorums* (1611) indicates,[9] by the time that she wrote the volume she was anxious to secure patronage.[§] This is the earliest female-authored volume discovered to date to make such an

* The heading is a misquotation of Flamineo's claim regarding his plot to prostitute his sister to assist his social advancement, in John Webster, *The White Devil*, III.i.33–4. See also Sir Thomas Wyatt's *How to vse the court and him selfe therin, written to syr Fraunces Bryan*, also known as 'A spending hand', lines 68–72.

† Henry Hunsden's mother, Mary (Boleyn), and his aunt, Anne, are considered to have been manipulated by their powerful family in precisely this way to create and maintain dynastic strength within the court.

‡ Discussing a similar attempt to gain royal favour by offering a young married woman to a local dignitary in Webster's *The White Devil*, for example, Wiggins notes that the brother performs the same role as his father had in selecting her husband, in 'exercising the same rights over the commodity of his sister's body'. Martin Wiggins, *Journeymen in Murder* (Oxford: Oxford University Press, 1991), p. 168.

§ See Part Four: 'The Woman Debate'.

overt bid for favour, whether for pecuniary or personal preferment. She includes nine individual dedications to prominent noblewomen, one addressed to 'Vertuous Ladies in Generall' and two addressed to the reader. In particular, the poem addressed to 'the Ladie Anne Countesse of Dorcet', the daughter of one of Lanyer's past patrons, belies its epideictic* intention in the terse undermining of the 'Titles of honour which this world bestows'.[10] It is difficult to believe that the poem did not offend its addressee, in its repeated denigration of rank and insistence on the equality of the spirit, meted out under the guise of Protestant admonition. Lanyer's prompts graciously to 'succour' and 'comfort [...] the comfortless', can be read as a scarcely-veiled petition, given her own privation and lack of status (l. 77).

Lanyer's country house poem, 'The Description of Cooke-ham', included in the volume, describes a pastoral vision which is often referred to as a female utopia. The poem's addressee, Margaret, Countess of Cumberland, it is revealed, inspired this poem and also commissioned *Salve Deus*. The poem continues the main poem's theme of the valorisation of women by association with Christian piety, charity and resemblance to Christ. In the opening lines, for example, the Countess is alluded to in the rhetorical figure of antanaclaysis,† 'Grace from that Grace where perfit Grace remain'd' (l. 2). The threefold repetition of 'Grace' evokes the Trinity and is, in fact, a loaded Protestant term denoting God's favour towards the Elect, who are chosen for heaven. Lanyer's praise acknowledges the patronage she received from her grace, the Countess, who is the embodiment of God's favour. The theme is developed as the narrative represents her in terms of equality in close proximity to Christ and other biblical figures, 'In these sweet woods how often did you walke, / With Christ and his Apostles there to talke' (ll. 81–2). The Countess's devotional exercises are enlivened by the conceit that she walks and meditates with Christ and the Old Testament patriarchs Moses, David and Joseph. The surrounding gardens, meanwhile, in willing servitude, create a sylvan court over which she reigns. Presented as courtiers, the

* Epideictic: a branch or rhetorical oratory concerned with praise or blame.

† Antanaclaysis: a figure which repeats the same word but has different meanings.

walks change into their summer livery, while trees bedeck themselves with leaves, flowers and fruit. In their finery the trees lean together to embrace, replicating the arches and canopies which framed royalty in the celebratory tableaux of state occasions and coronation pageants (ll. 21–7). The Countess's power over nature is further illustrated as birds and animals are tamed by her presence; the source of her power is not the classical Orphean lute, however, but her renowned religious devotion.

This pastoral idyll, while it obviously shares some Arcadian elements, also incorporates moral and pious tenets found in Mantuanesque eclogue.[*] Interestingly, despite a diametrically different final solution, Marvell's 'The Garden' demonstrates a similar reconciliation between nature and religion. Despite *Salve Deus*'s call to re-evaluate women's designated role in society, Lanyer's gardens celebrate female isolation and non-participation in a world dominated by worldly affairs. The estate of Cooke-ham, inhabited only by like-minded women, offers a Utopian respite in which to contemplate God and nature, somewhat akin to the Beguine[†] Houses of the medieval Netherlands. Marvell's wit surfaces in his praise of solitude and appreciation of creation as, quite paradoxically, his paradise is predicated on an absence of women, declaring, 'Such was that happy garden-state, / While man there walked without a mate' (ll. 57–8).[‡]

The underpinning issue beneath Lanyer's volume is that of patronage, experienced and denied, as she attempts to negotiate changed circumstances, both personal and political. Throughout the volume, Lanyer's frequent appeals and laments underline her inability to maintain both the elevated life style and social relations with her patrons, 'Whereof depriv'd, / I evermore must grieve, / Hating blind Fortune, carelesse to relieve' (ll. 123–5). Despite her strategies of praise, no doubt sincere in some parts, berating and solicitation, there is no

* See Part Three: 'Pastoral to Epic'.

† Beguine: a member of a religious sisterhood which is not bound by strict laws, nor enclosed. The first Beguine Houses were founded in the Netherlands in the twelfth century and were protected by the Vatican.

‡ See Andrew Marvell, 'The Garden' in Part Three: 'Pastoral to Epic'.

convincing evidence that her material conditions or status were improved by the publication of the volume. Indeed, it foregrounds the stasis of subjection, in underlining the courtier's lack of agency and unwilling subjection. From classical times the rustication from court has produced poetry of bucolic praise, sometimes in the form of lament, but more often as barbed satire.

The Dangers of Court versus a Quiet and Restful Rustical Life

The precariousness of life at court during the reign of Henry VIII erupts in Sir Thomas Wyatt's works, many of which invite reading as records of personal experience.[11] His '*V. Innocentia Veritas Viat Fides*' ('Innocence Truth Wyatt Faith') graphically captures the terror of powerlessness in desperate life-threatening circumstances.* It is believed to have been written whilst he was imprisoned in the Tower of London as a result of the accusations against Queen Anne Boleyn in 1536. From his window he is said to have witnessed the executions of his companions at court and the queen herself, believing that he would follow, hence, the reference to 'These bloody days [which] have broken my heart' (l. 11). The forceful message, written large in the poem, is that power equals danger. The wise man stays out of the public eye and avoids 'all favour, glory, or might' (l. 19), knowing that neither wit nor innocence can save an individual from the whim or castigation of the monarch.

'Mine own John Poins' is believed to have been written shortly after '*Innocentia Veritas Viat Fides*', when Wyatt was dismissed from the court and obliged to return to his father's estate in Kent. The poem is in the form of a letter written to a courtier friend and, whilst being inspired by

* The full title of the poem is '*V. Innocentia Veritas, V[W]yat Fides Circumundederunt me inimici mei*'. The latter part is from Psalm 16:9 and translates as 'My enemies surround me'. It is also known by its refrain as 'Circa regna tonat': 'It thunders through the realms'. The poem is influenced by, and repeats lines from, Seneca's *Phaedra*, a drama about a young man, Hippolytus, who is desired by his stepmother and meets a tragic death brought about by his father's rage. The story also appears in Ovid's *Metamorphoses*, where Hippolytus similarly protests his innocence, 15: 500–45.

the classical and Italian satires, creates a brusque speaking voice that seems to be recognisably his own. The poem ostensibly celebrates the honesty and integrity of life in the country, but the persistent enumeration of the manifold deceits habitually demanded by court life generates a bitter and resentful tenor. The speaker deplores the habitual duplicity, which labels a person a rustic 'that cannot lie and feign' (l. 73). His personal ethos, the speaker declares, forbids him to pander to others in hope of advancement, to encourage lust under the name of love, and to be grateful for foolish drunken advice. His moral rigour refuses the self-abasement similarly identified by Hythloday in Sir Thomas More's *Utopia*, to 'Grin when he laugheth that beareth all the sway, / Frown when he frowneth and groan when is pale' (*Innocentia Veritas Viat Fides*, ll. 53–4).

As Elizabeth Heale remarks, however, the section in which the speaking voice – which the reader is encouraged to read as Wyatt – protests his forthright plain manner, rejecting the obsequious eloquence of the court, is promptly followed by a passage which demonstrates Wyatt's literary artistry in its re-working of a section of Luigi Almanni's *Satire X* (1532).[12] Heale reads this as the establishment of two quite different speaking voices, one of which is the 'hail, fellow, well met' ingenuous and honest character, who lives to 'hunt and to hawk' (l. 80), and the other a more sophisticated, classically-trained and articulate 'political commentator'.[13] The dichotomy is structured through subtly manipulative language, which vilifies it own strategies in the midst of its most overt display. Perhaps Wyatt's intention is wittily to illustrate contemporary opinion that it is not possible to unlearn the dissemblance of court life.

Francis Bryant was a contemporary of Wyatt's and his *The Dispraise of the life of a Courtier, and a commendacion of the life of the labouring man* (1548) treads this familiar ground, with the added emphasis of the necessity of voluntary rejection of the calling.[14] The work lies within the tradition of Horatian satire, celebrating the pleasures of the countryside by contrast with the dangers and worries of the town.*

* See Horace, *Satires* Book II, satire VI, which includes the story of the town mouse and the country mouse.

Apparently basing observation upon experience, Bryant's counsel cautions that to return home vowing to 'leave the cursed life of the court' and yet still yearn towards it is 'a continuall death'.[15] The reformation of the court habitué to become the 'sage and grave' country gentleman is an arduous undertaking, he warns ominously – 'vices enter laughing and go them out from our house wepyng and lamentyng'. Emphasising the serious enterprise, he decries the lack of judgement of those that lead 'wilde and wanton' lives for twenty or thirty years and then expect to rehabilitate themselves in 'one year or two' (*D vii recto*).

Bryant's country gentleman enjoys the relaxed atmosphere of the village, where one can please oneself when and with whom to eat, enjoying conversation with good fellows, out of the way of the annoyances of the 'crying of pages', the complaints of stewards and 'the babbling of Cookes'. Peace of mind is engendered by the absence of beguiling women, 'crafty knaves' and judges who pursue and persecute (*E v recto*). Even at this early stage of London's development, an awareness of the effects of slum-dwelling is evident in the speaker's observations that overcrowding in the city generates pockets of corrupt air and disease in the narrow and overshadowed streets (*E vii recto*). As a result of his removal, therefore, the reformed courtier can look forward to a healthier lifestyle; in the village he will be 'lesse sicke' than in the city as 'the ayre is better, the sunne more clere, the yearth [earth] more swete'. The emphatic speaker makes the exaggerated claim that in the city commonly a half of a man's income is lost in fees paid to apothecaries and physicians. Villagers don't even know the names of 'common town remedies', syrups or pills, never having need of them, he points out, and seldom or never suffer from 'French pockes', palsy or gout (*E viii verso*). An amusing, if alarming, reflection on the newly-qualified doctors of the capital is that the absence of 'yong Phisitians' in the countryside is seen as contributing to improved health (*E viii verso*).

Despite the idealised depiction of country life which Bryant wishes to present, the positive advantages are often indirectly alluded to, in the negative reports of city residence, rather than straightforwardly celebrated in their own right. Reading aslant, as it were, we discover that the quiet life of peace is extolled, not so much as intrinsically desirable, but because no callers can be expected. This requires less expenditure but the theme of acting as unwilling host also provides an alarming insight into uninvited city marauders. Bryant goes on to suggest that in the country, at least, the womenfolk of the household are not prey to seduction and defilement (*E iiii verso*).

Concern to avoid unnecessary financial outlay continues in Bryant's observations on the comfortable and practical attire used in the countryside, which is fit for purpose but without ostentation. The only necessities (for a man, presumably) are 'an honest Spanish cloak and a pair of leather shoes' (*E vi verso*). Whereas rustics dress for warmth, even in a quaint 'furred gown' if the weather demands, in the city one invites scorn if not outfitted in the most fashionable hose and modern sword and 'hacbut'* (*E vi recto*). Courtly conventions, such as retaining maids and pages, to 'maintain honour' and indicate status, and equipping one's horse in the latest fashion, are not only redundant in the country but actually undesirable. The austerely principled speaker is concerned that the profligate habits of the city are not imported into rural localities, warning 'avoid prodigal apparel, superfluous ba[n]quettes, delicate meates and strong or precious wynes' (*E ii recto*).

As was the case with Wyatt's dual perspective in 'Mine own John Poins', despite the apparent sincerity of the advice, Bryant's proselytising cannot be taken at face value. His exceptionally successful career is often considered to have been built on precisely the self-seeking and opportunistic strategies that he identifies as endemic at the court of Henry VIII, 'A dissembling heart that under a prete[n]ce to be clere an loyal, make men to judge that hypocrisy is devotio[n]' (*D i verso*). According to contemporary opinion, the negative portrait described in *Dispraise of the life of a courtier* matches quite well his own ambitious and disloyal tactics towards preferment, which eventually gained him the prestigious post of Lord Chief Justice of Ireland the year after his volume was published. Indeed, Wyatt's own comment

* Hacbut, hackbut and arquebus are all names for the firearm which predated the musket.

on Bryant's ceaseless political activities, despite his own advice to the contrary, may be a sardonic reference to his unquenchable ambition:

> To thee therefore, that trots still up and down
> And never rests, but running day and night
>
> From Realm to Realm, from city, street, and town,
> Why dost thou wear thy body to the bones ...
> ('A spending hand', ll. 11–14)

Neither writer shies from criticism of the personal foibles of the monarch, nor his governance, at a time when this was clearly unadvisable, as Wyatt knew to his cost. In 'Mine own John Poins', to use his own idiom, Wyatt's speaker plays with fire, refusing to condone tyranny, 'To be the right of a prince's reign [...] No, no, it will not be!' (ll. 75–6).* The juxtaposition of 'lecher' and 'lover' immediately before the reference to 'a prince's reign' (l. 74) would need little deciphering at the court of the libidinous Henry VIII. Frequent more focused acerbic criticism of the monarch and his agents arises amid general denigration of court life, in, for example, the suggestion that the divinely-appointed ruler 'like God on earth alone' preys wolf-like upon 'these sely† lambs' (ll. 26–7) and a regime of cruelty is masked by calls for 'justice' (ll. 68, 69). Despite his claim not to 'scorn or mock', nor deny the right of governance of the monarch, nonetheless, its very articulation invites speculation. He claims instead to distinguish between the role and the inner man, as in the medieval concept of the monarch's two bodies:

> It is not for because I scorn or mock
> The power of them, to whom fortune hath lent
> Charge over us, of right, to strike the stroke.
> But true it is that I have always meant

* In Wyatt's 'Som fowls there be' the speaker recognises the fascination and danger of the 'fire', generally considered to be Anne Boleyn, but equally as possibly the king, and yet still proceeds into the flame. See Part Three: 'Sonnet and Amatory Verse'.

† Sely: innocent.

> Less to esteem them than the common sort,
> Of outward things that judge in their intent
> Without regard what doth inward resort. (ll. 7–13)

Quite how his service to the crown might be expected to proceed under these terms is ambiguous, however, when he categorically states his inability to 'crouch nor kneel to do so great a wrong, / To worship them' (ll. 25–6). Although Wyatt's work is customarily read within the classical parameters of Horatian satire, and can be understood as the plain talking of a humanist adviser, in the model of More's Hythloday, there are, nonetheless, the seeds of treason and rebellion here.

It may be useful to remember that Wyatt was one of the clandestine religious reform sympathisers at the Henrician court, which included Anne Boleyn herself, the Duchess of Suffolk, John Cheke, Sir Nicholas Bacon, Roger Ascham, William Cecil and, most importantly, Thomas Cromwell, who eventually became Henry's Vicar General.* Within the Continental movement for reform new concepts of duty and obedience were being formulated and circulated in publications of varying degrees of notoriety. Influential texts which contributed to this debate included Martin Luther's *Appeal to the German Nobility* (1520) and *On Secular Authority* (1523), the controversial *Vindiciae contra Tyrannos* (*Defences against Tyrants*) (1579), an anonymous French Huguenot tract, and John Calvin's 'On Civil Government' which appears in *The Institutes of the Christian Religion* (1536).[16] The uniting aspect of these and similar contemporary texts, which examine the right of resistance to the ruler, is the changed concept of individual religious culpability which the Reformation of the Church inculcated. Under this broad banner a subject might follow his/her own conscience in situations which undermined religious doctrine. This radical concept undermined accepted theories of order which emphasised a concept of society as an inter-dependent body, within which every element was required to perform rank and calling with unquestioning obedience.

* See Anne Locke's involvement with this circle in Part Three: 'Religious Verse'.

'We ought to obey God rather than men' (Acts 5:29)[17]

This Continental influence on perceptions of obedience and permissible resistance is often termed the 'Calvinist theory of resistance', due to the reformer's opinions, which are found most succinctly in *The Institutes,* Book 4. Despite its later use to justify anarchical removal of figures of authority, including an anointed king, Calvin's perspective frequently returns to the divine appointment of all figures of authority, well-grounded in such biblical provenance as, 'By me [God] kings reign, and princes decree justice. By me princes rule, and nobles, even all the judges of the earth' (Proverbs 8:15–16) and 'Whosoever, therefore, resisteth the power, resisteth the ordinance of God' (Rom. 13:1–2).[18] Despite outspoken censure of individuals who seek to cause schism and civil unrest, Calvin does permit, however, that the responsibility of appointed magistrates includes action against superiors who act impiously. Throughout this chapter Calvin labours to explain the divine purpose in setting tyrants over men and their duty to accept adverse conditions without rebellion. The chapter does gradually introduce fragmented observations which serve as introductions to the final controversial proposition. Amid many, these clues include 'Solomon says, "It is an abomination to kings to commit wickedness"' (4:20, 10) and the distinction that magistrates' authority is not primarily from the ruler, but from God (4:20, 23). Despite earlier manifold conventional admonishments, the final section destabilises the earlier pronouncements with the one caveat: 'We are subject to the men who rule over us, *but subject only in the Lord*. If they command anything against him let us not pay the least regard to it nor be moved by all the dignity which they possess as magistrates' (4:20, 32, added emphasis). Such resistance theories of the sixteenth century opened up the gateway to a plethora of radical interpretations which would find their most fervent expression in the political upheavals of the reign of Charles I.

Civic Obedience and Civil War

The rebellion against the monarchy in the 1640s was an anathema to received theories of order, perpetrated throughout the reigns of the Renaissance monarchs by the rhetoric of governance endorsed by the Church of England in, for example, the *Homily of Obedience.** The proliferation of tracts and pamphlets associated with the Civil War and the unprecedented number of first-time authors, written by both sides of the rift, is extraordinary. For this reason, historians are accustomed to designate it the first great outpouring of popular political debate. The concept of rebellion was clearly very troubling to many individuals caught up in the confrontation of Parliament against the king, and found its way into their arguments and defences published as tracts and pamphlets for a popular readership. These propagandist documents capture the urgent atmosphere of the time in their fast response and publication, often taking the form of a dialogue between Parliamentary and Royalist sectors, as was the case of Henry Parker's *Observations upon some of his Majesties late Answers and Expresses* (1642). As the crisis escalated, Parliament, supported by the army, claimed that, although their actions were technically illegal, they acted as 'lesser magistrates' bound by their duty to protect the people from exploitation. The argument is familiar from Calvin's pronouncements on secular authority cited above, but after the creation of the New Model Army (1644) the religious factor of the resistance became pronounced, as four of its generals were ardent Puritans.

Andrew Marvell's poetry bears evidence of a complex response to the political turmoil of his times. In 1651 he became tutor to the daughter of Thomas, Lord Fairfax, taking up residence at [Nun] Appleton House in North Yorkshire. Despite his prestigious post as a Parliamentary General, conscientious objection to the execution of Charles (1649) and the subsequent invasion of Scotland had prompted Fairfax to resign his post and retire to his country estate.

* *Book of Homilies*, 'An Exhortation concerning good Order, and Obedience to Rulers and Magistrates', STC 13675, available online via the Anglican Library, administered by the University of Toronto.

Marvell's loyalties are quite ambiguous. Along with the loyal poets of the court, Thomas Carew, Richard Lovelace and the dashing John Suckling, he seems to have held royalist sympathies as a young man, despite his Yorkshire Calvinist stock. Puritan sentiments lie just beneath the surface of the seemingly pastoral poem 'The Mower Against Gardens' for example, and yet the apparent eulogy of Oliver Cromwell in celebration of his military victories has intimations of regret for the regicide committed by the Parliamentarian forces. In the nineteenth century Marvell was enjoyed in relatively simple terms as a 'Nature poet' but contemporary criticism, by contrast, relishes the inconsistencies and contractions found in his works.

As Thomas Healy points out, a constant in the seventeenth century imagination is the recognition that no matter how idyllic the vision of the pastoral, it is at best a poor reflection of Eden: 'Ideal nature has in reality been lost and must be "recreated" by gardeners, poets, and painters.'[19] A glimpse of the disillusionment with the new regime may be apparent in this sentiment. For many individuals, existing alongside the Puritan insistence of the pervasiveness of the consequences of original sin, was the extreme disappointment of the dream pursued but revealed as a chimera. A political regime installed through anarchy and bloodshed, ruled by an austere and powerful individual, and enforced by martial law, fell far short of the vision of liberty which had been its instigation. Marvell's ambivalence of vision and expression has been attributed to the insecurities of the era, in many respects ironically paralleling the hazardous life of a courtier of earlier reigns.

'Sweet fields do lie forgot'

In 'The Mower Against Gardens'[20] Marvell's underlying Puritan sentiments emerge in the veiled allegory of the opulence and indulgence of the court as a decorative and unproductive walled garden:

> A dead and standing pool of air,
> And a more luscious earth for them did knead,
> Which stupefied them while it fed. (ll. 6–8)

His imagery builds upon the reader's *a priori* understanding of the biblical account of the Creation and the Fall from Eden, painting a garden of pleasure which does not mirror the perfection of Paradise, but offers up a vision distorted by corruption and vice. Hence, the flowers and fruits have lost their wholesome innocence and natural attributes, instead appearing as painted strumpets and the infertile products of illicit unions. This discourse draws upon horticultural terminology and interacts with the topical enthusiastic interest in gardening as a genteel occupation. While Continental taste was exported throughout Europe in the fashionable 'French' style, based upon geometric designs, adventurers such as John Tradescant travelled the world collecting exotic plants, creating thriving businesses supplying rare specimens to the nobility and gentry. Such excess is denigrated in the frivolity of risking life and fortune for mere novelty in Marvell's: 'Another world was searched through oceans new, / To find the marvel of Peru' (ll. 17–18). Fascination with exotica had similarly gripped the Netherlands in the 1630s in the form of 'Tulip madness', when the rarest single bulbs exchanged hands for sums of money amounting to the annual income of wealthy merchants.[21] It is precisely this decadent phenomenon that Marvell singles out in his condemnation of the flower as a 'tinctured' courtesan:[*]

> And flowers themselves were taught to paint.
> The tulip white did for complexion seek,
> And learned to interline its cheek,
> Its onion root they then so high did hold,
> That one was for a meadow sold … (ll. 12–16)

The court was the centre of civilised society, but Marvell's poem suggests over-cultivation favours artifice over nature. Moreover

* See also Thomas Tukes's cosmetics which are 'brought into use by the devil […] therewith to transform human creatures of faire, making them ugly, enormious and abominable' (8) in *A Discourse Against Painting and Tincturing of Women* (published 1616), available via EEBO, STC 24316a. 8.

'Luxurious'* man's appetite for novel sexual gratification in 'Forbidden' and clandestine liaisons, threatens concepts of natural order itself, by blurring division of rank and kind, grafting 'upon the wild the tame' (ll. 1, 22, 24). Although precise details are obscured by time, condemnation of the lax morality and voracious sexual appetites of the royal circle is readily apparent. In Marvell's vision, mankind's fixation with ornamental horticulture is symptomatic of a wider acceptance of similitude, in which sincerity and honest values have been lost beneath the façade of exhibitionism: a forthright criticism of court and king. Marvell's stance is conventional in terms of poetic satiric revelation, but also aligns with the cautionary advice to rulers found in William Baldwin's popular *Mirror for Magistrates* at the end of the sixteenth century. The quite conventional vilifying tactics used by Baldwin to represent Richard II, for example, a sovereign deposed for his 'evyll governaunce', might equally indicate Henry VIII or Charles I:

> I am a Kyng that ruled all by lust,
> That forced not of vertue, ryght, or lawe,
> But alway put false Flatterers most in trust,
> Ensuing such as could my vices clawe:
> By faythful counsayle passing not a strawe.
> What pleasure pryckt, that thought I to be just.
> I set my minde, to feede, to spoyle, to j[o]ust,
> Three meales a day could skarce content my mawe,
> And all to augment my lecherous minde that must
> To Venus pleasures alway be in awe. (*xvii recto*)[22]

The cohesive critical examinations of perceptions of royal privilege in both texts anticipate the outspoken and outrageous satires of John Wilmot, second Earl of Rochester, in the era of the Restoration of the monarchy. John Wilmot was a young, witty and irreverent libertine, much indulged by Charles II when he regained his father's throne in 1660. Rochester's satires and lampoons scandalised, titillated and

* Luxurious: lecherous.

affronted a coterie audience of wits at court, regulating neither subject matter nor language for any target or reader – including the king. Although there may be the vestiges of the humanist attitude to the role of the poet, in the responsibility to reveal corruption and therefore urge change, this is radically undermined by his exuberance in the licentious material. His 'Satyr Against Reason and Mankind' rejects prevailing concepts of reason and wisdom, arguing for a more honest attitude to life, and goes on to expose mankind's Hobbesian* self-interest in general, but especially at court:

> And to whose morals you would sooner trust.
> Be judge yourself, I'll bring it to the test:
> Which is the basest creature, man or beast?
> Birds feed on birds, beasts on each other prey,
> But savage man alone does man betray.
> Pressed by necessity, they kill for food;
> Man undoes man to do himself no good.
> With teeth and claws by nature armed, they hunt
> Nature's allowance, to supply their want.
> But man, with smiles, embraces, friendship, praise,
> Inhumanly his fellow's life betrays … (ll. 126–36)

The caustic attack condemns contemporary culture which promotes cruel self-promotion at others' expense, duplicity, pride and foolish self-regard. Although utilising a more violent semantic field, there are parallels between the courtier's customary duplicitous performance in the 'Satyr' and the self-conscious display endorsed in Castiglione's influential *The Book of the Courtier* (1528), a guide to 'self-fashioning' for aspiring courtiers.† Edward Hundert perceptively draws attention to the contemporary understanding of the terms 'person' and 'persona', according to Hobbes's definition, 'Persona in latin signifies the disguise,

* Hobbesian: relating to the theories of Thomas Hobbes (1588–1679), philosopher, political theorist and author of *Elements of Law, Natural and Politic* (1640) and *Leviathan* (1651).

† See Part Three: 'Life Guides, Mother's Advice and Conduct Books'.

or outward appearance of a man, counterfeited on the Stage', a man, in fact, acting his own self.[23]

The unifying aspect of these portraits of the courtier, despite their oppositional approaches, is the necessity of adopting a concealing code of behaviour to cloak the desire for personal advancement in a potentially hostile environment. In wider society the decline of familial support and inter-dependence, due to migration to the cities, helped to promote a sense of individualism and decline in traditional values. The Machiavellian outlook, adopted by some individuals caught in the machination of power, is therefore unsurprising in a city of such extremes of paucity and excess.

Overt satire and Mantuanesque eclogue may have helped to regulate the most extreme excesses of court life, but it is well to remember that they are always written from within the system and have a vested interest in maintaining the status quo. As the case of Sir Francis Bryant's *Dispraise of the Courtier* illustrates, the innocent and rustic life is a fine subject for literature, but not necessarily one to aspire to unless one is obliged. London life may have had its dangers but for the average rural worker it represented freedom from the laborious toil of everyday country life. The lure of the city was such that from the beginning of Henry VIII's reign to 1700, the population grew to over 500,000, more than doubling its size in a century.[24] Demographics altered as a result of the flood of all classes towards the cities, especially London, weakening ties not only to family but also to the past and localised hierarchical systems of authority. In this respect the city offered opportunity and the hope of self-advancement. Most of the canonical literary figures studied today could not have reached their potential if they had not left their provincial homes to establish themselves in the capital. It was the only place in the country affluent enough to support permanent playhouses and where the general population had recreation time enough to demand constant entertainment in the written and spoken word.

Notes

1 Ben Jonson, *Epigrams* (c. 1610) Book I, number 134, 51–2.
2 See *The Lisle Letters, An Abridgement*, Muriel St Clare (ed.), selected and arranged by Bridget Boland (London: Secker and Warburg, 1983), vol. 3: 529; Richard Norton to Lady Lisle; vol. 4: 881, John Husee to Lady Lisle; vol. 1: 71, William Seller to Lady Lisle.
3 Sir Francis Bryant, *A dispraise of the life of a courtier, and a commendacion of the life of a labouring man* (1548), translated from French. Available via Early English Books Online, http://eebo.chadwyck.com.home, Short Title Catalogue number (STC) 12431. Francis Bryant's name was sometimes written minus the final 't', see also later discussion of his 'Dispraise of the Life of a Courtier'.
4 The heading is from Miho Suzuki's fascinating study, *Subordinate Subjects, Gender, the Political-Nation, and Literary Form in England*, 1588–1688 (Aldershot: Ashgate, 1988), p. 9.
5 See Paul S. Seaver, 'Declining Status in an Aspiring Age: The Problem of the Gentle Apprentice in Seventeenth-Century London' in *Court, Country and Culture, Essays on Early Modern British History in Honor of Perez Zagorin* (New York: University of Rochester Press, 1992), pp. 129–47, p. 134 and *passim.*
6 Suzuki, pp. 28–30.
7 Isabella Whitney, *A Copy of a Letter, lately written in meeter, by a yonge gentilwoman to her unconstant lover. With an Admonition to al yong gentilwomen and to all other mayds in general to beware mennes flattery* (1567), available via EEBO, STC 25439, pages randomly unnumbered. For the seventeenth century see Part Four: 'The Woman Debate'.
8 Isabella Whitney, *A sweet nosegay, or pleasant posy, containing a hundred and ten phylosophicall flowers &c.* (1573), available via EEBO, STC 25440, pages often unnumbered. The 'wyll' appears at p. *E iii recto*. Note, '*recto*' denotes the right hand page and '*verso*' denotes the left. Numbering is therefore i recto, i verso, ii recto, ii verso, etc., pages may also be bound in sections alphabetically, as A i recto, A ii verso, etc.
9 The full test of *Salve Deus* is available through the Aemilia Lanyer Homepage site, administered by the University of Arizona.
10 Lanyer, *Salve Deus*, dedication 'To the Ladie Anne, Countese of Dorcet', l. 25.
11 Sir Thomas Wyatt, '*V. Innocentia Veritas, Vyat Fides*', l. 11.

12 Elizabeth Heale, *Wyatt, Surrey and Early Tudor Poetry* (London: Longman, 1998), p. 133.

13 Heale, p. 135.

14 Bryant, Chapter 5, header, *E iiii verso*. Note, the pages of the volume are randomly unnumbered and 'recto' denotes the right hand page while 'verso' denotes the left.

15 Bryant, Chapter 3, unnumbered, *C vii recto*. The work is an 'Englished' version of a French translation of a Castillian work, originally by Antonio Guevara (1542) and dedicated to the King of Portugal.

16 John Calvin, 'On Civil Government' in *The Institutes of the Christian Religion* (1536), Book 4: 20.

17 Calvin, *Institutes* 4:20, section 4, 32.

18 Calvin, *Institutes* 4:20, section 6, 23.

19 Thomas Healy, 'Marvell and the Pastoral' in *Early Modern English Poetry, A Critical Companion,* Patrick Cheney, Andrew Hadfield and Garrett A. Sullivan (eds) (Oxford University Press, 2007), pp. 302–14.

20 Andrew Marvell, 'The Mower Against Gardens', line 32, available online via the Luminarium Renaissance site.

21 See Anne Goldgar's *Tulipmania: Money, Honour, and Knowledge in the Dutch Golden Age* (Chicago: University of Chicago Press, 2007).

22 *A myrroure for magistrates* (published 1559 but started during the reign of Mary I), 'Howe kyng Richarde the seconde was for his evyll governaunce deposed from his seat, and miserably murdred in prison', available via EEBO, STC 1247. Note, '*myrroure*' is usually modernised to 'mirror' in modern orthography.

23 Thomas Hobbes, *Leviathan*, chapter 16, 'Of Man', ed. by C. B. Macphearson, (Harmondsworth: Penguin, 1968), pp. 217–18, cited in Edward Hundert, 'Performing the Enlightenment Self: Henry Fielding and the History of Identity' in *Court, Country and Culture, Essays on Early Modern History* (New York: University of Rochester Press, 1992), pp. 223–44, p. 227.

24 Vanessa Harding, 'Families and Housing in Seventeenth Century London', *Parergon* 24.2 (2007) pp. 115–38, p. 115.

The Woman Debate

In the 1970s the scholarship of feminist literary critics began to rediscover 'lost' texts written by Renaissance women in an endeavour, which Elaine Showalter identified as an aspect of 'Gynocritics'.* It is through the dedicated work of these and subsequent feminist scholars that the work of many women writers previously unknown to twentieth-century academia were re-published and put back into circulation. They were also interested in widening the canon of studied works to include genres not previously studied as 'high' literature, such as Mother's Advice books and polemic tracts. As part of their endeavour, however, they also studied male-authored texts noting and interrogating their representations of women. The popular pamphlets, which together comprise the seventeenth-century 'Woman Debate' or *Querelle des Femmes*, exemplify this enterprise in that they are often considered to be on the margins of 'literature' and are also very much concerned with representations of women. The underlying base line of Swetnam's *The Arraignment*† *of Lewde, idle, forward, and unconstant women* is the idealised construct of femininity endorsed by a patriarchal society, which

* Gynocritics: a term coined by Elaine Showalter to describe a dual feminist approach: to examine male-authored texts from a female perspective and to retrieve works by female authors which have been disregarded by male domination of high literature, resulting in their loss from the canon.

† Arraignment: trial.

he vividly illustrates most women do not meet. The female-voiced responses attempt to counter his attacks, from within the same discourse, however, accepting the unrealistic expectations of a male-dominated culture predicated upon contemporary theological belief. In the terms of Althusser,* they are interpellated within the system and world-view. Jean Luis Vives's *De institutione foeminae Christiana* (*The Instruction of a Christen Woman*) (1523, trans. 1529) is an example of the type of mainstream texts which assisted the process.

Educating Women: 'Preceptes and rules howe to lyve'

In the Renaissance as now, education played a central role in women's ability to achieve informed opinions on topical issues such as politics, exploration and national identity, trade and colonisation, besides more pious and domesticated issues. Apart from in the most exceptional circumstances, women, according to the early modern idealised model of femininity, were not encouraged to voice or even hold opinions on the majority of these subjects.† They were considered incompatible with their private and domesticated role. However, from accounts of women's private reading, translation exercises and eventual publishing of tracts, diaries and letters, it is obvious that as the sixteenth and seventeenth centuries progressed, women were increasingly well-informed and, in some cases, eager to participate in public debate.

Even as early as the reign of Henry VIII progressive humanist thinkers were devising educational programmes specifically for women,

* Louis Althusser (1918–90): Marxist philosopher. 'Interpellation' is the process by which an individual is drawn into a system, absorbing and accepting its ideology.

† Juan Luis Vives's intention was to write a manual of female Christian life, from infancy to adulthood. The beneficiary of his instruction was Princess Mary, the first daughter of Henry VIII, later becoming Mary I. Vives was her tutor as a child and in the service of her mother Catherine of Aragon. The work was translated from Latin to English by Richard Hyrde, Sir Thomas More's household tutor, in 1529, under the title, *A very frutefull and pleasant boke called the Instructio[n] of a Christen woma[n]*. The above quotation is from Valerie Wayne's chapter on the work in *Silent But For The Word, Tudor Women as Patrons, Translators, and Writers of Religious Works*, Margaret P. Hannay (ed.) (Ohio: Kent University Press, 1985), pp. 15–29, p. 16.

although predicated upon contemporary perceptions of female nature and cultural prescription. Educators such as Vives, Thomas More, Roger Ascham and Richard Mulcaster promoted women's education to varying degrees and condoned different fields of activity. Vives's aforementioned influential work takes as its foundation the safeguarding of a woman's virtue whilst training her in godliness.[1] Predictably, his choice of study texts is scriptural and morally uplifting. He endorses study as a useful distraction from more dangerous pursuits and a valuable resource for promoting good living, which may safely be encouraged if the young woman is 'truely and surely chaste'.[2] Vives reiterates the common understanding of the malleability of the female intellect, claiming that the 'study of lerning' wholly occupies the mind and 'infecteth' it with worthwhile knowledge. Vives maintains that access to only religious works would 'plucketh' the mind from dwelling on the corrupt, to focus it steadfastly on godliness and morality.[3] Historically, the female mind had been considered weak to the extent of permeability, its absorbent nature underlined in texts such as Boccaccio's *De mulieribus claris* (*Of famous women*) (*c*.1362), which advised parents 'at the beginning they are so flexible that with little effort they can be guided almost at will'.[4]

Despite Vives's foresight and sincere approval of education for women, throughout his text is a cautious undercurrent which decrees, for example, that a young woman must not be left to her own devices in her choice of subject and that her course of study must be directed by a 'sober' and pious man. These are precautions against 'the light fantasies of maydes' which delight in 'songes daunces / and such other wanton and pevyshe playes'. The purpose of young women's education is to 'enstruct their maners and enfurm their lyving', to teach a good and holy life.[5] Most specifically, Vives advises against permitting the reading of works dealing with love and romance as insidiously corrupting to the moral outlook, suggesting that such works are introduced to girls by young men specifically to further their amatory exploits. So alarmed by their influence is he that he resolutely declares that if the pupil is persistent in her 'delyte', and rejects alternative, more appropriate works, she should be prevented from reading at all until she has lost the skill.[6]

Clearly, to the Renaissance patriarch, female and male brain functions were different; the masculine was free-ranging and capable of inspirational ascendance, whilst the female followed prescribed pathways and had difficulty with retention.

The repercussions of women's perceived responsibility for mankind's Fall endorsed male governance, in all respects, and was reiterated by Church worthies in contemporary marriage manuals:

> God requireth subiection of a wife to her husband, the wife is bound to yeeld it. And good reason it is that she who first drew man into sin, should be now subiect to him, lest by the like womanish weaknesse she fall againe.[7]

In this era a daughter's education, just as her mother's obedience, was directed and enforceable by the male head of the family. In both cases the moulding of the female to male-prescribed parameters of knowledge, activity and even thought, in some degree, is the privileged male prerogative. The dictated sphere of knowledge and condoned intellectual activity, of course, has implications for the content of the creative output of those women who went on to write themselves. Unsurprisingly, religious works far outnumbered any other genre in the work of early Renaissance women writers, and published works which involved the imagination and original thought were rare.

Protestantism and the Equality of the Spirit

In many circumstances increased female educational opportunity was linked to a reformed religious outlook, as Protestantism promoted the concept of spiritual equality. This permitted some negotiation of the heavy burden of Eve's sin.* With the advent of state Protestantism in the reign of Edward VI (1547), it was considered essential that all members of society, regardless of rank, calling or sex, were able to read the Bible, for the sake of their own salvation. In this early period the humanist tenet of increasing access to education and the Protestant aim

* See Part Three: 'Life Guides, Mother's Advice and Conduct Books'.

of promoting literacy as a religious tool, were in harmony. The establishment of grammar schools and informal household programmes of reading instruction were both of great spiritual importance but also made a significant contribution to national literacy figures. Girls were mostly educated within the context of the household, however, whether within their own home or as attendants in the service of wealthy households of higher social status. Such an arrangement could be particularly advantageous to young women of middling class as they could have the advantage of sharing the educational programme of the women of the family. Aemelia Lanyer and Isabella Whitney are both thought to have benefited from such arrangements.

As humanist influences percolated into mainstream society even women of gentry or middle class status might receive tuition in the classics, one or two modern languages and, as is apparent from their writing, perhaps even in rhetoric. It was generally believed that women could be trained in desirable qualities by the close study of serious religious works. Such texts were therefore particularly recommended for the translation exercises of women with linguistic skills. Despite the fact that the term itself was often a misnomer, as 'translations' were often quite loose paraphrases, a further advantage of this type of literary occupation was that the act itself was considered a derivative exercise, rather than creative. For this reason translation was considered a 'feminine' and less commendable form of writing, even for men. John Florio famously regarded his translation of Montaigne's *Essayes* (1603) a 'defective edition (since all translations are reputed femalls)'.[8] Mary Ellen Lamb terms the activity 'degraded' in this respect and remarks that it is therefore particularly appropriate to dedicate a translation to a female patron. The skill demonstrated a type of mechanical competency, rather than a literary gift or (virile) intellectual brilliance. A further advantage of this genre was that the woman's own opinion remained undisclosed, protecting her privacy from the intrusive gaze of her readers; if a woman must write, translation was for this reason considered a more modest activity. This ultra-sensitivity to issues of female privacy and the protection of virtue reveals the reasoning behind the damaging common assertion that a published woman was a 'public' woman.

Shunning the 'Praise of the public'

A woman's education was mainly intended to create a capable and agreeable companion for her future spouse; her abilities were therefore to be celebrated in the privacy of familial contexts. Sir Thomas More's very gifted and highly-educated daughter, Margaret More Roper, excelled in translation and 'wrote eloquently in prose and verse in both Greek and Latin'. She also evidently studied 'medical science', religious works and astronomy, underpinned by her father's direction in humility, virtue and Christian charity.[9] Elaine Beilin examines accounts of Roper's extraordinary abilities, drawing attention to her father's own sympathy that due to her sex her talents would be questioned or simply not believed.[10] He urges her to accept this as praise, which is further deserved by her modesty in not seeking it:

> ... you do not seek for praise of the public, nor value it overmuch if you receive it, but [...] you regard us – your husband and myself – as sufficiently large circle of readers for all that you write.[11]

The issue of 'modesty' linked to virtue – or its lack – arises insistently in the debate about women's lives generally, but especially in the case of women writers during the era. A frequent observation of the time was that a woman's sole value lay in her 'honesty', meaning not only absence of immorality but also freedom from *suspicion* of any kind of behaviour judged to be inappropriate to her gender.

In the earliest part of the sixteenth century if women wished to broadcast their work among friends or family it was circulated in manuscript copies; loose pages were bound into books which were handwritten and laborious to prepare. The ability to produce literary texts is not only predicated upon a sufficient degree of education and the indulgence of male members of the family, but also on a certain amount of leisure time and level of affluence. Paper was expensive and often of irregular quality, sufficient light, inks and writing implements could be difficult and expensive to acquire, while the burning of candles in order to read and write in ill-lit Renaissance homes was an extravagance that only relatively privileged women could afford. Publication of such works was a contentious issue, as the widespread distribution to an unknown audience was considered vulgar in higher social circles, even for men. In the case of a woman writer, this could be particularly damaging to her reputation, as the suggestion is that she seeks public voice, which was anathema to the contemporary construct of a 'good' woman. The plethora of prefatorial male-endorsed recommendations, letters of explanation and assurances of piety, humility and godliness, bear evidence to this anxiety in numerous female-authored texts of the time.

Anne Locke's 'Songe'

Anne Vaughan Locke (*c.*1534–after 1590), whose early work is discussed in the religious verse chapter of Part Three, was from a wealthy merchant background of extreme Protestant sympathies. She was fortunate to be educated, along with her brother and younger sister, by a tutor who was learned in Latin and Greek. She was also fluent in French. Locke's entry into print culture was the direct result of her reformed faith and an avid desire to further its embattled cause. Her first volume traces her development as a writer, advancing beyond the prescribed genre of religious translation to include original poetry and an allegorical polemic in her dedicatory letter.* Her volume, quite surprisingly for its early date, does not offer any apologies for

* Locke's volume, *Sermons upon the Song that Ezechias made after he had been sick and afflicted by the Hand of God*, was written during her religious exile in Geneva while the Catholic Mary I was Queen of England. It was published upon her return, after Elizabeth I had acceded to the throne, in January 1559/60. Nonetheless, the preface to the sonnets states they were 'delivered [her] by a friend', rather than being written by Locke herself. Lexical analysis of her translations, and later volume *Of the Markes of the Children of God* (1590), has convinced modern scholars that they were written by Locke, however. See Susan Felch (ed.), *The Collected Work of Anne Lock* (Tempe, Arizona: Arizona Center for Medieval and Renaissance Studies & Renaissance English Text Society, 1999), p. liv.

publication nor utilise the 'modesty topos', of lack of expertise or a work badly rendered.* She also writes her own uncompromising dedicatory letter, rather than relying on male endorsement of her work, although her authorship is only signalled in initials, rather than her full name, which disguises her gender to the wider reading public.

The genre of religious translation may seem relatively uncontroversial but in translating four of Calvin's sermons on Isaiah 38 from French Locke gave her English-speaking co-religionists direct access to his new reformed† interpretation. She was present in Geneva as the sermons were delivered and had access to the transcriptions made in shorthand by an organised body of stenographers. Hence, she was at the forefront of the Calvinistic cause, her translations were modern, lively and colloquial, and not dry exercises in the classics, re-working familiar material prescribed by male educators.

Her volume's dedicatory epistle is to a celebrated and controversial heroine, the Duchess of Suffolk, who also went into religious exile during the reign of Mary I. The letter takes as its theme spiritual health, which is developed into an allegorical prescription for life, a large part of which denigrates the 'false' practitioner who misleads and fails his 'patient'. She describes the various symptoms and their true and false remedies in an outspoken polemic against Catholic doctrine, offering instead what she regards as a wholesome medicine for the soul, writing herself into its dissemination from the 'heavenly Physitian' through Calvin as a 'most excellent Apothecarie'.[12] She writes as one confident in her calling as one of the Elect which decrees her duty to admonish and teach; neither of which align well with conservative models of feminine decorum. In this respect her faith provides a public platform for her contentious address and a vehicle

* The publisher's dedication of Anne Cooke (Bacon)'s translations of Bernadino Ochino's sermons (*c.*1551), for example, praises her virtue and modesty and assures of her genteel status. See Elaine Beilin, 'Building the City: Women Writers of the Reformation' in *Redeeming Eve*, pp. 55–61, p. 56.

† In this volume the term 'reformed' is used broadly to distinguish the 'old' faith, Catholicism, from the new religious reform movement of the Continent, associated with Martin Luther in Germany, Huldrych Zwingli and Heinrich Bullinger in Switzerland, and Jean (John) Calvin in Geneva.

for self-definition within the confrontational context of an outlawed religion.

Locke's text implicitly assumes an equality of the soul, although it does not overtly interrogate prevailing notions of gender hierarchy and avoids any discussion of perceived female inadequacy. Male-authored literary defences of women engage with these concepts but in a manner that is not necessarily enabling, as their endorsement of innate female virtue, faithfulness and willing service to man or God is predicated upon the same set of patriarchal values as the misogynistic attacks which they counter. Whether historical examples of 'good' wives, passive virgins or wise queens throughout history, or celebrations of contemporary paragons, for the most part, whether classical, medieval or Renaissance, the 'Defences of Women' did not offer significant alternatives to accepted theories of the female capabilities nor – therefore – their prescribed sphere of activity.* As Pamela J. Benson points out, 'They argue about how successfully woman is chaste, obedient and silent, not about whether she ought to be [...] none argues for a change in women's social role'.[13]

Agrippa's sixteenth-century 'Defence', *On the Nobility and Pre-eminence of the Female Sex* (1529), broke new ground in the genre, in that it questioned and reinterpreted the foundations by which the concept of female inferiority was justified, rather than being just a collection of exemplary lives.[14] Although he illustrated his theories with reference to famous women, his arguments also interrogated the basic principles of ancient classical works of medicine and philosophy, legal precepts, both modern and ancient, and contemporary understanding of biblical material. Modern critical response, however, makes diverse claims for this work. Some scholars suggest that it was in fact satirical, rather than being intended as a vindication of women. Agrippa's pervasive arguments, nonetheless, furnished rebuttals of female defamation in the pamphlet war known as the *Querelle des*

* Boccaccio's *De mulieribus claris* (*c*.1362) was the first of this type of European text devoted solely to the praise of good women and had a strong influence on all subsequent works, including Geoffrey Chaucer's *Legend of Good Women* (*c*. 1385) and Christine de Pisan's *The Book of the City of Ladies* (1405).

*Femmes** of the following century. Some of his conclusions, restated by later writers such as Aemilia Lanyer, Rachel Speght and the women-voiced pamphlets of the Swetnam controversy, suggest that Eve's physical substance was more perfect and her innocence greater than Adam's, that his sin was greater as she was not warned against eating from the Tree of Knowledge, and that women were both favoured by Christ and have a special bond with him through the maternal role of the Virgin Mary.[15]

Aemilia Lanyer's plea: 'Let us have our Libertie againe'

Lanyer's volume of original poetry, *Salve Deus Rex Judaeorum* (1611), does include the praise of pious women, familiar in male-authored women's defence literature, but her main focus is the re-interpretations of scriptural events.† Although Agrippa had rehearsed similar arguments, for a female author of this time its uncompromising claims are exceptional. As Janel Mueller points out, in the accounts of the betrayal, condemnation and killing of Christ, Lanyer's narrative strategies represent men as consistently misunderstanding or deliberately misrepresenting him and not being aware of the significance of their own actions. Lanyer specifically exposes male duplicity in the calculated manipulation of language, in for example, 'They tell his Words, though farre from his intent, / And what his Speeches were, not what he meant.'[16] In an era of male-dominated discourse which barred women from much self-expression and specifically public speech, this is a significant point.

Despite allegedly adhering to patriarchal constraints of subject matter and condoned female literary activity, *Salve Deus* is nonetheless transgressive.[17] Although the work is essentially biblical paraphrase and

* Literally: 'The Women Quarrel', but more appropriately 'The Women Controversy' or 'The Woman Debate'.

† The title alludes to a biblical quotation, from Matthew 27, which records the Latin text, 'Hail King of the Jews', erected over Christ's head when he was crucified; two editions were printed in the same year, with slightly different dedications. The heading is a quotation from line 825.

the sources are scriptural, her tableaux of biblical events enhance women's roles and denigrate male actions, while forcefully disputing conventional interpretation of both. She presents strong arguments against the cultural stereotyping of women as evil, a condemnation of the misinterpretation of Eve's actions, and a call to recognise the true value of women's contribution to both biblical events and contemporary life:

> Then let us have our Libertie againe,
> And challenge to your selves no Sov'raigntie;
> You came not in the world without our paine,
> Make that a barre against your crueltie;
> Your fault beeing greater, why should you disdaine
> Our beeing your equals, free from tyranny?
> If one weake woman simply did offend,
> This sinne of yours, hath no excuse, nor end. (ll. 825–32)

As Barbara Lewalski noted, the overall structure of the work achieves the remarkable feat of drawing together the contemporary noblewomen of the numerous dedications, the author and the biblical heroines of the poem in a 'community of good women'.[18] Within the main section of the volume, the poem *Salve Deus*, Lanyer's religious material is prefaced by, and interwoven with, addresses to the Countess of Cumberland. The effect is somewhat controversially to create a dialogue between the addressee and events described, elevating her spiritual status to an onlooker at the Passion, and so one of the Daughters of Jerusalem.* Lanyer's forceful rehabilitation of women through reinterpretation of the sources of their subjection is extraordinary for its time and it is often termed proto-feminist. Nonetheless, a modern reader can identify the fact that some of her literary strategies incorporate elements of medieval

* The volume falls into three sections: an extensive group of dedications to women of the court, *Salve Deus*, and a 'A Description of Cooke-ham', which may be the first English Country House poem. See Part Four: 'City, Court and Country'.

female mysticism, whether deliberately or unconsciously.[*] Lanyer may have been familiar with such works through her (Catholic) Italian heritage, despite her own Protestant faith. It is interesting to consider that she may have consciously sited her work within this female writing tradition.

Echoes of this tradition are found in Lanyer's alignment of Christ's patience under affliction with women's long-suffering chastisement for Adam's sin. Despite adamant assertions of injustice and strident demands for retribution, however, Lanyer speaks from within prevailing concepts of natural order. Although arguing for a re-examination of the ingrained misogyny of her society, she nevertheless does not seem to wish to subvert of concepts the gender hierarchy, accepting Adam as the 'Lord of all' (l. 780), who cannot be ruled by his wife:

> And then to lay the fault on Patience backe, / That we (poore women) must endure it all / [...] If he would eate it, who had powre to stay him? (ll. 793–4, 800).[†]

Theories of gender hierarchy were perpetrated in sermons, medical texts, legal documents and other authoritative sources, while contemporary songs, jokes, and received wisdom of all kinds promoted the belief that women were weak, irrational and prone to evil and immorality if left to their own devices. This had important ramifications for the role of women in society and especially for women writers, who lacked personal authority and were constantly reminded of their supposed limitations in every area of activity.

* Lanyer's feminising of Christ and the semi-erotic imagery of spiritual fulfilment both frequently appear in the work of medieval female mystics. Bridal-mysticism was a significant aspect of the visionary experiences of some female mystics, such as Margery Kempe and Hadewijch of Brabant.

† Alternatively, it is possible to read this cynically as a knowing manipulation of the cultural codes to the advantage of women.

Swetnam's Baiting of 'Lewde, idle, forward, and unconstant women'

Joseph Swetnam's diatribe, published four years after Lanyer's volume, rehearsed a catalogue of negative opinion about women, ranging untidily through misquoted biblical and philosophical sources and delivering a liberal dose of adversarial comment, to present a hotchpotch of contemporary misogynistic thought. The antagonistic title of his pamphlet was *The Arraignment of Lewde, idle, forward, and unconstant women* (1615), and its aggressive stance may have been a commercial strategy, in that its outrageous claims invited response. The work is not innovative in content but collects together negative anecdotes, adages, jokes and disparate references to women and their failings from a wide variety of sources, including contemporary marriage guides, defences of women and earlier satires, such as Edward Gosynhill's *Schole house of women* (1541).[19]

Swetnam's arguments are illogical, fragmented and difficult to analyse, partly due to their inconsistencies and anecdotal presentation. He frequently creates lists of short citations which ostensibly illustrate the direction of his thought but, in fact, often have only tenuous links with the issue in hand, or are so obviously manipulated and reductive that his perspective is demonstrated to be seriously flawed. There is the possibility that he wrote in full appreciation of this, as a mockery of the works or their adherents, specifically for his appreciative male readership. Dianne Purkiss has commented on what she terms his 'rhetoric of citation', maintaining that the work's extraordinary popularity was at least in part due to this authorial strategy, which relied on the reiteration of the familiar.[20]

In his introduction Swetnam claims to have written the work in an idle moment and in angry response to maltreatment by women, warning any who read it that to reply to his 'monstrous accusations' would clearly indicate that the defamations were accurate and deserved:

> ... whatsoever you think privately, I wish you to conceal it with silence, lest in starting up to find fault you prove yourselves guilty ...[21]

His intended audience is primarily male, as the extended title of the work indicates in the centred and prominent typeface which specifically recommends the text as 'pleasant' and 'profitable' to married and single men. In the relative whisper of smaller print, it does, however, also address '*the common sort of Women*' in its final line. Although Swetnam hedges his term with the explanatory note that he does not deal with the best or worst examples of the sex, aiming at the typical, the descriptor is suspect. Despite – or perhaps because of – his protestation the reader registers the possible readings of 'common', including 'vulgar' or 'held in common', meaning 'of shared ownership': a prostitute. The innuendo is perpetrated in the following paragraph which utilises the *double-entendres* of 'bitten' and 'touch':

> I know I shall be bitten by many because I touch many [...]. And those which spurn if they feel themselves touched prove themselves stark fools in betraying their galled backs to the world, for this book toucheth no sort of women but such as when they hear it will go about about to reprove it. (Introduction)

This type of male humour is diffused throughout the text, alluding to a shared discourse of misogynistic thought in which women are commodified as the source of sexual pleasure. Swetnam's assertion is that the respectable facades adopted by most women are either bogus or open to negotiation and that all women, of every status, have their price:

> And women are easily wooed and soon won, got with an apple and lost with the paring [...] women's bright beauty breeds curious thoughts; and golden gifts easily overcome wantons' desires [...] and being once delighted therein, continues in the same without repentance. (Chapter 2)

Swetnam's diatribe reveals a pervasive insecurity in its insistent returns to the expression of female sexuality, which is perceived as excessive, manipulative and deceitful. In a section dwelling on the lust of 'unmarried wantons', which shifts focus from male 'victim' to female perpetrator, Swetnam adopts the liturgical tone of the Puritan sermon, calling upon women to wash away their sins 'with the crystal tears of true sorrow and repentance', enhancing his prose with ostentatious exclamation and apostrophe. Within this discourse of essentialised female lasciviousness, the only hope of delivery from 'this foul leprosy of nature', he indicates, is through prayer and divine intervention (Chapter 2). In an allusion to the fallen nature of women, moreover, Swetnam counts his licentious version of womanhood as less than human, denying her a place in the social organisation of human society as she cannot be accommodated in the culturally available roles available to women: she is no longer a maiden but not fit to be either a wife or widow. Whether this is a specific recollection or simply a reiteration of popular opinion is unclear, but his pattern of thought echoes that of Shakespeare's Duke in *Measure for Measure* (1604). When Mariana is confronted by Duke Vincentio her ambiguous response prompts his question 'Why you are nothing then:– neither maid, widow or wife?' This is closely followed by Lucio's inevitable pronouncement on a woman who cannot be adequately lodged in any of these categories, 'she may be a punk [prostitute]; for many of them are neither maid, wife nor widow'.[22] This reductive summary of the roles available to women in a patriarchal society is frequently quoted by feminist critics who point out that contemporary legal texts give legitimacy to the attitude. T. E.'s *The Lawes Resolutions of Women's Rights* (1632), for example, clearly identifies both married women's lack of rights in law and the expectation that 'All of them are understood either married or to be married'.[23]

Although no doubt intended to entertain his male readership, Swetnam's depiction of marriage is a miserable affair, predicated upon a misogynistic belief in women's natural inclination to infidelity and her voracious self-interest. A recurring concern in his portrait is women's profligacy, which is identified as a contributing factor to their inclination to sexual adventure, in that their delight in personal display not only attracts potential lovers, but also wastes the husbands' estate:

> … if she be decked up in gorgeous apparel, then a thousand to one but she will love to walk where she may get acquaintance […] if a woman love gadding but that she will pawn her honor to please her fantasy. (Chapter 2)*

The trope of cuckoldry, which seems to have been so prominent in the era, maintains a distrustful presence and can be read as an indication of 'anxious masculinity', in its humiliating evidence of a failure of patriarchal authority.

Swetnam's third chapter introduces itself as a 'remedy' against love and the hasty decision to marry, nonetheless, advising how to choose a wife if the bachelor cannot be deterred. The latter part might be considered to share common ground with the marriage manuals of the time, but the underlying sentiment, of course, is not celebratory of the marital union. Domestic advice books, often written by religious figures and especially Puritan divines, sought to stabilise society from its unit of the family. Theories of order and authority are enshrined within the mechanism of daily life which influence personal and cultural attitudes, ultimately ensuring the maintenance of the status quo. Purkiss perceptively points out that the opposition between Swetnam's misogyny and 'the more general conception of patriarchy or a patriarchal social order' is often overlooked (p. 73). Her point is that in its opposition to the social conditioning and normalised institutions of patriarchy, *The Arraignment* is actually subversive. Swetnam's text endorses the casual attitude to sex that is expressly condemned by outraged prelates, articulated in their pious literature and spoken sermons: 'it is counted no sinne at all, but rather a pastime, a dalliance,

* A similar concern with the preservation of the husband's goods and wealth is outlined in popular domestic advice books, which frequently underline a wife's duty to preserve, rather than squander. See William Whately's *A Bride-Bush* (1617), discussed in Part Three: 'Life Guides, Mother's Advice and Conduct Books'.

and but a touch of youth: not rebuked, but winked at: not punished, but laughed at.'[24]

The interactions between man and wife depicted by Swetnam are also radically different to the ideal created in such texts as William Whately's domestic Conduct Book, *A Bride-Bush: or, a direction for married persons Plainly describing the duties common to both, and peculiar to each of them* (1617).[25] *The Arraignment*'s devaluation of the institution of marriage and endorsement of alternatives to the stable and productive family unit encourage exactly the immorality and self-seeking pleasure decried in the *Homily Against Whoredom and Adultery* (1562–3), preached from the pulpits and absorbed into notions of public morality. This influential sermon explicitly links 'filthy and unlawfull love' with 'the utter destruction of publik wealth' and social breakdown which causes poverty and criminality.[26]

Rachel Speght: 'The talent God doth give, must be employ'd'

Swetnam's polemic prompted a number of retaliatory pamphlets, the first of which was written by Rachel Speght. This is the only response which can reliably be attributed to a female author, as the others are signed with pseudonyms and for this reason they are termed 'woman-voiced', although they are written from a female perspective.[27] Speght's background is similar to Anne Locke's in that she was from a middle-class family of staunch Calvinist sympathies and lived in the Cheapside merchant district of London.* Despite the support of family and 'carefull friends', she risked her reputation as a respectable unmarried young woman by the decision to publish her rejoinder, *A Mouzell for Melastomus the Cynicall Bayter of, and foule-mouthed Barker against Evahs Sex* and *Certaine Quares* [queries] *to the bayter of Women* (1617) under

* Her father was the rector of two churches which were within the Cheapside mercantile area; St Mary Magdalene on Milk Street and St Clement on Eastcheap, both of which can be easily traced on the map of early modern London. James Speght's ministries cited in *The Polemics and Poems of Rachel Speght,* ed. by Barabara Lewalski (Oxford: Oxford University Press, 1996), p. xi.

her own name.* In her second volume, *Mortalities Memorandum* (1621), she boldly addresses the detractors who claimed that the earlier text was beyond her capabilities, yet acknowledges that a public act always attracts censure (p. 45).

The prefatory verse dream vision of the second text follows Lanyer's precedent, engaging with the familiar patriarchal discourse which held that Eve's inappropriate pursuit of knowledge was the cause of mankind's Fall. Speght is careful to authorise her undertaking with biblical glosses, and boldly asserts her right to make use of her literary gifts: 'The talent God doth give, must be employ'd' (l. 133, p. 53). Her adopted cause is the issue of women's enforced ignorance and denial of access to knowledge, asking 'wherefore shall / A woman have her intellect in vaine, / Or not endevour / *Knowledge* to attain' (ll. 130–2, p. 53). Somewhat surprisingly, however, she presents her persona as the heroine of a quest, somewhat akin to a female knight of the chivalric romance.†

Accompanied by encouraging female muses, she encounters a 'full fed Beast' [Swetnam], which 'foamed filthie froth' on women, most evocative of the Redcrosse Knight's final confrontation with the monster named 'Erroure' in Book I of *The Faerie Queene*. This creature similarly vomits 'A floud of poison horrible and blacke' (Book I: 172–3) over its victim which, incidentally, contains published 'bookes and papers'.[28] Further evidence of the work's topical intertextuality appears in Speght's incorporation of other woman-voiced responses to Swetnam's polemic in the allegory. She relates her own earlier battle with the 'Beast', in which she used a 'Mouzel to bind his chaps' (p. 246), the 'selfe-conceited' Ester Sowernam's attempt to overcome him (pp. 248–52) and Constantia Munda's eventual gagging, 'to make him hold his tongue' (pp. 255–64).[29] Despite a gesture to modesty in

* The two texts seem to have been intended to be bound together as one volume, evidenced in their continuing pagination, but may also have at some time been published separately. See Lewalski's fascinating research, including discussion and reproduction of hand-annotations in one text which may have belonged to Swetnam himself: *The Polemics and Poems of Rachel Speght*, pp. xxxii–xxxiv and 91–106.

† See Spenser's *Faerie Queene* in Part Three: 'Pastoral to Epic', and Ariosto's *Orlando Furioso* (1532). Both feature a female knight.

the conventional reference to her 'insufficiency in literature and tendernesse in yeares', the works exhibit her impressive literary skills, wide learning and thorough knowledge of the scriptures. Her pleasure in study is also alluded to in her 'Dreame' vision and in this she was supported not only by her father, but also her godmother, Mrs Marie Moundford, whom she thanks and praises as a paragon in the prefatory epistle of *Mortalities Memorandum*.

Elizabeth Carey: 'They are much deluded, / Who think that learning's not for Ladies fit'

The case of Elizabeth Carey, Lady Falkland (*c.*1585–1639), was far removed from Rachel Speght's experience. Despite her elevated status, she incurred the hostility of her own and her young husband's family for pursuing her delight in reading.* A biography produced by one of her daughters indicates that she read widely in many different genres, in English, modern foreign languages, Latin and also Hebrew. Attempting to curb her excessive passion, her mother adopted the practical strategy of limiting her supply of candles and when, aged around nineteen, Carey was forbidden reading material by her mother-in-law, she apparently began to write her own original works.[30]

Her wide-ranging knowledge and interests led her to produce such diverse work as translations from French and Latin, including a detailed geographical text and Seneca's epistles, a humorous epitaph, a verse rendition of the life of the fourteenth-century emperor 'Timur the Lame',† verse 'lives' of female saints, contemporary religious translations, Mother's Advice-type writing for her children and two plays. This oeuvre ranges through the relatively condoned genre of translation of

* The heading quotation is the first two lines of 'Another', one of the anonymous poems which preface Elizabeth Carey's translation of *The reply of the most illustrious Cardinall of Perron*.

† Amir Timur, also known as 'Timur the Lame' and 'Tamerlane', was a ruthless fourteenth-century conqueror from the area now known as Uzbekistan. To the English Renaissance audience he was immortalised in Christopher Marlowe's popular play *Tamburlaine*.

religious works to more overtly male-dominated genres, such as original verse, drama and history.

Although innovative ventures for a female author, both of Carey's plays could be said to be conforming to cultural expectation to some degree, in that *The Tragedy of Mariam* is a closet drama* and *Edward II* is presented in a blended prose and dramatic form, presenting direct challenge to neither genre. Her negotiations of literary parameters and cultural givens can be read as subversive, however. Her daughter's biography reveals the difficulties Carey faced in attempting to uphold her strong sense of matrimonial and paternal duty whilst remaining true to her own high principles of behaviour and religious outlook. As her biography relates, she had 'Be and Seem' engraved on her daughter's wedding ring. This was understood by her daughter as meaning that external appearance should confirm inward resolution. It may, however, be interpreted as delivering the radically different and opposing advice of presenting a *façade* of conformity, whilst preserving one's own integrity.[31] In *Mariam*, for example, within the overarching frames of a male-authored historic text and inherited classical tragedy conventions, Carey presents a female perspective on domestic subjection and oppression.

Similarly, Carey's 1630 translation of the French Cardinal Perron's response to James I, which falls within the parameters of religious translation, is actually a defence of Catholicism addressed to the late monarch, head of Protestant state religion.[32] The prefatory epistle to the reader in this work also disrupts familiar humility conventions associated with female-authored works. Although Carey draws attention to her female sex, suggesting that this should excuse any deficiency within the work, by far the most striking aspect is the lack of false modesty. Her satisfaction with the translation is evident in her pragmatic point that she would not be foolish enough to permit its publication if it were not well done. Moreover, the familiar modest claim that her motivation was not vainglory is undermined by her assertion that, if this were the case she would choose a work more 'Antique' and taxing – implying that this enterprise hardly strained her abilities. Her dexterity in French is

* Closet drama: intended for private performance.

underlined in her claim that it took 'fower times as long' to transcribe as translate, which is confirmed in a prefatory poem marvelling at the rapidity of preparation, which amounted to only one month. The three prefatory poems, rather than being male-endorsements of her humility, piety and moral invulnerability avoid issues of morality, but immoderately draw attention to her learning and brilliance. Finally, Carey dismisses the disingenuous conceit of female authors that they were persuaded to publish, never having intended the work for the public gaze, instead claiming personal authority and self-determination. In voicing Perron's argument in English, she espouses the role of Catholic apologist, confident that she does God's work: 'reade Peron; And when that is done, I have my End, therest [*sic*] I leave to Gods pleasure'.[33] It would seem that Carey's belief was that the Catholic argument was self-evident and only needed expression to be accepted. Her bold assertion may also suggest that she accepted and even invited the castigation which might follow.

If the issue is obscured by the original work's Catholicism, Carey's unequivocal loyalty to the prohibited faith is made clear in her address 'To The Reader' in which she courageously states that she does not wish it to be 'guessed at' forthwith. The court circle of Queen Henrietta-Maria, to which Carey had belonged, was covertly sympathetic to Catholicism. When the details of Carey's conversion were publicised in 1626, however, she was abandoned by her husband and placed under house arrest, her children and servants were sent away and she was denied all material support, including heating, food and money.[34] The bold gesture of self-determination in publishing her convictions in Perron's reply in 1630 led to reprisals from the king and official censorship by Archbishop Abbot, who decreed that all copies imported from France be seized and burned.

Her biography seems to indicate that Carey's strong sense of duty towards her husband conflicted with her own religious convictions, causing severe psychological ill-health and eventual material poverty. Her undeniable piety and commitment to the spiritual direction of her children is evidenced in the extreme solution of smuggling several to France to enter the Catholic Church ministry. The glimpses of her determination and independence of spirit, gained through her biographical and literary remains, however, were anomalous to the meek and subservient construct of ideal womanhood defined by contemporary opinion of her day. Carey's self-governing and transgressive behaviour which defied her husband, the hierarchy of the Church, and finally her king, condemned her to ignominy on the margins of her society and an impoverished death. Whether her independence was nurtured by her studies in theology, philosophy and history, or her determined character would have prevailed had she not taken such passionate recourse in study, is unclear. Nonetheless, it is not difficult to imagine the tenor of conservative responses to her 'crimes', framed by the prevailing patriarchal mindset.

As the seventeenth century progressed, the period of the Civil War and interregnum made different demands on women of all classes, increasingly requiring them to participate in public life. As male family members of both sides were required to campaign away from home, the management of estates, businesses and familial interests were left under the governance of mothers, wives, sisters and daughters. A combination of increased educational opportunity, practical necessities, and an atmosphere of upheaval which interrogated cultural and religious values, was liberating for many women. Patricia Crawford's research, for example, revealed a marked rise in all editions of works published by women from 1640 onwards, with a particularly high incidence of first publications in the interregnum.[35] The rise of published women's works and the greater breadth of genres in which they were able to write reflects the social and ideological changes of the era.

Notes

1 Richard Hyrde's English translation of *De institutione foeminae Christiana* is available via Early English Books Online, STC number 24856.5.

2 Vives, Chapter 4, 'Of the lernyng of maydes', *E i verso.*

3 Vives, Hyrde's translation, Chapter 4, 'Of the lernyng of maydes', *E i verso.*

4 Boccaccio, *De mulieribus claris* (*c.*1362) (pp.173–4), cited Pamela Joseph Benson, *The Invention of the Renaissance Woman* (Pennsylvania:

Pennsylvania State University Press, 1992), p. 19.

5 Vives, Chapter 4, 'Of the lernyng of maydes', *E i verso.*

6 Vives, Chapter 5, 'What bokes be to be redde and what nat' [*sic*;], *F ii verso.*

7 William Gouge, *Of Domesticall Duties* (1622), STC 12119, p. 269. See also Part Three: 'Life Guides, Mother's Advice and Conduct Books'.

8 John Florio, Preface to Montaigne's *Essayes* (1603), cited in Mary Ellen Lamb, 'The Cooke Sisters: Attitudes Toward Learned Women in the Renaissance', in *Silent But For The Word*, pp. 107–25, pp. 115, 116.

9 Thomas Stapleton's *Life and Illustrious Martyrdom of Sir Thomas More* (1588), p. 112 cited in Elaine V. Beilin, *Redeeming Eve*, *Women Writers of the English Renaissance* (Princeton, New Jersey: Princeton University Press, 1987), p. 19 and *Letters of Sir Thomas More*, 105, cited pp. 21, 22.

10 Beilin, *Redeeming Eve,* p. 23

11 *Letters of Sir Thomas More,* 155, cited in Beilin, *Redeeming Eve,* p. 24.

12 Anne Locke, Prefatory Letter to the Duchess of Suffolk in *The Collected Works of Anne Vaughan Lock*, Susan Felch (ed.) (Tempe, Arizona: Arizona Center for Medieval and Renaissance Studies in conjunction with Renaissance English Text Society, 1999), pp. 4–8, p. 5.

13 Pamela Joseph Benson, *The Invention of the Renaissance Woman, the Challenge of Female Independence in the Literature and Thought of Italy and England* (Pennsylvania: Pennsylvania State University Press, 1992), p. 213.

14 Heinrich Cornelius Agrippa von Nettesheim's *De nobilitate et praecellentia foeminei sexus declamatio* or *Declamation On the Nobility and Pre-eminence of the Female Sex* (oration 1509, published in 1529).

15 See Rosemary Radford Ruether, *Women and Redemption: A Theological History* (London: SCM Press, 1998), pp. 129, 130; also Barbara Newman, 'Renaissance Feminism and Esoteric Theology: The Case of Cornelius Agrippa' in *Viator* 24 (1993), pp. 337–56.

16 Lanyer, *Salve Deus*, lines 655, 656. Janel Mueller, 'The Feminist Poetics of Aemila Lanyer's *Salve Deus Rex Judeaorum*' in *Feminist Measures: Soundings in Poetry and Theory*, Lyn Keller and Cristanne Miller (eds) (Ann Arbor: University of Michigan, 1994), pp. 208–36, pp. 218–22.

17 The title page announces its uncontroversial content as, '1. The Passion of Christ, / 2. Eves Apologie in defence of Women. / 3. The Teares of the Daughters of Jerusalem. / 4. The Salutation and Sorrow of the Virgine Marie.'

18 See Barbara K. Lewalski, 'Imagining Female Community: Aemilia Lanyer's Poems' in *Writing Women in Jacobean England* (London: Harvard University Press, 1993), pp. 213–41, p. 213.

19 Edward Gosynhill, *Here begynneth a lytle boke named the Schole house of women wherin euery man may rede a goodly prayse of the condicyons of women*

(1541), available via EEBO, STC 12104.5.

20 Dianne Purkiss, 'The Seventeenth-Century Woman Debate' in *Women, Texts and Histories, 1575–1760* , Clare Brant and Dianne Purkiss (eds) (London: Routledge, 1992), pp. 72, 73.

21 Joseph Swetnam, 'Introduction', *The Arraignment of Lewde, idle, forward, and unconstant women Or the vanity of them, choose you whether, With a Commendation of wise, virtuous, and honest women, Pleasant for married Men, profitable for young Men, and hurtful to none,* unnumbered. Full text available via the University of Oregon-hosted site: http://www.uoregon.edu/~dluebke/WesternCiv102/SwetnamArraignment1615.htm.

22 William Shakespeare, *Measure for Measure* (1604), V.i.177–80.

23 T. E., *The Lawes Resolutions of Womens Rights* ('The Women's Lawyer') (1632), p. 6, cited Catherine Belsey, *The Subject of Tragedy, Identity and Difference in Renaissance Drama* (London: Methuen, 1985), p. 153.

24 The *Homily Against Whoredom and Adultery* (1562–3).

25 William Whately, *A Bride-Bush: or, a direction for married persons Plainly describing the duties common to both, and peculiar to each of them*, available via EEBO, STC 25296. See also Part Three: 'Life Guides, Mother's Advice and Conduct Books'.

26 The *Homily Against Whoredom and Adultery* (1562–3) pages unnumbered.

27 Ester Sowernam, *Ester hath hang'd Haman: Or, An Answere to a Lewd Pamphlet* (1617), Constantia Munda, *The Worming of a mad Dogge: Or a Soppe for Cerberus* (1617). See also *Swetnam the Woman-Hater, Arraigned by Women, A New Comedie* (1620) and the anonymous pamphlets of the cross-dressing controversy, *Haec Vir and Hic Muelier* (1620).

28 Edmund Spenser, *The Faerie Queene*, Book I: 172–3. See also Part Three: 'Pastoral to Epic'.

29 Ester Sowernam, *Ester hath hang'd Hama* (1617), Constantia Munda, *The Worming of a mad Dogge* (1617).

30 *The Lady Falkland, Her Life* (c.1655) may have been written by her daughter Anne, a Benedictine nun. See 'The Tragedy of Mariam, Elizabeth Carey, Viscountess Falkland', in *Renaissance Drama by Women, Texts and Documents,* S. P. Cerasano and Marion Wynne-Davies (eds) (London: Routledge, 1996), pp. 43–75, p. 45. *The Lady Falkland: Her Life,* p. 8, cited in Elaine V. Beilin's 'Elizabeth Carey (1585–1639)' in *Readings in Renaissance Women's Drama; Criticism, History, and Performance 1594–1998*, ed. by S. P. Cerasano and Marion Wynne-Davies, pp. 167–81, p. 169.

31 *The Lady Falkland,* p. 16, Cerasano and Wynne-Davies, p. 170.

32 *The reply of the most illustrious Cardinall of Perron, to the answeare of the most excellent King of Great Britaine the first tome. Translated into English* (Douay, France, 1630), available via EEBO, STC 6385.

33 Carey, 'The Epistle Dedicatorie', *The reply of the most illustrious Cardinall of Perron*, STC 6385, pages unnumbered.

34 See Barbara Lewalski's *Writing Women in Jacobean England* (London and Cambridge, Mass.: Harvard University Press, 1993), p. 186.

35 Patricia Crawford's chart of first and other editions for the period 1600 to 1700, appears in James Fitzmaurice, Josephine A. Roberts, Carol L. Barash, Eugene R. Cunnar and Nancy A. Gutierrez (eds), *Major Women Writers of Seventeenth-Century England* (Ann Arbor: University of Michigan Press, 1997), p. 3.

Exploration and New Worlds

Miranda's entranced 'O, brave new world / That has such people in't' (*The Tempest*, V.i.183–4) has often been associated with the exploration of the Americas. In fact, as indicated in the plot, logically the geographical location of her island home had to be between the coasts of Tunis and southern Italy, but Shakespeare's play is imbued with allusion to the Atlantic voyages of discovery. During the sixteenth and seventeenth centuries public imagination was engaged by the possibilities of the 'New World', as the explorers' accounts were published, reinterpreted and translated into English. Although the term 'New World' is widely accepted as referring to the American continent, of course, it was only 'new' to the foreign explorers. The unquestioning acceptance of the term points to a Eurocentric perspective which subtly privileges the known and 'otherises' the alien. Postcolonial criticism interrogates this perspective in which European culture and its values are centralised and considered 'normal', relegating all others to marginalised or exceptional status. Critics such as Frantz Fanon* and

* Frantz Fanon (1925–61) was a leading figure in the development of postcolonial theory. Originally from Martinique and a psychiatrist, his published work most famously included *Les damnés de la terre* [*The Wretched of the Earth*] (1961) which critiqued French colonisation of Algeria.

Edward Said* rejected this world view and the implied universalism which measured other cultures by inappropriate standards and found them lacking.[1]

This modern view was anathema to most Renaissance Europeans, however, who held that the unknown lands, their produce and potential as trading posts, were available for appropriation and 'civilisation' as part of (the Christian) God's plan. Less than twenty years prior to Sir Thomas More's idealised account of the island of *Utopia* (1516) Christopher Columbus had claimed equally implausible swathes of the 'New World' on behalf of Spain.

Mapping the World, Mapping the Imagination

In the late fifteenth and the earlier decades of the sixteenth century, classical notions of the world were still perpetrated by an education system which endorsed a Ptolemaic perspective. Ptolemy was a respected second-century astronomer, mathematician and cartographer. His treatise *Geographia* was remarkable for its detailed instructions in the art of cartography and its correlation of existing geographical knowledge in Roman times. His discussion encompassed only three continents, however, and both the Mediterranean and the Indian Ocean were considered to be enclosed seas. To the south of the globe, including the area which in the present day is known as Antarctica, he outlined a vast uncharted land which gained the name *Terra Australis Incognita*. Vestiges of belief in this undiscovered southern territory continued into the eighteenth century, even after it was discovered, as suggested by Ptolemy, that Africa did not connect with this landmass.

The *Terra Incognita* theme finds expression in literature of mysterious fictional lands such as More's *Utopia*, the island of Defoe's *Robinson*

* Edward Said (1935–2003) was born in Palestine and completed his education in the United States. His most influential publication was *Orientalism* (1978) in which he investigated ideological manifestations apparent in aspects of western culture, including literature. Originally an examination of western attitudes to the east, its influences have been widespread and his theories are now commonly applied to other discourses of oppression, including patriarchy.

Crusoe (1719) and the lands discovered by the eponymous hero of Jonathan Swift's *Gulliver's Travels* (1726). More specifically, Joseph Hall's *Mundus alter et idem*[*] (1605) presents a dystopic vision of an alternative world south of Africa, where contemporary notions of order are 'topsy-turvied' in carnivalesque fashion.[2] Apart from the countries where gluttony and inebriation are *de jure*,[†] in the second book, 'Shee-landt, or Womandeçoia', Hall creates a land ruled by women, according to contemporary concepts of women's trespasses and failings. Chapter seven is 'Of Shrewes-bourg', where the dress codes and the social roles of men and women are reversed. Hall's narrator mistakenly believes that he has escaped Womandeçoia and his relief turns to amazement as he is presented with the unpalatable notion that the sexes are interchangeable:

> … when all came to all, I was flat cousned[‡] with a borrowed shape: for in this countrie women weare britches, and long beards, and the men goe with their chinnes all naked, in kirtles and peticoates; spinning and carding wooll, whilest their wives discharge the maine affaires of the state. (p. 113)

Male authority is eroded here to such an extent that men are not permitted to be alone in the house without a female overseer and must seek permission of their wives to even 'wipe their mouthes [and] (saving your presence) goe pisse [and] passe a word with their best friend' (p. 114). The misogynistic humour perpetrated in this second book interacts with contemporary anxieties about gender instability, evident in James I's royal proclamation decrying the fashion for masculine female and effeminate male attire and the later parodic pamphlets *Hic mulier* and *Haec Vir* (1620).[§ 3] Although writers of imaginary lands exploited the gaps in empirical knowledge, the 'Great

* Latin: Other and Same World.

† Latin: Required by law.

‡ Duped.

§ Inaccurate Latin: *Mannish Woman* and *Womanish Man*. See also Henry Neville's *Isle of Pines, A late Discovery of a fourth Island in Terra Australis, Incognita* (1668).

Unknown', within which their fictional lands were located, was as much political, moral or cultural as geographical, and reflected topical issues closer to home.

Navigation both Spiritual and Physical

In the centuries between the production of Ptolemy's *Geographia* and the Renaissance venture to re-create a visual representation of his world view, no map accompanied his discursive likeness. The very concept of a visual plan of the entire world was alien to most people and the mathematical instruments and knowledge required to present an organised and accurate representation of space were lacking at this early stage. The earliest true maps were often quasi-religious artefacts, compiled principally from biblical sources with information from classical literature, national histories and military records, more than experiential evidence. As the era of European exploration began to provide fragmented first-person accounts of far-flung domains these were stitched into the existing fabric of topographical 'knowledge'.

The extraordinary discoveries generated a spirit of optimism and wonder which seemed to point to even richer diversity and greater wealth of possibility. Even into the sixteenth and seventeenth centuries outlandish claims continued to be made by Europeans of the people, fauna, produce and mineral wealth of lands which they considered newly 'discovered'. Strangely, grotesque creatures of the 'new' lands often bore striking resemblance to the monsters described in biblical or classical sources. When Sir Walter Ralegh repeated accounts of the fearsome Ewaipanoma of Guyana, for example, he described the selfsame monsters who peopled the pages of Pliny's *Natural History* of the first century. These creatures, in Pliny's catalogue bearing the name Blemmyae, laboured under the inconvenience of having no heads and instead having their features upon their abdomens.[4] Misinformation and a lack of tested knowledge presented a serious threat to early explorers; as Christopher Columbus remarked, Plato and Seneca 'affirme that

India is no long tracte by sea distant from Spaine'.* Many missions embarked upon hazardous long-term voyages of terrible hardship with remarkably erroneous concepts of the inhabitants and physical geography of their intended destinations.†

Partly decreed by the necessity of providing travellers with practical and life-preserving knowledge of alien regions, European accounts of exploration and discovery are usually presented as meticulous practical observations of vital information such as coastlines and safe harbours, fresh water sources, and lists of edible fauna, fish, fruit and vegetables. The writers' roles of reconnoitring and recording, as the forerunners of their compatriots, are evident, whether their documentation is intended to assist crews of subsequent trading vessels or as the basis upon which to found new colonies. Amongst many such observations, for example, Columbus noted that on the island which he had named Hispaniola, except for 'three kindes of little conies' [rabbits], there was a lack of small game. Clearly alert to colonisers' need for equivalent sustenance, he shortly follows this deficiency with a detailed report on several different types and sizes of Popinjay domesticated by the indigenous people:

> ... bigger than pheasants ... having their brestes, and bellies of purple colour, and their winges of other variable colours ... As we bring up capons and hennes to franke and make them fat, so do they there bigger kindes of Popinjays for the same purpose.[5]

He also provides information on the invaluable new grain that later so crucially sustained the early colonisers, which was 'as bigge as a man's arme: the grains whereof are set in a marvellous order, and are in forme, somewhat like peas'. Evidently having had some dialogue with the inhabitants of the island, he records, 'this kind of graine they call *Maizum*' (p. 10).

* Columbus's account is contained within Michael Lok's 1612 translation of five books of Peter Martyr's *De novo orbe, or the historie of the west Indies contayning the actes and aduentures of the Spanyardes* (1516). Michael Lok (Lock, Locke) was the brother-in-law of Anne Locke whose work is discussed in Part Three: 'Religious Verse'.

† The French National Library online catalogue contains videos of the beginnings of cartography.

Although Columbus's accounts of his voyages often demonstrate a positive attitude towards the indigenous Americans, his testimonies also introduce the theme of cannibalism, so often repeated in later literature of the Indies. The 'meek and humane' people native to one of the islands, for example, are reported to live in fear of raiding parties by neighbouring cannibal or 'Caribe' tribes, who steal their children for food:

> ... such children as they take they geld to make them fat,
> as we doe cocke chickings and young hogges, and eate them
> when they are wel fedde ... (p. 10)

Some insight into the Caribs' resource management is provided with the note that, although the entrails and extremities of the unfortunate children provide immediate sustenance, the fleshy torsos were 'powdered for storage, as we do pestels of porke, and gammondes of bakon' (p. 10). Columbus suggests that adult men were equally under threat, despite their relative toughness, as a visit to the 'kychens' found 'mans flesh, duckes flesh, & goose flesh, all in one pot' and parts of other victims on the spits ready to be 'layd to the fire' (p. 11). Women, however, escaped this terror, as the Caribs 'doe absteyne from eating of women, and count it vile' (p. 10). Columbus's crew are also said to have found thirty child captives, destined 'to bee eaten' whom they released and later trained as interpreters (p. 13).

Published travel narratives served a number of purposes, whether as patriotic evidence of the courage and talents of home-grown adventurers – to encourage commercial investment in trade ventures – or as literary projects intended to divert and enthral, as the section above illustrates. The many different versions and reprintings of a plethora of travel documents in the late sixteenth and seventeenth centuries attest to their great popularity.[6] As might be expected, given the shared classical terms of reference of a generation of grammar-school educated readers, allusions to Greek and Roman works abound. Whether mythological, philosophical or geographical, these references run as a subtext of similitude to the narratives, employed either to measure new discoveries against or to endorse the relatively alien. As Wiktor Stoczkowski points out, voyagers' imaginations were already preconditioned by their world views and, in this sense, they re-discovered, rather than discovered, much of the 'New' World.[7]

A report of Columbus' second voyage, for example, painstakingly defines the location of an island north of Guadaloupe, measuring the number of days' sailing, the approximate distance and precise direction from the Canary Isles. Beyond this, however, the veracity of the account is called into question as it is blurred by hearsay and 'validated' by mythical precedent. *Martininos*, or Martinique, which he did not visit, is recorded as an 'Iland of women' whose social arrangements bear a strong resemblance to that of the 'Amazones in the Iland of Lesbos'. Only enduring the male cannibals' presence at designated times of the year, these warrior women fiercely repulse uninvited men 'with bowes and arrowes' (pp. 13–14). This theme of independent unruly women rejecting male authority became a commonplace in tales of adventure and seems to have had enduring fascination throughout history. As original accounts, perhaps whimsical in places, were translated, gathered and re-presented in many different forms, exaggerations and misrepresentations were enshrined and repeated. Without doubt, some records of terrain explored were exaggerated to generate public interest, noble patronage or financial backing.

El Dorado and '*The great and golden City of Manoa*'

In 1595 Sir Walter Ralegh, spurred by an urgent need to regain the favour of Queen Elizabeth, embarked upon a voyage to 'Guiana' [Guyana]. His welcome at court had been severely curtailed after his involvement in two failed attempts to colonise what is now North Carolina, compounded by his secret marriage to Elizabeth Throckmorton.* Encouraged by Spanish

* The colony at Roanoke was 'planted' in 1585 but failed, due to a combination of problems centring on a lack of provisions, and was subsequently repopulated in 1587. All inhabitants of the first colony disappeared and their fate is a matter of speculation. DNA testing is presently being used to try to discover if there was intermarriage with indigenous groups. Ralegh sponsored and planned the expeditions and colonies but was not permitted to travel himself.

discoveries of great wealth in Mexico, his aim was to return with a fleet laden with gold. His published account of the voyage bears evidence to the anxiety generated by a damaged reputation which was further reduced by his return minus the promised abundance of treasure. The grandiose title of his work was *The Discovery of the large, rich, and beautiful Empire of Guiana; with a Relation of the great and golden City of Manoa, which the Spaniards call El Dorado.*[8] In fact, rather than the envisaged glittering holds of pure gold from El Dorado, he returned with a humiliating lack of riches, only emphasised by the dubious provenance of his samples of 'ore'.

His aggrieved epistle 'To the Reader' has two aims. Firstly, to assert authenticity for his claims to have at least discovered gold and, secondly, to justify his perceived failure and lack of profit. His reasons for not having further pursued the quest are a combined lack of time, man-power and resources, which prevented a large scale mining enterprise:

> … whosoever hath seene with what strength of stone, the best golde oare is invironed, he will not thinke it easie to be had out in heapes, and especially by us who had neither men, instrumentes, nor time (as it is saide before) to performe the same … (p. 3)

Ralegh is at pains to guarantee that the gold exists, however, and will amply repay further investigation and investment. Hence the narrative is complex with sometimes conflicting aims. It is presented as a Shangri-la of unimagined wealth, as a pragmatic navigational aid, a guide for possible colonisers and bid for financial backing.[9]

In his preface 'To the Reader' Ralegh tersely disparages 'An Alderman of London and an officer of her majesties minte' who had pronounced that the 'good oare brought from Guiana […] is of no price' (p. 2). After a digression on Trinidadian marcasite,* which embellishes the discourse and distracts from his lack of success, he makes the expansive claim that in Guyana 'all the rocks, mountaines, all stones in the plaines,

* Marcasite is iron sulphide, FeS_2; it was often confused with white iron pyrite (Fool's Gold) which, in turn, was mistaken for gold.

in woodes, and by the rivers side are in effect thorow shining, and appeare marveylous rich'. While the dazzling imagery captivates the imagination, Ralegh claims that the luminescence is a certain marker of rare mineral deposits and is termed by the Spaniards '*El madre del oro*' (the mother of gold) (p. 2).

The prefatory letter describes in detail the extraction of a type of white stone with 'daggers, and with the heade of an axe', recounting its difficult retrieval from a cleft in rocks at the mouth of a river. This, Ralegh claims, in the manner of revelation, is the 'sparre'* which he has had examined by named, known, respected and knowledgeable goldsmiths, 'extractors' and royal servants of London: Masters Westwood, Bulmer, Dimocke and Palmer. Records of the ratios of gold content in each of the samples appear to verify Ralegh's claims; nonetheless, malicious rumours circulated that 'the same oare was had from barbery' (the Barbary Coast in Africa) and conveyed to Guyana in order to perpetrate a grand deception (p. 7).

The notion of Guyana's inestimable and retrievable wealth is perpetrated in Ralegh's narrative, as he predicts the acquisition of 'no lesse quantities of treasure, then the king of Spayne hath in all the Indies, east and west' (p. 8). He bolsters the veracity of his account with meticulous lists of topographical detail, compiled from his own observations, which he maintains extended to approximately four hundred miles from his ship's anchorage. The records are blended, however, with a collection of Spanish letters seized by 'Captaine *George Popham*' the previous year. This can either be viewed as endorsing or destabilising his own account, depending on the reader's perspective. The transcribed sections of the letters inform of negotiations and battles with the native inhabitants of the Orinoco basin, and estimates the vast wealth of the area: 'Golde to be there in most abundaunce, Diamondes of inestimable value, with great store of pearle' (p. 111). Ralegh annexes these supposed discoveries with the notice:

* Gold is found within such mineral veins in the area which Ralegh explored. The 'sparre' was probably feldspar or calcite, named by Edmund Gosse as quartz. See Edmund Gosse, *English Worthies, Ralegh* (1886), ed. by Andrew Lang (2008) available online.

> One other thing to bee remembred is that in these letters the Spanyards seeme to call *Guiana* and other Countries neere it, bordering uppon the river of *Orenoque*, by the name of *Nuevo Dorado*, because of the greate plentie of Golde there, in most places to be founde. Alluding also to the name of *El Dorado* which was given by *Martines* to the greate Citie of *Manoa*. (p. 104)

Ralegh dexterously adopts this 'evidence', further authenticating it by the report of the exotic-sounding '*Cayworaco*, the sonne of *Topiawary* now chiefe Lord of the saide *Aromaya*' who is said to have witnessed the activities of the Spaniards (p. 103).* Ralegh's adroit manipulation of fact belies the fact that the river Orinoco, mentioned frequently, was not within Guyanan territory, but formed the northernmost boundary of the country, with Venezuela, and was already claimed by the Spaniards. The transcribed letters clearly indicate that all of the surrounding territory had been claimed (twice) by the Governor, Anthony Campe, assisted by Francisco Carillo, in the name of 'king *Don Phillip* [his] master' (p. 106). By this time Ralegh already had a reputation as a privateer, and was no doubt inured to battle and plunder on the oceans. One can only assume that the intention was to pursue a similar method of acquisition along the shores of the Caribbean coastline.

'Greate plentie of Golde [...] in most places to be founde'

Perhaps the most interesting, damning and revealing aspect of Ralegh's venture, however, is a map intended to accompany his narrative in *The Discovery*. As a surrogate for the expected tangible evidence of exotic treasure, he uses cartography to authenticate his verbal montage. The map is thought to have been drawn by Ralegh himself and, like the discursive account of the voyage, some sections are laden with verified topographical information. Ralegh's 'great and golden citie of Manoa (which the spanyards call El Dorado)' appears on the shores of an impressive lake fed by numerous tributaries. As D. K. Smith remarks,

* Cayworaco was a Native American taken to England by Ralegh himself.

however, this is entirely fictitious.[10] One can only imagine the desperation with which Ralegh finally turned from the Caribbean to return to England and which prompted him to fabricate evidence, perpetrating the myth of the 'greate plentie of Golde there, in most places to be founde'.*[11]

At this distance it can be difficult to separate empirical records from enthusiastic exaggeration or antipathetic opinion from recorded fact, and both from creative literary strategies. The curiosities, hypothetical wealth and chilling depravities depicted in the travel narratives, nonetheless, worked on the popular imagination. In Peter Barry's terms, distant lands became 'the repository or projection of those aspects of themselves which [they] did not wish to acknowledge' whilst also paradoxically being 'a fascinating realm of the exotic'.[12] Hence, the Eurocentric vision presented the Caribbean peoples as inferior, uncivilised, immoral, pagan and, in some cases, less than human. Bermuda, in particular, wreathed in lethal rocks and tossed by hurricanes, gained the soubriquet 'the Devil's Isles'.[13]

Establishing Jamestown and 'the starving time'

At the beginning of James I's reign a commercial venture was established to try again to colonise the area known as Virginia on the west coast of America. Two companies, based in Plymouth and London, were granted royal charters to establish settlements but, again, experienced overwhelming difficulties.† The London Company oversaw the more successful colony, under John Smith, of Pocahontas fame, and established Jamestown in honour of the king. Within a short time, this

* Ralegh's eventual execution, in the reign of James, was directly linked to his inability to make good similar promises in 1616, when he once more led an expedition to search for El Dorado and again returning empty-handed, having attempted to plunder Spanish galleons *en route*.

† The Plymouth settlement was built on the marshy land between Chesapeake and Delaware Bays and, although sharing the name with the later settlement of the Pilgrim Fathers, this location was in the area of Maine, rather than the more northerly Cape Cod.

company absorbed the area designated for the Plymouth settlers. Although successful in some respects, the inability to be self-sufficient in food production was a major problem and the first colonisers experienced prodigious hardship and wide-spread starvation before provisions arrived from England in 1610.

The voyage of mercy to provision the Virginian colony set sail in the summer of 1609, under the command of Sir George Somers. Just eight weeks later, disaster befell the 'Sea Venture' when it was separated from the other ships of the fleet amid a hurricane, gaining itself and the admiral of the venture a permanent place in history and literature. Upon this vessel were not only George Somers but also Sir Thomas Gates, appointed Governor of Virginia, William Strachey of the Virginia Company and Silvester Jourdain.* All of these names have become associated with the subsequent accounts of the wreck of the 'Sea Adventure' and the survivors' impressions of Bermuda in their 'reporatories'.

William Strachey's *A true reporatory of the wracke* (1610)† was one of the accounts of English navigation collected and popularised by Samuel Purchas in the fourth volume of his extensive compilation, *Purchas his pilgrims* (1613–25).[14] Strachey's accounts are frequently cited as one of Shakespeare's sources and excerpts are often appended to editions of *The Tempest*. There is a close resemblance between Strachey's notes on the storm's 'Sea-fire', for example, described as an 'apparition of a little round light, like a faint Starre trembling and streaming along with a sparkeling blaze' and Ariel's description of his own manifestation to the mariners (*The Tempest*, I.ii.198–206).[15] Popular imagination was captivated by the gory, tempestuous and dangerous supposed attributes of the Caribbean, including untamed women, flesh-eating men and treacherous seas and hurricanes. It is these shared concepts to which Shakespeare alludes in *The Tempest*, in his mysterious island which is

* John Rolfe who married the legendary Pocahontas, after John Smith's return to England, was also on board. Pocahontas converted to Christianity and took a Christian, as opposed to 'pagan', name before her marriage in 1614 and two years later visited the English court with her husband under the name Rebecca Rolfe.

† 'True report of the wreck'.

associated with a transgressive female exile, her wild son Caliban and the hurricanic storm which acts as a catalyst to the action.

As Somers's resourceful castaways numbered shipwrights among their company, within less than a year they were able to build two new vessels and continue their delayed journey to the Jamestown colony. The initial colonising of Bermuda, discovered to be 'habitable and commodious' despite its notorious reputation, was therefore achieved by default, as a number of individuals were left behind to maintain the English presence on the island when the rest of the mission set sail for Virginia.*

Attempts to impose strict codes of obedience and religious observation in the colonies are apparent in published relics of governance, such as William Strachey's later tract *For the colony in Virginea Britannia. Lawes divine, morall and martiall* (1612).[16] This was of paramount importance, as the original colonisers were not of the most law-abiding or God-fearing citizens. Sir Francis Bacon later commented that this was a major error which directly contributed to the failures of the early colonies and Strachey's authoritarian code, published in England upon his return, was uncompromising.[17] Blasphemy was punished by death and disrespect to ministers of religion incurred three public whippings followed by humble requests for forgiveness made on three subsequent Sabbaths (p. 3). Twice daily attendance at church was a legal requirement, the disregard of which upon the first instance resulted in loss of rations for the day. The appalling historical context, not apparent to a modern reader, is that this community had experienced such severe famine before the arrival of the Somers provisions that two members were publicly starved for the theft of food and another was believed to have eaten his wife. Subsequent non-attendance at church earned a whipping and a third offence saw the unfortunate, presumably male, condemned to row in the galleys for six months (p. 4). Predictably, Sunday observations were enforced with even greater severity and, in this case, the final punishment for a third offence was quite simply execution (p. 4). The austere governance indicates a social organisation which differs little from a theocracy and serves as a prelude to the later Puritan settlements.

* Bermuda is often called the Somers Islands in subsequent literature.

'Another world was searched, through oceans new'

Andrew Marvell's 'Bermudas' alludes to the Pilgrim Fathers exemplified in his line, 'Safe from the storms, and prelate's rage' (l. 12); the poem is presented as the thanksgiving voiced as the non-conformists row towards the island from the vessel which transported them from persecution in England.* The island is envisioned not only as a haven of religious toleration, but as paradisiacal, in terms akin to the medieval Land of Cockayne.† Marvell's land of plenty enjoys a perpetual spring and God's solicitude for his subjects, which illustrates that they are his chosen people, produces an over-abundance of temperate-zone fruits:

> He hangs in shades the orange bright,
> Like golden lamps in a green night,
> And does in the pomegranates close
> Jewels more rich than Ormus shows;
> He makes the figs our mouths to meet,
> And throws the melons at our feet. (ll. 17–22)

The currents of the ocean, the abundant fruit and fowl, are all commanded by the divine Governor of His colony – or a Prospero-like enchanter – for this isle bears more resemblance to the wish-fulfilment folk tales of Europe than the genuine Bermuda islands. The horticultural plenitude is matched by natural geographic wonders: a resonating cave takes on the character of a great cathedral, which amplifies their praise. But the much-sought mineral wealth of the Americas is transformed into 'jewels' of pomegranate seeds and the 'pearl' of the gospel (ll. 19, 30). The allusion to the gospel serves to remind the reader of extreme Protestantism's evangelising nature and the colonial endeavour to win

* The dissenters initially left England for Holland and established a separatist church in Leiden, but eventually sailed for America to preserve their group's religious identity. They settled at Cape Cod in 1620, the colony becoming known as Plymouth, although in a more northerly location to the land licensed to the Plymouth Company by James I in 1606.

† See the *Utopia* section in Part Three: 'Humanist Prose and Rhetoric'.

souls for the 'true' religion. Juxtaposed with this evocation of the gospel is a veiled aside on the religious conversions of the Native Americans by the Spanish Conquistadors in Mexico. The joyful praise of the pilgrims resounds to heaven and echoes back down the east coast to the Catholic-occupied Bay of Mexico area (ll. 33–6). Whether this is simply defiance of the Spaniards' religious enterprise or in competition to win souls to their own cause, is not clear. As Smith points out, this poem was written during the English Civil War and so may represent a desire to see beyond the immediate turmoil, political and religious discord, to a stabilised future moderated by the tenets of a sober faith.[18] Nonetheless, the poem is informed by the allegorical possibilities of the New World.

'Divine Tobacco', a Cure for Wounds, Chilblains and Hysteria

As accounts of exotic places coloured the public imagination, traces of the new discoveries found their way into common knowledge and parlance and thence into works of literature and performance. In Book III of Spenser's *The Faerie Queene*, for example, Belphoebe searches the woods for an astringent medical remedy to apply to Timeas's deep wounds, subsequently grinding the leaves and applying the juice to treat the swelling:

> There, whether it diuine *Tobacco* were,
> Or *Panachæa*, or *Polygony*,
> She found, and brought it to her patient deare
> Who al this while lay bleeding out his hart-bloud neare.
> The soueraigne weede betwixt two marbles plaine
> She pownded small, and did in peeces bruze,
> And then atweene her lilly handes twaine,
> Into his wound the juyce thereof did scruze, [squeeze]
> And round about, as she could well it uze,
> The flesh therewith she suppled and did steepe,
> T'abate all spasme, and soke the swelling bruze …
>
> (Book III, canto 5, lines 277–88)

The character shows an easy familiarity with tobacco as a medicinal plant, paralleling its powers with the similarly panacean home-grown herb, '*Panachæa*, or *Polygony*'.* *The Faerie Queene* was originally published in 1590 and Spenser's treatment seems to indicate, by this time, a reasonably widespread medical usage of tobacco and popular recognition of its properties.

Nicolás Monardes's *Historia medicinal* was a catalogue of all the medicinal usages of products discovered in the Spanish West Indies. It was originally published in Castilian and subsequently introduced to an English readership by John Frampton, an English merchant. Four years lapsed between Monardes's first and second volumes, during which time the Native American use of tobacco's healing properties been observed and documented. The most commodious claims are made for tobacco, these included the cure of chilblains, wind, aching in the joints, swellings, toothache, hysteria ('the mother'), worms and 'the evill breathing at ye mouth of children, when they are over filled with meate'.[19] Spenser's Belphoebe prepares the tobacco leaves in exactly the same manner as observed among Native American people and recorded in Monardes's *Historia medicinal*.

Amatory Verse Mapping the Virginal 'New-found-land'

More generalised awareness of the wider world, and new territories available for colonisation, arises in contemporary poetry in the perennial trope of the battle of love. Shakespeare's *The Rape of Lucrece* (1594) employs cartographic imagery to chart the 'unconquered' terrain of the eponymous heroine's body. Her 'ivory globes circled with blue', evoke the spherical promise of adolescent breasts, but evade easy interpretation, prompting the question, why should the breasts be *encircled* by blue? Shakespeare's oblique gesture is to Geradus Mercator's renowned double-sphere projection of the world

* Also known as Solomon's Seal this herb is used to cure wounds that were newly-inflicted or difficult to heal.

in his *Orbis terrae of* 1569.* In this innovative projection the known world is depicted as the orb of the 'old world' on the right, twinned by the complimentary sphere of the 'new' world on the left. The projections (perhaps an intentional Shakespearian pun) are encased within a filigree-patterned framework of gold upon an azure background, not so dissimilar from the figured brocade of the bodice of a woman of status. This section of the poem contains tacit acknowledgement of the violence and destruction in annexed territories, however, as the lexis of exploration, and allusion to 'worlds unconquered' in the poem directly prefigure Lucrece's violent rape and subsequent suicide:

> Her breasts like ivory globes circled with blue,
> A pair of maiden worlds unconquered,
> Save of their lord no bearing yoke they knew,
> And him by oath they truly honoured.
> These worlds in Tarquin new ambition bred,
> Who like a foul usurper went about
> From this fair throne to heave the owner out. (ll. 407–13)

The semantic fields employed in John Donne's discourse of love and amorous play similarly demonstrate his interest in geographical discoveries and the colonising of new 'worlds'. In the elegy 'To His Mistress Going to Bed', the anticipation of exploring a female lover's voluptuous body is expressed as a scarcely-contained Ovidian voyage of discovery:

> License my roving hands, and let them go,
> Behind, before, above, between, below.
> O my America! my new-found-land,
> My kingdom, safeliest when with one man man'd,

* See Rumold Mercator's double sphere image in *Orbis terrae compendiosa description* (1587); the method builds upon his father Gerardus's work in cartography, especially his ground-breaking projection in the 1569 world map, available online. This observation is indebted to Robert L. Sharp's 1954 discussion of the influence of cartography on Donne's 'Good-Morrow', see endnote 20.

My mine of precious stones: my emperie,
How blest am I in this discovering thee! (ll. 25–30)

His aubade 'The Sun Rising' takes the form of an apostrophe to the sun, rather than a more conventional lament addressed to the beloved. Again, the lover is described in a lexis of topography and acquisition, as the speaker's hyperbole transports and transforms 'both th' Indias of spice and mine' from the external world to assume the body of the woman (ll. 17–18). In these terms she is objectified, no matter how attractively, and becomes a virgin territory to be possessed and occupied, in the same way as Virginia. The imagery of 'The Good Morrow' once more revolves around the discovery of new love, using conceits generated by Donne's knowledge of cartography. The middle stanza of the poem employs a similar trope to the final lines of 'The Sun Rising', synecdochically representing the lovers' room as the outside world: 'And makes one little room an everywhere' (l. 11).* The introduction of the new worlds of the 'sea-discoverers', however, instigates an abstracted conceit which Robert L. Sharp deciphered so perceptively in 1954:[20]

Let sea-discoverers to new worlds have gone;
Let maps to other, worlds on worlds have shown;
Let us possess one world; each hath one, and is one.

My face in thine eye, thine in mine appears,
And true plain hearts do in the faces rest;
Where can we find two better hemispheres
Without sharp north, without declining west? (ll. 12–18)

Sharp claims that Donne's concern with interlocking and mirroring images, in 'worlds on worlds' and 'each hath one, and is one' and especially the notion of mirrored hemispheres, evokes the forms of double 'cordiform' maps.[21] These sixteenth-century projections created mirrored heart-shaped figures, very apt for Donne's project, touching or

* Donne, 'The Sun Rising', 'Shine here to us, and thou art everywhere; / This bed thy centre is, these walls thy sphere', lines 29, 30.

intersecting to depict 360-degree visualisations of the world.[22] Facing each other, Donne's lovers become part of the visual image of the other, reflected in the beloved's eyes, 'My face in thine eye, / Thine in mine appears' (ll. 15, 16). The similitude is emphasised by the assonance which equates 'thine' and 'mine'; a doubling pursued in the cartographic analogy of two hemispheres presented as face[t]s. The inspirational most certainly arises from the Mercator maps of father and son, but specifically draws to mind the Gerardus Mercator image of 1569 which, at first glance, bears a resemblance to echoed curved moth wings.[23] Importantly, due to the projection, the 'north' (or top) of the chart is therefore empty; there is therefore no 'sharp north', as Donne claims. The north is 'sharp' due to its association with the needle of the compass, necessary for navigation, but also the ice and harsh winter winds, familiar through accounts of expeditions to discover the North-West passage to India.* The 'declining west' is metaphorically associated with loss of vigour and death, as the setting of the sun in the west signals the onset of cold night. Hence, in a densely-textured few lines, Donne's imagery evokes metaphors of exploration and navigation to chart an emotional terrain, which then he tries to fix within the timeless unchangeability of a mathematical diagram:

> My face in thine eye, thine in mine appears,
> And true plain hearts do in the faces rest;
> Where can we find two better hemispheres
> Without sharp north, without declining west?
> Whatever dies, was not mix'd equally;
> If our two loves be one, or thou and I
> Love so alike that none can slacken, none can die. (ll. 15–21)

* During Donne's childhood Martin Frobisher attempted to discover the route in three separate expeditions in 1576, 1577, and 1578 and Sir Francis Drake took up the quest in 1579.

Poet and Priest 'adventuring' for Virginia

Alongside the aesthetic aspects of Donne's allusions to exploration in his love poetry, he was also active on the behalf of the Merchant Adventurers Company. In 1622, now Dean of St Paul's, rather than 'Jack Donne' of the risqué amatory verse, he addressed himself to the 'Honourable Company of the Virginian Plantation'. In the published version of an earlier requested sermon he clearly defines his partiality towards the venture, 'By your favours I had some place amongst you before but now I am an adventurer if not to Virginia yet, *for* Virginia' (added emphasis).

The design becomes apparent with the revelation that his pericope for the sermon, drawn from Acts 18, promotes the evangelising of the faith 'unto the uttermost part of the earth'. The text is particularly prescient within the context of American colonisation, given the European mission to seize assets, souls and territory:

> … you shall give satisfaction to all to the citie to the Country to the calumnyising adversary and the naturals of the place to whom you shall present both Spirituall and Temporall benefit to. (p. 4)[24]

The semantic field of the opening phrase aligns the enterprise of trade with the ethics of spiritual duty, uniting commercial and theological justification. To 'give satisfaction' is to repay a debt, articulated as being to 'citie and Country'. Given the phenomenal financial outlay required to discover and establish commercial ventures, one would imagine financial considerations and possibilities of 'Temporall benefit' were not far from the thoughts of the original audience. The payment of a duty was also to 'give satisfaction' and, in this sense, the colonisers viewed their projects as benefiting the 'naturals of the place' by introducing European culture and notions of civilised life. Just as Shakespeare's Milanese nobles considered that they educated Caliban and 'taught him speech', for the greater part colonisers privileged European culture and religion, assuming the role of benefactors in their enforcement. The London merchants had long been associated with the most staunch Protestantism, even Calvinism, long before the faith was accepted as the state religion. It therefore requires little stretch of the imagination to identify the Spanish as 'calumnyising adversary', whose own enterprise was equally to harvest souls and merchandise for the glory of nation and faith.

The Munificence of Merchants: Sugar loaves, Nutmegs and Cloves

The lucrative nature of trading opportunities presented in western expansion is evident in the merchants' munificent sponsorship of civic celebrations and pageants in London. Thomas Middleton was engaged to create the Lord Mayor's pageant three times between 1613 and 1622; his 1613 *tour de force* was outstanding in its immense expenditure (approximately twice comparable amounts) and its long-term meticulous planning. The spectacle included 'native' monarchs who drifted down the Thames upon five Spice Islands; other props included a 'ship, chariots … and fireworks'.[25] The total cost of all the construction and painting was the enormous sum of £1,300.[26] This does not include the payment to Middleton, typically £40, or the extremely desirable and expensive 'favours' thrown to the crowd, documented as including 'nutmegs, cloves, dates, ginger and peppers'.

George Chapman's *Masque of the Middle Temple and Lincoln's Inn*, sponsored as part of the wedding celebrations of Princess Elizabeth, James I's daughter, and the Elector Palatine in 1613, similarly employed spectacular costumes and effects based on the theme of Virginian exploration. Characters included Virginian priests, princes and sun-worshippers and baboons dressed in courtly finery. The lavish costumes were designed by Inigo Jones and utilised quantities of exotic feathers, butterfly wings, jewelled crowns and luxurious fabrics of silver and gold. The preliminary torch-lit procession through the city to Whitehall Palace, in the darkness of a London February night, must have resembled a magical apparition to the gathered populace.[27]

Celebrations of material advancement in successful London society and of fortunes made through lucrative foreign investments, however, largely mask the narratives of wrecked lives and desperate circumstances of individuals at the raw edges of the so-called 'Age of Discovery'. The more spiritually-motivated of the contemporary authors tend to distinguish between ethically-motivated endeavours and those which become overtaken by the lust for commercial gain. At both ends of this spectrum, however, extreme hardship generated its own brand of misery.

Michael Lok (Locke) provides a good example of a well-educated and connected gentleman from a wealthy background who lost both pecuniary assets and his previously unassailable public standing for the cause. The huge losses sustained by ventures he had underwritten ruined him and marred his reputation, so necessary for trading. He endured continual harassment, including imprisonment, into his seventies for debts incurred funding Frobisher's north-eastern ventures.[28]

Although the Lok family themselves were ardent and quite extreme Protestants, they were one of the foremost of the London mercantile families. By contrast, the New World project of the Bradstreets was founded firmly on ethical and spiritual aspiration. Aged eighteen, Anne Bradstreet travelled to America as a young wife with her husband, a Puritan minister.* The family were of gentry status and held prominence in the community of Ipswich, Massachusetts. Both her father and husband were involved in the government of the colony. Despite the New World setting and her extensive education, her poetry for the main part reflects the intense domesticity of a woman's role lived within the stringent confines of female Puritan conformity. It very noticeably does not document the new land in the mode of the visiting explorers – in terms of wonder and effusive comments on its plenitude. Amid the poems of Christian reflection upon her love for her husband and

* Although her work was published in England and without her permission, Anne Bradstreet (*c.*1612–72) is claimed to be the first American female poet. Her brother-in-law, John Woodbridge, with the co-operation of her sister, had the first volume published in 1650 as *The Tenth Muse Lately Sprung Up in America, By a Gentlewoman of Those Parts*, available via EEBO, Wing (1994) / B4167.

children and the misfortune of many close family bereavements and personal illness, all endured with pious fortitude, there does sometimes appear glimpses of her pioneering life.

As Marvell's *Bermudas* noted the ambergris* thrown upon the shore, similarly Bradstreet's encomium to the sea in her 'Four Elements' speaks of 'gallant rich perfuming Amber-greece […] lightly cast a shoare as frothy fleece'. The same poem also acknowledges the 'rowling grains of purest massy gold / Which *Spaines Americas*, do gladly hold'.[29] The tenor of most of the poems is less sanguine, however, perhaps reflecting the bleak isolation of her later surroundings.[30] Given the experiential nature of her verse, it is difficult not to read as biographical her observations on 'Fevers, Purples, Pox and Pestilence […] / Whereof such multitudes have di'd and fled, / The living scarce had power to bury dead'.[31] Her description of the hurricanes, for which the coast was so feared, also presents a vivid picture of lives pitted against the elements:

> … of my tempests felt at sea and land,
> Which neither ships nor houses could withstand,
> What wofull wracks I've made […]
> Again what furious storms and Hurricanoes
> Know western Isles, as *Christophers, Barbados*,
> Where neither houses, trees nor plants I spare;
> But some fall down, and some fly up with air.
>
> ('The Four Elements' (Air), p. 21)

Despite her protestation that her verse cannot attempt to 'sing of Wars, of Captaines, and of Kings, / Of Cities founded, Common-wealths begun' in the 'Dialogue Between Old England and New', this is precisely her intention.[32] In a remarkably outspoken condemnation, she offers frank and negative opinion on England's political, social and religious matters. Just as the early explorers defined themselves in comparison to the 'savage' races, Bradstreet and her co-religionists affirmed their self-image by adopting a similar contrariety. In designating

* Ambergris is a product from the sperm whale which had medical use, but was and is chiefly known as a fixative for perfumes.

Old England as corrupted 'Other', they confirm their own society as a moral commonwealth. If not a 'brave new world', they perceive their accomplishment as the establishment of an uncorrupted New England.

Notes

1 See Peter Barry, *Beginning Theory, An Introduction to Literary and Cultural Theory* (Manchester: Manchester University Press, 1995), 'Postcolonial criticism', pp. 191–201; Edward Said, excerpt from 'Orientalism' in David Lodge (ed.), *Modern Criticism and Theory, A Reader* (London and New York: Longman, 1988), pp. 295–309.

2 Joseph Hall, *Mundus alter et idem siue Terra Australis* (1613 edn), available via Early English Books Online (EEBO) STC 12686.3. The work was originally published anonymously, subsequent editions bear Hall's name.

3 These are customarily read alongside the '*Querelle des Femmes*' pamphlets, see 'The Woman Debate' in Part Four of this volume. The texts are available via the University of Arizona site and they are also discussed on Norton Topics Online.

4 See Wiktor Stoczkowski, *Explaining Human Origins, Myth, Imagination and Conjecture* (1994), Mary Turton (trans.) (Cambridge: Cambridge University Press, 2002), p. 3.

5 Michael Lok's 1612 translation of five books of Peter Martyr's *De nouo orbe, or the historie of the west Indies contayning the actes and aduentures of the Spanyardes* (1516, the same year as More's *Utopia*), available via EEBO, STC 650, 'The First Decade', p. 13. Note, Columbus's name is given as 'Colonus'.

6 See Richard Haklyut's famous collections, *Divers Voyages Touching the Discoverie of America* (1582) available via EEBO, STC 12624, and *The Principal Navigations, Voiages, Traffiques and Discoueries of the English Nation* (1598–1600), STC 12625.

7 Stoczkowski, pp. 1–3. In this context, see Jonothan Culler's astute observations in 'Semiotics of Tourism' in *American Journal of Semiotics* 1 (1981): 127–40.

8 Available, EEBO STC 20634.

9 See D. K. Smith's insightful discussion in *The Cartographic Imagination in Early Modern England, re-writing the world in Marlowe, Spenser, Ralegh and Marvell* (Hampshire: Ashgate Publishing Ltd., 2008), pp. 136–46.

10 Smith, p. 145.

11 Ralegh, *The Discoverie,* Part Three, 'An Abstract taken out of certaine Spanyardes Letters concerning *Guiana* and the Countries lying vpon the great riuer *Orenoque*', p. 104.

12 Peter Barry discussing Edward Said's *Orientalism* (1978) in *Beginning Theory: An Introduction to Literary and Cultural Theory* (Manchester: Manchester University Press, 1995), p. 192.

13 For a more rational approach see Michel de Montaigne's 'Of the Caniballes', in *The essayes or morall, politike and millitarie discourses*, 3 vols (1580), translated by John Florio (1603), Book 1, p. 103, available via EEBO, STC 895.16.

14 An excerpt from Strachey's *A true reporatory of the wracke* is available online, in 'Purchas, his Pilgrims' via the Canadian Libraries online resource 'Internet Archive'.

15 *A true reporatory of the wracke and redemption of Sir Thomas Gates Knight; upon, and from the Ilands of the Bermudas: his coming to Virginia, and the estate of that Colonie then, and after, under the government of the lord La warre, July 15 1610. written by William Strachy, Esquire*, published in Volume four, Book 9, Chapter 6 of *Purchas his Pilgrimes* (1625), excerpt as 'Appendix 1: Strachey, *A True Reporatory*', in *The Tempest*, Arden Shakespeare edition, ed. by Virginia Mason Vaughan and Alden Y. Vaughan (Surrey: Thomas Nelson and Sons Ltd, 1999), p. 292.

16 William Strachey, *For the colony in Virginea Britannia. Lawes divine, morall and martiall* (1612) EEBO STC 23350.

17 See Sir Francis Bacon, 'Of Plantations', in *The essayes or counsels, civill and morall* (1625), chapter xxxiii, available via EEBO, STC 618.12, pp. 198–204.

18 Smith, pp. 157–88.

19 Nicolás Monardes's *Historia medicinal*, Frampton, 1580 edition, STC 18006, p. 37.

20 Robert L. Sharp, 'Donne's "Good-Morrow" and Cordiform Maps', *Modern Language Notes*, Vol. 69, No. 7 (Nov. 1954), pp. 493–5.

21 See Gerardus Mercator's double cordiform map at the University of Pennsylvania Library website.

22 Sharp, p.293.

23 See example on the Norman B. Leventhal Map Center, Boston Public Library site.

24 'A sermon Preached to the Honorable Company of the Virginian Plantation, 13 November 1622. By John Donne Deane of St Pauls, London', John Donne Sermon Database, available: http://www.lib.byu.edu/.

25 Amongst other expensive and coveted luxury items, sugar loaves, nutmegs and cloves were supplied by the merchants' guild to be thrown to the crowd during Middleton's Lord Mayor's Shows. See 'Other People, Other Lands' in Julia Briggs, *This Stage-Play World, Texts and Contexts, 1580–1626* (Oxford: Oxford University Press, 1997), pp. 79–107, p. 94.

26 Gary Taylor and John Lavagnino (eds), *Thomas Middleton, The Collected Works* (Oxford: Oxford University Press, 2007), p. 965.

27 Briggs, p. 91.

28 See James McDermott, 'Lok, Michael (*c.*1532–1620 x 22)', *Oxford Dictionary of National Biography*, Oxford University Press, Sept 2004; online edition Jan 2008.

29 Anne Bradstreet, 'The Foure Elements' (of water) in *Several poems compiled with great variety of wit and learning, full of delight wherein especially is contained a compleat discourse, and description of the four elements, constitutions, ages of man, seasons of the year, together with an exact epitome of the three by a gentlewoman in New-England* (1678, published posthumously), available via EEBO, Wing / B4166, p.15.

30 See the Celebration of Women Writers Project: University of Pennsylvania website.

31 Bradstreet, 'The Four Elements' (Air), p. 21.

32 Bradstreet, 'Prologue'.

Religious Works and Controversy

Even a glancing survey of Consistory* records of the era firmly reveals the pervasive nature of religion in everyday life during the medieval and early modern periods. As the documents confirm, the Church calendar, as much as the rhythms of nature, decreed times of leisure and of work; abstinence and indulgence. The obligation to fast on a weekly basis, besides on specific religious holidays such as Lent, was simply a way of life, decreed and regulated by the Church. Except in cases of particular infirmity, when it might be possible to obtain special dispensations, fish was the only animal protein which could be eaten on Wednesdays, Fridays and on Saturday evening, prior to compulsory Sunday worship. Canonical law was regularly violated, however, as accounts of individuals accused and punished demonstrate. From the ecclesiastical records it is difficult to ascertain if these incidents were calculated disregard by those opposed to Church doctrine, or simply a matter of lack of resources. A family member employed by Lady Lisle, for example, wrote soliciting a gift of fish for Lent, in order that the family avoid 'more penance for our sins against our will'.[1]

Further evidence of the elision of boundaries between religious obligation and civic responsibility is found in the published handbooks of the bishops' visitations to the parishes within their dioceses throughout the Tudor reigns. These published tables of questions to be

* Consistory: an ecclesiastical court.

asked were presumably sent abroad to all the parishes, prior to the inspection, facilitating a degree of conformity to be enacted in order to avoid undesirable conflicts. Searching questions were posed not only regarding the professional conduct of the ministers of religion and the precise manner in which they fulfilled their obligations, as might be expected, but also about the parishioners themselves. Ministers were required to report on a variety of unacceptable attitudes and behaviours observed within the flock. These might include unwilling religious observance or possible dissent, taking the form of deliberately defaced or torn prayer books, for example, but also included matters which concerned public order and social regulation. The 'Articles' to be inquired of during the visitation of Thomas Cooper, Bishop of Lincoln, in 1574, quite predictably included the monitoring of church attendance and the religious instruction of children. It also delved into the unconventional living arrangements of the parishioners, asking of married couples if any 'lived asunder', were married before proper notification or more suspiciously, at night or 'before clere light of day'. This article was most thoroughgoing in its rooting out of immoral practices, beginning with the demand to inform if any were 'infected with notorious vice, as Whoredom' or kept 'suspicious houses'. It closes with a concatenation of evil-doers to be exposed: 'adulterers, swearers, dronkerds, sla[n]derers of their neighbours, or any suchlike'.[2] Life at all levels of society was monitored and governed by the Church, both Catholic and the later Protestant.

The amalgamation of theological scraps, vivid affective practices and rituals of action and word, often found in lay piety of the late fifteenth and early sixteenth centuries, can seem at extreme variance with orthodox belief systems today. The affective prayers and meditations, in their metaphorical language, number symbolism and cult following, often seem to encourage a mysticism that contemporary thought more readily associates with the occult. Prayers from the popular Books of Hours, or 'Primers', increasingly available in printed editions in the later fifteenth and early sixteenth centuries, often incorporated numerical symbolism. Through the cult of the five wounds of Christ, the number five became mysticised, so that beliefs associated with the number developed in its observances. Believers attempted to amplify the effectiveness of prayers by the creative application of ritualised repeated actions focusing on the numerical significance. Eamon Duffy illustrates the use of number symbolism in the record of a woman's bequest for five masses of the five wounds to be said on five consecutive days before the high altar, illuminated by five small candles, for example.[3] Similarly, a Somerset legacy was made of five gowns given to five poor men, further enhanced by the gift of five pence given on each Friday (considered to be the fifth day) for a year (p. 246). The shared imagery and its associations were so proverbial that they constituted a mutual language of piety lost to a twenty-first century imagination. The purpose of such elaborate masses was to elicit mercy upon the souls of the deceased, but protection from more prosaic harm was sought not only in cult prayers, but by wearing holy amulets and in the multitude of blessings available for different purposes, some combined with ancillary assistance from holy water, the sign of the cross or appeals for angelic protection.

Folk religion often blurred the boundaries between religion and magic, but the orthodox Church clearly endorsed some of these customs and encouraged emotional investment in like practice. Keith Thomas's valuable overview, *Religion and the Decline of Magic*,[4] indicates numerous overlaps between the ostensibly contradictory perspectives, illustrated by the following single example: drawing attention to the magical powers of protection claimed for the *agnus dei* (Lamb of God) amulets, 'originally made from paschal candles and blessed by the Pope', he enumerates the scope of their defences against evil. Most importantly thwarting the attacks of the omnipresent devil, the talismen also protected against natural disaster, such as tempest and flood, and the dangers of childbirth.[5] Popular religion of the late fifteenth and early sixteenth centuries maintained a raft of such miraculous associations, as Thomas relates, 'holy' men were thought to 'prophesy the future, control the weather, provide protection against fire and flood, magically transport heavy objects, and bring relief to the sick' (p. 28). Prayer scrolls of apparently orthodox provenance, for example, might use the power of naming to protect the bearer, intermixing ancient names for God and the angels with signs of the cross and apotropaic* requests.[6]

The diocese visitations of the prelates early in Henry VIII's reign frequently discovered tight-knit communities which had evolved their own forms of worship, often heavily involved with such practices, especially among the illiterate. Bishop Longland's visitation to the parishes of Lincoln in 1521, for example, revealed in Burford a family named Collins which was at the centre of unorthodox piety within the village. For at least two generations there had been a tradition of owning illicit English-language religious works and the oral teaching of children and neighbours.† Alice Collins and her daughter were regarded as assets to the group due to their powers of memory, as they were able to recite prayers and passages from the Bible at the meetings of the village conventicle.‡ John Foxe records the 'crimes' which Alice was accused of as being the ability to 'recite unto them the declaration of the ten commaundementes & the Epistles of Peter and James', while her daughter had mastered:

> … the Ten Commaundementes, the seven deadly sinnes, the seven woorks of mercy, the five wittes, bodely and ghostly, the eight blessings, and five chapters of St James Epistle.[7]

The pervasive influence of the family's commitment to evangelism is found within Bishop Longland's records as the threads of heterodoxy spread out through familial and neighbourly connection to other towns and villages. One Mr Edmundes sought out Richard Collins in order to place his daughter within the household as a maid so that she could benefit from the learning 'God's law'. Agnes's competence in reciting 'the X commaundements, the five wits, bodely and ghostly and the 7 deadly sins' may have been a credit to the Collins family's instruction,

* Apotropaic: to protect from evil.

† Most religious works under Catholicism were written in Latin, and English Bible translations were outlawed from the end of the fourteenth century, on pain of death, as a result of the work of the Wycliffe group. See following discussion.

‡ Conventicle: a secret religious meeting

but earned her the punishment of elaborate rituals of penance and the enduring sentence to fast on only bread and ale every Friday and *Corpus Christi*[*] of her life.

Until the stirrings of Lutheran thought seeped into English life at the beginning of the sixteenth century, to all intents and purposes, 'Christian' meant Roman Catholic. This is not to say that there were no voices of dissent, or negotiation of parameters, but contentious factions still largely defined themselves as belonging within the faith, albeit with a desire for modification of doctrine, liturgy or vision. Dissenters were often accused of Lollardy. This was used as a generic and derogatory term, originally referring to those who were influenced by John Wycliffe's teachings. The fourteenth-century 'Wycliffe Bible' was central to this controversy, although now recognised as not being wholly Wycliffe's work. In a time when religious texts and services were in Latin, it was inspired by the egalitarian belief that people should have a vernacular Bible which they could read and interpret themselves, rather than relying upon the priesthood to disseminate its teachings to the laity. Opinion is divided, but some scholars maintain that the strong thread of Lollardy formed a sub-current in popular belief which nurtured the new reformed religion later in the reigns of Henry VIII and his son, the boy king Edward VI. The Lollard stance is broadly in concurrence with later Reformation doctrine in the demand for a vernacular Bible and other fiercely-held tenets, which aimed to redefine or eradicate the monopoly of the Catholic Church, and questioned the foundations of revered rituals and concepts. As Wendy Scase underlines, modern scholarship questions the notion of an organised and coherent Lollard system of thought, however, suggesting rather that this concept arises as the result of 'the anxieties of the Church and the monarchy' rather than being an organised movement of like-minded individuals.[8]

The official Church court records of articles raised against two Lincolnshire brothers accused of Lollardy, illustrate both the concerns

* Latin: 'Body of Christ'. This Catholic Feast which occurs the Thursday after Trinity celebrates the Eucharist, commemorating the Last Supper and the miracle of the transformation of the body and blood of Christ into the bread and wine. This was a particularly contentious issue to dissenting Christians, who denied the miracle.

of the authorities and lay resistance to aspects of orthodox religion.[9] Several of their responses involve a discerning attitude to interpretation of the term 'idolatry', strongly forbidden in the Bible but, in the eyes of the Sparke brothers, enforced by the Catholic Church. The theme consistently arises in the examinations of similar unfortunates, suggesting either a shared familiarity with outlawed texts or, at least, widespread discussion of them. The Sparke brothers maintain, for example, that pilgrimages to the sites of saints' burials are ineffective and 'a waste of money' and that crosses and other images at the altar should not be worshipped, as they are 'only stocks and stones'. Their responses resonate with Lollard attitude, as confirmed by *Wyclife's Wicket*'s immovable, 'God lyvynge is not lyke to golde, sylver, ether any graven thynge, or paynted by crafte' and the controversial pronouncement 'God despisethe' such religious imagery (*A iiii verso*).*

The Sparke brothers' statements also undermine sacramental office, questioning the need to pay the priests for services including burial, insisting that confession to a like-minded lay person is 'more soul-healing than confession made to a priest', and denying the sanctity of consecrated ground. They interrogate the right of the Church to ordain fasts, which included times of celibacy, imposing them on married and 'working men'. Their arch-heresy, however, is the denial of the miracle of transubstantiation. This doctrine became fundamental to later inquisitions of faith and was a touchstone for identifying orthodox Catholic and Protestant belief systems. Simplistically, the debate revolves around whether the bread and the wine used to celebrate Mass actually *became* the body and blood of Christ, or whether they were metaphorical representations. *Wyclife's Wicket* again interrogates this essential tenet, suggesting tentatively in parenthesis, '(it semeth)' that the 'bread of life' which Jesus gave to the Apostles at the Last Supper was his message, rather than the material substance:

* In an attempt to clarify the Church's position on sacred art, the second Council of Nicea of 787 had reintroduced the veneration of icons, but prefiguring the Protestant position, the Lollards adamantly rejected all religious imagery. The issue would continue to be debated by the counter-reformation Council of Trent's 25th session in 1563.

> … for the materiall breade hath an ende, as it is wrytten in the gospell of Mathew. xv. that Christ saide all thynges that a man eatethe goethe downe into the wombe, and is sent downe into the draughte awaye, and it hathe an ende of roottynge, but the blessynge of Christe kept his discyples and apostels bothe bodelye and gostely.[10]

According to the records of their arraignment, the Sparke brothers drily, if dangerously, upheld:

> A priest has no more power to make 'the body of Christ' than the wheat-stalk has. After the words of consecration the bread remains only bread as before; and, in fact, is debased by having had such spell-words pronounced over it.[11]

Although articulated in a simple idiom, the basic creed presented in the ecclesiastical records of these trials of common people interacts with important contemporary theological debate, founded on scriptural sources, and interacts with the grand metanarratives of Roman Catholic belief, ratified in ecumenical Councils' impositions.[12]

If discovered, 'heretics' freely admitted their fault and asked forgiveness, as in the case of William and Richard Sparke, they were saved from excommunication but required to perform public penances which usually included self-abasement and beatings, alongside ritualised exhibitions of contrition. The brothers in question were required to shoulder the customary faggot of wood on their shoulders – a reminder of the pyre on which they would burn, should they withdraw their admission of guilt – and make the circuit of the market places of two nearby towns on a crowded market day and, on a day when there was a large religious procession, similarly exhibit themselves around the churchyards of two other parishes, carrying the faggot and a candle each. At every corner during both penances they were to be publicly beaten with rods by the priests, who were commanded loudly to proclaim the reason for their punishment.[13] If a dissenter later relapsed into former practices, as happened in several cases of the Burford conventicle identified above, he or she was committed to public execution by burning at the stake. John Foxe particularly notes of this group that the children of John Scrivener and William Tilesworth were 'compelled to set fire unto their father ... The example of whiche cruelty, as it is contrary both to God and nature' (pp. 838, 774).

Greg Walker remarks that, in many circumstances, when put to the test such individuals often could not describe their own or others' religious affiliations, not recognising that their own beliefs were nonconformist.[14] There is no doubt that some of those executed for their faith were naive in their religious affiliations, rather than actively dissenting. 'Evidence' of offending actions or memorised responses can be found in records of testimonials or judicial procedures, but they are open to distortion and can be manipulated to reflect the perspective of the recorder. The fact that they still exist at all is verification that they served someone's purpose. John Foxe's Protestant martyrology, *Actes and Monuments* (1563), although often simply accepted as a record of factual information, is actually a prime case of *compiled* legal records, letters and testimonials with a precise agenda. Although the evidence presented is historically correct, the documents are, of course, edited and arranged to optimum propagandist effect.

Perhaps surprisingly, as the episcopal examinations of parish clergy revealed, the spiritual leaders of local areas were often as uninformed as their flocks.[15] In some cases even the most rudimentary precepts of the faith, such as the *Pater Noster* (Lord's Prayer) or the Ten Commandments, were mistaken or unknown. In a visitation made to Gloucester as late as Edward VI's reign, in 1551, eight basic questions posed to more than three hundred local clergymen obtained dire results. In this examination eight hapless individuals apparently could not answer any of the questions and two hundred and sixty-one could not answer the full quota. Even those who did respond often had only a woolly understanding, as in the case of one vague individual who offered that 'he knew the number of commandments was ten, but nothing else', subsequently being unable to recite any.[16] Concern over this widespread lack of theological knowledge and training of many of the ministry, combined with extensive malpractice and corruption, fuelled the call for the reformation of the Church throughout Europe.

'Tickets to heaven'

Martin Luther was the German Augustinian monk who initiated the movement which became the Continental Reformation and instigated the advent of Protestantism. The catalyst which prompted him to call for open debate was the scandal of papal 'indulgences', then being sold near Saxony by Johann Tetzel, a respected itinerant Dominican preacher. Orthodox Catholicism accepted that the exemplary lives lived by Christ and the saints had earned a fund or 'Treasury', of merit, which was administered by the Pope.* This sanctity was sold in the form of 'indulgences', which popular misrepresentation held had the power to reduce the length of time the buyer spent in Purgatory, atoning for sins not adequately addressed on earth. Distinction between indulgences to assist the living and the deceased were blurred, however, which contributed to their infamy. According to papal ordinance, in order to be effective the indulgence needed to be accompanied by full and contrite confession. As this was obviously not possible in the case of the deceased, Tetzel was gravely at fault in maintaining, as he did, the efficacy of remission from sin in such situations. Termed by detractors 'tickets to heaven' the indulgences were vilified by reform-minded individuals as verification of the corruption of the Church, encapsulated in scathing rhymes on the theme, 'As soon as the gold into the coffer rings, / The rescued soul to heaven springs'.†

Funds raised from the sale of indulgences throughout Europe were used to complete the building of St Peter's basilica in Rome, begun during the life of Pope Leo's predecessor. To Luther the notion of pecuniary outlay equating remission from sin in any circumstance epitomised the Church's loss of direction. Objecting strongly to the concept that salvation could be traded, he proposed discussion of ninety-five related topics, the audacious eighty-sixth of which was 'Why does not the pope, whose wealth is today greater than the riches of the richest, build just this one church of St Peter with his own money, rather

* At this time Pope Leo X.

† See the online Catholic Encyclopedia for more information on this subject.

than with the money of poor believers?' The deliberations were posted for response on the castle church door at Wittenburg in 1517, becoming notorious as the 'Ninety-five Theses'.*

'Only faith'

Although Luther intended to promote debate and reform from within the Catholic Church, the basic tenets which he proposed as primary to the Christian life brought him infamy and excommunication. Above all, he taught that salvation could not be bought or earned by charitable works, nor any personal agency, but was possible only through faith, hence, the doctrine of Justification by Faith, or '*Sola Fides*'.† He urged popular understanding and engagement with the scriptures in their entirety, rather than the then fragmented approach to worship through selected biblical passages, collections of prayers and hagiographies. Prior to Luther's radical new approach to preaching, sermons were usually based upon occasional pericopes,‡ chosen for thematic harmony with the Church calendar or special events. They were often embellished with extensive allegory and based upon the rhetorical principals of oration, which Luther denigrated in his own early practice with the comment, 'I used to be so fluent that I almost talked the whole world to death'.[17] His disapproval of over-elaborate sermons, which only mystified the listeners and stoked the vanity of the preacher, is evident in his humorously understated advice on preaching, 'First you must learn to go up to the pulpit. Second, you must know how to stay there for a time. Third you must get down again.'[18]

By contrast to the embellished orthodox Catholic sermons which often resembled learned scholastic oration, the reformers' guiding principles were to promote understanding and knowledge of the scriptures, through teaching with clarity and with continuity through

* Luther's ninety-five theses are available online via Project Wittenberg.

† Latin: 'Only Faith'.

‡ A pericope is a biblical section chosen for elucidation in the sermon, such as 'Love thy neighbour as thy self' (Leviticus 19:18; Mark 12:31).

the Bible. As the century progressed, throughout Europe coherent bodies of vernacular teachings were formed in the reformed centres, centring upon Luther in Wittenberg in Germany, Huldrych Zwingli in Zurich, Switzerland, and John Calvin in Geneva (at that time an independent city-state). The democratic impulse was to enfranchise all levels of society, enabling them to take responsibility for their own salvation through direct contact with the Word. This plain approach to scriptural exegesis was also eminently suitable for publication, to facilitate private Bible study in the home, which became one of the defining features of the personal religious routines of later extreme Protestantism.

The insurmountable problem with the egalitarian spirit of the 'priesthood of all believers', implied by Luther's dismissal of the intermediary offices of the priests, was that the onerous charge of responsibility for one's own salvation was laid upon every citizen's shoulders. Humanist educational strategies had ensured that many more boys were taught to read in the newly-founded grammar school, and the reformers urged householders to teach their dependents to read using religious primers and biblical passages. The mere mechanical process of reading does not ensure assimilation or comprehension of complex or subtle content, however. For this reason there was opposition in some quarters to the availability of religious works, especially the Bible, in the common tongue. Sir Thomas More was not alone in his concern that the common man should be protected from possible error – which may cause his damnation for eternity. Hell was a real place and the devil was ever alert to gather the souls of the unwitting. If erudite scholars who had immersed themselves in biblical study for most of their lives could not reach consensus of opinion, how misled might a carpenter, a farmer – or a woman – become? The issue of religious translation was extremely contentious, partly for this reason, causing great discord in humanist scholarly circles, despite a more general interest in the retrieval and re-translation of classical works.

Erasmus of Rotterdam, a good friend of Sir Thomas More, produced a pioneering new edition of the New Testament in 1516, which provided readers with the original Greek in a table beside a new, more accurate, translation in Latin. In itself this was extremely controversial as it rejected the hallowed St Jerome Vulgate Bible as corrupt and inaccurate. The wider implication was that the myriad of sacred works throughout the centuries, which had expounded and theorised upon its content, were now exposed as inauthentic. Although the revelations of Erasmus's Greek-Latin New Testament were not intended for the common man, but only those who were able to read Latin, the work was tremendously influential throughout Europe, opening the floodgates to many vernacular works which were subsequently influenced by or based upon it.

William Tyndale, in extreme contrast to Sir Thomas More, but in concord with Erasmus and the reformers, stated that his desire was to teach even the rustic ploughboy theology.[19] Unable to gain support in England, where the Pope had recently dubbed Henry 'Defender of the Faith' for his polemic against Luther, Tyndale eventually entered voluntary exile and sailed for Hamburg in 1524.* As John Foxe's martyrology dryly recounts, the publication of Tyndale's English translation of the Greek New Testament was fraught with unwanted adventure and danger. Tyndale was obliged to publish his finished work in Cologne, as he was unable to return to England due to his dangerously unorthodox sympathies, which Sir Thomas More and Cuthbert Tunstall, Bishop of London, labelled 'Wycliffite'.[20] Details of the printing of six thousand copies, with which to flood England, were discovered by a passionately anti-Lutheran Colognian pamphleteer who alerted the city authorities, causing the print shop to be raided and the work in progress to be impounded. Tyndale was fortunate to escape with loose sheets which were then reprinted in both large and small formats (for easy concealment) by a German printer in Worms. Further disruptions ensued, however, as the books were being prepared to be smuggled into England. As Foxe reports, a mercer named Augustus

* Stephen Vaughan was the diplomat later engaged by the king to attempt to persuade Tyndale to return to England. He was an avid but clandestine supporter of the Reformation himself and the father of Anne [Vaughan] Locke. See discussion of Anne Locke's Protestant works in Part Three: 'Religious Verse' and 'The Woman Debate' above in Part Four.

Packington was commissioned by the unwitting Bishop of London to seek out and buy as many copies of the work as possible, to be shipped to England for burning. In fact, Packington was a reform sympathiser himself and set about his project with humour. He followed Tunstall's directions implicitly, entering into an agreement with Tyndale to procure all the remaining copies of the text – at a generous price – which funded the printing of an improved and corrected edition.[21] Tyndale had great support and some close allies within the English merchant community of Antwerp, where he lodged in their 'English House', which was overseen by Thomas Poyntz, 'a grocer of London'.[22]

Tyndale's work is quite extraordinary in its close attention to style and philological scrutiny. In his 'Prologue to Leviticus' in the Pentateuch* which followed the New Testament in 1530, he states that the writers of the Old Testament had to employ 'likenesses, riddles, proverbs, and dark and strange speaking' to convey their message. This is as a result of mankind's fallen nature and reduced acuity, which leaves it only able to perceive God's Word 'but through a cloud'.[23] His duty, he felt, was to dispel the allegories and ambiguities which encrusted the true teachings of the Bible. This, of course, entailed not only translation but also interpretation, a contested domain, which was the crux of the dispute between Sir Thomas More, William Tyndale, and their followers. A furious and increasingly caustic published dialogue ensued over three years between the two ardent but opposed Christians, ranging over issues of scriptural interpretation, religious doctrine and considerations of Church hierarchy.†

* The Pentateuch: the first five books of the Bible: Genesis, Exodus, Leviticus, Numbers and Deuteronomy.

† More's *Dialogue Against Heresies* (1529) was aimed squarely at Luther and Tyndale, whom he saw as being of the same camp. Tyndale responded with *An Answere to Sir Thomas More's Dialogue* (1531) to be rebuffed the following year by *A Confutation of Tyndale* (1532). Despite his loyal support, More himself was eventually martyred by beheading by Henry VIII in 1532. As an ardent Catholic, his conscience rejected the absolute authority of the king and his heirs over the Church of England. This was later formally entailed in the Act of Supremacy (1534).

'Juggling and conveying craftily'

More was anxious about the process of translation itself, maintaining, as many devout members of both camps did, that the active and living truth of the scriptures was embedded within the words themselves and could be damaged or lost.[24] More pragmatically, the process of translation was fraught with problems and open to deliberate manipulation. To create an English translation of biblical material may require transposing meaning (which itself was often contested) through the incompatible semantics of Greek or Hebrew into English, in some cases, travelling through Latin first. Moreover, the task of expressing the mysteries of the faith in English, a language considered lacking in the necessary subtleties, was considered complex and even dangerous. Grammatical slips or aberrations in translating the classical languages could alter the perspective of a passage and subsequent doctrine built upon it. William Tyndale took Cardinal John Fisher to task on precisely these grounds, citing the latter's interpretation of a verse of St Paul's Letters to the Galatians (5:6).* As the grammatical structure of the passage alters when it is articulated in Latin from the Greek and Hebrew, the resulting 'translation' may arrive at either of these conflicting conclusions: salvation is dependent upon faith, good works and love; or faith gains salvation which is evident in the subsequent love and performance of good works.[25] The difference is crucial as it underwrites the seminal salvific† doctrines of both Catholic and Protestant ecclesiology.

More was also of the mind that man's intrinsic fallibility disqualified most from a reliable interpretation of religious works, exemplified in

* The Greek New Testament latter part of Galatians 5:6 translates literally as 'but faith working through love', but the Latin Vulgate Bible has 'sed fides quae per caritatem operatur' which translates literally as 'but faith that worketh by Charity'. Tyndale's version has 'but faith which by love is mighty in operacion'. The emphasis of the Vulgate implies that faith comes through charity, in accordance with the Catholic doctrine of good works, necessary to achieve salvation. Tyndale achieves a closer relationship with the more ancient Greek text and avoids any connection with Catholic doctrine, instead emphasising love for God and fellow man. See Brian Cummings, *The Literary Culture of the Reformation: Grammar and Grace* (Oxford: Oxford University Press, 2002), p. 191.

† Salvific: relating to the doctrine of salvation.

Tyndale's 'heretical' elucidations. In a concerted programme of re-evaluation and adjustment, Tyndale had substituted theologically-loaded terms in common use, such as 'priest' for 'elder', 'Church' for 'congregation', 'penance' for 'repentance', 'charity' for 'love', and modified 'confession' into the acknowledgement of sin. His strategies forced readers to read the scriptures afresh, without the pre-conceived lexical significations of, for example, 'good works', confession and penance. Tyndale's semantic realignment succeeds in fracturing the union of Catholic doctrine with the message of the Greek and Hebrew sources of the Biblical works. He also re-aligns connotation by removing terms which have specific doctrinal weight for Protestants, such as 'grace', connoting God's spiritual gift of belief, essential for faith and so salvation.[26] In a confidently democratic gesture, he also urges the conscious participation of his reader in interrogating the language of the religious works. Etymological notes on the ancient sources appeared in the marginalia, to facilitate personal interpretation, and some of his works were provided with glossaries in a range of ancient languages, including English, Hebrew, Latin and Greek. The gesture was typical of the new religion's levelling and inclusive ethos, encouraging all to participate in their own spiritual rehabilitation and salvation – and this was precisely its danger.*

Preaching 'Against disobedience and willful rebellion'

The prospect of the general populace questioning and perhaps ousting fundamental tenets of state religion was extremely threatening to the mechanisms of secular power in both Europe and England. Hence, the hard-line approach to religious dissent.

During the reign of Henry VIII, Archbishop Thomas Cranmer created the first officially-endorsed book of homilies,† although they

* By 1534 Tyndale had been betrayed and discovered. Despite determined intervention by the Merchant Adventurers of the English House, including Stephen Vaughan, he was burned for heresy in Vilvorde, close to Antwerp, in 1536.

† Homilies: approved regulated sermons.

were not published and put into service until the reign of Edward VI, in 1547. By rigidly inscribing the parameters of permitted teaching, the sermons sought to safeguard against religious non-conformity, but also served a major political purpose. Theories of social hierarchy and civic order were intertwined with concepts of religious conformity in these discourses, which were delivered from the pulpit when no calendar-relevant sermon was given by the preacher. Besides the more expected subjects such as prayer, the relevance of Good Friday and the necessity of good works, others carried such titles as 'Against Swearing and Perjury', 'An exhortation to Obedience' and 'Against Strife and Contention'. A second book of Homilies was added to these during Elizabeth I's reign, including two 'Against Idleness' and 'An Homily Against Disobedience and Willful Rebellion'.*

The sermon against idleness was a powerful vehicle which yoked notions of Christian duty and obedience with the necessity to work productively, for one's master and the community, in the calling to which one was destined. Self-indulgent inactivity benefited neither society nor the individual, and as such was both 'repugnant' and 'a grievous sinne'. Significantly, the sermon's vehement condemnation identified the 'intolerable evil' of immoral or seditious activities which arose through too much leisure and temptation to pleasurable, but sinful, activity. The mind and body were to be kept fully occupied by application to 'honest labour and businesse, which [...] is enjoyned unto man by GODS appointment'.[27] Under later Protestantism these decrees would be further developed, leading to what is commonly referred to as the 'Protestant work ethic', in Max Weber's terms, 'the providential interpretation of profit-making justified the activities of the business man' and provided the 'ethical justification of the [...] division of labour'.[28]

* The first three homilies named above are numbers VII, X and XII of the first collection and the latter two are homilies XIX and XXI from the second book. Both books are available edited by Ian Lancashire (1994), on the University of Toronto-managed Anglican Library website.

From 'Catholicism without a Pope' to the approved English Bible

Henry VIII's new-founded Church of England performed the unthinkable in first weakening and ultimately deposing the Pope as Supreme Head of the Church, but in many ways remained conservative.* The *Ten Articles* of the faith of 1536 were said to be written by the king himself, but he was no doubt assisted by Archbishop Cranmer and Thomas Cromwell, the new Vicar General. They were intended to clarify the theological precepts and 'to stablysh Christen Quietnes', stabilising the new dogma. They retained confession and absolution, maintained that charitable works were necessary for salvation, and upheld the doctrine of Purgatory. Church adornment in imagery of the saints and the Virgin Mary was to remain and the saints' intercessory role was still recognised. Most importantly, the bread and wine of the Eucharist were understood as the actual body and blood of Christ, not metaphorical representations.[29] Due to its *via media* † approach, scholars have termed Henry's Church 'Catholicism without the Pope'. Despite the many traditionalist elements, as the reign progressed there was greater consensus towards the need for an English-language Bible. Pressure from Cranmer and Cromwell eventually saw Myles Coverdale commissioned to provide an English translation from the standard Latin Vulgate Bible in 1534. Ironically this version, itself a foundation for others, relied heavily on both Luther's and Tyndale's outlawed works. A compilation of this and Tyndale's near complete Bible formed a further popular version, known as the Matthew's Bible but, in fact, assembled by Tyndale's friend and assistant, John Rogers under the pseudonym. The king approved this Bible, no doubt unaware of its provenance, and it was made freely available for general perusal by a royal injunction demanding its provision in every church by 1537.

* The main impetus for the break with Rome was to enable Henry to gain an annulment of his marriage to Catherine of Aragon and enable him to marry Anne Boleyn. Leviticus 20:21 was cited as evidence that divine disapproval had caused the monarchy to be without an heir during his 20-year marriage.

† Latin: middle path.

The *Valor Ecclesiasticus*

The impetus towards a reformed religion gathered force as much through financial considerations as pious conviction. Thomas Cromwell instigated a visitation to the monasteries which was to have a devastating effect not only on their inhabitants, but on a whole sector of society. The *Valor Ecclesiasticus** estimated the comparative wealth and holdings of the religious house, prior to the seizure of their assets and dissolution. *The Dissolution of the Lesser Monasteries* Act (1536) and *The Act of Suppression* (1539), which closed the smaller then the larger monasteries and other religious houses, had two lasting effects, apart from the intended great advantage of enriching Henry VIII's royal coffers. Firstly, as the religious houses had traditionally aided the poor and tended the sick in their hospitals, the impact on the impoverished was immediate and continued to be felt throughout the rest of the Tudor reigns. This was especially true of the periods of poor harvests which exacerbated their miserable conditions during the Elizabethan period. There were also innumerable cases of ex-members of the religious orders, male and female, being left homeless or without adequate provision. Secondly, the confiscated monastic lands and properties were used as very desirable inducements or rewards for favoured courtiers and diplomats. Individuals of the rising middle class, such as the wealthy merchants employed about court business at home and abroad, were therefore able to establish themselves as landed gentry. In an era which saw the erosion of the assets of the nobility, new money increasingly married into higher social strata, contributing to the shift in the demographics of the era.

When he acceded to his father's throne in 1547, the young Edward VI avidly embraced Protestantism, inviting prominent theologians and scholars from the Continent, including Martin Bucer and Peter Martyr, to assist in its establishment as the state religion.† His reign also encouraged the return of reform-minded individuals who had taken

* *Valor Ecclesiasticus*: Latin 'Ecclesiastical Valuation'.

† As Edward was still in his minority, aged only ten, his powerful uncle, Edward Seymour, Duke of Somerset, who was also a staunch reformist, was installed as Lord Protector.

voluntary exile on the Continent, where they had experienced the new religion in Germany and Switzerland. As the Catholic bishops and preachers were retired from their positions, they were replaced by ardent Protestants, such as John Hooper, Myles Coverdale, Nicholas Ridley and John Knox, many of whom would suffer persecution or execution during the following reign when Catholicism was reintroduced. Under the new regime the regulatory Book of Common Prayer was produced, partly by Bishop Cranmer, and introduced in 1549. It was basically a working manual to enforce concurrence of practice on all church services. It decreed the precise form of all types of worship and religious observance, including daily worship, religious festivals, weddings, baptisms and burials. The following year an Act of Uniformity further enforced its sole use in the kingdom, to prevent any vestige of Catholic observance being practiced.

The far-reaching effects of this and the second edition of the Edwardian Prayer Book cannot be over-emphasised.* The services of the stages of life, especially of marriage and burial, provided a plethora of memorable phrases which found their way into everyday speech as adages, and so into the literature of the day. These include familiar axioms such as 'We brought nothyng into this worlde, neyther may we carye any thyng out', 'In the myddest of lyfe we be in death', 'Ashes to ashes, dust to dust', 'in sickenesse and in health', 'so long as you bothe shall live' and 'to have and to holde', among numerous others. The patterning and terms of the litanies were also absorbed into the public imagination, affording example and imagery with which contemporary speech was littered.

During the period between 1533 to 1558 Mary I re-established Catholicism in England, rejecting the Protestant reforms and introduction of vernacular forms of worship. The Protestant bishops were replaced, High Mass resumed and a vast programme of religious spectacles through the capital was begun. The diary of an eye-witness, Henry Machyn, records local parish clergy processions on alternate

* The rejection of the use of *The Book of Common Prayer* in Scotland in 1637 was also one of the catalysts which contributed to the Puritan uprising against Charles I in 1645, when Parliament declared war on the king.

weekdays and astonishingly opulent and impressive larger processions, involving hundreds of participants in penitential costume and carrying candles, several times a year. His diary entries of 1555 record two such processions in January, three in May and one each in June and August.[30] Since such persuasions to convert did not persuade staunch Protestants, increasingly fierce retribution was meted out upon them, culminating in the burning at the stake of around three hundred dissenters in just three years of Mary's reign. Many non-conformists sought religious exile in Europe in the great centres of reform, Emden, Wesel, Frankfort, Strasbourg, Basel, Zurich and Geneva. During their years spent in Geneva, John Calvin's theocracy, prominent and gifted translators and writers of the English exile community prepared the monumental new Geneva Bible. Incorporating the earlier work of reformists, Tyndale and Coverdale, the text was printed in more easily readable Roman font, presented an accessible format of chapters and verses and with copious marginalia to assist self-study. Printed in 1560, shortly after Elizabeth I's accession to the throne and hailing her as a saviour of the 'true' religion, this is the Bible of the Elizabethan era.

The Elizabethan Thirty-nine Articles were intended to standardise religious belief and practice, but were vociferously interrogated by a significant Puritan presence within the Church. Contested areas included the articles of the faith, wording of the liturgy, the prescriptions of the Book of Common Prayer and the vestmental requirements. When James I acceded to the throne he was persuaded to hold a religious inquiry to discuss these concerns, at which he presided most knowledgeably for three days. One of the outcomes of the inquiry was the decision to commission a new Bible. By June 1604 outstanding biblical translators were being contacted to assist in the great national undertaking. These were eventually reduced to an approved fifty-four scholars who were grouped into six teams, with bases at the two universities and Westminster.[31] The most prominent of these gifted linguists was the Dean of Westminster, Lancelot Andrewes. He had studied under one of the great humanist scholars, Richard Mulcaster, at the Merchant Taylors' School, along with Edmund Spenser. His prodigious accomplishments included the mastery of fifteen languages, including ancient and modern, and a gift of exceptional eloquence.[32] The writing team was keen to emphasise the continuity of the Bible with its predecessors, although it was not at first accepted by the stalwart Puritans who remained faithful to the Geneva Bible. The King James Bible was printed in 1611 and its contribution to the development of English language was quickly recognised in its cadences, adopted from Greek and Hebrew, native Anglo-Saxon vocabulary and engaging diction. A century later, Joseph Addison wrote of it, 'Our language has received innumerable elegancies and improvements [thereby] ... They give a force and an energy to our expressions'.[33]

During this period the Bible was read as a storehouse of histories and exempla by which to define one's own path through life, encouraging close personal engagement. The all-pervasive nature of religion and the obligatory Church attendance ensured that the sacred works outlined above had a profound effect upon their literally captive audience. Their well-known phrases and terminology, intoned weekly from the pulpits and encountered in personal pious reading routines, permanently etched themselves on the mind. As is evident from publications of all genres, people habitually expressed themselves in borrowed biblical references, framing their experience of life to the examples contained within its pages. Bruce Gordan, writing of the reformers, points out that they 'saw themselves and their enemies reflected' in the Bible, but this stands firm for the embattled on both sides of the theological divide at different times.[34]

Literature reflects the mindset of the author but also accommodates the prejudices of its intended audience. Hence, as a result of the religious strife of these reigns, intensely anti-Catholic sentiments can be discovered embedded in Elizabethan and Jacobean poetry and drama. Book I of Spenser's *The Faerie Queene* uses apocalyptic imagery, painting a lurid portrait of Duessa the 'Whore of Babylon'* and introducing, as an adversary to the 'true' faith, a monster named 'Erroure'.† Arising from a similar impulse, the Jacobean Revenge Tragedies are habitually

* A common Protestant term of abuse for the Catholic faith in sixteenth and seventeenth-century England.

† See Part Three: 'Pastoral to Epic'.

set in Catholic countries, Spain and Italy, implying that the monstrous crimes of passion – calculated murder, familial prostitution and incest – could only occur in such lawless and 'godless' places. By extension, opulence, decadence and ornamentation were distrusted through their associations with the iconography of the Catholic Church.

It is often assumed that once the reformation of the Church was underway in mid-sixteenth and seventeenth-century England that 'religion' was synonymous with Protestantism. This is misconceived, however, as it suggests a clean break with the practice and beliefs of earlier times. In reality, the entrenched and habitual cadences of the older traditions lingered from the medieval past, and beneath seeming conformity was a blend of practice and belief, acknowledged and rejected to differing degrees. The popular Psalms of the new faith frequently used existing traditional (Catholic) melodies, but substituted more fitting reformed lyrics, epitomising the fusion of both faiths in aspects of contemporary worship. During the reigns of Edward VI and Elizabeth I, when Catholicism was outlawed, there was a steady flow of religious works from over the Channel which provided spiritual solace to the persecuted. Meditations and contemplations by Catholic theologians Luis de Granada and François de la Sales and the Spiritual Exercises of the Jesuit St Ignatius de Loyola were particularly sought after and popular.[*] These and indigenous medieval meditations, such as the 'Meditations on the Life of Christ', subsequently influenced Protestant prayer and devotional meditation, despite their seeming contrariety. Vestiges can often be identified in the vivid pictorial imagery employed, or empathic focus on Christ's crucifixion, for example, as in Anne Locke's affective *Meditation of a penitent sinner* or sections of Aemilia Lanyer's *Salve Deus Rex Judaorum*.[†] Above all, the personal religious strife endured by committed Christians of both faiths should not be forgotten, as they were forced to comply with the demands of a

* See Louis L. Martz, *The Poetry of Meditation: A Study in English Religious Literature* (New Haven and London: Yale University Press, 1954), p. 7. The English translations that Martz cites in this context date mainly from the 1580s and the beginning of the next century, though the original works circulated in Europe from 1548 onwards.

† See Part Three: 'Religious Verse' and Part Four: 'The Woman Debate'.

changing state religion through the reigns of the Tudor monarchs. From the medieval Roman Catholicism of the beginning of Henry VIII's reign, this ranged through his creation of the (conservative) Church of England, to the extreme Protestantism of Edward VI, back to re-instated Catholicism under Mary I, and then to Elizabeth's moderate Protestantism. Many individuals lived through these tempestuous decades of religious strife and were obliged to choose between their conscience and their livelihood or, in some desperate cases, their life.

Notes

1 Muriel St Clare (ed.), *The Lisle Letters, An Abridgement*, selected and arranged by Bridget Boland (London: Secker and Warburg, 1983), vol. 3, William Seller to Lady Lisle, p. 132 (emphasis added).

2 Article 18 of *Articles to bee Enquired of within the Diocesse of Lincolne* (1574) (in the reign of Elizabeth I), available via Early English Books Online, http://eebo.chadwyck.com.home, STC 102229.

3 Eamon Duffy, *The Stripping of the Altars, Traditional Religion in England 1400–1580* (New York and London: Yale University Press, 1992), p. 246.

4 Keith Thomas, *Religion and the Decline of Magic, Studies in Popular Beliefs in Sixteenth- and Seventeenth-Century England* (London: Penguin, 1971, repr. 1991).

5 Thomas, p. 33.

6 Duffy, p. 270.

7 John Foxe, *Actes and Monuments* (1587 edn), Chapter 7, p. 834.

8 Wendy Scase, 'Lollardy' in *The Cambridge Companion to Reformation Theology*, David Bagchi and David C. Steinmetz (eds) (Cambridge: Cambridge University Press, 2004), pp. 15–21, pp. 16–17.

9 'Xl Proceedings, 1457, against the brothers William and Richard Sparke', of Somersham, Lollards, at the instance of John Chedworth bishop of Lincoln', Lincoln diocese documents, 1450–1544 / edited, with notes and indexes by Andrew Clark, available online via Corpus of Middle English Prose and Verse, digitalised by the University of Michigan's Digital Library Production Service.

10 *Wycliffe's Wicket*, reprinted in 1546, available via EEBO, STC 25590, p. *A v recto* (although unnumbered).

11 'Xl Proceedings, 1457, against the brothers William and Richard Sparke', p. 103.

12 See Scase's discussion of the ecumenical Council of Constance (1414–18) and the Lateran Council of 1215, p. 17.

13 'Proceedings, 1457, against the brothers William and Richard Sparke', p. 103.

14 Greg Walker, *Persuasive Fictions, Faction, Faith and Political Culture in the Reign of Henry VIII* (Aldershot: Scolar Press, 1996), pp. 125–6.

15 Luther began these examinations in Wittenberg, Saxony, and the practice was extended throughout the reformed areas. The visitations were intended to assist by advising on all aspects of the ministry, including the religious education of children, care of the poor and sick, and the administration and standardisation of ceremonies. See Thomas M. Lindsay, *A History of the Reformation,* Vol. 1, (Edinburgh: T. and T. Clark, 1963), pp. 410–16.

16 Lindsay, vol. 1 p. 406, n.2.

17 Martin Luther, *Table Talk*, no. 1317, p. 135, Volume 54 of Luther's *Works*, H. T. Lehmann (ed.) (St Louis: Concord, 1955). Luther is referring to his *Dictata super psalterium* of 1515.

18 Martin Luther, *Table Talk*, no. 5171b recorded by John Mathesius (August, 1540), p. 393.

19 Both Erasmus's Preface to the 1516 edition of his Greek New Testament and Myles Coverdale's the prefatory notice to *Goostly psalms and spirituall songes drawen out of the holy Scripture, for the co[m]forte and consolacyon of soch as love to rejoyse in God and his Worde* (London, *c.*1535) use similar analogies. *Goostly psalms* is available via EEBO, STC 5892.

20 See W. J. Shiels, *The English Reformation 1530–1570* (Harlow: Longmans, 1989), p. 1 and Document 4, Letter of the Bishop of London to More requesting that he write against Tyndale, in which he uses the same terms, p. 81.

21 See Foxe, *Actes & Monuments* (1563), p. 443. Elsewhere Packington is identified as one who 'passed and repassed the seas' to collect and distribute outlawed books, see John Strype, *Ecclesiastical Memorials relating Chiefly to Religion and the Reformation of it* (Oxford: Clarendon Press, 1822), pp. 255–6.

22 See William Tyndale, *Doctrinal Treatises to Different Parts of the Scriptures*, H. Walter (ed.), Parker Society (Cambridge: Cambridge University Press, 1848), pp. lxv–vii.

23 Tyndale, 'A Prologue unto the third book of Moses, called Leviticus', vol. 1, *Work of William Tyndale*, ed. by G. E. Duffield (Appleford, Berks: Sutton Courtney Press, 1964), p. 59.

24 William Tyndale's remark upon John Fisher's translation of Galatians 5:6 which appears in *Doctrinal Treatises*, pp. 221–2, also cited in Brian

Cummings, *The Literary Culture of the Reformation, Grammar and Grace* (Oxford: Oxford University Press, 2002), p. 191.

25 See Cummings, p. 191.

26 See Tyndale's 'Epistle to the Reader', originally intended as a prologue to the 1525 translation but published separately as *A Pathway unto the Holy Scripture*. See David Norton's *A History of the Bible as Literature from antiquity to 1700*, vol. 1 (Cambridge: Cambridge University Press, 1993), p. 97. For a detailed and lengthy discussion of the soterial doctrine see *The Collected Works of Sir Thomas More*, vol. 6, part II, pp. 512–16.

27 'Homily against Idlenesse', Homily XIX, Second Book of Homilies, as above, also available via EEBO, STC 13675.

28 Max Weber, 'Ideas and Religious Interests, The Religious Foundation of Worldly Asceticism' in *Theories of Society, Foundations of Modern Sociological Theory*, Talcot Parsons *et al* (eds) (New York: The Free Press, 1960), pp. 724–9.

29 See Lindsay, vol. 2, pp. 333–4.

30 Henry Machyn, *The Diary of Henry Machyn, A London Citizen, 1550 to 1563*, edited by John Gough Nichols for the Camden Society, Vol. 42 (London: J. B. Nicholson and Son, 1848), pp. 80, 81, 86, 89, 92.

31 See Benson Bobrick, *The Making of the English Bible* (London: Weidenfield and Nicholson, 2001), p. 224.

32 Bobrick, pp. 224, 225.

33 Addison, *Spectator*, No. 416 (27 June 1712), cited in Bobrick, p. 264.

34 Bruce Gordan (ed.), *Protestant History and Identity in Sixteenth-Century Europe*, vol. 2 (Aldershot: Scolar Press, 1996), p. 4.

Part Five
References and Resources

Timeline

	Historic Events	Literary Events*
1492	Christopher Columbus lands in the 'New World'	
1501	Catherine of Aragon is formally married to Prince Arthur in London	
1502	Prince Arthur dies aged 16	
1507		Amerigo Vespuci's account of his voyages to America published
1509	Death of Henry VII the first Tudor monarch; accession of Henry VIII and marriage to Catherine of Aragon, his brother's widow	
1515–16		Thomas More's *Utopia* published in Latin in Louvain, France
1517	Martin Luther nails his 95 theses on the doors of Wittenberg cathedral	
1531	Henry VIII broke away from the Roman Catholic Church and proclaimed Supreme Head of the Church of England	
1536	The Catholic insurrection named the Pilgrimage of Grace centred on York in the north of England; Anne Boleyn beheaded; Wyatt imprisoned in the Tower of London	John Calvin's *Institutes of the Christian Religion* published in Geneva

* Some of the dates of literary works are still contested.

	Historic Events	Literary Events
1537	Birth of Edward VI and death of his mother Jane Seymour	
1542	Henry VIII proclaimed King of Ireland	
1543		Nicolaus Copernicus's *On the Revolutions of the Heavenly Spheres* published
1547	Edward VI accedes to the throne, aged 10; the Duke of Somerset becomes Lord Protector	*First Book of Homilies* published and adopted
1549	The Act of Uniformity enforces the use of the *Book of Common Prayer* in all church services; Peasants' Rebellion	*Book of Common Prayer* issued Wyatt's metricised version of the *Penitential Psalms* published
1551		More's *Utopia* translated into English
1552	Edmund Spenser born	
1553	Edward VI dies and his half-sister Mary Tudor is crowned; an abortive attempt to seize the throne for Lady Jane Grey results in her execution; Catholicism is re-established as the state religion	Thomas Wilson's *Arte of Rhetorique* published
1554	Mary I marries Philip II of Spain; Sir Philip Sidney born	
1556		The *Genevan Psalter* is printed by exiles in Geneva
1557		Tottel's *Miscellany* published
1558	England loses Calais to France; Mary I dies and Elizabeth, her half-sister, is crowned. Protestantism restored as the state religion	John Knox's *Against the Monstrous Regiment of Women* published
1559	Act of Uniformity passed; Elizabeth I takes the title of Supreme Head of the Church of England	*Book of Common Prayer* re-issued

	Historic Events	Literary Events
1560	Church of Scotland founded	*Geneva Bible* published by exiles in Geneva; Anne Locke publishes *Sermons of John Calvin, Upon the Songe that Ezechias made*
1561	Mary Sidney born; Mary Stuart (Queen of Scots) begins her reign in Scotland	Thomas Hoby's translation of Castiglione's *Il Cortegiano* as *The Courtier* is published; Calvin's *Institutes of the Christian Religion* translated into English by Norton
1562	French wars of religion	
1563	Massive death toll from the plague in London and throughout Europe	John Foxe's *Acts and Monuments* (Foxe's *Book of Martyrs*) published
1564	Christopher Marlowe, William Shakespeare and Galileo Galilei born; John Calvin dies	
1565		Arthur Golding's translation of Ovid's *Metamorphoses*, Books 1–5 published
1566	Mary Stuart of Scotland delivered of a son who would become James VI of Scotland and James I of England	
1567	Mary Stuart abdicates under threat	
1568	Mary Stuart flees to England seeking protection	The *Bishop's Bible* printed
1569	Catholic insurrection in the north of England is suppressed	
1570	The Pope excommunicates Elizabeth I	Roger Ascham's *The Scholemaster* published
1572	John Donne and Ben Jonson born	
1576	The Theatre opens in Shoreditch under Burbage in London; The Children's company playing at Blackfriars	

	Historic Events	Literary Events
1577	Francis Drake starts his voyage to circumnavigate the globe; The Curtain theatre opens in London	Ralph Holinshed's *Chronicles of England, Scotland and Ireland* published
1578	James VI begins his reign in Scotland. Marriage negotiations between Elizabeth I and the French Duc d'Alençon begun amid much Protestant opposition	Lyly's *Euphues* published
1579	Francis Drake circumnavigates the world, and names and claims New Albion in California for Elizabeth I	Edmund Spenser's *The Shepheardе's Calendar* published anonymously
1580	French marriage negotiations between Elizabeth I and the Duc d'Alençon end; Francis Drake arrives back in England; John Webster is born	The first of Michel de Montaigne's *The essayes or morall, politike and millitarie discourses* (3 vols) published, including 'Of the Caniballes'; John Stow publishes *Chronicles of England*
1581		Seneca's *Tragedies* are translated into English by Thomas Heywood; Richard Mulcaster's *Positions* is published; Philip Sidney probably writes *Arcadia*
1582	An English colony is founded in Newfoundland	Richard Hakluyt begins collecting and writing his accounts of discovery under the title *Voyages;* Philip Sidney writes *Astrophil and Stella* and *Defence of Poesy*
1583	The Queen's Men formed; English trade expands to the Middle East and India; The Queen's Players acting company founded	The Puritan Philip Stubbes publishes *An Anatomy of Abuses* attacking the theatre
1584	Walter Ralegh names and claims Virginia for Elizabeth I	Thomas Lodge writes *Scylla's Metamorphosis* (1584–8)

	Historic Events	Literary Events
1585	Declaration of war with Spain; Edward Alleyn leads the Lord Chamberlain's Men and the Lord Admiral's Company of actors	William Shakespeare arrives in London to make a living, initially as actor, poet and playwright Christopher Marlowe writes *Dido, Queen of Carthage*, perhaps with Thomas Nashe (1585–6)
1586	Sir Philip Sidney dies of a wound sustained fighting the Protestant cause in Europe; Mary Stuart of Scotland tried	Christopher Marlowe translates Ovid's *Amores* and *Passionate Shepherd to His Love*, around this time, whilst a student at Cambridge
1587	Mary Stuart executed; Rose playhouse built	
1588	England defeats the Spanish Armada	
1589		Richard Hakluyt's *The Principal Navigations of the English Nation* published; Thomas Lodge publishes *Scylla's Metamorphosis*; George Puttenham publishes the *Arte of English Poesie*
1590		Early Shakespeare plays and Christopher Marlowe's *Tamburlaine* performed; Sir Philip Sidney's *Arcadia* published; Edmund Spenser publishes *The Faerie Queene*, Books I–III
1591	Robert Dudley, Earl of Essex, leads an expedition to the Netherlands to assist Henry IV in religious war against Catholicism	Edmund Spenser's *Complaints* published

	Historic Events	**Literary Events**
1592	Protracted outbreak of plague in London causing theatres to be closed. Little respite until 1594	Philip Henslowe's *Diary* documenting his theatre business is started. Kyd's *Spanish Tragedie* performed; Daniel's *Delia* published; Marlowe's *Dr Faustus* performed
1593	Christopher Marlowe killed in a street brawl; plague in London; George Herbert born	Shakespeare publishes *Venus and Adonis* and probably working on the *Sonnets*; Marlowe's *Hero and Leander* written
1594	Shakespeare's *Lucrece* published	Plague in London
1595	Swan playhouse built	Edmund Spenser's *Amoretti, Epithalamion* and *Colin Clout comes Home Again* published; Sir Walter Ralegh publishes *The Discovery of the large, rich, and beautiful Empire of Guiana*; first of Shakespeare's *Sonnets* probably written
1596		Spenser publishes *The Faerie Queene*, Books IV–VI
1597		Francis Bacon publishes his *Essays*
1598		Marlowe's *Hero and Leander* published; Sir Philip Sidney's collected works posthumously published by Mary Sidney Herbert, Countess of Pembroke
1599	Death of Spenser; Globe Playhouse built	
1600	East India Trading Company founded	

	Historic Events	Literary Events
1603	Death of Elizabeth I and accession of James I of England (James VI of Scotland) unites Scotland and England; very bad outbreak of plague	Montaigne's *Essays* translated by John Florio
1605	The Gunpowder Plot to assassinate James I thwarted	Francis Bacon publishes *The Advancement of Learning;* Joseph Hall's *Mundus alter et idem* about a fictional world published
1606	The Virginia Company founded	
1607	Colonisation of Virginia	
1608	John Milton born	
1609		Shakespeare's *Sonnets* published
1610		William Strachey's *A true reporatory of the wrack* published
1611		King James Bible published; Aemilia Lanyer publishes *Salve Deus*; Shakespeare's *The Tempest* probably written 1610–11, this is also the latest estimated date for *The Winter's Tale*
1612		William Strachey's tract *For the colony in Virginea Britannia*; *Lawes divine, morall and martiall* published; John Webster's *The Duschess of Malfi* performed ? (before 1614)

	Historic Events	Literary Events
1613	The Globe playhouse burns down; Princess Elizabeth marries the Elector Palatine	Elizabeth Carey's *Tragedy of Mariam* published; Samuel Purchas's first volume of *Purchas his pilgrims* (1613–25) printed; Thomas Middleton creates a New World-inspired Lord Mayor's pageant and George Chapman's masque to celebrate the marriage of Princess Elizabeth uses similar Virginian images
1614		Sir Walter Ralegh publishes his *The History of the World*
1615		Joseph Swetnam's *Arraignment of Lewde, idle, forward and unconstant women*
1616	William Shakespeare dies	Dorothy Leigh, *A Mother's Blessing* published
1617		Rachel Speght publishes *A Mouzell for Melastomus*; Esther Sowernam publishes *Esther hath hang'd Haman* and Constantia Munda publishes *The Worming of a mad dogge* all in response to Swetnam's diatribe; William Whateley's *A Bride-Bush* marriage guide published
1620	Pilgrim Fathers leave for Europe and then America	
1621	Andrew Marvell born; death of Mary Sidney Herbert; John Donne becomes Dean of St Paul's	
1622		William Gouge's *Of Domesticall Duties* marriage guide published; Elizabeth Joscelin's *Legacy to her Unborn Child* published

	Historic Events	Literary Events
1623		Shakespeare's *First Folio* published
1625	Death of James I and accession of his son Charles I; bad outbreak of plague; death of John Fletcher	Francis Bacon, 'Of Plantations', in *The essayes or counsels, civill and morall* published
1629	Charles dissolves Parliament, personal rule for 11 years	
1631	Death of John Donne	Richard Braithwaite's *The English Gentlewoman* conduct book published
1633	Death of George Herbert	William Prynne publishes *Histriomatrix: or the Player's Scourge* attacking the theatre; George Herbert's *The Temple* published
1634	Death of John Webster	
1637	Death of Ben Jonson	
1640	The Long Parliament meets	
1642	The Civil War begins as Charles declares war on Parliament; all theatres are closed; death of Galileo	
1645	The *Book of Common Prayer* banned	
1646	The office of bishop abolished	
1649	Charles I executed; England is declared a Commonwealth, monarchy and the House of Lords are abolished	
1650		Marvell writes 'An Horatian Ode upon Cromwell's Return from Ireland
1653	Oliver Cromwell is named Lord Protector	
1656		Francis Osborne's *Advice to a Son* published

	Historic Events	Literary Events
1660	Restoration of the monarchy and Charles II accedes to the throne; the House of Lords and the office of bishop restored; the Royal Society for the promotion of Science founded; the theatres are re-opened with actresses taking female roles for the first time	
1662	Act of Uniformity	*Book of Common Prayer* re-issued
1667		*Paradise Lost* published by John Milton
1674	John Milton dies	
1678	Death of Andrew Marvell	

Further Reading

Historical Overviews and General Resources

Briggs, Julia, *This Stage Play World: English literature and its background, 1580–1625* (Oxford: Oxford University Press, 1983)
This is a very useful general contextualisation of the literature of the period, with nine chapters on such topics as change and continuity, order and society, women and family, religion and education

Brigden, Susan, *New Worlds, Lost Worlds: The Rule of the Tudors 1485–1603* (London: Penguin, 2001)
This is a valuable introduction to all aspects of the Tudor period from the reign of Henry VIII to Elizabeth I, with discussion of religious strife, the contemporary 'world-view' and exploration

Dollimore, Jonathan, *Radical Tragedy, Religion, Ideology and Power in the Drama of Shakespeare and his Contemporaries* (New York and London: Harvester Wheatsheaf, 1984, repr. 1989)
Parts 1 and 2 of this seminal work provide invaluable contextual information for the era. This includes discussion of contemporary ideas of gender, Providentialism and the concept of Natural Law, notions of identity and the political implications of literature

Hill, Christopher, *The World Turned Upside Down: Radical Ideas During the English Revolution* (Harmondsworth: Penguin, 1975)
Examines the conditions which gave rise to radical groups during the period leading up to the Revolution, including Diggers, Ranters and Levellers

Hinds, Hilary, *God's Englishwomen, Seventeenth-Century Radical Sectarian Writing by Women* (Manchester: Manchester University Press, 1996)
The first section is a very valuable discussion of contextual and theoretical aspects of the study followed by discussion of the work of individual Quaker authors

Kelly-Gadol, Joan, 'Did Women Have a Renaissance?'
This influential essay has been reproduced in many publications, including

Becoming Visible: Women in European History, Renate Bridenthal and Claudia Koonz (eds) (Boston: Houghton Mifflin Company, 1977), pp.148–52

Kraye, Jill (ed.), *The Cambridge Companion to Renaissance Humanism* (Cambridge: Cambridge University Press, 1996, repr. 1998), especially Clare Carroll 'Humanism and English Literature in the Fifteenth and Sixteenth Centuries', pp. 246–68

This very useful overview contains essays on the origins of Renaissance humanism, its political and religious significance, its influence on science, the arts and literature and discussion of the importance of rhetoric

Mendelson, Sara and Crawford, Patricia, *Women in Early Modern England 1550–1720* (Oxford: Clarendon Press, 1998)

This is an excellent sourcebook for all stages of women's lives in the seventeenth century, including a useful section which introduces the medical, legal and religious contexts

North, Marcy L., *The Anonymous Renaissance* (Chicago and London: University of Chicago Press, 2003)

This fascinating study explores the contemporary concepts of 'author' and 'authorship' from the medieval to Renaissance eras, within the context of texts partially or completely unsigned

Rivers, Isabel, *Classical and Christian Ideas in English Renaissance Poetry, A Student's Guide*, 2nd edn (London: Routledge, 1992)

Rivers outlines the influential classical and Christian ideas which were absorbed into Renaissance culture and literature, providing excerpts from the original works and relating them to Renaissance literature

Stone, Lawrence, *The Family, Sex and Marriage in England 1500–1800* (Harmondsworth: Penguin, 1977, repr. 1985)

An interesting and wide-ranging study of family life in the sixteenth and seventeenth centuries

Zunder, William, and Suzanne Trill (eds) *Writing and the English Renaissance* (London: Longman, 1996)

A useful range of essays which discuss the work of Edmund Spenser, Christopher Marlowe, Mary Sidney, George Herbert, Andrew Marvell and John Milton, besides more generalised themes such as masculinity, identity, popular culture, preaching and prophesy

Website

The Agas Map, hosted by the University of Victoria, is searchable and a valuable resource for developing a sense of early modern London http://mapoflondon.uvic.ca/

Literary Genres

Verse

Bate, Jonathan, *Shakespeare and Ovid* (Oxford: Clarendon Press, 1993, repr. 2001)

An insightful examination of the influence of Ovid on a wide range of Shakespeare's works both poetry and drama

Burrow, Colin (ed.), *William Shakespeare: The Complete Sonnets and Poems* (Oxford: Oxford University Press, 2002)

This is a very useful work as it includes all of Shakespeare's poetry, including poems attributed to him in anthologies. The introduction is excellent

Callaghan, Dympna, 'Comedy and Epyllion in Post-Reformation England', *Shakespeare Survey*, Vol. 56: Shakespeare and Comedy (2003), pp. 27–38

Available via Cambridge Collections Online: Digital Object Identifier 10.1017/CCOL0521827272.002

Carey, John, *John Donne, Life, Mind and Art* (London: Faber and Faber, 1981)

An excellent biography which also incorporates detailed readings of Donne's poetry

Chedgzoy, Kate, 'Marlowe's men and women' in *The Cambridge Companion to Christopher Marlowe*, Cheney, Patrick (ed.) (Cambridge: Cambridge University Press, 2004) also available via Cambridge Collections Online

Discusses gender and sexuality in *Hero and Leander*

Cheyney, Patrick (ed.), *The Cambridge Companion to Shakespeare's Poetry* (Cambridge: Cambridge University Press, 2007)

Besides essays on specific poems, this work has chapters on Shakespeare's place in the development of Renaissance poetry, the reception and influence of his works and their contemporary religious and political contexts

Cheyney, Patrick, Hadfield, Andrew and Sullivan, Garrett A., Jr (eds), *Early Modern English Poetry* (Oxford: Oxford University Press, 2007)

Twenty-eight essays by prominent scholars on every genre of early modern verse. An excellent introduction written specifically for students, it organises its contents by author and also thematically

Clark, Sandra (ed.), *Amorous Rites: Elizabethan Erotic Verse* (London: Everyman, 1994)

Provides a useful introduction and detailed readings of several epyllia, including Shakespeare's *Venus and Adonis* and Marlowe's *Hero and Leander*

Dawson, Terence and Scott Dupree, Robert (eds), *Seventeenth-Century English Poetry* (New York and London: Harvester Wheatsheaf, 1994)

A very useful annotated anthology featuring the work of forty writers, including prominent and lesser-known poets

Healy, Elizabeth citing Nohrnberg, *The Faerie Queene: A Reader's Guide* (Cambridge: Cambridge University Press, 1987)

A very readable and interesting guide which is particularly useful to newcomers to the epic

Ovid, *Metamorphoses: A New Verse Translation*, translated by David Raeburn, (London: Penguin, 2004)

Metamorphoses was a core text for Renaissance scholars and this is a very readable and attractive edition

Roche, Thomas P., Jr, *The Kindly Flame: a Study of the Third and Fourth Books of Spenser's Faerie Queene* (Princeton: Princeton University Press, 1964)

A well-known and very useful detailed exploration of the third and fourth books, Chastity and Friendship

—, *Petrarch and the English Sonnet Sequences* (New York: AMS Press, 1983)
A seminal text on the Italian influence on the English sonnet, including discussion of the work of Sidney, Greville, Daniel and Shakespeare

Spiller, Michael R. G., *The Development of the Sonnet* (London: Routledge, 1992)
An excellent introduction to the genre, tracing the development from the earliest known examples through the work of prominent Renaissance poets, including Wyatt, Sidney and Shakespeare

Waller, Gary, *English Poetry of the Sixteenth Century* (Harlow: Addison Wesley Longman, 1986, second edn 1993)
Chapters include discussion of patronage, the poets' world, women's poetry and detailed readings of the work of individual poets

Website

The Spenser Home Page, based at the University of Cambridge, hosts the Spenser Journal, an annual scholarly journal, and the Spenser Society
http://www.english.cam.ac.uk/spenser/

Prose

Davies, Kathleen M., 'The Sacred Condition of Equality: How Original Were Puritan Doctrines of Marriage?' in *Social History*, Vol. 2, No. 5 (May, 1977), pp. 563–80
A perceptive study and one of the few discussions of marriage guides available

Duncan-Jones, Katherine and Van Dorsten, Jan (eds), *Miscellaneous Prose of Sir Philip Sidney* (Oxford: Clarendon Press, 1973)
The editors link Sidney to prominent European writers and their theories of literature, such as Hubert Languet and Henri Estiene

Javitch, Daniel (ed.), *Baldesarre Castiglione's The Book of the Courtier* (Norton Critical Edition (New York and London: W.W. Norton and Company, 2002)

This edition includes ten critical essays, including Kelly-Gadol's [above] and a study of *The Book of the Courtier*'s influence abroad

Logan, George M., *The Meaning of More's 'Utopia'* (Princeton: Princeton University Press, 1983)

Logan's study reads *Utopia* through its classical influences

More, Sir Thomas, *Utopia*, Norton Critical Edition, translated and edited by Robert M. Adams (New York and London: W. W. Norton and Company, 1975, second edn 1975)

As with all Norton Critical editions, this text provides contextualising 'Backgrounds' and is followed by a selection of critical essays by leading scholars

Ryan, Lawrence V., 'Book Four of Castiglione's Courtier: Climax or Afterthought?' *Studies in the Renaissance*, 19 (1972), pp. 156–79

A useful discussion of Neo-platonic theories of love within a court context

Website

John Donne Sermon Database is the digitalised ten-volume *Sermons of John Donne*, edited by George Potter and Evelyn Simpson (University of California Press, 1953–62) hosted by Brigham Young University: http://www.lib.byu.edu/dlib/donne/

Key Debates

New Worlds and Nationalities

Barber, Peter, 'The Evesham World Map: A Late Medieval English View of God and the World', in *Imago Mundi*, Vol. 47 (1995), pp. 13–33

Interesting discussion of the insights gained about fourteenth-century map-making and medieval perceptions of the country and the world

Brigden, Susan, *New Worlds, Lost Worlds: The Rule of the Tudors 1485–1603* (London: Penguin, 2001), chapter 9: 'New World Ventures and the Coming of War With Spain in the 1580s', pp. 274–94

This is a valuable introduction to all aspects of the Tudor period from the reign of Henry VIII to Elizabeth I, with specific focus in chapter 9 on the implications of exploration and colonisation

Briggs, Julia, 'Other People, Other Lands' in *This Stage-Play World, Texts and Contexts, 1580–1626* (Oxford: Oxford University Press, 1997)

This section provides insights into English Renaissance attitudes to foreign lands and nationalities

Smith, D.K., *The Cartographic Imagination in Early Modern England, re-writing the world in Marlowe, Spenser, Raleigh and Marvell* (Hampshire: Ashgate Publishing, 2008)

A thought-provoking study which traces the development of the art of cartography and its influences on the imagination and perceptions of national identity

Sharp, Robert L., 'Donne's "Good-Morrow" and Cordiform Maps', *Modern Language Notes*, Vol. 69, No. 7 (Nov., 1954)

A perceptive discussion of the influence of cartography on Donne's imagery in this poem

Website

Norton topics Online, The 16th Century, 'Renaissance Exploration, Travel, and the World Outside Europe'

This site has an overview which provides an introduction to the theme and some explorer's voyages, but also excerpts from the original narratives of exploration and a list of other useful internet links

http://www.wwnorton.com/college/english/nael/16century/topic_2/welcome.htm

Religious Controversies

Duffy, Eamon, *The Stripping of the Altars, Traditional Religion in England 1400–1580* (New York and London: Yale University Press, 1992)

An important text which contextualises the reformation of the English Church beside the existing religious beliefs of the era

Ebner, Dean, *Autobiography in Seventeenth-Century England* (Paris: Moulton, 1971)

Traces the development of autobiographical writing through accounts of spiritual awakening

Hamlin, Hannibal, *Psalm Culture and Early Modern English Literature* (Cambridge: Cambridge University Press, 2004, repr. 2007)

Provides a survey of English Metrical Psalmody in the first section, followed by close attention to the treatment of three important Psalms (23, 51, 137) in the work of several authors

Hannay, Margaret (ed.), *Silent But For The Word: Tudor Women as Patrons, Translators, and Writers of Religious Works*, (Ohio: Kent State University Press, 1985)

Another seminal work in the rediscovery of female authorship of the period

Stachniewsky, John, *The Persecutory Imagination: English Puritanism and the Literature of Religious Despair* (Oxford: Clarendon Press, 1991)

An insightful study of the agonising self-doubt and despair often caused by extreme Protestant belief

Walter, H. (ed.), William Tyndale, *Doctrinal Treatises to Different Parts of the Scriptures*, Parker Society, (Cambridge: Cambridge University Press, 1848)

Provides real insight into Tyndale's motives and practice

Gordan, Bruce (ed.), *Protestant History and Identity in Sixteenth-Century Europe*, Vol. 2 (Aldershot: Scolar Press, 1996)

A perceptive study which considers the means by which Protestants sought to provide their religion with credibility and history in the face of Catholic denigration

Society and Culture

Suzuki, Miho, *Subordinate Subjects, Gender, the Political-Nation, and Literary Form in England*, 1588–1688 (Aldershot: Ashgate, 1988)

This fascinating study considers marginalised members of society in historical record and literary representation

Kunze, Bonnelyn Young and Brautigan, Dwight D. (eds), *Court, Country and Culture, Essays on Early Modern British History in Honor of Perez Zagorin* (New York: University of Rochester Press, 1992)

Wide-ranging study of the political, cultural and intellectual contexts and influences of the English Civil War

Websites

The Aemilia Lanyer Homepage is administered by the University of Arizona and provides full text versions of Aemilia Lanyer's work online, including all of the many dedications to *Salve Deus*
http://www.ic.arizona.edu/ic/mcbride/lanyer/lanyer.htm

The complete Tudor *Books of Homilies* are available via the Anglican Library, administered by the University of Toronto
http://www.anglicanlibrary.org/homilies/

Ben Jonson's 1692 collected folio of works, including the *Epigrams* http://hollowaypages.com/jonson1692epigrams.htm

The Woman Debate

Boesky, Amy, and Crane, Mary T. (eds), *Form and Reform in Renaissance England: essays in Honor of Barbara Kiefer Lewalski* (London: Associated University Presses, 2000)

The essays are presented in three sections which reflect the interests of the prominent scholar, Barbara Lewalski: the interaction between religion and political position, women writers, and Milton's epic

Brant, Clare, and Dianne Purkiss, *Women, texts and histories, 1575–1760* (London: Routledge, 1992)

Essays by prominent feminist scholars discuss the Woman Debate, women's utopian writing and works by individual female authors

Coolahan, Marie-Louise, 'Review of Heather Wolfe, *Elizabeth Cary Lady Falkland: Life and Letters*' in *Early Modern Literary Studies* 9.1 (May, 2003):11, pp. 1–6

A detailed discussion of *The Lady Falkland, Her Life* (*c*. 1655)

Crawford, Patricia and Gowing, Laura (eds), *Women's Worlds in Seventeenth-Century England* (London and New York: Routledge, 2000)

This valuable resource provides readings from historical sources illustrating ten areas of women's lives, including spirituality, work, marriage and protests

Fitzmaurice, James, *et al.* (eds), *Major Women Writers of Seventeenth-Century England* (Ann Arbor: University of Michigan Press, 1997)

Includes a useful introduction and discussion of Aemilia Lanyer, Elizabeth Cary, Aphra Behn and the Woman Debate pamphlets, among others

Hannay, Margaret (ed.), *Silent But For The Word: Tudor Women as Patrons, Translators, and Writers of Religious Works* (Ohio: Kent State University Press, 1985)

This is a seminal work for the study of early modern women writers including Margaret Roper, Mary Sidney Herbert, Anne Askew, Aemilia Lanyer and Elizabeth Cary

Lewalski, Barbara, *Writing Women in Jacobean England* (London and Cambridge, Mass.: Harvard University Press, 1993

This important text includes discussion of the work of Elizabeth Cary, Aemilia Lanyer, Rachel Speght and Mary Wroth

Ruether, Rosemary Radford, *Women and Redemption: A Theological History* (London: SCM Press, 1998)

Provides detailed analysis of the biblical roots of Renaissance patriarchal attitudes to women

Website

A Celebration of Women Writers Project provides digitalised versions of the work of women writers from 3000 B.C. to the twentieth century. It focuses mainly on work in English and is hosted by the University of Pennsylvania
http://digital.library.upenn.edu/women/

Critical Theory

Barry, Peter, *Beginning Theory: an Introduction to Literary and Cultural Theory* (Manchester and New York: Manchester University Press, 1995, repr. 2002)

A very practical and understandable text designed for students new to literary theory

Eagleton, Terry, *How to Read a Poem* (Oxford: Wiley-Blackwell, 2006)

A new work by the prominent Marxist theorist, which includes discussion of theoretical approaches and practical assistance for analysing poems, including some worked examples

Gallagher, Catherine and Stephen Greenblatt, *Practicing New Historicism* (London: University of Chicago Press, 2000)

A more advanced exploration of New Historicist theories used in the interpretation of various objects, artefacts, and cultural practices, including paintings and religious ritual

Greenblatt, Stephen, *Renaissance Self-Fashioning: from More to Shakespeare* (Chicago and London: University of Chicago Press, 1980)

This much-quoted text was one of the earliest New Historicist approaches to the era. It is particularly useful for the study of Wyatt and Sir Thomas More

Lodge, David (ed.,) *Modern Criticism and Theory: A Reader*, third edition (London: Longman, 2008)

Provides excerpts from influential essays representing major schools of literary theory

Said, Edward, *Orientalism* (1978) introduced in *Beginning Theory: An Introduction to Literary and Cultural Theory* (Manchester: Manchester University Press, 1995)

A useful introduction to post-colonial concepts in literature

Selden, Raman, *Practising Theory and Reading Literature* (London: Longman, 1989)

This is an excellent book for anyone starting to use literary theory. It explains not only the theories themselves, but how to use them

Index